The Canadian Oral History Reader

CARLETON LIBRARY SERIES

The Carleton Library Series publishes books about Canadian economics, geography, history, politics, public policy, society and culture, and related topics, in the form of leading new scholarship and reprints of classics in these fields. The series is funded by Carleton University, published by McGill-Queen's University Press, and is under the guidance of the Carleton Library Series Editorial Board, which consists of faculty members of Carleton University. Suggestions and proposals for manuscripts and new editions of classic works are welcome and may be directed to the Carleton Library Series Editorial Board c/o the Library, Carleton University, Ottawa K1S 5B6, at cls@carleton.ca, or on the web at www.carleton.ca/cls.

221 *Surveyors of Empire*
Samuel Holland, J.F.W. Des Barres, and the Making of The Atlantic Neptune
Stephen J. Hornsby

222 *Peopling the North American City*
Montreal, 1840–1900
Sherry Olson and Patricia Thornton

223 *Interregional Migration and Public Policy in Canada*
An Empirical Study
Kathleen M. Day and Stanley L. Winer

224 *How Schools Worked*
Public Education in English Canada, 1900–1940
R.D. Gidney and W.P.J. Millar

225 *A Two-Edged Sword*
The Navy as an Instrument of Canadian Foreign Policy
Nicholas Tracy

226 *The Illustrated History of Canada*
25th Anniversary Edition
Edited by Craig Brown

227 *In Duty Bound*
Men, Women, and the State in Upper Canada, 1783–1841
J.K. Johnson

228 *Asleep at the Switch*
The Political Economy of Federal Research and Development Policy since 1960
Bruce Smardon

229 *And We Go On*
Will R. Bird
Introduction and Afterword by David Williams

230 *The Great War as I Saw It*
Frederick George Scott
Introduction by Mark G. McGowan

231 *The Canadian Oral History Reader*
Edited by Kristina R. Llewellyn, Alexander Freund, and Nolan Reilly

The Canadian Oral History Reader

Edited by Kristina R. Llewellyn, Alexander Freund,
and Nolan Reilly

CARLETON LIBRARY SERIES 231

McGill-Queen's University Press
Montreal & Kingston · London · Ithaca

ISBN 978-0-7735-4495-6 (cloth)
ISBN 978-0-7735-4496-3 (paper)
ISBN 978-0-7735-8352-8 (ePDF)
ISBN 978-0-7735-8363-4 (ePUB)

Legal deposit second quarter 2015
Bibliothèque nationale du Québec

Printed in Canada on acid-free paper that is 100% ancient forest free
(100% post-consumer recycled), processed chlorine free

McGill-Queen's University Press acknowledges the support of the
Canada Council for the Arts for our publishing program. We also
acknowledge the financial support of the Government of Canada
through the Canada Book Fund for our publishing activities.

Library and Archives Canada Cataloguing in Publication

The Canadian oral history reader / edited by Kristina R. Llewellyn,
Alexander Freund, and Nolan Reilly.

(Carleton library series ; 231)
Includes bibliographical references and index.
Issued in print and electronic formats.
ISBN 978-0-7735-4495-6 (bound). – ISBN 978-0-7735-4496-3 (pbk.). –
ISBN 978-0-7735-8352-8 (ePDF). – ISBN 978-0-7735-8363-4 (ePUB)

1. Oral history – Canada – Case studies.   I. Llewellyn, Kristina R.,
1976–, author, editor   II. Freund, Alexander, 1969–, author, editor
III. Reilly, Nolan, editor   IV. Series: Carleton library series ; 231

D16.14.C35 2015   907.2'071   C2015-901193-0
                                    C2015-901194-9

Set in 10.5/13 Minion Pro with Libertad
Book design & typesetting by Garet Markvoort, zijn digital

Contents

Acknowledgments · ix

Introduction · 3
Alexander Freund, Kristina R. Llewellyn, and Nolan Reilly

SECTION ONE: METHODOLOGY

1 Methodology for Recording Oral Histories in the
  Aboriginal Community · 25
  Brian Calliou

2 Sharing Authority with Baba · 53
  Stacey Zembrzycki

3 Oral History and Ethical Practice after *TCPS2* · 73
  Nancy Janovicek

4 Legal Issues Regarding Oral Histories · 98
  Jill Jarvis-Tonus

SECTION TWO: INTERPRETATION

5 Reflections on the Politics and Praxis of Working-Class
  Oral Histories · 119
  Joan Sangster

6 Productive Tensions: Feminist Readings of Women Teachers'
   Oral Histories · 141
   Kristina R. Llewellyn

7 A Canadian Family Talks about Oma's Life in Nazi Germany:
   Three-Generational Interviews and Communicative Memory · 159
   Alexander Freund

8 Oral History, Narrative Strategies, and Native American
   Historiography · 180
   Julie Cruikshank

SECTION THREE: PRESERVATION AND PRESENTATION

9 Hidden from Historians: Preserving Lesbian Oral History
   in Canada · 201
   Elise Chenier

10 Oral History as Process-Generated Data · 218
    Alexander Freund

11 "When I Was Your Age": Bearing Witness in Holocaust Education
    in Montreal · 239
    Stacey Zembrzycki and Steven High

12 Listening and Learning with Life Stories of Human Rights
    Violations · 266
    Bronwen Low and Emmanuelle Sonntag

SECTION FOUR: ADVOCACY

13 Narrative Wisps of the Ochēkiwi Sīpi Past: A Journey in
    Recovering Collective Memories · 285
    Winona Wheeler

14 I Can Hear Lois Now: Corrections to My Story of the Internment
    of Japanese Canadians · 297
    Pamela Sugiman

15 Contested Memories: Efforts of the Powerful to Silence
Former Inmates' Histories of Life in an Institution for
"Mental Defectives" · 318
Claudia Malacrida

16 "Don't Speak for Me": Practising Oral History amid the
Legacies of Conflict · 335
Joy Parr

Postscript · 347
Ronald J. Grele

Additional Readings in Canadian Oral History: 1980–2012 · 361
Kristina R. Llewellyn and Dana Nowak

Contributors · 373

Index · 377

Acknowledgments

This *Reader* was born out of our desire to build an identifiable oral history community among scholars within Canada and to have Canadian oral history scholarship gain greater recognition on the international stage. Our collaboration toward this goal began through our roles as co-editors of *Oral History Forum d'histoire orale*, the journal of the Canadian Oral History Association (COHA). We were grateful to inherit a journal with a long-standing record due to the dedication of past editors. We wish to acknowledge those who sustained the journal – pioneers in Canadian oral history – including Leo LaClare, Richard Lochhead, Allen W. Specht, James Morrison, Ronald Labelle, and Patricia Skidmore. Our time as co-editors has come to an end, but work on this *Reader* has provided us with rich opportunities to further our research in the field and to cultivate our friendship.

The strength of COHA and its journal has waxed and waned over time. This turbulence has in part been the result of scholars' lack of self-identification as oral historians, despite engaging in oral history methodology. With a recent surge in the popularity of recording and hearing people's memories of the past, Canadian scholars are increasingly staking their claim as oral historians. Now is the time for Canadian oral historians to strengthen as a community and share their scholarship that has transformed, and will continue to transform, historical knowledge and the role of the historian. The contributors to this *Reader* have, among others, committed themselves to the growth of oral history in Canada and elsewhere – challenging accepted practices, developing innovative projects, and enhancing the democratizing potential of oral history. Many of them have heavily revised and rewritten previous publications to reflect the rapidly changing ideas and contexts that shape oral history today. We thank them for their support for this *Reader*.

Given that a portion of this *Reader* is developed from previously published material, we relied on financial support from several organizations for its publication. We sincerely appreciate the Small Projects Grant awarded by the History Education Network/Histoire et éducation en réseau. We also recognize the generous funding provided by the Oral History Centre at the University of Winnipeg, as well as institutional grants from the University of Winnipeg and Renison University College at the University of Waterloo. Lastly, this project was made possible thanks to funding for our ongoing research by the Social Sciences and Humanities Research Council of Canada.

We extend our sincere thanks to research assistants Dana Nowak, Shauna McLean, and Kimberley Moore, who culled publications for possible inclusion and formatted chapters for publication. We also extend appreciation to the anonymous reviewers who provided valuable suggestions for a more concise and accessible *Reader*, as well as to our copy editor, Jane McWhinney, who provided a skillful review of the final manuscript. To Jacqueline Mason, our editor at McGill-Queen's University Press, we are grateful for your enthusiastic support for the *Reader* throughout production.

As oral historians regularly acknowledge, oral history is made possible by the people who generously share their time and stories in order to keep memories alive for future generations. We wish to thank the many narrators on whose participation our research relies.

Kristina Llewellyn: Thank you to my co-editors who have supported my work as an oral historian in so many ways. To my parents, Karen MacKay Llewellyn and Hallett Llewellyn, and my sister, Jennifer Llewellyn, thank you for teaching me that storytelling about and from human experience is a primary path to social justice. And, to my partner, Todd Arsenault, and two children, Ethan Arsenault and Gavin Llewellyn, your understanding for juggling family time with publishing is a testament to the gift of your love.

Alexander Freund: Thanks to my co-editors' hard work and great sense of humour, our collaboration was always enjoyable. I thank my family – Gisela and Michaela in Hamburg, Judith, Isabel, and Gabriela in Winnipeg – for their love, support, and encouragement.

Nolan Reilly: I wish to thank my co-editors, Kristina Llewellyn and Alexander Freund, who made this collection possible, and my family, Sharon, Darryl, Sarah, and Leanne.

PERMISSIONS

For their kind permission to reprint previously published material, acknowledgment is made to the following publishers. We give special acknowledgment to the journal editors and managers who processed permissions. In case of unintentional omission or error, an appropriate acknowledgment will be placed in future editions of this book.

Reprinted with permission from the Canadian Oral History Association: Jill Jarvis-Tonus, "Legal Issues Regarding Oral Histories," *Oral History Forum d'histoire orale* 12 (1992): 18–24; Alexander Freund, "A Canadian Family Talks about Oma's Life in Nazi Germany: Three-Generational Interviews and Communicative Memory," *Oral History Forum d'histoire orale* 29 (2009): 1–26; Kristina Llewellyn, "When Oral Historians Listen to Teachers: Using Feminist Findings," *Oral History Forum d'histoire orale* 23 (2003): 89–112; Winona Wheeler, "Narrative Wisps of the Ochēkiwi Sīpi Past: A Journey in Recovering Collective Memories," *Oral History Forum d'histoire orale* 19–20 (1999–2000): 113–25.

Reprinted with permission from the Canadian Historical Association: Joy Parr, "'Don't Speak for Me': Oral History Among Vulnerable Populations," *Journal of the Canadian Historical Association* 21, no. 1 (2010): 1–12.

Reproduced with permission of Palgrave Macmillan: Pamela Sugiman, "I Can Hear Lois Now: Corrections to My Story of the Internment of Japanese Canadians – For the Record," edited by Anna Sheftel and Stacey Zembrzycki, *Oral History Off the Record: Toward an Ethnography of Practice* (New York: Palgrave Macmillan, 2013).

Reproduced with permission of Springer Science + Business Media: Nancy Janovicek, "Oral History and Ethical Practice: Toward Effective Policies and Procedures," *Journal of Academic Ethics* 4 (2006): 157–74.

Reproduced with permission of Taylor & Francis Group: Julie Cruikshank, "Oral History, Narrative Strategies, and Native American Historiography: Perspectives from the Yukon Territory, Canada," edited by Nancy Shoemaker, *Clearing a Path: Theorizing the Past in Native American Studies* (New York: Routledge, 2002); Claudia Malacrida, "Contested Memories: Efforts of the Powerful to Silence Former Inmates' Histories of Life in an Institution for 'Mental Defectives,'" *Disability & Society* 21, no. 5 (August 2006): 397–410; Bronwen Low and Emmanuelle Sonntag, "Toward a Pedagogy of Listening: Teaching and Learning from Life Stories of Human Rights Violations," *Journal of Curriculum Studies* 45, no. 6 (2013): 768–78.

Reprinted with permission from University of Toronto Press (www.utp journals.com): Stacey Zembrzycki, "Sharing Authority with Baba," *Journal of Canadian Studies* 43, no. 1 (2009): 219–38; Stacey Zembrzycki and Steven High, "'When I Was Your Age': Bearing Witness in Holocaust Education in Montreal," *Canadian Historical Review* 93, no. 3 (2012): 408–35.

Reprinted with permission from GESIS – Leibniz-Institut für Sozialwissenschaften: Alexander Freund, "Oral History as Process-Generated Data," *Historical Social Research* 34, no. 1 (2009): 22–48.

The Canadian Oral History Reader

Introduction

Alexander Freund, Kristina R. Llewellyn,
and Nolan Reilly

If oral history cannot conclusively establish pre-sovereignty
(after this decision) occupation of land, it may still be relevant to
demonstrate that current occupation has its origins
prior to sovereignty.
Chief Justice Antonio Lamer[1]

I call myself a chronicler, a collector of people's tales and stories.
Really what I am is a collector of people.
Barry Broadfoot[2]

For several decades, scholars in various disciplines have used oral
history methods as a means of both reclaiming the history of the
marginal and silenced and centring women's lives.
Franca Iacovetta[3]

Those familiar with the field of oral history will realize that the term carries different meanings, according to context, historical period, and the
purpose of the researcher. To some people, it denotes knowledge about
the past that has been relayed by word of mouth from one generation to
the next. To others, it is the practice of recording, archiving, and analyzing
eyewitness testimony and life histories. Some use it as a tool for political activism, to disseminate knowledge, or to raise awareness. For many,
including the editors of this volume, it is a global social movement for
democratizing history; that is, for making the telling and writing of history more inclusive. In this view, oral history is a powerful tool to engage
people in the discovery and making of history and in the critical assessment of how stories about the past are created.

The Canadian Oral History Reader seeks to make oral history accessible to a broad public. It is structured as a guide that takes the reader from a general introduction to the method of oral history (Section One) to questions about the interpretation of oral narratives (Section Two), the preservation of oral history interviews (Section Three), and the role of oral history in advocacy work (and vice versa) (Section Four). The *Reader* addresses diverse audiences. It introduces novice researchers to the rich heritage and diversity of Canadian oral history practices. It provides a resource for teachers, community and public historians, and more advanced scholars, building the foundation for a renewed dialogue among Canadian and global oral history movements. Newcomers and experienced practitioners alike will benefit from reading (and re-reading) the following articles, which explore a range of methodological and theoretical aspects of oral history.

As a resource for students, researchers, and activists to learn about Canada-based scholarship, *The Canadian Oral History Reader* provides the tools for joining the international movement to democratize history. In this introduction, we distinguish among different understandings of oral history, review the development of oral history in Canada, position it in its global context, and explain how the individual chapters in this collection advance our knowledge of oral history. After surveying the state of the art of oral history in Canada, we conclude by reflecting on potential future challenges for the field.

Oral history has been practised for a long time, in different cultures and countries, and in many disciplines – from academic historians, sociologists, and ethnographers to archivists, museum curators, and other public historians, to journalists and activists.[4] Defining oral history is therefore not easy; nor is it necessarily desirable, because any definition will exclude certain practices and practitioners. In the 1970s, for example, the Canadian oral history movement was severely hindered by squabbles among academics, archivists, teachers, journalists, activists, and others about what constituted oral history.[5] Canadian oral historian, writer, and activist Michael Riordan, who has been interviewing people from around the world since the 1970s, was once told by an academic at an oral history summer institute that what he did was not oral history. He later wrote: "I did wonder at the enormous human capacity for dogma ... Even in this endeavour that all of us at the institute were celebrating as one of the most democratic vehicles possible for human expression, here was someone designating what does and what does not count."[6] Clearly, definitions can easily be misunderstood or misused in an attempt to exclude.

Nevertheless, definitions can help to clarify communication, raise consciousness, and bring practitioners together. For decades in Canada, even as oral history movements were flourishing around the world, many Canadians creating and using oral sources did not consider their work oral history or themselves as oral historians. As a result, they worked in isolation instead of collaborating, sharing, and meeting. With this background of uncertainty about Canadian oral history identity in mind, we have assembled this *Reader* for oral historians broadly defined; that is, not only historians using oral sources, but rather everyone – from inside and outside of academia – who collects, creates, studies, or preserves oral history or oral tradition or both. Yet, despite such inclusiveness, we must also ask: What brings and holds all these disciplines and practices together?

Here is one inclusive framework for thinking about the methods used in oral history: We can think of it as: a method for creating historical sources (methodology); a method for using and making sense of what we learn from eyewitnesses (interpretation); a method for archiving and presenting memories of our individual and collective past (preservation and presentation); and a method for disseminating knowledge and raising awareness about past and present injustices and inequalities (advocacy). This categorization – methodology, interpretation, preservation and presentation, and advocacy – serves as the outline of this *Reader*. Let us look more closely at these four methods of oral history.

Modern oral historians often point to ancient Chinese and Greek historians as their predecessors, because the ancient scribes relied extensively on eyewitness accounts to write their histories. Others, using oral history to signify the traditions and knowledge orally transmitted from one generation to the next, point to African *griots* and indigenous storytelling practices to emphasize the deep roots of oral narratives in human cultures.[7] Social reformers of the nineteenth century used journalistic interviewing methods to learn about the living and working conditions of the poor in European and North American urban slums, while historians and sociologists interviewed immigrant settlers.[8] By the late 1880s, when the first recording machine (the Edison Perfected Phonograph) became available to the public, researchers recorded "sounds of historical and cultural value to Canadians."[9] Among these sound historians were ethnologists and folklorists like Marius Barbeau, who recorded indigenous songs and stories for Canada's National Museum of Man before the First World War.[10]

Historians of Canada understood that "old-timers" had valuable knowledge to share – long before Allan Nevins "invented" oral history at

Columbia University in 1948. In an address to the organizational meeting of the Regina Historical Association in 1922, Arthur S. Morton, a historian of Western Canada and later the founder of Saskatchewan's provincial archives, explained:

> We are now at the beginning of a movement to preserve the early history of this province. We have conducted an experiment in Saskatoon by which a small group of only five, of which some were old-timers and some professors of the university, meet regularly with a typist present. Some old-timer is the guest of the evening. We all sit around and smoke and ask questions about the early days and after a while the old-timer's tongue is loosened and he tells us of things that happened while the typist takes it down in shorthand. Finally copies are given to each member of the group. It is felt that some such machinery for gathering the stories of our pioneers should be set up in the different districts of the province and this year we are trying to do it.[11]

In the first half of the twentieth century, journalists as well as social scientists refined their recording and interviewing methods. Journalists, working for the CBC and its predecessor, the Canadian Radio Broadcasting Commission (CRBC), recorded "historical broadcasts," "oral memoirs and interviews," and "the sounds of war" during the 1930s and 1940s. Social scientists seeking "objective" forms of interrogation for polls and surveys developed standard questionnaires and formulas for posing questions. In the 1940s and 1950s, university-based North American oral historians developed methods with which they might document people's lived experiences more extensively. By the 1960s oral historians in the United States and Canadian archivists, as well as CBC journalists and NFB filmmakers, had completed large projects and created a number of guidelines for oral history interviewing.[12] They also developed standards for preservation and archiving, including best practices for transcription, which became more widely accessible in the 1970s.[13] The early Canadian oral history movement was driven and shaped by provincial and national archivists. National archivist Leo LaClare headed the Oral History Committee of the Canadian Historical Association, which became the Canadian Oral History Association (COHA). LaClare was COHA's first president. Archivists were instrumental in organizing annual national conferences throughout the 1970s and they founded the COHA Journal (in 1995 renamed Oral History Forum d'histoire orale).[14]

At conferences and in the pages of the journal, Canadian oral historians hotly debated best practices, the status of oral history as historical evidence, and the role of the interviewer in the creation of the source and in the relationship with the interviewee. The contentious status of oral history was evident from the start. In the 1970s, practitioners could not even agree on a name for their professional association: Was it the "Aural" or the "Oral" History Association? Archivists from the Aural History division of the Provincial Archives of British Columbia, among others, advocated "aural history," because it was the "more encompassing term," including oral histories, other oral sources, and other historical sound (aural) material.[15] Those advocating "oral" history, however, quickly won the argument, renaming the association at the second national conference held in St John's, Newfoundland, in 1975.[16]

Despite such disagreements and disparate approaches, objectives, and practitioners (including archivists, historians, geographers, ethnographers, ethnomusicologists, folklorists, educators, museum curators, journalists, broadcasters, and authors), oral historians have developed a widely shared methodology for conducting interviews. While "methodology" covers a broad spectrum of tools, tactics, strategies, and approaches, a number of established steps in creating excellent oral history interviews are generally accepted. Before interviewing informants, oral historians conduct preliminary research in public and private archives and libraries to learn more about the interviewees and the historical context in which they lived. During the interview, interviewees may wish to share personal documents such as correspondence, photographs, diaries, or government documents. For project-related interviews, historians develop a research question that goes beyond documenting the interviewees' lived experiences. Oral historians may open interviews with a broad, open-ended question, such as "tell me your life story" or "tell me about your childhood" or begin in a more structured way, asking closed questions such as "when and where were you born?"[17] Either way, they will attempt to stimulate the narration of stories that provide richly detailed accounts of lived experiences rather than simply recording short responses as in a questionnaire or survey. Brian Calliou's article, which opens this *Reader* (chapter 1) provides an excellent overview and introduction to the method of interviewing. Unlike standard guides, however, Calliou's article considers particularly the Canadian indigenous perspective, from which both beginners and seasoned practitioners will benefit.

From the 1950s forward, oral historians found that in their relationship with interviewees they could not claim to be detached and objective.

In the context of the postwar dominance of positivism and quantifica-
tion in the social sciences, this was no longer an easy assertion to make.
Nevertheless, oral historians argued that the interview was an interactive
communication and an interpersonal, human experience that often left
both parties changed. With the rise of social history and the move from
elite interviewing to interviewing marginalized groups, historians became
increasingly concerned about the ethics of the interviewer/narrator relationship. In 1974 Pauline Jewett, then president of Simon Fraser University, in her welcoming address to the first national gathering of oral
historians in Canada and the constituting meeting of the Canadian Oral
History Association, pointed to "the unique moral bond between interviewer and interviewee":[18] "Aural historians have a special obligation to
their informants which does not exist in other forms of research. The tape
recorder obtains information from a living person whose recollections
can then be utilized and interpreted in a variety of ways that the subject
may not have considered."[19] One response in the direction of negotiating this "moral bond," as the US American oral historian Michael Frisch
proposed in 1990, was the acknowledgment of "shared authority."[20] From
giving interviewees a chance to edit their interview transcripts and providing them with copies of recordings, this type of collaboration has since
been expanded to include interviewees in the research and ownership of
the projects. In "Sharing Authority with Baba," chapter 2 of this *Reader*,
Stacey Zembrzycki explores the methodological problems of sharing authority in the interviewing process. She considers some of the challenges
faced by interviewers whose involvement goes beyond giving back to the
community to their becoming dependent on community insiders to gain
access to interviewees and who wish to shape the research and its outcomes according to their own agendas.

Concerns about the "moral bond" and "sharing authority" were mostly
negotiated between the interviewer and interviewee. In the 1990s, however, ethics became a major preoccupation at universities in North America. Before the 1980s, medical and clinical experiments on human subjects
and fieldwork research among indigenous cultures had sometimes com-
promised the dignity of men and women participating in the research,
particularly if experiments or research were conducted without their
knowledge or consent. Minority and oppressed populations and social
groups – women, working-class, ethnic and racial minorities, immigrants,
the populations of the Global South, and indigenous people – were particularly vulnerable to exploitation by researchers.[21] In Canada, the three
major research councils established a tri-council policy in research ethics

in 1998. While important for ethical research, the strict new guidelines at times threatened the integrity of oral history projects, particularly when ethics review boards asked researchers to anonymize interviews and destroy them at the end of the project. In chapter 3, Nancy Janovicek writes about these concerns in the Canadian context. For this *Reader*, she extensively revised an earlier article on the subject to correspond with the newest version of the tri-council policies known as *TCPS2*.[22]

Like ethical concerns, legal questions have loomed large in oral history research, particularly in the United States. Until recently, Canadian researchers had no guidance specific to the Canadian legal system, except for a short article by Jill Jarvis-Tonus published in the *Forum* in 1992. For this *Reader*, Jarvis-Tonus has substantially revised and updated her original article, which appears as chapter 4. It now serves as the only guide for oral historians to legal issues, such as copyright and ownership, confidentiality and privacy, and libel and slander, pertaining to Canadian context. Together, these four chapters in the first section of the *Reader* address the many sides of oral history as a research method and offer introductory guidance to orient novices, provide reference for experienced practitioners, and illuminate Canadian practices that will be useful to both national and international audiences.

In our second section we turn our attention to the uses to which oral history can be applied. Historians and researchers employ oral history interviews for several purposes, using both extant collections and their own interviews, and paradigm shifts have taken place in the way historians have used and considered oral history interviews.[23] Until the late 1970s, the most widespread approach to interpreting oral histories was to mine them for factual information about the past. Oral history interviews provided information where established archives were silent. Social historians particularly began to interview women, workers, migrants, and other minorities to find out about the experiences of groups that had been traditionally marginalized and oppressed. While state documentation in criminal and court records, welfare agency records, health records, and immigration records provided information about members of these groups as soon as they became a "problem" for the state, there was little in these sources that revealed the personal perspectives of these people or told us about their everyday lives. Oral histories provided a great resource for these personal perspectives, even though historians knew that they could not simply take their narrators' words at face value. As with all other sources, they needed to examine the reliability and credibility of their informants' words. Nevertheless, the possibility of learning about the past from people's memories, particularly in the absence of other (reliable) sources, has continued to be a major motivation for researchers. Despite the massive growth of academic and public history since the 1970s, researchers continue to document the experiences of groups previously overlooked.

With the rise of critical theories such as Marxism, structuralism, and feminism, oral historians began to view their sources through new lenses. In the 1970s, following the lead of ethnographers, anthropologists, linguists, and other cultural studies scholars who were emphasizing the importance of language in conveying one's perception of the world, oral historians began to view the narratives they recorded no longer simply as pools of factual information about the past, but rather as narratives constructed in the moment of the interview and in a dialogic (rather than monologic) format. US American historian Ronald J. Grele called these oral history dialogues "conversational narratives." He also asked how oral histories could help us understand the way ideologies shaped worldviews.[24] Italian oral historian Luisa Passerini explored the silences of Italian working-class narratives, while her compatriot colleague Alessandro Portelli illuminated the peculiarities of oral history and pondered the meaning to be found in "misrememberings" or factually inaccurate memories.[25] Increasingly, oral historians paid attention to the dynamics of the interviewer-interviewee relationship to make sense of the stories they were told.[26]

Despite these important changes and turning points in the understanding of oral history, the development has not been as linear and as much of a "story of progress" as Canadian and international oral historians have at times implied.[27] Not only were labour and working-class historians at the forefront of theorizing history but they were often pioneers of oral history as well. Gil Levine's 1977 interview with union leader Patrick Lenihan is as much a testimony to this long and rich tradition as the project from the early 1980s by a group of retired coal miners from Vancouver Island, who wrote a book and a play based on their oral histories with over a hundred miners.[28] As Joan Sangster demonstrates in chapter 5, the earlier "recovery" approach to history was much more reflective and theoretically enriched than is often assumed. Considering the complex ways in which working-class historians in Canada have used oral histories over the past half century, Sangster argues that the narratives that activist historians wrote about their interviewees were shaped by concerns about ethical and political responsibilities as well as relationships with interviewees.

Similarly, and often in connection with working-class history, women's historians rewrote history from a theoretical perspective that employed feminist theories as well as a more self-reflective approach to interviewing. Several early research and archival projects focused on the experiences of pioneer women and female unionists. By the 1980s, feminist historians such as Denyse Baillargeon, Julie Cruikshank, Franca Iacovetta, Joy Parr, and Joan Sangster gave the field its major impetus.[29] In chapter 6, Kristina Llewellyn explores how different feminist theoretical frameworks can be used and combined to interpret oral history interviews – in this case, interviews with school teachers – in more nuanced ways. She draws both on a materialist feminist framework, which Sangster also embraced, as well as on post-structuralist approaches, which are particularly apt for studying language, narrative, and identity. Other chapters, including those by Zembrzycki, Elise Chenier, and Pamela Sugiman, illuminate the variety of ways in which oral history has contributed to writing women's and gender history.

Other social historians have used oral history to write the history of immigrants and ethnic groups. Since 1976, for instance, the Multicultural History Society of Ontario has collected over nine thousand hours of interviews with members of over sixty ethnocultural groups. Correspondingly, the Canadian Museum of Immigration at Pier 21 in Halifax, Nova Scotia, has been collecting interviews with immigrants, as have many other public archives and private collections. In chapter 7, Alexander Freund investigates both the memories of migrants and the migration of memories. On the basis of individual interviews and a group interview, he considers how family members of three different generations collectively construct a family memory around the oldest generation's experiences of growing up in Nazi Germany and migrating to Canada in the 1950s. The chapters by Zembrzycki and Sugiman offer further glimpses into Canada's rich immigrant and ethnic history.

More recently, in Canada perhaps more than anywhere else, research in indigenous oral history has brought important new perspectives to the field. One prominent aspect of this new perspective is the Canadian Supreme Court's decision to admit First Nations' oral tradition as evidence in land claims cases. This decision from 1997 has led to a flurry of oral history recordings, conducted by a wide range of researchers.[30] Brian Calliou's chapter in this book gives a good introduction to this decision and demonstrates that indigenous peoples are increasingly conducting research into their own oral histories. In 2014, for example, the Oral History Centre and the Indigenous Studies Department at the University of

Winnipeg brought to a conclusion the project "ininiwag dibaajimowag: First Nations Men's Digital Stories on the Intergenerational Experiences of Residential Schools," funded by the Aboriginal Healing Foundation. Indigenous scholars used digital storytelling and oral history to help the children of survivors of Indian Residential Schools understand their own experiences and those of their parents. The researchers developed a teaching kit that is available to communities free of charge.[31]

Much other work on indigenous oral history was influenced by folklorists and anthropologists rather than by historians and archivists because, while the latter continued to view oral history mostly as a means of filling gaps in historical knowledge, the former were seeking a more complex understanding of oral history as a source of multiple layers of meaning about the past and the present. Indigenous understandings of what ought or ought not to be recorded challenged Western historians' assumptions about the necessity of preserving all information in the form of textual archives. Mi'kmaq scholars, for example, noted that the writing down of oral tradition was perceived as a threat to their communities, because it erased the need to pass information on orally to the next generation.[32] Julie Cruikshank, in her chapter on Native American narrative strategies (chapter 8), explores the disparate ways in which stories were told, used, and shared among elders in the Yukon Territory. In this case, narrative content was not transparent in itself but depended on the narrative form and the situation in which stories were told and shared. The chapters by Calliou, Cruikshank, and Wheeler give important insights into the diverse understandings of oral stories in indigenous cultures and societies. Indeed, the focus on indigenous oral history and oral tradition is a theme that runs through this *Reader* and sets it clearly apart from other national and international oral history collections.

Folklorists and ethnographers, who stood at the inception of oral history in Canada, have continued to exert an important influence on historians' understanding of spoken and sung word as linguistic and cultural symbols; as symbols, texts were neither transparent windows onto the past nor unbroken reflections of past realities. Symbols needed to be decoded; thus, greater attention to language and culture was required. French Canadian scholars in particular became interested in collecting life stories. As in Canadian historiography at large, French-Canadian oral history developed separately from English Canadian oral history, and English-speaking historians took little note of the works of their Francophone colleagues. This disconnect between Anglo-Canadian and Franco-Canadian research is evident not only in this *Reader* but also in the pages of the *Oral History Forum d'histoire orale*, which, despite its bilingual name, has not yet succeeded in becoming a bilingual journal.[33]

The focus of the third section is preservation and presentation, particularly the archiving of interviews. Issues related to archiving have been integral to the whole field of oral history and perhaps constitute what most sets it apart from other social science and humanities interviewing. Oral historians strive to transcribe – or at least summarize – their interviews and make them available to other researchers and later generations. Since the 1960s, they have developed standards and best practices. This emphasis was especially pronounced in Canada, where the oral history movement was led by archivists from the early 1970s until the early 1990s, when federal budget cuts forced many archivists out of the field. In those two decades, archivists ensured that oral history collections, such as those of the CBC, were properly preserved and made accessible to researchers. Archivists also conducted their own interviews, thus adding important records to their archives. The Sound Heritage program at the Provincial Archives of British Columbia, for instance, collected oral histories and made them accessible through publications and recordings.[34] There has long been a debate among oral historians as to whether transcribing – which is the most time-consuming and thus most expensive aspect of oral history projects – is the best way to use sparse funds. New digital technologies have raised hopes in some quarters that interviews – increasingly captured on video rather than audio – can be indexed and thus made more accessible without transcription. While Elise Chenier in her chapter on creating an archive of lesbian oral history (chapter 9) explores the importance of preserving extant collections, Alexander Freund (chapter 10) illuminates the ways scholars in the social sciences and humanities can make use of extant collections.

One major use of collections or presentation of previously created oral histories has been in the field of education. From the 1960s, teachers like Margaret Andrews at Capilano College and Alfred and Jessie Haché have used oral histories in the classroom, and archives collaborated with teachers' unions to create teaching materials that incorporate oral histories.[35] They quickly appreciated the power of the voice. To amplify this lesson, they often brought eyewitnesses into their classrooms to speak to their students. Some even involved students in the production of oral history interviews. More recently, scholars have delved more deeply into the ramifications of using oral history for educational purposes. In chapter 11, Stacey Zembrzycki and Steven High explore the experiences of Holocaust

survivors who migrated to Canada and became active in Holocaust education. Rather than focusing on their survival stories, they investigate their
postwar lives and in particular their experiences of telling their stories to
young Canadian students. As in the case of using oral history for research,
oral history in the classroom is not a source that can be used without providing context. Oral sources are never self-evident. And even if a class
of students listens to the same story, they will all hear different stories,
depending on their own background, experiences, and listening skills. In
chapter 12, Bronwen Low and Emmanuelle Sonntag develop a pedagogy
of listening to the stories of refugees. They introduce readers to innovative
curriculum reforms happening in Quebec that will highlight the need for
oral history to have a central place in human rights education.

With the rise of social history and historians' increasing concern for writing a more inclusive, democratic history, oral history since the 1960s has
been championed as a tool of activism and advocacy, the "mehod" to
which we turn in the fourth section. The title of Paul Thompson's book,
The Voice of the Past, became the mantra of much of the early movement. "Giving voice" to the silenced became an important objective in
the work of social historians and activists. Sharing authority was another
mantra – and collaborative work another imperative – of activist oral history. Academics questioned the role of scholars and their claims of scientific objectivity. Furthermore, the unequal relationship of power inherent
in any oral history interview – usually privileging the academic who has
access to funding, skills, and knowledge, and who builds a career on the
harvest of his research – called into question any easy claims at sharing
authority.[36]

Scholars from several groups made it clear that there was no single
solution to these complex ethical and political dilemmas. Among them
were indigenous scholars, who, as Winona Wheeler shows in chapter 13,
grappled with the role of settler archives and the lack of oral tradition in
their attempt to reconstruct and write indigenous history. While oral historians may have felt good about giving back to the community – whether
in the form of recordings or skills – they quickly came up against certain limits if, as Pamela Sugiman details in chapter 14, their interviewees
had their own agendas that did not correspond to or even contradicted
those of the historian. And when historians encountered powerful state
institutions, especially in the health sector, they sometimes had to negotiate other relationships of power, as Claudia Malacrida demonstrates in
chapter 15. Her chapter is one of the few contributions to the field of oral

history that intersects with disability studies.[37] Finally, as Joy Parr argues in the concluding chapter, the whole idea of a scholar initiating a process of sharing authority – at least with someone from a "vulnerable population" – is highly problematic, because it presumes the narrators' wish or intention to collaborate when in reality all the historian can and should do is to stand by and hear the testimony. Parr challenges the very role of the oral historian as advocate.

All chapters in this *Reader* engage with issues that affect oral history practitioners around the world. They do so from a specific space and place, informed by local, regional, national, and global perspectives. Thus, these are Canadian contributions to global debates that affect practices in specific locales.

This *Reader* seeks to stimulate dialogue and debate among Canadian oral history practitioners. It provides an institutional memory of past and current practices by presenting some of the best oral history work produced in Canada over the past quarter century. Over the past few decades, a number of English-language readers, anthologies, and handbooks have showcased the diversity of oral history theory and practice in the United States, Great Britain, Australia, New Zealand, France, Germany, Argentina, and other countries. Canadian oral history, however, has been noticeably absent from these collections. Some readers may be familiar with the internationally successful *Oral History Reader*, edited by Robert Perks and Alistair Thomson and in its second edition since 2006. Of the sixty-two articles published in the *Oral History Reader*'s two editions, however, only two were written by Canadian authors and none are represented in the second edition. Similarly, the two editions of *Oral History: An Interdisciplinary Anthology* included no text by Canadian authors. The two recently published handbooks to the practice include not a single text by a Canadian author.[38] These books, which have set the standards for the international field of oral history, entirely bypass the developments of Canadian scholarship. As a result, Canadian perspectives are virtually absent from international debates on oral history. The publication of a Canadian reader, therefore, brings an important addition that has been neglected by the international oral history movement. But this is not an exercise in nationalism. If Canadians had nothing to say about oral history or could contribute nothing meaningful to the international debate, we would not have bothered to assemble this *Reader*. Over the course of several years, as we talked about the state of oral history in Canada, however, we agreed that Canadians had much to contribute to the debate.

Some of it has been published in the *Oral History Forum d'histoire orale*, and more in various collections.[39]

Until now, Canadian students and teachers discussing oral history in seminars, and researchers and practitioners wishing to learn about oral history theories and methods in Canada, have had no resource to guide them. We hope our *Reader* will overcome this lack. It is the first comprehensive collection of articles on oral history within the Canadian context and by Canadian scholars. The collection will be of use to a growing number of students and educators in high school through to adult education and provide a resource for practitioners in the areas of community research and public policy development. Our goal is to raise awareness both within and outside Canada about Canada's contribution to the field. At the same time, we hope that this *Reader* will serve as a springboard for new debates within Canada and as a bridge to re-connect Canadian practitioners with their colleagues throughout the Americas, Europe, the Commonwealth and other parts of the world where oral history is flourishing. We hope also that *The Canadian Oral History Reader* will awaken in the broader Canadian public a new awareness of oral history, and acquaint a global audience with the rich sources of Canadian oral history.

The *Reader* comes at a time that sees a renaissance of oral history in Canada, with a string of new institutions, projects, and initiatives that provide stimulus and innovation beyond Canada's boundaries. As elsewhere in the world, there has been a significant growth of oral history in Canada over the past two decades. Despite continued skepticism in a few small quarters of traditional historians, oral history – along with life histories, storytelling, and testimony – has become a mainstay in documentaries, museum exhibits, multimedia and online presentations, education, therapy, and even business and administration. Permanent institutions such as the Canadian Museum of Immigration at Pier 21, the Canadian War Museum, the Canadian Museum for Human Rights, the Centre for Oral History and Digital Storytelling at Concordia University, and the Oral History Centre at the University of Winnipeg, as well as large projects such as the Truth and Reconciliation Commission on Indian Residential Schools, the Montreal Life Stories Project (Concordia University), and Nindibaajimomin – Digital Storytelling on the Inter-generational Experiences of Residential Schools (University of Winnipeg) – are just a few among dozens of new publicly and privately funded initiatives that envisage documenting the lived experiences of Canadians.[40] As in other parts of the world, Canadian society now acknowledges and cherishes subjective individual experiences as integral to understanding Canadian history and culture as well as to charting Canada's political, social, cultural, and even economic development in the future.

Much of this new interest in oral stories is driven by digital technologies. Recording people's memories, archiving them, and disseminating them online has become affordable and feasible for almost everyone. An increasing number of Canadians flock to oral history workshops, buy guides or look them up online, and seek guidance from oral historians in their attempts to reconstruct the histories of their families and communities. Students of all ages now regularly interview people and create oral history projects, as do community historians and activists. This flurry of activity presents oral historians with new questions and challenges about the practical, ethical, and legal aspects of their methods, the meanings of their sources, the technologies for archiving and disseminating their research, and the role oral history plays – or should play – in advocacy. We hope that this *Reader* provides the base and the beginning for a renewal of the conversation among Canadian oral historians, a conversation that needs to be integrated into a larger global discussion about the new aims of oral history in the twenty-first century.

NOTES

1 *Delgamuukw* v. *British Columbia*, 11 December 1997, 1075–6. Chief Justice Antonio Lamer explaining why oral history is admissible as evidence in court.

2 "Interview with Barry Broadfoot, reprinted from *Access Magazine*, winter 1978," *Oral History Association Journal* 3, no. 2 (1978): 26–8, quote 28.

3 Franca Iacovetta, "Post-Modern Ethnography, Historical Materialism, and Decentring the (Male) Authorial Voice: A Feminist Conversation," *Histoire sociale/Social History* 32, no. 64 (1999): 275–93, at 285–6.

4 For a survey of the use of oral sources in global historiography, see Daniel Woolf, *A Global History of History* (Cambridge: Cambridge University Press, 2011); the most extensive overview of the development of oral history is in Paul Thompson, *The Voice of the Past: Oral History*, 3rd edition (Oxford University Press, 2000), 25–81; on the beginnings of oral history as a research method in the United States, see Jerrold Hirsch, "Before Columbia: The FWP and American Oral History Research," *Oral History Review* 34, no. 2 (2007): 1–16; Allan Nevins, "Oral History: How and Why It Was Born," *Wilson Library Bulletin* 40 (March 1966): 600–1; Louis Starr, "Oral History," *Encyclopedia of Library and Information Sciences* 20 (New York: Dekker, 1977), 440–63; a recent critical analysis of the development of oral history worldwide is provided by Alistair Thomson, "Four Paradigm Transformations in

Oral History," *Oral History Review* 34, no. 1 (2007): 49–70; for an attempt to position the development of the oral history interview in the broader scope of modernity, see Alexander Freund, "Confessing Animals: Toward a Longue Durée History of the Oral History Interview," *Oral History Review* (spring 2014): 1–26; surveys of oral history in Canada include Ronald Labelle, "Reflections on Thirty Years of Oral History in Canada," *Oral History Forum d'histoire orale* 25 (2005): 7–14; Alexander Freund, "Oral History in Canada: A Paradox," in *Canada in Grainau/Le Canada à Grainau: A Multidisciplinary Survey after 30 Years*, edited by Klaus-Dieter Ertler and Hartmut Lutz (Frankfurt am Main: Peter Lang, 2009), 305–35.

5 Richard Lochhead, "Three Approaches to Oral History: The Journalistic, the Academic, and the Archival," *Canadian Oral History Association Journal* (from here: COHA *Journal*) 1 (1975–76): 5–12.

6 Michael Riordan, *An Unauthorized Biography of the World: Oral History on the Front Lines* (Toronto: Between the Lines, 2004), 1–2.

7 Donald Ritchie, *Doing Oral History: A Practical Guide*, 2nd edition (Oxford: Oxford University Press, 2003), 18–22; Valerie Raleigh Yow, *Recording Oral History. A Practical Guide for Social Sciences*, 2nd edition (Thousand Oaks, CA: Sage, 2005), 2.

8 James Bennett, *Oral History and Delinquency: The Rhetoric of Criminology* (Chicago: University of Chicago Press, 1988); Robert Sellar, *The History of the County of Huntingdon and of the Seigniories of Chateaugay and Beauharnois, From Their First Settlement to the Year 1838* (Huntingdon, QC: Canadian Gleaner, 1888), preface reprinted in COHA *Journal* 4, no. 1 (1979): 22–3; Heinz Lehmann, *The German Canadians, 1750–1937: Immigration, Settlement and Culture*, translated, edited, and introduced by Gerhard P. Bassler (St John's: Jesperson Press, 1986).

9 Leo LaClare, "Introduction," COHA *Journal* 1 (1975–76): 3.

10 Leo LaClare, "Directions in Canadian Aural/Oral History," *Sound Heritage* 4, no. 1 (1975): 6.

11 Quoted in Ian E. Wilson, Provincial Archivist, "Foreword," in Krzysztof M. Gebhard, *Community as Classroom: A Teacher's Practical Guide to Oral History* (Saskatchewan Archives Reference Series; 5), (Regina and Saskatoon: Saskatchewan Archives Board, 1985), iii; "About the Archives," Saskatchewan Archives Board website, http://www.saskarchives.com/about-archives (accessed 23 June 2014).

12 LaClare, "Directions," 6; Richard Lochhead, email correspondence with Alexander Freund, 26 June 2008; W.J. Langlois, Derek Reimer, Janet Cauthers, and Allen Specht, eds., *A Guide to Aural History Research* (Victoria, BC: Provincial Archives of British Columbia, 1976); Willa K. Baum, *Oral History for the Local Historical Society* (Stockton: Conference of California Historical Societies, 1969).

13 Willa K. Baum, *Transcribing and Editing Oral History* (Nashville: American Association of State and Local History, 1977).

14 Wilma MacDonald, "Some Reminiscences of COHA," *Oral History Forum d'histoire orale* 25 (2005): 15–28, 16.

15 W.J. Langlois, "Notes from Aural History," *Sound Heritage* 4, no. 1 (1975): 1.

16 MacDonald, "Some Reminiscences," 16.

17 Almut Leh, "Ethical Problems in Research Involving Contemporary Witnesses," translated by Edith Burley, *Oral History Forum d'histoire orale* 29 (2009): 1–14; Alexander von Plato, "Contemporary Witnesses and the Historical Profession: Remembrance, Communicative Transmission, and Collective Memory in Qualitative History," translated by Edith Burley, *Oral History Forum d'histoire orale* 29 (2009): 1–27; Linda Shopes, "Oral History and the Study of Communities: Problems, Paradoxes, and Possibilities," *The Journal of American History* 89, no. 2 (September 2002): 588–98.

18 Langlois, "Notes," 2.

19 Pauline Jewett, "Foreword," *Sound Heritage* 4, no. 1 (1975): v–vi, v.

20 Michael Frisch, *A Shared Authority: Essays on the Craft and Meaning of Oral and Public History* (Albany: SUNY Press, 1990); more recently, see High et al., "Sharing Authority: Community-University Collaboration in Oral History, Digital Storytelling, and Engaged Scholarship," special issue of *Journal of Canadian Studies* 43, no. 1 (winter 2009), guest edited by Steven High, Lisa Ndejuru, and Kristen O'Hare.

21 Will C. van den Hoonaard and Deborah K. van den Hoonaard, *Essentials of Thinking Ethically in Qualitative Research* (Walnut Creek, CA: Left Coast Press, 2013); Robert Borofsky, *Yanomami. The Fierce Controversy and What We Can Learn from It* (Berkeley: University of California Press, 2005).

22 All university-based researchers are required to complete the TCPS2 Tutorial Course on Research Ethics (CORE), which provides excellent documentation of unethical research in the past: http://www.ethics.gc.ca/eng/education/tutorial-didacticiel (accessed 23 June 2014). For a critique of such institutional research ethics processes, see Will C. van den Hoonaard, *Seduction of Ethics: Transforming the Social Sciences* (Toronto: University of Toronto Press, 2011); see also: Rosamond Rhodes, "Rethinking Research Ethics," *The American Journal of Bioethics* 10, no. 10 (2010): 19–36; Greg Koski, "'Rethinking Research Ethics,' Again: Casuistry, Phronesis, and the Continuing Challenges of Human Research," *The American Journal of Bioethics* 10, no. 10 (2010): 37–9.

23 Thomson, "Four Paradigm Transformations," 2007; Ronald J. Grele, "Commentary," *Oral History Review* 34, no. 2 (2007): 121–3.

24 Ronald J. Grele, *Envelopes of Sound: The Art of Oral History*, 2nd revised and expanded edition (Chicago: Precedent Publishing, 1985).

25 Luisa Passerini, "Work Ideology and Consensus under Italian Fascism," *History Workshop Journal* 8, no. 1 (1979): 82–108; Alessandro Portelli, "The Peculiarities of Oral History," *History Workshop Journal* 12, no. 1 (1981): 96–107; Alessandro Portelli, *The Death of Luigi Trastulli and Other Stories: Form and Meaning in Oral History* (Albany: SUNY Press, 1991).

26 Eva M. McMahan and Kim Lacy Rogers, eds., *Interactive Oral History Interviewing* (Hillsdale, NJ: Lawrence Erlbaum, 1994); Eva M. McMahan, "A Conversation Analytic Approach to Oral History Interviewing," in *Handbook of Oral History*, edited by Thomas L. Charlton et al. (Lanham, MD: AltaMira Press, 2006), 336–56.

27 Thomson, "Four Paradigm Transformations," 2007; Grele, "Commentary," 2007; Steven High, "Sharing Authority in the Writing of Canadian History: The Case of Oral History," in *Contesting Clio's Craft: New Directions and Debates in Canadian History*, edited by Chris Dummitt and Michael Dawson (London: Institute for the Study of the Americas, University of London, 2009), 21–46; Bryan D. Palmer, "Review of *Contesting Clio's Craft*," *American Historical Review* 115, no. 2 (April 2010): 497–8.

28 Riordan, *An Unauthorized Biography*, 200–2; Derek Reimer et al., "Industry, Labour and the Professions in British Columbia," COHA *Journal* 6 (1983): 21–32; Steven High, *Industrial Sunset: The Making of North America's Rust Belt: 1969–1984* (Toronto: University of Toronto Press, 2003).

29 Franca Iacovetta, "Post-Modern Ethnography, Historical Materialism, and Decentring the (Male) Authorial Voice: A Feminist Conversation," *Social History/Histoire sociale* 32, no. 64 (1999): 275–93; Freund, "Paradox," 313–14; Alexander Freund, *Oral History and Ethnic History*, Immigration and Ethnicity in Canada Series, 32 (Toronto: The Canadian Historical Association, 2014), 15–18.

30 Lori Ann Roness and Kent McNeil, "Legalizing Oral History: Proving Aboriginal Claims in Canadian Courts," *Journal of the West* 39, no. 3 (2000): 66–74; Chris Preston, "A Past of Tragic Stories: The (Non-)Treatment of Native Peoples' Oral Histories in Canada," *Undercurrent* 2, no. 1 (March 2005): 54–64; Mary Ann Pylypchuk, "The Value of Aboriginal Records as Legal Evidence in Canada: An Examination of Sources," *Archivaria* 32 (1991): 51–77; Joan Lovisek, "Transmission Difficulties: The Use and Abuse of Oral History in Aboriginal Claims," in *Papers of the Thirty-Third Algonquian Conference*, edited by H.C. Wolfart (Winnipeg: University of Manitoba Papers of the Algonquian Conference, 2002); Brian Thom, "Aboriginal Rights and Title in Canada After 'Delgamuukw,' Part 1: Oral Traditions and Anthropological Evidence in the Courtroom," *Native Studies Review* 14, no. 1 (2001): 1–26; Brian Thom, "Aboriginal Rights and Title in Canada After 'Delgamuukw.' Part 2: Anthropological Perspectives on Rights, Tests, Infringement and Justification," *Native Studies Review* 14, no. 2 (2001): 1–42.

31 For further information, see http://www.oralhistorycentre.ca/projects/ininiwag-dibaajimowag-first-nations-men-and-inter-generational-experiences-residential.

32 Isabelle Shay, "Interviewing Tribal Elders and Native Women," COHA *Journal* 9 (1989): 4–5.

33 Freund, "Paradox," 316, 326. *Oral History Forum d'histoire orale* is an open-access journal available at www.oralhistoryforum.ca.

34 Richard Lochhead, "Directions in Oral History in Canada," COHA *Journal* 6 (1983): 3–6; Freund, "Paradox," 313, 316.

35 For early examples in Canada, see "Aural History in B.C. Studies," *Sound Heritage* 4, no. 1 (1975): 8–15; "Aural History in Primary and Secondary Schools," *Sound Heritage* 4, no. 1 (1975): 16–19; Alfred and Jessie Haché, "Oral History at Petite Riviere Elementary School, Nova Scotia," COHA *Journal* 14 (1994): 11–20.

36 Frisch, *A Shared Authority*, 1990; High et al., "Sharing Authority"; Anna Sheftel and Stacey Zembrzycki, eds., *Oral History Off the Record* (New York: Palgrave, 2013); Freund, "Confessing Animals," 2014.

37 But see the innovative, oral history–based film, "The Inmates Are Running the Asylum," available on YouTube: https://www.youtube.com/watch?v=Jwya RU1svrA (accessed 23 June 2014). Lanny Beckman and Megan Davies, "Democracy Is a Very Radical Idea," in *Mad Matters: A Critical Reader in Canadian Mad Studies*, edited by Brenda A. LeFrançois, Robert Menzies, and Geoffrey Reaume (Toronto: Canadian Scholars' Press, 2013), 49–63.

38 David K. Dunaway and Willa K. Baum, eds., *Oral History: An Interdisciplinary Anthology*, 1st and 2nd editions (Walnut Creek, CA: AltaMira Press, 1984, 1996); Sherna Berger and Daphne Patai, eds., *Women's Words: The Feminist Practice of Oral History* (New York and London: Routledge, 1991); Alistair Thomson and Robert Perks, eds., *The Oral History Reader*, 1st and 2nd editions (New York: Routledge, 1998/2006); Thomas L. Charlton et al., *Handbook of Oral History* (Lanham, MD: AltaMira Press, 2006); Donald A Ritchie, ed., *The Oxford Handbook of Oral History* (Oxford: Oxford University Press, 2011).

39 The complete run of the journal is freely available online at www.oralhistoryforum.ca. Recent collections with significant Canadian content include Alexander Freund and Alistair Thomson, eds., *Oral History and Photography* (New York: Palgrave, 2012); Sheftel and Zembrzycki, *Oral History*, 2013.

40 On the Montreal Life Stories project, see Steven High, *Oral History at the Crossroads: Sharing Life Stories of Survival and Displacement* (Vancouver: UBC Press, 2014).

SECTION ONE

Methodology

1

Methodology for Recording Oral Histories in the Aboriginal Community[1]

Brian Calliou

> Every time an Elder dies, it is like
> a library has burned down.[2]

Among social scientists and in the courts, there is a growing awareness and acceptance that oral histories are credible sources of information. Many academic disciplines – history,[3] anthropology,[4] political science,[5] education, [6] Native studies,[7] and law,[8] and others – have begun to explore their value. Particularly in cases involving Aboriginal issues, courts have moved toward accepting oral histories as viable sources for understanding and interpreting the past. In the 1997 *Delgamuukw* decision, for instance, the Supreme Court of Canada made significant pronouncements about the utility of Aboriginal oral histories, stating that oral histories of Aboriginal peoples are to be given consideration and weight equal to other forms of evidence.[9]

The importance of Elders' knowledge in the Aboriginal community[10] cannot be over-emphasized. Their testimony can assist Aboriginal communities in their struggles to assert their rights in courts or in claims negotiations for Aboriginal or treaty rights. Elders' knowledge can also be used to rewrite history to include an Aboriginal perspective, which until recently has largely been overlooked.[11] Further, because the traditional storytelling method of learning is slowly being lost, this information can be recorded for future generations to learn traditional teachings and stories.

The objective of this commentary is to assist Aboriginal communities and other researchers in documenting the vast knowledge held by Elders and others. It is designed to guide researchers through many aspects of the interview process. These guidelines will also be of use to students interested in obtaining information through interviews in the Aboriginal community. This chapter also provides information on how to conduct and document oral histories. The format guides researchers from pre-interview arrangements and background research to the interview, and on to analyzing post-interview data, cataloguing evidence, writing a final report, and making the data available for further use. It also addresses proper protocols for approaching Elders, as well as other cultural factors. Before setting out this methodology, however, the need for oral histories and the way in which academics and the courts have dealt with oral histories as sources of historical knowledge will be discussed.

THE NEED FOR ORAL HISTORIES

Most oral history projects aim to supplement or complement written information. However, they can also provide primary research material where written evidence is lacking.[12] In Aboriginal communities, Elders are a wealth of information; they have knowledge of significant events, personal reminiscences, genealogies, and traditional knowledge.

Interviews with Elders provide primary sources of knowledge on various issues. These primary sources can be used for a variety of purposes. One important contemporary issue is First Nations' understanding of treaties with the Dominion government. What did our ancestors understand about the negotiations and processes with respect to treaty making? What benefits did they expect to receive through the treaties? What would they have expected to give in return? These questions have largely been ignored by non-Aboriginal historical and legal interpretations of the Canadian treaty-making process.[13] Answers to them can be found, in part, through community Elders.

There is very little, if any, written information about what our forefathers actually understood about their contact and relationship with European newcomers. Non-Aboriginals have almost exclusively written the history with little regard for Aboriginal peoples' perspectives and understandings. Indeed, Bruce Trigger noted that much information about Indians originated as propaganda and only later in works of history.[14] There is a need to tap into the vast reservoir of Elders' knowledge, some of which has been passed down from generation to generation, so that the other side of the story can be told. Elder knowledge can supplement, complement, or contrast with written history, and thereby put forth Aboriginal perspectives of history. Blair Stonechild conducted one example of this historical research method in *Saskatchewan Indians and the Resistance of*

1885: Two Case Studies.[15] In his introduction, Stonechild argued that "the study of the North West Resistance of 1885 is only complete if the role of the Indian people of the time is included." Because most accounts focus on the Métis and Dominion Government response, Stonechild revisited the history of the North West Resistance of 1885 to write a First Nations perspective of the event, focusing on the role that First Nations played. In reference to his methods, he added: "the account in this book, using Indian oral history and original source materials, takes a retrospective look at the Resistance from the perspectives of Indian peoples."

A better understanding of the past can create change. Citing recent civil rights cases as examples, historian Robert Shafer states that historical knowledge has often been used as a tool for change.[16] Through the use of Aboriginal history, similar types of change can be made. And as Aboriginal perspectives become more widely known, a clearer understanding of contemporary Aboriginal claims and grievances will emerge. We are more likely to be closer to the historical truth of the relationship between Aboriginal and non-Aboriginal peoples when both sides of the story have been told and understood.

Elders' knowledge is also useful in litigation, as well as in negotiating claims.[17] Indeed, as the *Simon* and *Delgamuukw* cases illustrate, Canadian courts have begun to accept oral histories as testimonial evidence in Aboriginal litigation.[18]

In the *Delgamuukw* case, Chief Justice Lamer reasoned that it was necessary for the Canadian legal system to "adapt the laws of evidence so that the Aboriginal perspective on their practices, customs and traditions and on their relationship with the land, are given due weight by the courts."[19] In practical terms, this meant that the courts had "to come to terms with the oral histories of Aboriginal societies."[20] The chief justice further pointed out that "those histories play a crucial role in the litigation of Aboriginal rights."[21] In fact, the Supreme Court of Canada allowed the Gitksan and Wet'suwet'en chiefs' appeal in part, because the trial judge failed to give sufficient weight to the oral histories. The earlier trial judge had erred in fact, Chief Justice Lamer stated, "by failing to appreciate the evidentiary difficulties inherent in adjudicating Aboriginal claims."[22] He reasoned that if oral histories were disregarded or given no weight, it would amount to imposing an impossible burden of proof for Aboriginal peoples to meet. The chief justice reviewed the rules of evidence and its exceptions, and recognized the challenges of using oral histories as historical proof. Nevertheless, he concluded that "the laws of evidence must be adapted in order that this type of evidence can be accommodated and placed on an equal footing with the types of historical evidence that courts are familiar with."[23] Chief Justice Lamer expressly acknowledged that, since Aboriginal societies did not keep written records at the time of contact and few did when sovereignty was asserted by the Crown, "it would be exceedingly difficult for them to produce" the conclusive evidence required to authenticate their practices, customs, and traditions.[24] It is interesting to note that the chief justice referred to and quoted the discussion of oral histories in the Report on the Royal Commission on Aboriginal Peoples and an academic article on Aboriginal oral histories and evidence law.[25] While acknowledging the difficulties of relying on oral histories, he concluded that exceptions to the rules against hearsay evidence allowed, and oral societies' special circumstances required, courts to give equal weight to oral histories because the latter are a "repository of historical knowledge" and "an expression of the values and mores of" a specific Aboriginal culture.[26] In the *Dick* case, a British Columbia Provincial Court judge stated that oral histories are "enclothed … with a cloak of trustworthiness" because of the authority that Elders are accorded as keepers of oral histories. The fact that each generation passes on those oral histories was further validation.[27] In the *Paulette* case, Justice Morrow stated that, with respect to the oral histories of Elders surrounding the treaty negotiations and signing, "their testimony was the truth and represented their best memory of what to them must have been an important event."[28] Thus, Canadian courts have given voice to those who were previously excluded, and have clearly proclaimed that oral histories are a primary source of information that must be considered.

ACADEMIC DEBATE ABOUT ORAL HISTORIES

Winona Wheeler (Stevenson), a Native studies scholar, has criticized historians who refuse to respect oral histories and rely solely on written documents. She argued that they "fear what they don't understand and so they 'other' Indigenous voices right out of their own histories."[29] She critiqued traditional historians who have spoken for her peoples' experiences without hearing their voices: "A large portion of my own research ponders why it is that many conventionally trained historians believe, subconsciously or not, that they can tell the stories of my peoples' experiences without talking to us, or valuing, or placing any credibility in, how we understand our past – how they can presume to represent our histories without ever hearing our side of the story."[30]

Angela Cavender Wilson, another Native studies scholar, also argued that Aboriginal sources are necessary for any Aboriginal peoples' histories. Indeed, she asks: "Would historians attempt to write a history of Germany without consulting any German sources? Would a scholar of Chinese history attempt to write Chinese history without consulting Chinese sources? Why is it that scholars in American Indian history have written so many academically acceptable works without consulting American Indian sources? Is it simply because most of our sources are oral rather than written?"[31]

Wheeler argued that historians must stop objectifying indigenous communities' pasts and learn to write history in collaboration and consultation with the communities in question.[32] She argued that, in order to better ensure that an Aboriginal voice comes through, ethnohistorians and other social scientists ought to pursue research questions and write Aboriginal peoples' histories under the direction of the Aboriginal communities being investigated.

The growing acceptance of oral histories as a credible source of information has not quieted the debate on oral histories, however. Many critics continue to view oral histories with skepticism. For instance, they raise concerns about the fallibility of human memory or the possibility of misunderstanding events as retold over a number of generations.[33] Historians, in particular, have suspected that oral history is incapable of providing any "truth" about the past.

Anthropologist Julie Cruikshank examined the history of anthropologists' views of oral traditions.[34] Originally, she explained, anthropologists saw oral traditions as having little or no value as historical evidence. Later, traditional accounts were treated as objects to be collected. Later still, they were viewed as more complex narratives that could only be understood in reference to the context in which they were told. More recently, anthropologists have begun to view oral traditions as narratives to be understood on their own terms. Anthropologists and ethno-historians now ask how people use the ideological, symbolic, and metaphoric meanings of oral traditions to talk about the past. These scholars are increasingly critical of the Western ethnocentric bias of written documents and now view them within the context in which they are written.[35]

It is imperative for academics, courts, and other Canadians to listen to the perspective of Aboriginal peoples on history and the relationship that our peoples had with the immigrant populations of this country. They must discard the rigid Eurocentric views and academic biases that have resulted in the oppression of non-European, non-literate societies. A good starting point is the acceptance and trust of the oral testimony of our Elders. There are legitimate reasons for Elders' beliefs and understandings. The histories they were told have been told and retold for generations. This is what gives them their air of truth.[36] The community can usually expose those who deceive or stretch the truth by comparing their words to other testimonies given by Elders.

DEFINING ORAL HISTORIES

Distinctions are made among academics regarding different types of oral history. First, there are "collective" histories that are the "official" group versions. Then there are "individual" histories, which are personal reminiscences shared with others. Historians hold that oral histories passed down over a number of generations are not as trustworthy as personal reminiscences because the former are hearsay while the latter are direct accounts. Both personal reminiscences and collective histories, however, provide valuable information that should be recorded and interpreted.

Bennett Ellen McCardle defined oral history as "evidence about past life, events, and traditions, taken from the spoken word of people who have personal knowledge of these facts."[37] Although this definition is adopted here for purposes of explanation, oral history can and should be broad enough to include Aboriginal peoples' definitions of oral history. Although differences exist in what oral history means to varying Aboriginal groups, there are enough similarities to form a core definition. A richer definition of oral history would include all types of narratives, stories, songs, and speeches passed along to successive generations to explain the past. The gathered materials – interview tapes or videos, notes, summaries, transcripts, and translations – constitute primary sources that historians and other researchers can utilize and interpret.

The concept of oral history also encompasses the "method of gathering a body of historical information in oral form."[38] Fred Kendal states that oral history involves "certain procedures and standards for the gathering and preservation of spoken memoirs in particular, and for their proper documentation and use in finished historical works."[39] A systematic approach that meets high academic standards and procedures reflects a method known as oral history.

If the views of Aboriginal peoples are presented in conjunction with other documentary evidence, a compelling reinterpretation of history – one that is fairer and more objective – emerges. By taking into account the views of a greater number of parties involved in a particular event, the resulting narrative will provide a more accurate reflection of past events.

RECOMMENDED METHODOLOGY FOR AN ORAL HISTORY PROJECT

Defining the Project's Goals and Objectives

What are the objectives for documenting oral histories? It is important to determine at the outset how oral history evidence will be used, because different purposes require different interviewing procedures and storage methods.[40] For example, if the evidence is to be used in court, a strict method of data gathering and storage may be required. One might also be required to have the Elder sign a declaration stating the truthfulness of their statement.[41] The audio or videotape might have to be stored in a place where only one person has access to it in order to ensure that tampering does not occur.[42] One would hate to have a comprehensive land claim fall through because a piece of evidence (the audio or videotape) was ruled inadmissible for lack of proper procedure or proper storage. If oral history evidence is intended for future legal action, a practising lawyer should be consulted before any interview takes place so that all necessary factors in the undertaking are considered.

If the objective is academic research,[43] the data collection method need not be quite as strict, but it is nevertheless rigorous. Most universities publish stringent guidelines for research using human subjects, including minimizing risk of harm to participants, full disclosure and informed consent, and respecting confidentiality and anonymity if requested.

If the objective is to record and store Elders' knowledge for the future (possibly to teach traditional stories to youth), then it is possible to follow less strict procedures for interviewing, recording, and storing data. However, a note of caution must be emphasized here. It makes sense to ask open-ended questions that will allow the elicited information to be used for a number of heretofore unknown and different purposes. Let the Elders' knowledge speak for itself. They should not be led to specific answers that the interviewer thinks are important. For the most part, the answers are already in the narration.

Both the academic community and the courts may disregard an Aboriginal perspective if the oral testimony is perceived to be politically motivated or if the Elder was "led" to a desired answer.[44] An example of a leading question is: "Your people were pressured into signing treaty, weren't they?" This question "leads" to a likely "yes" response. Rather, the question should be open-ended, such as: "What are some of the factors, if any, that might have influenced your people to sign treaty?" or "What happened at the treaty negotiations?" The latter questions invite a variety of responses, so that the Elder's views, not the interviewer's, are recorded. The perception of bias in an interview can taint otherwise useful and accurate data. Such data would be too one-sided and not present a balanced view. For a closer approximation of the truth, many sides of an issue must be presented. Data will be viewed as carrying more weight – that is, be more persuasive – if it is objective and balanced, if it is not too biased or one-sided. Thus, the interviewer must use open-ended questions so that the Elder can answer according to the way he or she feels.[45] If approached in this way, the recorded testimony will more closely reflect what the Elder thought was important.

Pre-Interview Preparation

Appropriate protocol must be followed before interviewing a member of an Aboriginal community. One cannot simply go to an Elder and begin questioning without preparing the ground.[46] First, the topic must be given much prior thought and consideration. Second, one must request and obtain permission from the local authority. Third, after it has been decided which Elders will be interviewed, their personal agreement must be sought.

Topic or Research Question

Giving a topic serious thought beforehand is a mark of respect for the Elders. They can tell immediately by the questions whether sufficient forethought has been given and, if they perceive the absence of prior research, may turn away an interviewer.[47] Therefore, it is important at the outset of the preparation to establish the goals and objectives.[48]

With respect to the research question, they must clearly reflect the project's goals and objectives. What is the issue? Where is it situated? What is to be accomplished with the gathered information? Is the information for a written report or for future use?

Once the goals and objectives are clarified, background research into the issue and community or territory in question must be conducted.[49] This is done so as to be prepared, and to ensure that the recorded material will be as valid to the issue as possible. One must ask intelligent questions that get to the issue addressed. It makes little sense to waste one's own time or the Elder's by asking poorly developed questions that yield non-pertinent information.

Information for background research is available at local public libraries or at the libraries of colleges, universities, or other post-secondary institutions. Legislature libraries also have excellent collections of materials and are open for public loan. Provincial archives or local museums may also be helpful. One might also consult Aboriginal organizations such as the Assembly of First Nations in Ottawa, Treaty and Aboriginal Rights Research (TARR) organizations, or Métis and Inuit organizations, all of which house a variety of materials in their libraries. The libraries of specific Canadian or provincial government departments also house information and materials. A researcher might contact the Fish and Wildlife, Forestry, and Parks and Recreation departments, for instance, to request materials on hunting, fishing, and trapping issues.[50] For primary written sources, the Library and Archives of Canada RG10 Series, or Missionary and Church records are invaluable. Local historical or genealogical societies can also be excellent sources of information.

While researching background material, it is a good idea to write brief summaries that can be reviewed at a later date if needed.[51] This step will save time at the stage of going over material in preparing the report. Notes should be taken to support one's arguments and to reference different sources of material.

Once the researcher has become somewhat familiar with the issue and the community or territory in which it is based, the focus of the enquiry must be narrowed.[52] Developing a set of questions to ask Elders accomplishes this. Let the questions sit for a couple of days and then critique them for being too closed, too vague and ambiguous, or too specific. An Elder is shown respect when one's topic has been subjected to considerable self-reflection.

LOCAL AUTHORITY

It is essential to obtain permission from appropriate authorities in order to conduct research in the community. For example, one might approach the Band Council on a reserve or the governing council of a particular Aboriginal community. Be prepared to make a presentation to convince them that the research is needed and will be of benefit to them.

It is important to note that members of an Aboriginal community have no obligation to cooperate with a researcher. It is possible, for instance, that some Elders may be tired of being interviewed. In some Aboriginal communities, resentment has built up over the years toward researchers who come in, interview the locals to "pick their brains," and then leave. In many cases, the community never sees or hears from the interviewer again. Preliminary contact with community members can help determine Elder willingness. For the most agreeable and mutually beneficial relationships, a "community-based research" approach should be adopted, whereby the researcher makes a commitment to full disclosure, full consultation with – and participation of – community members, and complete access to information; and, ideally, undertakes to return a copy of the finished report to the community.[53]

CONTACT WITH ELDERS

If the researcher does not know the Elders to be interviewed, it is helpful to use an intermediary as a go-between.[54] It is necessary to first establish a trusting relationship. If the Elder knows and trusts the intermediary, he or she will likely extend that trust to those whom the intermediary knows and trusts. The Elder will be that much more at ease when it comes time for the interview.

If possible, a preliminary meeting should be set up to meet the Elders before any interviews.[55] Proper protocol should also be observed by offering the Elder a gift of tobacco or cloth, or a small monetary gift.[56] This protocol is a traditional practice in many Aboriginal communities and is always followed when one seeks the sharing of an Elder's knowledge. This gesture demonstrates respect for their knowledge and gratitude for their generosity in sharing it.

If the Elder is not an adherent of traditional customs, but, rather, for example, a Catholic, ask the community about the best way to approach him or her. In my experience of interviewing Elders in northern Alberta, even devout Catholics accept traditional gifts because they are well aware of the traditional protocol. In order to not offend anyone, it would be wise to find out from preliminary community contacts what is acceptable practice in a particular locale.

The preliminary meeting provides an opportunity to fully disclose the research's purpose, who or what agency is sponsoring the research, and what uses it will be put toward. At such a meeting, the researcher's goals, objectives, and the important contribution that the Elder's knowledge will make to the project must be clearly explained.[57] One might also emphasize how important their stories and knowledge will be when passed on to the youth. One should also clarify to the Elder each step to be taken in the research process.

This is also a good moment to ask the Elder for permission to record the interview. If the Elder is unfamiliar with such equipment, one could perhaps illustrate its use. If the Elder does not wish to be recorded, either take notes as he or she speaks – as long as they agree – or make notes immediately afterwards.

This preliminary meeting gives an opportunity for the two parties to get to know each other a little so that at the formal interview the Elder is likely to be more at ease and speak more openly. Further, the Elder will have had time to think about the topic and its objectives and had a chance to refresh his or her memory before the actual interview.[58]

As a researcher, be prepared to disclose the interview's purpose and intent. The information provided by Elders "belongs" to them, so they must first "release" it to the researcher.[59] To confirm this, it may be advisable to request that the interviewee sign a release form.[60] This form must be retained for future reference, so it should be filed with the transcript and audiotape. One might be able to get around the need for a form by letting the Elder know that he or she may edit anything out that they feel should not be released.[61] Also, there may be no need for a release form if what is given is "general information."[62] Generally, however, it should be made a practice to obtain release forms to avoid problems.

Equipment preparation comes next. An interviewer must gather and become familiar with any equipment that will be used.[63] Video recording will require even more preparation and familiarization than audio recorders. Video recordings, like sound recordings, require an area for good sound quality, but the former also require additional testing for adequate lighting and picture quality. No matter what type of recording is made, the equipment should be tested and a trial run made so that a sample can be viewed to check the recording quality. Purchase the best quality equipment or the end product will suffer. Be sure that cords, lights, batteries, and microphones are all gathered and in good working order before heading out into the field. Do not waste the Elder's time by being unprepared or having equipment that does not function properly. Mentally run through the interview and try to determine if anything has been left out. Also create a checklist of additional things that need to be done.

THE INTERVIEW PROCESS

Choose a quiet, comfortable spot for the interview. Background noise or interruptions can cause serious problems at the stage of playing the audio back for transcription. (Note that a bare room tends to echo and affect sound quality.)[64]

Try to create a relaxed atmosphere. Put yourself and the Elder at ease by perhaps beginning with some small talk. Then set up the equipment and get everything ready. Allowing the Elder to feel at ease will enable the conversation to flow as between friends. As with interviewees in any oral interview, Elders may be more quickly put at ease and engage in more relaxed discussion if they are shown material objects such as old photographs or maps and invited to talk about their contents – who the persons involved were and what events were connected with them.

The taping session begins by recording the names of the interviewer and the Elder, and the project, interview location, and date.[65] Ask specific biographical questions first, and then proceed to the prepared questions on the topic.[66] It is not necessary to follow the question list strictly. If the Elder talks freely on the subject without prompting, let him or her speak freely. Obviously the information singled out to be related is important. On the other hand, if an Elder is quiet, then further questioning might offer encouragement. Note, however, that pauses of up to a few minutes are not uncommon for an Aboriginal Elder. This is because the Elder is developing the answers, so care must be taken not to interrupt the silence. The interviewer will require great sensitivity in gauging the situation to determine regular lengths of pauses so as to not break the Elder's train of thought by interrupting too soon.[67]

An interviewer's attitude and behaviour are very important. Show great respect and give full attention to the Elder as he or she speaks.[68] One person related a story to me about a friend who had written everything down while interviewing an Elder.[69] The Elder later enquired, "What is wrong with your friend's mind?" The Elder thought that the interviewer's mind was not working properly because everything had to be written down and the interviewer seemed not to be paying attention. Remember that an interview is a recorded conversation, so partake in it by listening intently, showing agreement, and asking for clarification when it is needed. Show respect by being involved in a conversation.

If the Elder makes hand gestures, then the interviewer must note the direction or size indicated, to supplement the sound recording. Without verbal clarification, anyone hearing it or reading the transcript later would not know what the Elder had meant. One can also ask the Elder to state aloud the specific direction or size, although to do so would require interrupting their train of thought.

If contradictory information is given, make a note and ask the Elder to explain the inconsistency at a later time, to avoid interruptions.[70] One must be cautious here. Do so in a respectful and polite manner, gently mentioning that something that was said one way at first seemed to have been said differently later. An intervention of this nature usually clears up the discrepancy and demonstrates that the interviewer is paying attention. For example, the Elder might earlier have referred to a place where an important event occurred, using different names. Often, places are known by more than one name, and there may be a specific name for a particular place in the Elder's language. The Elder might inadvertently refer to the same place by two different names. It is also the case with many Indian people that they themselves are known both by a name in their language and a Christian name. A seeming discrepancy can usually be resolved by asking for clarification.

Another situation in which an inconsistency might occur is when the Elder's statement does not correspond to what other Elders have stated. Ill feelings may be caused among Elders if an interviewer names particular Elders who have made differing statements.[71] Rather than provide names, simply mention what another person has said and then let the Elder respond. Much can be explained when the Elder is given a chance to clarify. There may be a good reason why this Elder views an event differently. It might be useful to understand an Elder's reasons for a contradictory interpretation of an event. Indeed, clarification of inconsistencies can tap a wealth of knowledge that might otherwise be buried. The essential point is that the interviewer listen intently and ask for clarification of any inconsistencies, because people can unconsciously state one thing while meaning another.

The interviewer must also keep an eye on the recording device to ensure there is sufficient storage. An interview can often run for hours. One does not want to have to ask the Elder to repeat much of what was said only because the recording device stopped unnoticed.

There is another interviewing model whereby several Elders are interviewed simultaneously. An excellent example of this is seen in the transcripts of the 1975 *Elders' Think Tank*, where a number of Elders were gathered together and recorded while responding to specific questions.[72] The discussion generated by this collective method can stimulate participants to remember various events. In such cases, the interviewer must be sure to take accurate notes of who is speaking at any time, so that when transcription is performed it will be clear who was speaking. Such open discussions, because they record a public and collective memory, generally provide an official version of events.[73]

The preceding description has portrayed the interview process as though any Elder can be interviewed in English. Most Elders in Aboriginal communities speak English as a second language; however, some may speak more freely and better express themselves in their native tongue. An interview with a Cree Elder, for example, may necessitate a Cree-speaking interviewer or the services of an interpreter. The chosen interpreter should be somewhat familiar with the topic, background research, and questions to be asked. Richard Lightning, a Cree interpreter who worked with the Indian Association of Alberta oral history project of the 1970s, pointed out the difficulty he experienced in trying to formulate questions to ask Elders.[74] This problem arises because "there is such a vast difference in grammatical structure" between Cree and English.[75] Furthermore, English words do not always easily translate into Cree or other Aboriginal languages, and an Elder may have difficulty grasping the concepts the questions convey. Nuances in language and voice intonation may also be lost in the translation.

For the uninitiated interviewer, the manner and structure of Elders' conversations may be a challenge to fathom. Elders "often commence a conversation with great depths of historical background information" and may need to be brought more into focus through further questions. However, this is the pattern of storytelling.[76] It may take some time for a researcher to learn to "hear" the stories and narratives told by Elders. Walter Lightning described the levels of complexity in Elders' narratives:

> The way that the Elder told the stories was a way of giving me information that would become knowledge if I thought about the stories in the right way. The stories were structured in such a way that each story's meaning got more and more complex and rich as I thought about it. The Elder knew that I was not ready to understand the deeper systems of meaning and could not take it all in at once, so he constructed the story so that its meaning would continue to unfold. It was not just the individual stories that did this, but the stories were all structurally related to each other, even though I did not necessarily realize that when each one was told.[77]

Thus, we must "learn to hear" our Elders before we are able to understand the full meaning of the knowledge that they pass on to us. Some Elders' stories may be somewhat repetitious, indicating an emphasis that the Elder places on certain topics. As the late Linda Akan pointed out, repetition may also serve to refocus the topic or check the learner's understanding: "Repetition in text is made for refocusing in (an)other context(s). There is an implication of maturity or stage-development changes, as repetition checks the learner's understanding of these. A 'good talk' has lots of repetition to help us draw verbal circles of existence."[78]

Elders may respond to only one or two questions, and with lengthy stories because, generally, they are not used to being asked a stream of questions.[79] One must appreciate the virtue of patience and learn to hear what the Elders say, because they may frame their responses in a way that differs from the way in which the question is framed.[80] It requires hard work on the interviewer's part. One has to go over and over the recorded testimony, but most answers can be found within it. Keep in mind during the interviews that this is a learning process. Do not hesitate to adjust the format or method as required. The interviews must produce the information sought or they will be of little use to the project.

POST-INTERVIEW PROCESS

Transcription

Once the interview is completed, the recording should be transcribed as soon as possible. Ideally, transcription is performed by the interviewer immediately after having completed the interview (or a few interviews). Although recordings should of course be transcribed as accurately as possible, minor editing, such as removing the "um's," "uh's," and "er's," or any other sounds used to fill silence, is allowable.[81] Some information can be bracketed – comments about gestures, laughs or chuckles, an interruption in the recording, or a ringing telephone. Pauses in speech or unfinished sentences are generally indicated by ellipses, as in: "Were you there when …?" or "I think that was in … about 1917." If a word or phrase cannot be understood during transcription, a blank space should be left in its place.

Julie Cruikshank described the technique that she used for transcribing the tapes on which she recorded Yukon Elders.[82] She and the translator began a word-by-word translation, and when that was completed they reworked it into Standard English. This usually required some juggling of words because the Aboriginal language and the English language have reverse sentence structures.[83]

When transcription is complete, the interviewer should read the transcript while listening to the recording to ensure that everything is properly written down. A proofreading should follow. If possible, it is advisable to let the Elder read (or have read to him or her) the transcript for accuracy and to seek their approval of the product. This is now a primary document that can be consulted for future use and should be complete and accurate. Once the first set of recordings is transcribed, go over them with the question set in mind to verify that the desired information has been obtained. If it is to be reused, the question list, with its goals and objectives, should be evaluated to ensure that it is serving its purpose. Adjust by adding, deleting, or reworking the questions.

The researcher can provide additional commentary to be attached to the raw data transcripts, providing background information about the interviews. For example, was the interview conducted in a relaxed atmosphere? How did the interviewee respond to certain questions? Was the interviewee feeling ill? Are there any details that may explain the situation in which the information was given? This can be valuable information to researchers using these materials in the future. Such commentary can also be useful to the interviewer when he or she evaluates the transcripts and other materials to write the report at a later date.

Cataloguing the Information

All materials must be clearly labelled – original recordings and transcripts, as well as copies of both. The label should include the project name, interviewer, interviewee (i.e., the Elder), date, and interview location.[84] Information is catalogued by creating an index of each and every piece of data.[85] If the information is broad, specific categories should be created. As long as everything is labelled and indexed, future researchers will have all the necessary information about the interviewees, when the interviews were recorded, and what issues were addressed. This is crucial because, as those who know about the contents of each recording move on, unidentifiable boxes of tapes, disks, videos, and transcripts could remain behind.

Making Copies

It is a good idea to make backup copies of the recording and safely store the original.[86] And it is an appreciated gesture to give a copy of the recording and transcript, as well as the final report, to the Elder or the community. To do so is to give something back to a community that has given so much to the research.[87] The interviewer might write a summary report of all the project's given testimonies. It might also contain mention of repeated themes, as well as discrepancies or inconsistencies.[88] This summary report can be put on file and referred to in the future as a quick reference for the transcripts.

Analyzing the Data

After completing the data collection (interviews, transcripts, photographs, maps, and books and articles relating to the topic) and having made copies of all needed documents, the researcher now must evaluate what has been done and consider what steps to take next.[89] Is more research necessary? Consultation with co-workers or professionals such as teachers, professors, librarians, archivists, Band or community officials, or lawyers will help determine if any important ideas or sources have been missed.

This is also the moment to decide on the nature of the finished report. Will it be a short account, a major report, or a legal statement of claim? After making these decisions, one can move on to analyzing the data and materials and writing the final report. Regardless of the final report type, it is important to detail the findings and pass on any recommendations. Since the reader may not be as well versed in the material as the author, writing a clear concise report will help.[90] Data analysis can be as elaborate as desired. The simplest analysis consists of evaluating and correlating responses.[91] This involves assigning a positive or negative value to a response for tabulation. For example, if a question generates a response such as "I understand we gave up our rights to water resources" or "I understand we did not give up our water rights," it is common practice to put a plus sign (+) for every "positive" response and a minus sign (–) for every "negative" response. Total the responses and comment in the report as to the overall outcome in the study.

Another analytical method is to "grade" the responses using a measure referred to as the Likert scale. Especially when open-ended questions are involved, the answers may differ in degree from one extreme to the other. Assign the number one (1) to an extreme response, two (2) to a slightly less extreme response, and continue to a chosen number to the response at the other extreme. For example, responses might be divided into five groups, with 1 assigned to one end and 5 to the response at the other extreme.

In order for the data to be meaningful to the reader, they must be accompanied by a narrative or story. A narrative is a way of explaining the analysis;[92] that is, a vehicle for presenting one's thoughts on the facts. Thus, if one concludes that, for the most part, the informants (Elders or other interviewees) understood that their people were giving up land only to the depth of the plough, then it must be explained clearly how that conclusion was reached, by taking the reader step by step through the tabulated and evaluated responses. One might also include a sampling of quotations to provide as evidence. Inconsistencies in the responses, if any, must also be explained.

A more difficult analytical process involves intuitive interpretation.[93] There are no strict rules for this method, but some of the following techniques are useful. Trends or themes in responses can be highlighted and explained. Direct quotations can be used to strengthen the argument or conclusion. Seek out and note any discrepancies and inconsistencies in responses. Do discrepancies occur only in discussions of specific topics? Is there one explanation that can cover all discrepancies? Look for meaning in all of the data. Also make note of the many implicit assumptions derived from the interview material. Much of what is communicated is often not stated explicitly. Assumptions need to be stated in the report.

Interview data can also be evaluated by comparing responses with written facts, maps, and photographs. For example, the validity of dates and locations must be confirmed. Just as written information derived from traditional sources is not always entirely accurate, so the information provided in oral histories should also be cross-referenced against other sources. Thus, when the oral evidence of a number of people consistently contradicts written evidence, the former may well be correct and the latter incorrect.[94] Critical examination of the data will ensure its reliability.

Writing the Report

The following steps will assist in writing almost any type of report.[95] First, make an outline that includes all of the important points or events in the gathered data. The table of contents of a well-researched, published book can be a possible guide to evaluating which issues or subtopics might need to be addressed. The important events in the research data will form the outline and usefully guide the writing.

Next, arrange all notes and documents according to the headings in the outline. Re-read the notes and documents and think about them. For each section, decide on the important facts that need to be conveyed to the reader. Begin with a brief introductory statement about the purpose of what is being written. Then, write each section by telling the story that the data have revealed. Just go ahead and get some thoughts on paper so that you have something to work with. Return later to fill in the details, fleshing out or editing as required.

Once a first draft is ready, revisions are necessary – at least three. It is counter-productive to submit a report that looks like a draft copy because it has not been revised. If the project is large, such as a local history of an Aboriginal community, then tackle one chapter at a time. The topic of each chapter depends on the outline. For example, a chronological series of chapters might be "The Fur Trade," "Entering into Treaty," and "The Impact of Industrial Development." Focus on one chapter alone until producing a draft that can be given to another person to read and offer comments. Then revise and redraft. After the chapter is essentially complete, turn to the next chapter soon. When the overall project is near completion, be prepared to go back again and make revisions to earlier chapters if necessary.

Next, a conclusion that sums up the findings in a few sentences or paragraphs is needed. Once that is in place, add any special material such as pictures, maps, or copies of important documents. These supplementary documents, or appendices, must be labelled Appendix A, B, C, and so on, and be attached to the end of the report.[96] At this point it can be reassuring to ask still another person to read the completed report to check for its clarity, and any parts that remain unclear should still be reworked.

The title page must include the report's title, the author's name, the date of the report's conclusion, and the party for whom the report was written (that is, the institution or organization that commissioned the study).

Lastly, make a copy of the final report, plus some extra copies. Store one copy in a safe place and catalogue it into an index for future retrieval. One copy should be presented to the Elders' community. They were highly involved in the project and the resulting report should be made available to them. It is also part of their heritage.

Making the Data Available for Future Use

Having finished the report and completed the project, do not let the materials languish somewhere in a box or on a shelf. Useful source materials have been gathered, but they are virtually useless if inaccessible. The recordings and transcripts ought to be made available to researchers, so that they can in turn hear and read what the Elders had to say.

By "re-educating" non-Aboriginals and presenting them with Aboriginal views of historical events, long-held misunderstandings may ultimately be rectified. It is through the dissemination of the Elders' own words, by presenting arguments in reports, academic writing, and court cases, and by educating the youth that a vision of a "just society" can be related to others. Therefore, the materials gathered should be well catalogued and carefully stored in an archival institution such as a provincial archive or an Aboriginal organization's library holdings, so that they can be easily accessed and consulted for future use and research.

Aboriginal communities are encouraged to develop archives, museums, and libraries to store their collections. Oral histories in written form, as well as original audiotapes and videos, could be housed in them, in addition to any other important documents. Another important step will be for more Aboriginal community members to become trained in archival and museum care and administration.[97]

One note of caution: some Elder knowledge should not be so readily accessible to the general public. Traditional healing knowledge and religious practices, for instance, are often closely guarded. Elders or their community must be allowed to add any restrictions or limitations on the information that they feel are necessary to guard this knowledge. The restrictions are to be noted on the release form and must be respected. One such case is the policy with regard to access of materials held at the Treaty and Aboriginal Rights Research library, which restricts access to information about any Bands or Reserves. Before access can be granted to any of their files, a letter or Band Council Resolution (BCR) from the Band Council in question must be obtained. In this way, Aboriginal communities can control and monitor access to their oral histories while still making them accessible to researchers.

CONCLUSION

This chapter began with a quotation: "Every time an Elder dies, it is like a library has burned down." This is an apt metaphor because Elders are indeed libraries of knowledge. The wealth of knowledge that Elders possess could be lost if it is not recorded or passed along. Today, Aboriginal communities rely less on oral traditions as a source of knowledge as they become a "literate" society – that is, as they come more and more to rely on the written word as a means of communicating knowledge. Furthermore, recordings of the Elders' personal reminiscences provide material that personalizes broader historical events by relating personal experiences and feelings to them. However, Elders with such valuable experiences and rich knowledge are aging and dying without passing their knowledge along to future generations. There is an urgent need to record and document that treasured knowledge.

NOTES

1 This is a revised version of a paper originally prepared for the Treaty and Aboriginal Rights Research (TARR) Department of the Indian Association of Alberta while I was employed as a consultant through the Indian Management Assistance Program at Edmonton, Alberta. I would like to thank both organizations for the opportunity to work on such an interesting and important subject. I would also like to acknowledge the many people who talked to me about their experiences and involvement in interviewing the Elders: the late John Foster, John Borrows, Richard Price, Wilma Jacknife, Sharon Venne, and Eileen Sasakamoose. I am also grateful to Cora Voyageur and Gerald Johnson, and to the two anonymous referees who read drafts and offered constructive criticism. Any deficiencies, of course, are my own.

2 An African proverb quoted in Barbara Allen and William L. Montell, *From Memory to History: Using Oral Sources in Local Historical Research* (Nashville: American Association for State and Local History, 1981), xii.

3 Walter Hildebrand, Sarah Carter, Dorothy First Rider, and the Treaty 7 Elders and Tribal Council, *The True Spirit and Original Intent of Treaty 7* (Montreal and Kingston: McGill-Queen's University Press, 1996); Deanna Christensen, *Ahtahkakoop: The Epic Account of a Plains Cree Head Chief, His People, and Their Struggle for Survival 1816–1896* (Shell Lake, SK: Ahtahkakoop Publishing, 2000); Angela Cavender Wilson, "Power of the Spoken Word: Native Oral Traditions in American History," in *Rethinking American Indian History*, edited by Donald Fixico (Albuquerque, NM: University of New Mexico Press, 1997), 101–16; Blair Stonechild and Bill Waiser, *Loyal Till Death: Indians and the Northwest Rebellion* (Calgary: Fifth House, 1997); Neil J. Sterritt, Susan Marsden, Robert Galois, Peter R. Grant, and Richard Overstall, *Tribal Boundaries in the Nass Watershed* (Vancouver: UBC Press, 1998).

4 Julie Cruikshank, "Oral Tradition and Oral History: Reviewing Some Issues," *Canadian Historical Review* 75, no. 3 (1994): 403–18; Bernard L. Fontana, "American Indian Oral History: An Anthropologist's Note," *History and Theory* 8, no. 3 (1969): 366–70; Julie Cruikshank, "Discovery of Gold on the Klondike: Perspectives from Oral Tradition" in *Reading Beyond Words: Contexts for Native History*, edited by Jennifer S.H. Brown (Peterborough: Broadview Press, 1996), 433–53; Brian Thom, "Aboriginal Rights and Title in Canada After *Delgamuukw*: Part One, Oral Traditions and Anthropological Evidence in the Courtroom," *Native Studies Review* 14, no. 1 (2001): 1–26.

5 Tom Flanagan, "Oral Traditions and Treaty 8," *Lobstick: An Interdisciplinary Journal* 1, no. 1 (1999–2000): 54–72.

6 Carl Garth Johnson, "The Nlha7kapmx Oral Tradition of the Three Bears: Interpretations Old and New," *Canadian Journal of Native Education* 25, no. 1 (2001): 37–50; A.M.J. Hyatt, "Teaching Oral History to Post-Secondary Students," *Canadian Oral History Association Journal* 14 (1994): 30–3; Millie Charon, "Teaching Ethnic Studies Using Oral History," *Canadian Oral*

History Association Journal 14 (1994): 21–9; Jo-ann Archibald, "Coyote Learns to Make a Storybasket: The Place of First Nations Stories in Education" (PhD dissertation: Simon Fraser University, 1997).

7 Winona Stevenson, "Introduction," *Oral History Forum d'histoire orale* 19–20 (1999–2000): 13–18; Rebecca Kugel, "Utilizing Oral Traditions: Some Concerns Raised by Recent Ojibwe Studies: A Review Essay," *American Indian Culture and Research Journal* 7, no. 3 (1983): 65–75; Saullu Nakasuk, Herve Paniaq, Elisapee Ootoova, and Pauloosie Angmaalik, *Interviewing Inuit Elders Vol. 1: Introduction*, edited by Jarich Oosten and Frédéric Laugrand (Iqaluit: Nunavut Arctic College, 1999); Mariano Aupilaarjuk, Marie Tulimaaq, Akisu Joamie, Emile Imaruittuq, and Lucassie Nutaraaluk, *Interviewing Inuit Elders, Vol. 2: Perspectives on Traditional Law*, edited by Jarich Oosten, Frédéric Laugrand, and Wim Rasing (Iqaluit: Nunavut Arctic College, 1999); Angela Cavender Wilson, "Walking into the Future: Dakota Oral Tradition and the Shaping of Historical Consciousness," *Oral History Forum d'histoire orale* 19–20 (1999–2000): 25–36; Neal McLeod, "Cree Narrative Memory," *Oral History Forum d'histoire orale* 19–20 (1999–2000): 37–61; Rob Innes, "Oral History Methods in Native Studies: Saskatchewan Aboriginal World War Two Veterans," *Oral History Forum d'histoire orale* 19–20 (1999–2000): 63–88; Nicole St-Onge, "Memorials of Métis Women of Saint-Eustache, Manitoba," *Oral History Forum d'histoire orale* 19–20 (1999–2000): 90–111; Winona Wheeler, chapter 13 in this *Reader*; John Boatman, *My Elders Taught Me: Aspects of Western Great Lakes American Indian Philosophy* (New York: University Press of America, 1992); Isabelle Shay, "Interviewing Tribal Elders and Native Women," *COHA Journal* 9 (1989): 4–5; Angela Cavender Wilson, "Grandmother to Granddaughter: Generations of Oral History in a Dakota Family," in *Natives and Academics Researching and Writing About American Indians* edited by Devon A. Mihesuah (Lincoln: University of Nebraska Press, 1998), 27–36; Peter Kulchyski, Don McCaskill, and David Newhouse, eds., *In The Words of Elders: Aboriginal Cultures in Transition* (Toronto: University of Toronto Press, 1999).

8 Brian J. Gover and Mary Locke Macaulay, "'Snow Houses Leave No Ruins': Unique Evidence Issues in Aboriginal and Treaty Rights Cases," *Saskatchewan Law Review* 60 (1996): 47–89; Clay McLeod, "The Oral Histories of Canada's Northern People, Anglo-Canadian Evidence Law, and Canada's Fiduciary Duty to First Nations: Breaking Down the Barriers of the Past," *Alberta Law Review* 30, no. 4 (1992): 1276–90; Paul Williams, "Oral Traditions on Trial," in *Gin Das Winan: Documenting Aboriginal History in Ontario*, Occasional Papers of the Champlain Society (No. 2), edited by S. Dale Standen and David McNab (Toronto: Champlain Society, 1996), 29–34; Sharon Venne, "Understanding Treaty 6: An Indigenous Perspective," in *Aboriginal and Treaty Rights in Canada: Essays on Law, Equality and Respect for*

Difference, edited by Michael Asch (Vancouver: UBC Press, 1997), 173–207; Michael Asch and Catherine Bell, "Definition and Interpretation of Fact in Canadian Aboriginal Title Litigation: An Analysis of *Delgamuukw*," *Queen's Law Journal* 19 (1994): 503–50.

9 *Delgamuukw v. British Columbia* [1998] 1 CNLR 14.

10 Although I am aware of the diversity of Aboriginal peoples in Canada, I will use the term "Aboriginal community" to refer to the collective "community" of Aboriginal peoples and persons and use the term "Aboriginal communities" to refer to the many communities made up of specific Aboriginal peoples.

11 Historian Wilbur Jacobs, "The Indian and the Frontier in American History: A Need for a Revision," *Western Historical Quarterly* 4, no. 1 (1973): 43, argues that there is a need for a "wider basis of truth" to better understand the past and that there is a need for the "Indian point of view." Wilbur Jacobs, in another article, "Native American History: How It Illuminates Our Past," *American Historical Review* 80, no. 3 (1975): 596, argues that examining the role of Indians in history provides "a fresh analysis of white frontier history by looking at the past from the perspective of native Americans."

12 W.J. Langlois, *Aural History Institute of British Columbia Manual* (Victoria, BC: Aural Institute of BC, 1974).

13 Two exceptions are Richard Price, ed., *The Spirit of the Alberta Treaties* (Montreal: Institute for Research on Public Policy, 1980) and Walter Hildebrand et al., *The True Spirit and Original Intent of Treaty 7*.

14 Bruce Trigger, *The Huron: Farmers of the North* (New York: Rinehart and Winston, 1969), 5, as quoted in *The Cultural Maze: Complex Questions in Native Destiny in Western Canada*, edited by John W. Friesen (Calgary: Detselig Enterprises, 1991), 27.

15 Blair Stonechild describes this method of historical research in *Saskatchewan Indians and the Resistance of 1885: Two Case Studies* (Regina: Saskatchewan Education, 1986). See also Stonechild and Waiser, *Loyal Till Death*.

16 Robert J. Schafer, *A Guide to Historical Method* (Homewood, IL: Dorsey Press, 1974), 19.

17 For an excellent review and critical analysis of which court cases (pre-*Delgamuukw*) allowed oral histories as evidence to be considered, see Clay McLeod, *Oral Histories Report*, unpublished report prepared for TARR (Treaty and Aboriginal Rights Research) at the Indian Association of Alberta 1992; see also a shorter published version: McLeod, "The Oral Histories of Canada's Northern People."

18 *Simon v. R.*, [1986] 1 CNLR 153 (SCC), where Chief Justice Dickson of the Supreme Court of Canada stated (p. 171) that because Mi'kmaq did not keep written records, it was necessary to admit oral traditions which he held to be "sufficient to prove the appellant's connection to the tribe covered by the

treaty"; *Delgamuukw* v. *British Columbia* [1998] 1 CNLR 14. Recent literature
on land claims includes: Bruce Granville Miller, *Oral History on Trial: Recognizing Aboriginal Narratives in the Courts* (Vancouver: UBC Press, 2011);
John Borrows, *Canada's Indigenous Constitution* (Toronto: University of Toronto Press, 2010); Ben Richardson, Kent McNeil, Shin Imai, eds., *Indigenous
Peoples and the Law: Comparative and Critical Perspectives* (Oxford: Hart,
2009); Ulla Secher, *Aboriginal Customary Law: A Source of Common Law
Title to Land* (Oxford: Hart, 2014).

19 *Delgamuukw* v. *British Columbia* [1998] 1 CNLR 14, 48.

20 Ibid.

21 Ibid.

22 Ibid.

23 Ibid., 49–50.

24 Ibid., 48.

25 *Report of the Royal Commission on Aboriginal Peoples. Vol. 1: Looking Forward, Looking Back* [RCAP] (Ottawa: Minister of Supply and Services, 1996);
see also McLeod, "The Oral Histories of Canada's Northern People."

26 See note 9, 49, in which Chief Justice Lamer is quoting McLeod's article "The
Oral Histories of Canada's Northern People."

27 *R.* v. *Dick* [1989] 1 CNLR 132, 1988 (BC Prov. Ct.).

28 *Re: Paulette et al. and Registrar of Titles* (No. 2) (1973), 42 DLR (3d) 8
(NWTSC), 12–13, rev'd *Re: Paulette et al. and Registrar of Titles* (1975), 63 DLR
(3d) 1 (NWTCA), aff'd *Paulette* v. *R* (1976), 72 DLR (3d) 61 (SCC).

29 Winona Stevenson, "Indigenous Voices, Indigenous Histories, Part I: The
Othering of Indigenous History," *Saskatchewan History* (fall 1998): 24.

30 Ibid.

31 Angela Cavender Wilson, "American Indian History or Non-Indian Perceptions of American Indian History?" in *Natives and Academics: Researching
and Writing About American Indians,* edited by Devon A. Mihesuah (Lincoln: University of Nebraska Press, 1998), 23–4.

32 Wheeler, chapter 13 in this *Reader.*

33 See, for example, Flanagan, "Oral Traditions and Treaty 8," and Alexander
von Gernet, Oral Narratives and Aboriginal Pasts: An Interdisciplinary
Review of the Literatures on Oral Traditions and Oral Histories, a report
submitted to the Department of Indian Affairs and Northern Development,
April 1996. Available online at: http://www.collectionscanada.gc.ca/
webarchives/20061209015030/http://www.ainc-inac.gc.ca/pr/pub/orl/
index_e.html (accessed 17 June 2014).

34 Julie Cruikshank, "Invention of Anthropology in British Columbia's Supreme Court: Oral Tradition as Evidence in Delgamuukw v. BC," *BC Studies*
95 (1992): 25–42.

35 Ibid., 37–9.

36 McLeod, "Oral Histories of Canada's Northern People," 1279.

37 Bennett Ellen McCardle, *Indian History and Claims: A Research Handbook* (Ottawa: Treaties and Historical Research Centre, Research Branch Corporate Policy, Indian and Northern Affairs Canada, 1983), 318.

38 Langlois, *Manual*, 1.

39 Jean Elaine Mann Kendal, "Oral Sources and Historical Studies," unpublished M.A. thesis (University of Alberta, 1976), 6.

40 McLeod, *Oral Histories Report*, chapter 6, Part B.

41 Ibid., chapter 6, Part E.

42 This point was raised by the Research Director of TARR for Treaty 8 in Northeastern British Columbia Peter Havlik in his presentation during the session, "Treaty Land Surrenders" at the TARR Land Claims Workshop held at the Continental Inn, Edmonton, Alberta, 10–12 May 1993.

43 I use the words "academic research" as a standard that research must meet. I am stating that if one wants research to be accepted by the academic community, it must meet the rigorous requirements that academics demand. I do not intend it to mean that all non-legal research is academic.

44 Telephone interview with Dr John Foster, professor of history at the University of Alberta, 17 June 1993. Dr Foster was at one time a consultant with TARR. See also McCardle, *Indian History and Claims*, 6.

45 McCardle, *Indian History and Claims*, 6. See also McLeod, *Oral Histories Report*, chapter 6, Part E.

46 McLeod, *Oral Histories Report*, chapter 6, Part E.

47 Ibid.

48 McCardle, *Indian History and Claims*, 219–25; Langlois, *Manual*, 3.

49 Carlotta Herman Mellon, "Preparatory Research Necessary for the Oral History Interview," in *A Guide to Oral History Programs*, edited by Richard D. Curtiss et al. (Fullerton: California State University, 1973), 59; see also Langlois, *Manual*, 5.

50 For an excellent review and explanation of how to use government departments or other archival institutions, see McCardle, *Indian History and Claims*, 11.

51 Ibid., 11; See also Langlois, *Manual*, 5.

52 McCardle, *Indian History and Claims*, 5–6; Langlois, *Manual*, 5.

53 For a discussion of community-based research see Susan Guyette, *Community-Based Research: A Handbook for Native Americans* (Los Angeles: American Indian Studies Center, University of California, 1983); for a discussion of the ethical issues involved in researching Aboriginal "human subjects," see Laurie Meijer-Drees, "Native Studies and Ethical Guidelines for Research: Dilemmas and Solutions," *Native Studies Review* 14, no. 1 (2001): 83; for a discussion of participatory action research and an example of the data it can produce, see Joan Ryan, *Doing Things the Right Way: Dene Traditional Justice in Lac La Martre, NWT* (Calgary: Arctic Institute of North America and University of Calgary Press, 1995), 7–22.

54 Telephone interview with John Borrows, professor of law, University of British Columbia, 27 May 1993. Mr Borrows has had extensive experience in interviewing Elders. For example, see John J. Borrows, "A Genealogy of Law: Inherent Sovereignty and First Nations Self-Government," *Osgoode Hall Law Journal* 30, no. 2 (1992): 291.

55 Ibid. See also Mary Ellen Glass, "A Technique in Oral History Interviews," in *A Guide to Oral History Programs*, edited by Curtiss et al., 65.

56 Interview with Aboriginal lawyer Sharon Venne of Edmonton, Alberta, at the offices of the Indian Association of Alberta, 17 June 1993. Ms Venne has extensive experience with interviewing Elders and shared many of her experiences with the author.

57 Langlois, *Manual*, 7.

58 Borrows interview.

59 Ibid. Professor Borrows stated that one should get a release form for storytelling because it is property-like information that is owned by the person or their family.

60 See Langlois, *Manual*, 29 and 31, for a discussion. A release form is merely a one-page document that states that the person grants the researcher or organization/institution permission to allow (restricted, limited, or open) public access to the oral history interview undertaken and to use portions of the interview in a report (or book) or excerpts of the audio in exhibit (for a museum). This document has the Elder's (or interviewee's) name printed in it and is signed by the Elder (or interviewee) and dated and witnessed.

61 Borrows interview.

62 Vern John, TARR director, related this to the author in the summer of 1993.

63 Anne Morgan Campbell, "Trappings of the Trade: Oral History Equipment," in *A Guide for Oral History Programs*, edited by Curtiss et al. See also, Edward D. Ives, *The Tape-Recorded Interview* (Knoxville: University of Tennessee, n.d.).

64 Ibid.

65 Langlois, *Manual*, 10.

66 Foster interview.

67 The author would like to acknowledge Gerald Johnson, a Cree graduate student at the time from Calling Lake, Alberta, for bringing out this point. Mr Johnson also acted as a translator and intermediary during the author's interviews with some Calling Lake Elders in August 1993.

68 Venne interview and Borrows interview.

69 Venne interview.

70 Langlois, *Manual*, 13–15.

71 Jan Vansina, "The Documentary Interview," *African Studies Bulletin* 8 (1965): 9–13, an excerpt of which was attached as Appendix VII to Kendal, "Oral Sources."

72 Treaty and Aboriginal Rights Research, *Elders' Think Tank*, 1975, on file at Alberta TARR's library holdings.

73 Jan Vansina, referring to a collective interview, notes: "the interviewer should be aware that their testimony reflects their knowledge about the events only in part, insofar as there is consensus between the interviewees about it. The very fact of a collective interview, however, points to the likelihood that there are variant versions and that the testimony is important enough in present-day life to warrant special protection, so that the 'official' statement only should be known." Jan Vansina, "The Documentary Interview."

74 Richard Lightning, "Problems in Doing Native Interviews," in *Spirit of Alberta Indian Treaties*, edited by Richard Price (unpublished manuscript copy), 18.

75 Ibid.

76 Ibid., 19.

77 Walter Lightning, "Compassionate Mind: Implications of a Text Written by Elder Louis Sunchild," *Canadian Journal of Native Education* 19, no. 2 (1992): 217.

78 Linda Akan, "Pimosatamowin Sikaw Kakeequaywin: Walking and Talking: A Saulteaux Elder's View of Native Education," *Canadian Journal of Native Education* 19, no. 2 (1992): 192.

79 Richard Lightning, "Problems in Doing Native Interviews," 19.

80 Venne interview.

81 Langlois, *Manual*, 40.

82 Julie Cruikshank with A. Sidney, K. Smith, and A. Ned, *Life Lived Like a Story: Life Stories of Three Yukon Native Elders* (Lincoln: University of Nebraska Press, 1990), as quoted by Walter Lightning, "Compassionate Mind," 228.

83 Richard Lightning, "Problems in Doing Native Interviews," 21.

84 Ibid. See also Nancy J. Hunsaker, "Processing the Oral History Interview," in *A Guide for Oral History Programs*, edited by Curtiss et al., 71–7.

85 Eugene D. Carlisle, "Cataloguing the Oral History Collection," in *A Guide for Oral History Programs*, edited by Curtis et al., 78–85; see also Langlois, *Manual*.

86 McCardle, *Indian History and Claims*, 15.

87 Ibid., 15.

88 Langlois, *Manual*, 18–21.

89 McCardle, *Indian History and Claims*, 11–15 and 286–9.

90 Ibid., 290.

91 Langlois, *Manual*, 20–1.

92 For a more detailed discussion on data analysis see Susan Guyette, *Community-Based Research,* and Earl Babbie, *The Practice of Social Research*, 4th edition (Belmont, CA: Wadsworth Publishing Co., 1986).

93 Langlois, *Manual*, 20–1.
94 Ibid., 21.
95 McCardle, *Handbook*, 291–2. I have based much of what I discuss here on McCardle's discussion of this topic.
96 For an example of the use of appendices in a book that utilizes oral histories and other sources of historical data see Neil J. Sterritt et al., *Tribal Boundaries in the Nass Watershed*, 253–71.
97 For an excellent review of the need for Aboriginal communities' involvement in archives and museums see Heather Devine, *Aboriginal Archives in Alberta: An Inventory and Needs Assessment*, A Report Prepared for the Historic Sites and Archives Service, Historic Sites and Cultural Facilities Division, Alberta Community Development (Edmonton: Alberta Community Development and the Historical Resources Foundation, 10 June 1994).

2

Sharing Authority with Baba[1]

Stacey Zembrzycki

When I began to research Sudbury's Ukrainians, I intended to consider the history of this community from a safe and objective distance. In particular, I planned to examine empirical and historically traditional evidence at local, provincial, and national archives before conducting a series of oral history interviews with Ukrainian men and women who lived in the Sudbury region in the first half of the twentieth century; Ukrainians began to settle in this area of Northern Ontario around 1901, and shortly thereafter, they formed a number of heavily polarized communities that were divided along political, ideological, and religious lines.[2] The end result of my project was quite different from my original intentions. When exhaustive searches at public archives produced few pertinent textual documents, I had to look elsewhere for sources that would enable me to document the history of Sudbury's Ukrainian community. Although the public archive seemed to indicate that this community lacked a history, I knew that this silence was a serious omission in the public record because I had grown up listening to my Ukrainian Catholic grandmother's, my Baba's, stories about it.[3] If Baba had spent most of her adult life telling stories about the Ukrainian community and her place in it, then I assumed that others had done the same. The creation of an oral record was, however, not without its complexities.

Shortly after acquiring clearance from Carleton University's ethics committee, I moved back to Sudbury to conduct interviews. Since I had yet to do an oral history interview, I figured that it would be best to start with my Baba. Within the familiar setting of her home, I would be able not only to practise my interviewing style and questioning techniques but also to test my equipment. When I pulled into Baba's driveway on

6 October 2004, she was raking the leaves in her front yard. On this cool, blustery day, Baba was dressed in layers of old work clothes and her hair was a mess. Before going inside to start the interview, she insisted on finishing her yard work. I placed my interview equipment on the front steps and proceeded to help this spry and determined seventy-seven-year-old woman stuff the last bunch of leaves into a garbage bag.

When we finally went inside, I set up my analog tape recorder and VHS video recorder and waited for Baba to finish some errands around the house. As she sat down, she quickly noticed the video recorder and excused herself from the room. When she reappeared ten minutes later, her hair was styled and she was dressed in her Sunday best. Baba was not going to look "shabby" in a video that would be seen by others. After a somewhat tense and relatively slow start – I fiddled with my equipment while trying to articulate my introductory remarks and questions – Baba became swept up in her stories for the next couple of hours, easily recalling the good old days of her youth.[4]

Although the interview went well, I spent the following week thinking about the experience and writing personal field notes about it. As I listened and re-listened to the interview and transcribed it, I thought about my role as an interviewer, my interview equipment, and my relationship with Baba. I soon realized that preparing for an oral history project and reading the necessary literature is very different from actually doing an interview.[5] Frustrated with my inability to "roll with the punches," I pledged to abandon my interview guide and work on being more spontaneous in the interview space. I would have to try to make a concerted effort to allow interviewees to take the lead in future interviews. I also realized that my tape recorder would have to be replaced by a digital recorder; I had no doubt that digital technology would improve the sound quality of my interviews and make listening easier. Lastly, I noted that it was going to be difficult to step back from this particular interview and analyze it because I had grown up listening to the stories that Baba had shared with me. Clearly, as my field notes state, I was biased. Despite the subjectivity that I brought to my interview with Baba, I had no reason to believe that this would become a major aspect of my oral history methodology. Little did I know that various circumstances would soon lead me to share authority with Baba. She would act not only as an interviewee but also as an interviewer in my project.

"Shared authority" has, according to Linda Shopes, "become something of a mantra among oral historians."[6] Coined by Michael Frisch in 1990, this neat phrase captures the essence of the oral history enterprise.

Emphasizing the collaborative nature of the discipline, the term forces us to think about how we may make oral history a more democratic cultural practice.[7] In essence, interviewers must make "a deliberate decision to give up some control over the product of historical inquiry," sharing power with their interviewees when it comes to the research, interpretation, and presentation phases of their projects.[8] There is no doubt that collaborative work is a personally and intellectually demanding process that, depending upon the project, can produce mixed results.[9]

Although I was familiar with Frisch's work prior to conducting interviews for my dissertation, I had no intention of engaging with it. While I recognized that collaboration was central to the interview process – interviewers and their interviewees work together to create a living history of the past – I did not plan to share authority with my interviewees in any other ways. A lack of funding, and hence a limited amount of time, forced me to establish a clear set of priorities. I planned to conduct a hundred single, life story interviews with fifty Ukrainian men and fifty Ukrainian women in a one-year period. Since the public archive was relatively silent when it came to the history of Sudbury's Ukrainians, I would use these oral histories to supplement the written record. It was not until I placed my first advertisement in the bulletin at Baba's church, St Mary's Ukrainian Catholic Church, and failed to receive a single response that I realized my priorities had to change. Whether I wanted to or not, I would, in the end, learn to share authority. Collaboration occurred not just with my interviewees – a more familiar methodological consideration – but also with a fellow interviewer who happened to be a member of my family: my Baba.

I grew up in Sudbury in a home with two working parents. Fortunately, my maternal and paternal grandparents resided in Sudbury, and there was never any need to send me to a babysitter. I spent a lot of time with each one of my grandparents, but most of my time was spent with Baba; she is my paternal grandmother. In fact, I spent so much time with her that the first language I was able to speak was Ukrainian. Although Baba is Canadian – she was born and raised in Sudbury in a strict Ukrainian Catholic household – her immigrant father insisted that his children speak Ukrainian in the home, stressing that they ought to know where they had come from. Like her father, Baba believed that it was imperative that I learn this language, so she only spoke Ukrainian when she babysat me. Unfortunately, I did not have an easy time transitioning from Ukrainian to English when my parents arrived home from work, so these early language lessons ended soon after I began to speak.

I have very few memories when it comes to recalling these preschool years. I remember neither what Baba and I would talk about, nor how we would spend our time together. My memory is fallible; with the passage of time I have either forgotten or transformed my experiences, basing them upon the stories that I have heard or the pictures that I have seen rather than upon the actual events themselves. This is not surprising or extraordinary, given the fact that "a memory is really a reconstruction of what is being recalled rather than a reproduction of [that recollection]."[10] Imperfections aside, my memories begin around the time I started grade one, at about the age of six. Baba and my grandfather, my Gigi, lived on Marymount Hill, a neighbourhood overlooking Sudbury's downtown core. We were close to everything, and so Baba and I walked everywhere together. Unless the weather was inclement, we strolled downtown every day whether Baba needed something or not. This was a social outing, giving us an opportunity to get out of the house and pass time in the afternoons. Baba is an outgoing and active lady – a lifelong member of St Mary's Ukrainian Catholic Church and various volunteer organizations within it – and therefore she has always known a lot of people in Sudbury. I cannot remember a single trip downtown in which we did not bump into someone Baba knew. Whether it was in Eaton's, the Toronto Dominion Bank, or the neighbourhood grocery store, it seemed like Baba knew just about everyone. Depending on who they were, she would speak to these men and women in either Ukrainian or English, sharing the latest news and reminiscing about past experiences. These daily excursions were never dull.

What made these trips downtown even more interesting were Baba's stories. As we walked down the hill, through the shopping centre, and then back up the hill and home, Baba would tell me stories about when she was young, vividly recalling her exciting Donovan days. The Donovan was a multicultural neighbourhood that was established around 1907 and located just northwest of the downtown core.[11] Miners, both single men and those with families, moved to this neighbourhood during the 1910s and 1920s because it was close to Frood Mine, which was owned by the International Nickel Company (INCO), the largest employer of men in the town. This was a neighbourhood filled with immigrants, boarding houses, and young families, and I never would have known this had it not been for Baba's stories. By the time I was a young child, the Donovan was a very different place. The ethnic breakdown of the neighbourhood had changed, those who had lived in the area had either died or moved away, and the buildings and the stores that had once been vibrant community centres had long since closed, been vandalized, or torn down. Baba's stories took me back to a time and a place that had ceased to exist. Although I never forgot these stories, as I grew older and spent more time away from Baba, I also distanced myself from them. It was not until I was well into my doctoral work that I returned to them, realizing that her memories about growing up as a Ukrainian-Canadian Catholic girl in a Northern Ontario mining town were important and needed to be preserved. In a manner corresponding to Martha Norkunas's experience, I began to view these stories, as well as my community and its citizens, "intellectually rather than emotionally."[12]

Unlike Baba, I did not grow up being an active member of Sudbury's Ukrainian community. Although I attended Ukrainian language school in the basement of St Mary's Ukrainian Catholic Church for a number of years, I, like so many other Ukrainian-Canadian children from third and fourth generations, became involved in non-Ukrainian activities, effectively disassociating myself from my ethnic roots. My connection to the community and my knowledge about it were therefore premised upon Baba's memories. Like Penny Summerfield and Carolyn Steedman,[13] I had participated imaginatively in Baba's world and had thus shared her vision of the past.[14] Historically, Ukrainian grandmothers have acted as important storytellers in their family units. Custodians of Ukrainian traditions, arts, and culture, they have played a central role in defining the Ukrainian identities of their descendants.[15] Had it not been for Baba, I would not identify as a Ukrainian today. Certainly, Baba's role in my life, her experiences within the Ukrainian Catholic community, and her stories about those experiences formed the basis of my identity and my imagined Ukrainian community. When I began this project, I believed that I was both a community insider and an outsider, maintaining not only a subjective connection to it through my Baba, but also a real distance from it because I had not participated in it. Despite this complex status, I was a Sudburian: I knew what it was like to grow up in this Northern Ontario mining community, where maintaining anonymity tends to be quite difficult. Knowing this, I hoped that my familiarity with Sudbury and my family's ethnic roots would help me solicit interviewees.

In hindsight, I was quite naïve to believe that, because I was Ukrainian and, most important, Olga Zembrzycki's granddaughter, I would invariably be welcomed by members of the community. After failing to receive a single response from my first advertisement to solicit interviewees, I quickly realized that my ethnicity and my relationship with Baba would not necessarily help me forge an easy connection to this community; after all, this connection was imagined, premised upon Baba's stories rather than upon my own participation in it. While my complex insider/outsider status was certainly not the sole reason why individuals did not come forward – shyness, apathy, and a tendency to devalue personal stories were among some of the other reasons – I nevertheless determined that if I was going to proceed with this kind of research, I would need help from someone who was not only familiar with the Ukrainian community but also trusted and known by the members of that community. Not surprisingly, I approached my Baba.

I first asked Baba if she had any friends who would be willing to share their memories with me. Eager to help, she not only gave me a parish directory, but also began to construct a list of her friends and acquaintances. Although I proceeded to telephone some of these individuals, few agreed to be interviewed; I suspect that in many cases poor hearing resulted in the impression that I was a telemarketer. Fearing that the project would come to an abrupt stop, I visited Baba once again and asked her how she thought I ought to proceed.

Since Baba had done pastoral visits at local hospitals and nursing homes on behalf of the church for thirty-five years, she suggested that I start by approaching the Ukrainians who lived in these places because their time was more limited. Because of the age of these men and women – most were well into their eighties and nineties – Baba offered to accompany me to these places to solicit potential interviewees. We both agreed that it would be easier for those who had vision or hearing problems to be introduced to my project by a friendly and familiar face. Baba and I decided to begin by recruiting interviewees at the Ukrainian Barvinok Retirement Home and Pioneer Manor, two long-term-care facilities in the city. In both places we met a number of Baba's friends. For the most part, they were friendly and thrilled to have visitors. Baba would greet them and then introduce me and my project. Instead of making an appointment for a return visit, they often insisted that we sit down and do the interview right there and then. Although I had planned to meet these interviewees at a later date, without Baba, I also did not want to miss the opportunity to interview them. Many were quite sick, and so if we visited them on a good day when they were feeling well, then we just stayed and interviewed them; a number of interviewees passed away shortly after being interviewed, driving home the importance of timing in this project.

I did not realize this at the time, but I was collaborating with Baba in the interview space. In these early interviews, she would spend the first part of the session getting reacquainted with interviewees, asking them how they were feeling, if they had had many visitors, and whether they enjoyed living in the long-term-care facilities. Baba and the interviewees would complain about being old and then they would start to reminisce about the good old days. There is no doubt that having Baba present put the interviewees as well as myself at ease. As an insider, she made the interview space feel like a meeting between old friends rather than an impersonal interview. We did not need to build trust; it was already there. The problem, however, was that Baba and the interviewees would get swept up in their conversations. They would tell anecdotal stories while I sat on the sidelines and watched. I actually felt quite powerless in these spaces at times, like a young granddaughter, not a trained historian. Although I would jump into the conversations from time to time and ask questions, interviewees would answer them and then proceed to speak with Baba, not me. At other times, I would ask questions, the interviewees would answer them, and then Baba would proceed to answer the questions as well, telling and retelling the stories that I had heard throughout my life. Since my dissertation focused on the interwar years, I would often ask interviewees to tell me about their Depression-era experiences. Had it been a difficult time for their families? How had their families coped during this period? Interviewees would answer these questions and then Baba would frequently recall her own memories, emphasizing that it had been a hard time for her family. Her father had had his shifts cut back at Frood Mine, and he had lost a boarding house that he had owned prior to the economic crash. Instead of remembering their own experiences, interviewees would get wrapped up in Baba's story. By interrupting them, Baba also effectively silenced interviewees and dominated the interview space.

Coming home and listening to the interviews was difficult and frustrating. Instead of hearing new stories, I would hear those recounted by Baba. Feeling like I was outside of the interview space listening in, I would recoup power by writing Baba's stories and frequent interruptions out of my transcripts. After a couple of these interviews, I began to think about the roles that Baba and I were playing in the interview space. I had to establish, with Baba and the interviewees, that I was not just a granddaughter; I was a historian, and this was my project. I would have to decide how authority would be shared. Collaboration "does not require agreement in all things, but a mutual commitment to talk things through, to reach a common understanding, and to respect considered differences."[16] Baba and I would have to learn how to collaborate before we would be able to listen to our interviewees. Certainly, we would have to share some of the same purposes if we were going to move forward.

Henry Greenspan states that "a good interview is a process in which two people work hard to understand the views and experiences of one person: the interviewee."[17] In this case, Baba and I had to come together to appreciate the significance of the stories that our interviewees recalled. After a couple of interviews, I decided to sit down with Baba and discuss the ways that she was both helping and hindering the interview process. I spoke about the trust that she brought to the interview space, the implicit power struggle between Baba and myself and between Baba and the interviewees, and Baba's frequent interruptions in the interview space. Although she vowed to listen more and speak less, Baba continued to behave in the same manner. Ukrainian grandmothers have been characterized as stubborn, highly individualistic, opinionated, and at times slightly irreverent beings, and certainly my Baba was not an exception.[18]

Convinced that Baba was hindering the interview process, I began to conduct interviews on my own. I soon realized, however, that although my interviews were going well, they were neither as rich nor as detailed as when Baba was present. Interviewees were shy, and although they warmed up to me, they did not seem to trust me completely. After a handful of these solo interviews, I decided to try to include Baba once again. I made this decision for two reasons. First, she had quickly become obsessed with documenting the history of Sudbury's Ukrainians. She thought about the project a lot, keeping notes about the memories that she had forgotten to tell me in her interview and making extensive lists of potential interviewees. Every evening she would make phone calls to solicit interviewees, arranging dates and times for interviews. She referred to herself as "my secretary" and unabashedly proclaimed that at the end of this project, she too would gain a PhD. During this whole process, Baba's kitchen table was laden with sticky notes containing information about interviewees, their contact information, and the dates we were to interview them. Without Baba, these interviews would have never taken place. She welcomed the chance to leave her home and visit with friends that she had not seen in years. Additionally, this project was a way for her to establish her relative worth. Just as Barbara Myerhoff discovered while exploring the process of aging among a group of elderly Jewish men and women, I began to see that this was a means through which Baba could demonstrate her existence in no uncertain terms.[19] I did not want to disconnect Baba from this process, and thus I walked a fine line when discussing her role in the interviews. Like the challenges discussed by Lorraine Sitzia, emotional attachments were central to this project, and our grandmother-granddaughter relationship had to be maintained throughout, whatever the cost.[20]

Baba brought a degree of trust into the interview space. Since my limited funding meant that I had to keep to a rigid schedule, I did not have time to develop this trust on my own by conducting multiple interviews with my interviewees. After discussing, yet again, the subtle ways that Baba could consciously and unconsciously change the dynamics of each interview space, I decided to give this methodological approach a second chance by bringing her to the interviews. This time, however, I stated that if Baba was going to accompany me she would have to agree to remain silent during the duration of the interviews. At the end of each interview, she could then ask any questions that she had and add any relevant memories of her own. I decided to keep the digital recorder on throughout this process, so that my exchanges and her exchanges could both be preserved. Collaboration, in this instance, had to be structured. Without a clear set of rules, Baba would have continued to act as though she was visiting with friends rather than conducting an interview. It took Baba and me many interviews to begin to share authority in a fruitful way; collaborative work takes time and practice to develop. We never perfected this three-way exchange, but we managed to transform it into a working relationship that eased my frustrations and suited my needs as well as those expressed by Baba and our interviewees.[21] While Baba and I had to learn to work together, I also realized that I had to trust my methodology. As a graduate student, I was worried about doing oral history properly. Unlike anthropologists, historians, concerned with maintaining a degree of objectivity, have spent little time reflecting upon their experiences in the field. This project has, however, taught me that oral history is a subjective craft that is made more interesting when unconventional approaches form its basis. There is no need to worry about breaking rules because there are none.

Baba may not have been a trained historian, but her questions and memories sometimes made a difference, enabling interviewees to recall stories that my questions had not brought forward. For instance, an interview that Baba and I conducted with Anne Matschke provided an important insight into a silence that I had found in the public record. There is no doubt that Baba's presence at the interview was essential to retrieving the gossip that enabled me to read past this silence.[22]

Citing a "lack of funds and co-operation from the church authorities," as well as "internal dissension," St Mary's Ukrainian Catholic Church closed its doors on 29 April 1931.[23] Three days after this closing, the *Sudbury Star* reported that the parish had reopened to the public and was under the leadership of a new priest.[24] I knew very little about this aspect of the community's history when I began to research Sudbury's Ukrainians. Neither Baba nor my other Ukrainian Catholic interviewees recalled a time when the parish had been closed. According to them, it had always been a successful and thriving ethnic space. An interview with Anne, however, provided some useful information about this forgotten moment in the community's history.

Although Baba had arranged this interview, she was diffident about accompanying me to it because she did not know Anne personally. Baba generally did not come to interviews when she did not know the interviewees. While Anne had lived in Sudbury as a youth, she had spent most of her life in Toronto and Baba, not recognizing Anne's last name, was thus hesitant about attending the interview. I persisted, however, arguing that her presence was needed for the sake of consistency, and Baba reluctantly agreed to accompany me; I also suspected that Baba would know Anne once she saw her, since she lived in the Ukrainian Seniors' Centre apartment building that Baba frequented from time to time. While the first half of this interview was relatively unmemorable, the dynamics of the interview space changed when Baba realized that she had grown up with Anne. The two women returned to their youth, reminiscing about the people they had known and the places that they had both patronized, and these shared memories quickly led to an interesting gossip session. Not surprisingly, my ears perked up when I heard the name of Father Bartman, the priest who had presided over the church when its doors had closed in 1931.

Anne did not remember the church's closure per se, but she did recall the gossip that had engulfed Father Bartman. In particular, one Sunday mass stood out in her memory. While she was seated beside her family in a pew in the front row of the church, Anne remembered, just as Father Bartman was about to begin his weekly sermon, a woman ran into the church with a baby, screaming, "It's his! It's his!" She then proceeded to place the baby on the church altar and run out of the building, shouting, "Don't listen to him, he's a liar!" Although Anne declared that this had been a "communist prank," she went on to point out that Father Bartman had had a child and when this news became public he was reduced to a lay state and became a lawyer; Ukrainian Catholic priests could not marry after they were ordained. Had Baba not been present during the interview, Anne might not have included this incident in her narrative. Baba's and Anne's parents had been founding members of the church, and it was their long-time connection and the gossip that shared that led Anne to discuss this memory.[25]

If Baba did not know an interviewee personally, I did not include her in the interview process; I recruited ten Ukrainian men and women through word-of-mouth networks and interviewed them alone. I did not want to overwhelm those who had granted me an interview with two strangers; one was enough. In these cases, I recognized that Baba and I were both outsiders, and that I would therefore have to earn trust. Since Baba was considered an insider by members of the Ukrainian Catholic community as well as those who belonged to the Ukrainian National Federation (UNF) and St Volodymyr's Ukrainian Greek Orthodox Church – frequent interactions with members of these organizations had allowed her to build relationships throughout her life – she accompanied me to the majority of the interviews that took place with individuals who belonged to these organizations. Baba was an outsider, however, when it came to the progressive community, and so I interviewed these Ukrainians on my own, often taking the time to conduct multiple interviews to get to know these interviewees and to develop a solid relationship with them.

As a child, Baba had always been forbidden to associate with the "communists" and their Spruce Street Hall; although they formed different communities, Catholic, Orthodox, and nationalist Ukrainians came together on occasion to rally against "evil" progressive Ukrainians and their organization. Hearing stories that portrayed members of the Ukrainian Labour Farmer Temple Association (ULFTA), later renamed the Association of United Ukrainian Canadians (AUUC), in a negative manner, I assumed that Baba had not formed relationships with progressives. Sustained conversations with Baba revealed, however, that the boundaries of her Ukrainian community were more fluid than I had imagined. Her strict Ukrainian Catholic father may have forbidden her to associate with members of the ULFTA, but that did not stop Baba from becoming friends with a number of progressives. Throughout her life, she formed relationships with Ukrainians who belonged to the ULFTA. She interacted with them in a variety of locations outside of the Catholic Church, in neutral spaces like schools, workplaces, and shopping centres. Clearly, Baba's status as both an insider and an outsider was quite complex, layered by her experiences and the multiple identities that she assumed over time. A "neighbourhood's bricks and mortar," as Talja Blokland has pointed out, can provide "the building blocks for the production of collective memories."[26] These places can also offer spaces in which relationships, like those maintained by Baba and a number of progressive Ukrainians, may flourish. In reflecting upon this project, I admit that it was foolish to believe that Baba's community was simply structured upon equalities and similarities. Baba's narrative about the past may have excluded progressives, but its silences, and specifically her relationships with members of this community, speak to a more complicated notion of the past and a broad view of the community to which she belonged.

Since the men and women I interviewed had been children during the interwar years, the period upon which my dissertation is based, the richest details to come out of these interviews related to childhood, and specifically to growing up as a first- or second-generation Ukrainian-Canadian child in Sudbury.[27] If I had been interviewing those who had held prominent roles in society, I would have been able to obtain details about their lives from the public archive before conducting interviews with them. There is, however, a significant difference when it comes to preparing for interviews with individuals who have lived private lives. Although I could familiarize myself with the context – the place and time – in which these individuals lived, I was unable to obtain any personal information about them from the public archive. Having Baba involved in these interviews was therefore quite invaluable, because we were interviewing people she had known for many years. In many respects, speaking with Baba was like doing research. Prior to an interview or on the way to it, she would give me a short briefing about the interviewee and her relation to them. Although these briefings were based on her subjective opinions and perspectives, and supplemented by the gossip she had heard over the years, they were usually quite helpful, allowing me to prepare my questions in advance. For instance, knowing the particular neighbourhood in which an interviewee grew up allowed me to examine interviews I had done with others from the same neighbourhood before going into the interview environment. I was then able to ask specific and contextual questions during the interview. Unless one conducts a series of interviews with an individual, a single life-story interview is a relatively short period of time for an interviewee to reflect upon his or her life.[28] This approach maximized my time with an interviewee, and the knowledge I brought to an interview showed the interviewee that even though I had not lived in the neighbourhood under discussion, I had reconstructed it nonetheless.

This approach also made the interviews as constructive as possible because I always knew what subjects and questions ought not to be discussed or which issues required sensitivity. Although I went into many interviews knowing something about each of my interviewees' pasts, I always gave them the opportunity to discuss freely whatever memories they deemed relevant. If they did not want to talk about a positive or a negative event that I had known about prior to the interviews, then I did not push them. Additionally, on a couple of occasions, the parts of the interviews that I believed were missing were not absent at all. There were times when Baba's briefings were completely inconsistent with the stories recalled by my interviewees. Certainly, discrepancies reminded me of the subjective and layered nature of memories and particularly of the importance of asking how variables like gender and class shape both the construction of historical memories and the telling of stories.[29] Specifically, it was at these junctures that I realized that Baba's subjective memories were valid but that they were not by any means complete or infallible. By having Baba present at the interviews, I was forced to separate myself from her subjective understanding of the past and what had been my imagined world since childhood. Listening to her stories as well as those told by my interviewees allowed me to reconceptualize my understanding of the past; I came to recognize that everyone experiences a time, a place, and a space differently, and that it is only in putting these memories together that we can attempt to reconstruct collectively what ceases to exist. Although each narrative may be unique, as Steven High notes, patterns of shared meaning and collective memories nevertheless emerge.[30]

Bringing Baba to these interviews also made me realize that an uneasy balance must be maintained when combining oral history with local history. Because Baba knew or was familiar with the individuals that we interviewed, she was able to pick up on subtleties that I would have missed in the course of an interview. Together, we were able to use these small details to begin to understand the silences or uneasy periods that had occurred during interviews; even when people leave major details out of their narratives, they drop hints and leave markers that can be pieced together if one is aware of what those major details are. Sudbury is a relatively small community, and it is hard to go into a public space and remain unknown or anonymous. These interviews revealed that the Ukrainian community within Sudbury is even smaller and more closely linked. Many of the immigrants who settled in Sudbury between 1901 and 1939 still have family members living in the region; so, even if a second-, third-, or fourth-generation Ukrainian-Canadian has not been involved in any aspect of organized life, there is a good chance that the majority of Ukrainians will nevertheless still be familiar with that individual's particular family or know him or her personally. People talk among themselves, and thus it was very difficult for an interviewee to get away with constructing a false or an embellished narrative during an interview.

The nature of the community made it quite easy to reflect upon the ways that individuals remember and reminisce about their experiences. Some people had little to hide, while others sought to protect family secrets and to ensure that their families' names would not be tarnished. This was, for instance, often the case when discussing bootlegging. Most interviewees readily admitted that they had known that there was bootlegging in their neighbourhood. In fact, they could often name the individuals in charge of these businesses and vividly describe the houses in which this activity took place. When it came to admitting whether their parents had bootlegged, however, most were silent; it must be noted that this was a survival strategy employed by many families, not just Ukrainians, during difficult times like the Depression. It was only through interviews with others who had lived in those respective neighbourhoods and discussions with Baba that I discovered when an interviewee had remained silent about an issue such as this.

Undoubtedly there will always be readers who think that I have gotten the story of Sudbury's Ukrainians wrong. My version of the past will not be consistent with what they believe to be the truth. However lamentable, this has never been one of my concerns. I have come to realize that the ways that people remember are sometimes more important than what it is they remember.[31] Memories may not be entirely reliable but they do nevertheless have their strengths. A truth is a highly subjective thing, and it is really only through an interviewee's embellishments or silences that we may gain a sense of the ways in which that person constructs and defines his or her past.[32]

While bringing an insider like Baba to the interviews had its benefits, there is no doubt that this methodological approach also made the interview space a more complicated place. Specifically, interviewees may have been quite selective in sharing their memories, given that Baba was present. For instance, there were a handful of interviewees who, according to Baba, had been victims of domestic abuse. Despite the horrendous stories that Baba had shared with me, interviewees never mentioned this aspect of their lives, choosing instead to focus upon the positive aspects of their relationships. Even when interviewees provided hints about the abuse that they had suffered, I consciously chose not to broach this subject. While I trusted that Baba would remain silent when it came to the content of each interview, I did not want to take a chance and risk ruining my interviewees' reputations; I did not want these private memories to become public. I also did not want to make interviewees uncomfortable by putting them on the spot. Had I conducted multiple interviews with interviewees, the first with Baba and subsequent interviews alone, I would have felt more comfortable asking these kinds of tough questions. Revealing difficult experiences is often easier when there is a commitment, on the part of interviewers, to engage in deep listening. Interviews cannot be interrogations. They require intimacy and thus a space where knowing with interviewees, rather than knowing from them, may occur.[33]

As we engage in oral history, we are often made "uncomfortably aware of the elusive quality of historical truth itself."[34] As Alessandro Portelli reminds us, oral sources "tell us not just what people did, but what they wanted to do, what they believed they were doing, and what they now think they did."[35] In other words, nothing is certain in oral history. This kind of source tells us less about events than about their meanings. It is therefore next to impossible to be objective, neutral, or balanced when it comes to doing oral history. In this instance, I built subjective links not only to my interviewees but also to my Baba, who acted as both interviewee and interviewer.

Although the decision to share authority with Baba was a difficult one to make, it was absolutely necessary in order to gain access to the Ukrainian community. Fortunately, once we worked through many of the problems that plagued the first few interviews by establishing boundaries as well as a set of rules, we developed a relationship that worked for us as well as our interviewees. There is no doubt that this relationship was tested on many occasions. A messy process, collaboration was demanding, "requiring," as Shopes asserts, "an ability – even courage – to deal with people and situations that can be difficult; a certain tolerance for ambiguity and uncertainty about how a project will work out; and a willingness to take risks, not follow established protocols, and make decisions based on the logic of the work itself."[36] Successfully sharing authority, especially with family members who act as interviewers, necessitates dialogue at every stage of a project. Conflict and consensus will result. These are healthy outcomes that allow us to not only develop personal relationships but also push the boundaries of the discipline.

NOTES

1 This chapter is based in part upon my doctoral dissertation, which has recently been published as *According to Baba: A Collaborative Oral History of Sudbury's Ukrainian Community* (Vancouver: UBC Press, 2014). I would like to thank Steven High, John C. Walsh, and Marilyn Barber for their comments on the original article. Earlier drafts of the article were presented at the

Canadian Historical Association's Annual Meeting, held at the University of British Columbia in 2008, and the "Sharing Authority: Building Community University Alliances through Oral History, Digital Storytelling, and Collaboration" conference, held at Concordia University in 2008. I would therefore also like to thank all those who offered astute comments throughout the proceedings of these engaging conferences. These insights, along with those of the *Journal of Canadian Studies*' anonymous reviewers, where this piece originally appeared, have enhanced this work. Above all, I am indebted to my Baba for the role she played as interviewee, interviewer, and "secretary" in this oral history project. Without her, the history of Sudbury's Ukrainian community would have remained unwritten.

2 My doctoral dissertation, "Memory, Identity, and the Challenge of Community among Ukrainians in the Sudbury Region, 1901–1939," uses new and critical theoretical and methodological approaches to personalized scholarship to redefine what constitutes a community study. Specifically, it views community as an important analytical category that is worthy of deconstruction; community is not a simple and static entity, but an imagined reality, a social interaction, and a process. The adoption of a fluid model enabled an examination of the varying ways in which Ukrainians attached different meanings to community. These meanings, as my dissertation argues, depended upon the geographic spaces that these citizens occupied, the social networks to which they belonged, and their real and imagined identities and experiences both within and on the margins of their communities. While the subjective but rigorously researched narrative of my dissertation provides a social history of this ethnic community, it also offers an epistemological discussion about the limitations of the public archive and the challenges of writing about and engaging with oral history. See Stacey Zembrzycki, "Memory, Identity, and the Challenge of Community among Ukrainians in the Sudbury Region, 1901–1939" (PhD dissertation, Carleton University, 2007).

3 The public archive is a complex and highly political site of knowledge and power that ultimately determines the national narratives we can and cannot write. For a discussion about the ways in which the power of a state is manifested in its public archive see, for instance, Jacques Derrida, *Archive Fever: A Freudian Impression*, translated by Eric Prenowitz (Chicago: University of Chicago Press, 1996), 4; Marlene Manoff, "Theories of the Archive from Across the Disciplines," *Libraries and the Academy* 4, no. 1 (January 2004): 9–11; Antoinette Burton, *Dwelling in the Archive: Women Writing House, Home, and History in Late Colonial India* (Oxford: Oxford University Press, 2003), 140; and Antoinette Burton, "Introduction: Archive Fever, Archive Stories," in *Archive Stories: Facts, Fictions, and the Writing of History*, edited by Antoinette Burton (Durham: Duke University Press, 2005), 1–24.

4 Olga Zembrzycki, interview with Stacey Zembrzycki, 6 October 2004, Sudbury, Ontario. Interview is in the author's possession.

5 For similar reflections see, for instance, Donald Ritchie, *Doing Oral History: A Practical Guide* (New York: Oxford University Press, 2003).

6 Linda Shopes, "Sharing Authority," *Oral History Review* 30, no. 1 (January 2003): 103.

7 Michael Frisch, *A Shared Authority: Essays on the Craft and Meaning of Oral and Public History* (Albany: SUNY Press, 1990).

8 Katherine T. Corbett and Howard S. Miller, "A Shared Inquiry into Shared Inquiry," *Public Historian* 28, no. 1 (Winter 2006): 20.

9 Daniel Kerr, "'We Know What the Problem Is': Using Oral History to Develop a Collaborative Analysis of Homelessness from the Bottom Up," *Oral History Review* 30, no. 1 (January 2003): 27–45; Wendy Rickard, "Collaborating with Sex Workers in Oral History," *Oral History Review* 30, no. 1 (January 2003): 47–59; Alicia J. Rouverol, "Collaborative Oral History in a Correctional Setting: Promise and Pitfalls," *Oral History Review* 30, no. 1 (January 2003): 61–85; Lorraine Sitzia, "A Shared Authority: An Impossible Goal?" *Oral History Review* 30, no. 1 (January 2003): 87–101; Corbett and Miller, "A Shared Inquiry into Shared Inquiry."

10 Neil Sutherland, "When You Listen to the Winds of Childhood, How Much Can You Believe?" in *Histories of Canadian Children and Youth*, edited by Nancy Janovicek and Joy Parr (Oxford: Oxford University Press, 2003), 23.

11 For a thorough discussion about the history of the Sudbury region, see the essays in C.M. Wallace and Ashley Thomson, eds., *Sudbury: Rail Town to Regional Capital* (Toronto: Dundurn Press, 1993).

12 Martha Norkunas, *Monuments and Memory: History and Representation in Lowell, Massachusetts* (Washington: Smithsonian Institution Press, 2002), 25.

13 Penny Summerfield, *Reconstructing Women's Wartime Lives: Discourse and Subjectivity in Oral Histories of the Second World War* (Manchester: Manchester University Press, 1998), x; Carolyn Steedman, *Landscape for a Good Woman: A Story of Two Lives* (New Brunswick, NJ: Rutgers University Press, 1986), 8–12.

14 For a related discussion also see Franca Iacovetta, "Post-Modern Ethnography, Historical Materialism and Decentering the Male 'Authorial Voice': A Feminist Conversation," *Histoire sociale/Social History* 32, no. 64 (November 1999): 275–93; Pamela Sugiman, "'These Feelings That Fill My Heart': Japanese Canadian Women's Memories of Internment," *Oral History* 34 (Autumn 2006): 69–84; and Olive Stickney, "My Mother's Trunk," in *Unsettled Pasts: Reconceiving the West Through Women's History*, edited by Sarah Carter et al. (Calgary: University of Calgary Press, 2005), 241–9. Although other scholars have used the memories of family members to construct their histories, they have spent very little time exploring their subjective link to the resulting narratives. See, for example, Leslie Robertson, *Imagining Difference: Legend, Curse, and Spectacle in a Canadian Mining Town* (Vancouver: UBC Press, 2005); Robert Bruno, *Steelworker Alley: How Class Works in*

Youngstown (Ithaca: Cornell University Press, 1999); Jennifer Scuro, "Exploring Personal History: A Case Study of an Italian Immigrant Woman," *Oral History Review* 31, no. 1 (2004): 43–69; Christine Georgina Bye, "'I Think So Much of Edward': Family, Favouritism, and Gender on a Prairie Farm in the 1930s," in *Unsettled Pasts*, edited by Sarah Carter et al., 205–37; and Yong Chen, "Remembering Ah Quin: A Century of Social Memory in a Chinese American Family," *Oral History Review* 27, no. 1 (2000): 57–80.

15 Frances Swyripa, *Wedded to the Cause: Ukrainian-Canadian Women and Ethnic Identity, 1891–1991* (Toronto: University of Toronto Press, 1993), 216–17.

16 Rouverol, "Collaborative Oral History in a Correctional Setting," 83.

17 Henry Greenspan, *On Listening to Holocaust Survivors: Recounting and Life History* (Westport: Praeger, 1998), xvii.

18 Swyripa, *Wedded to the Cause*, 241–3; Karen Dubinsky, "'Who Do You Think Did the Cooking?': Baba in the Classroom," in *Changing Lives: Women and Northern Ontario*, edited by Margaret Kechnie and Marge Reitsma-Street (Toronto: Dundurn, 1996), 193–7.

19 Barbara Myerhoff, *Number Our Days* (New York: Simon and Schuster, 1978).

20 Sitzia, "A Shared Authority." Although the purpose of Katherine Borland's project was very different from mine, she also reflects upon the challenges of working with her grandmother. See Katherine Borland, "'That's Not What I Said': Interpretive Conflict in Oral Narrative Research," in *Women's Words: The Feminist Practice of Oral History*, edited by Sherna Berger Gluck and Daphne Patai (New York: Routledge, 1991), 63–75.

21 Together, Baba and I conducted seventy-two life story oral history interviews, between October 2004 and June 2005, with Ukrainians who were either born in, or raised in, or came to the Sudbury region prior to 1945; I conducted ten other interviews on my own. Of these interviewees, fifty were women and thirty-two were men. Moreover, twenty-three grew up in Manitoba and Saskatchewan, while forty-nine grew up in Northern Ontario; the ten remaining interviewees grew up elsewhere, usually in Eastern Europe. As for political affiliations, nine interviewees identified as progressives, six were members of the Orthodox community, fourteen did not identify with any Ukrainian community, and fifty-three were Ukrainian Catholics; fourteen Ukrainian Catholics reported that they also belonged to the Ukrainian National Federation. While Baba's involvement in the Ukrainian Catholic community explains why the majority of interviewees belonged to this community, it is also important to note that this community remains the most vibrant today. Sudbury's Orthodox, progressive, and nationalist Ukrainian organizations have largely disbanded and struggle to remain alive. Members have either died or have disconnected themselves from these organizations, and thus locating willing interviewees was difficult.

22 For a discussion about gossip and rumour and the ways in which they can be used by historians see, for instance, Franca Iacovetta, "Gossip, Contest, and Power in the Making of Suburban Bad Girls," *Canadian Historical Review* 80, no. 4 (December 1999): 585–624; and Lynne Marks, "Railing, Tattling, and General Rumour: Gossip, Gender, and Church Regulation in Upper Canada," *Canadian Historical Review* 81, no. 3 (September 2000): 380–402.

23 *Sudbury Star*, "Lack of Funds Forces Church to Close Doors," 29 April 1931, 23.

24 *Sudbury Star*, "Parish Control Is Transferred," 2 May 1931, 1.

25 Anne Matschke, interview with Stacey and Olga Zembrzycki, 7 May 2005, Sudbury, Ontario. Interview is in the author's possession.

26 Talja Blokland, "Bricks, Mortar, Memories: Neighbourhood and Networks in Collective Acts of Remembering," *International Journal of Urban and Regional Research* 25, no. 2 (June 2001): 279.

27 Childhood is a separate and socially constructed stage of existence that complicates the creation of a memory text; in terms of age, all of my interviewees were under the age of thirteen prior to 1939. Since, as Neil Sutherland notes, adults tend to use childhood memories that are "really a reconstruction of what is being recalled rather than a reproduction of it," we must focus upon the form, content, and silences that result during these kinds of interviews. Sutherland, "When You Listen to the Winds of Childhood," 23. See also Neil Sutherland, *Growing Up: Childhood in English Canada from the Great War to the Age of Television* (Toronto: University of Toronto Press, 1997).

28 For a detailed discussion about the life story approach employed by oral historians, see Robert Atkinson, *The Life Story Interview* (Thousand Oaks, CA: Sage, 1988).

29 See, for instance, Joan Sangster, "Telling Our Stories: Feminist Debates and the Use of Oral History," *Women's History Review* 3, no. 1 (March 1994): 5–28.

30 Steven High, *Industrial Sunset: The Making of North America's Rust Belt, 1969–1984* (Toronto: University of Toronto Press, 2003), 42.

31 Alessandro Portelli, *The Death of Luigi Trastulli and Other Stories: Form and Meaning in Oral History* (Albany: SUNY Press, 1991), 50.

32 Personal truth is revealed through the collective threads of an interview. It is the way in which interviewees subjectively represent their lives through stories. For a Canadian discussion about self-representation and truth see, for instance, Marlene Epp, "The Memory of Violence: Soviet and East European Mennonite Refugees and Rape in the Second World War," *Journal of Women's History* 9, no. 1 (Spring 1997): 58–87; Epp, *Women without Men: Mennonite Refugees of the Second World War* (Toronto: University of Toronto Press, 1999); Paula Draper, "Surviving Their Survival: Women, Memory, and the Holocaust," in *Sisters or Strangers? Immigrant, Ethnic, and Racialized Women in Canadian History*, edited by Marlene Epp, Franca Iacovetta,

and Frances Swyripa (Toronto: University of Toronto Press, 2004), 399–414; Pamela Sugiman, "Passing Time, Moving Memories: Interpreting Wartime Narratives of Japanese Canadian Women," *Histoire sociale/Social History* 37, no. 73 (May 2004): 51–79; Sugiman, "These Feelings That Fill My Heart"; Sangster, "Telling Our Stories"; Alexander Freund and Laura Quilici, "Exploring Myths in Women's Narratives: Italian and German Immigrant Women in Vancouver, 1947–1961," BC *Studies* 105–6 (spring–summer 1995): 159–82; and Michael Riordon, *An Unauthorized Biography of the World: Oral History on the Front Lines* (Toronto: Between the Lines, 2004). For an international discussion, see Luisa Passerini, *Fascism in Popular Memory: The Cultural Experience of the Turin Working Class*, translated by Robert Lumley and Jude Bloomfield (Cambridge: Cambridge University Press, 1987); Paul Thompson, *The Voice of the Past: Oral History* (Oxford: Oxford University Press, 1988); Alessandro Portelli, "The Peculiarities of Oral History," *History Workshop* 12, no. 1 (1981): 96–107; Portelli, *The Death of Luigi Trastulli*; Frisch, *A Shared Authority*; Kathleen Blee, *Inside Organized Racism: Women in the Hate Movement* (Berkeley: University of California Press, 2002); and Raphael Samuel and Paul Thompson, eds., *The Myths We Live By* (New York: Routledge, 1990).

33 Henry Greenspan and Sidney Bolkosky, "When Is an Interview an Interview? Notes from Listening to Holocaust Survivors," *Poetics Today* 27, no. 2 (2006): 432.

34 Portelli, *The Death of Luigi Trastulli*, viii–ix.

35 Ibid., 99.

36 Shopes, "Sharing Authority," 106.

3

Oral History and Ethical Practice after *TCPS2*[1]

Nancy Janovicek

In 2010 the three major Canadian federal funding agencies for health, sciences, and humanities[2] released the second edition of the *Tri-Council Policy Statement: Ethical Research Involving Humans* (TCPS). The revised policy, known as TCPS2, evolved from a three-year consultation between the Interagency Panel on Research and Ethics (the Panel) and researchers who were critical of the earlier imposition of a medical model on qualitative and quantitative research in the social sciences and humanities. The original version of this chapter elaborated on the submission to the Panel that I wrote on behalf of the Canadian Historical Association with Sarah Carter and Peter L. Twohig.[3] This chapter argues that TCPS2 has addressed many of the barriers that the original policy created for qualitative research identified by academics in the social sciences and humanities during consultations, but that despite these improvements, concerns about liability still influence the decisions of some university research ethics boards (REBs) at the institutional level.

When I first published on this issue, I had two major criticisms of the original TCPS and the impact of its interpretation by REBs on historical research: (1) its emphasis on privacy and confidentiality; and (2) the implications of its proposed "good practices for research involving Aboriginal people" for research involving women and marginalized members in First Nations communities. The revised policy has addressed key criticisms from oral historians. Under the first policy, many oral historians became embroiled in debates with institutional REBs about anonymity and the preservation of oral histories. TCPS2 provides good guidelines for disclosing the identity of research participants, guidelines that reflect ethics in oral history theory and practice.

A noteworthy improvement in the policy is its widening of the discussion of research involving First Nations, Inuit, and Métis peoples. The initial policy insisted that researchers acquire written consent from Aboriginal leaders, preferably Chief and Band Council, as a good practice that promoted collaborative research. Ultimately, this requirement created barriers for researchers, especially graduate students working with less powerful members of Aboriginal communities. Taking into account the Panel's consultations with Aboriginal communities, the current policy still maintains that cooperation and consultation are best practices. However, the new guidelines also recognize the potential for research to further marginalize women and other vulnerable individuals, and advise researchers to take diverse voices into account in their research programs. To ensure that researchers incorporate diverse views, the new policy has broadened its definition of Aboriginal leadership to include political groups that advocate on behalf of Aboriginal people who have lost their connection to their communities.

I begin this chapter with a comparison of the core values of the original and the revised ethics policies. The revised policy offers an expanded definition of research and consequently a more comprehensive analysis of ethical dilemmas in diverse contexts. I then summarize debates about the relationship between researcher and subject in the oral history literature. When the field gained popularity in the 1970s, oral historians argued that giving voice to marginalized people was one way to restore pride and dignity to groups who had been excluded from the historical narrative. Subsequent discussions of oral history offered more critical analysis of the relationship between historians and informants, and of the nature of the evidence gleaned from interviews. The question of how much analysis to impose on life stories has become an important ethical concern for historians.

I go on to examine how *TCPS2* addresses the concerns I discuss in regard to the original document: privacy and confidentiality, free and informed consent, and research involving Aboriginal peoples. I conclude with thoughts on the relationship between researchers and REBs at the institutional level, which still seem to be distrustful rather than committed to ethical practice. The Panel initiated a vigorous national discussion about ethics that led to the implementation of an improved policy. This conversation needs also to take place at the institutional level to ensure that the policy is implemented in a manner that protects research participants and promotes ethical research.

THE EVOLUTION OF THE CORE VALUES OF FEDERAL ETHICS POLICIES

The implementation of the *TCPS* in 1998 made historical research more complicated. Under that policy, research involving oral histories and privately held records came under the purview of university REBs. Historians had to struggle to convince social science researchers of the merit of disclosing the identity of research participants (an issue I discuss in greater detail below). Moreover, many researchers believed that REBs were more concerned with legal liability than with ethical responsibility. Perhaps the most significant implication of the imposition of bureaucratic oversight on historical research was that, in order to avoid debates with overprotective REBs, scholars became disinclined to interview people. Graduate students were particularly reluctant to take on oral history projects because of new expectations from faculties of graduate studies for timely completion; the application for ethics approval often delayed research for too long.

A fundamental criticism of the *TCPS* on the part of researchers in the social sciences and humanities was its restrictive definition of research, which was based on a medical model. The United States was the first country to introduce ethics policies to regulate biomedical research. Their purpose was to strike a balance between patient risk and the reputations of doctors and medical research institutions. This medical model was later extended to govern research in the social sciences and humanities,[4] and when other national research funding agencies implemented their own research ethics policies, they followed the American pattern.[5] Qualitative researchers have argued that one of the consequences of imposing the medical model on all research is that ethics policies have preferred research methods and ethical practices that work best for experimental research models designed to produce generalizable data from large databases.[6]

The initial Canadian policy made concessions for oral history, but REBs tended to interpret the policy in a manner that did not address tested collaborative research methodologies and participatory action models that were widely practised by qualitative researchers. *TCPS2* espouses an expansive definition of research involving humans that "is as boundless as the human imagination."[7] Under this policy, research is "an undertaking intended to extend knowledge through disciplined or systematic investigation."[8] By adopting a broader definition of research, the revised policy provides for a much more comprehensive discussion of the ethical considerations that may arise in various research settings. The policy also includes guidelines for assessing emerging methodologies that develop in the course of a research program, and it offers greater flexibility for adapting recruitment strategies and interview topics on the basis of research findings and conversations with research participants.

The fundamental guiding principle of both policies is respect for human dignity. The initial policy adopted eight guiding ethical principles: respect for human dignity; respect for free and informed consent; respect for vulnerable persons; respect for privacy and confidentiality; respect for justice and inclusiveness; balancing harms and benefits; minimizing harm; and maximizing benefit.[9] In practice, however, a result of identifying harm and risk as ethical principles was that REBs often conflated ethics with potential liability to the institution. Researchers were critical of the chill that this tendency cast on all research, and especially research on controversial topics. Furthermore, positing privacy and confidentiality as ethical principles obliged oral historians to explain how identifying narrators was ethical practice and to defend the historian's obligation to preserve research data.

TCPS2 follows three core principles to promote human dignity: respect for persons; concern for welfare; and justice.[10] The policy allows room for differences between academics and communities, and acknowledges that researchers must often make difficult choices to balance the protection of research participants and the requirements of research. Significantly, TCPS2 replaced the term "research subject" with "research participant," thereby emphasizing the reciprocal relationships that inform community-based research and oral history. This recognition that research participants play an active role in scholarly endeavours promotes the dignity of people who agree to join research projects.

The core values of the revised policy comply with many of the underlying assumptions of ethical concerns among oral historians. In comparison to the initial policy, the TCPS2 guidelines are more compatible with oral history theory and practice. The discussion of qualitative research projects addresses oral historians' criticisms of the original policy, but only briefly mentions oral history. The following section reviews the question of ethical practice and oral history.

ETHICAL CONCERNS FOR ORAL HISTORIANS

When oral history gained credibility in the 1970s, its most vocal advocates were scholars who were dedicated to writing history from the bottom up.

Oral history gave people who had not written memoirs or produced documents an opportunity to provide their accounts of the past. Historians studying racialized minorities, women, workers, poor people, and grassroots activists believed that oral history would give marginalized groups the opportunity to direct historical research. By listening carefully, historians could learn what issues were most important to ordinary people. They believed that, by organizing their research questions according to what they learned from interviews rather than from archival documents, they could construct a new historical narrative that better reflected the day-to-day lives of less powerful people. Paul Thompson, one of the most well known proponents of the new field, argued that oral history democratized the discipline because it brought history into the community, radically transformed the social meaning of history, and encouraged greater understanding between generations. At the personal level, the process of conducting oral history enhanced individuals' sense of dignity and self-confidence. Oral historians' commitment to restoring the dignity and self-confidence of people by making them central to history obliged researchers to conduct their interviews in an ethical and respectful manner.[11]

Enthusiastic endorsements of oral history as an unmediated articulation of the past were subsequently tempered, however, by analyses of how oral histories reflect the politics and agendas of both researcher and interviewee.[12] Historians, influenced by debates in the social sciences, began to pose more critical questions about the unequal relationship between researcher and subject. Asking who benefits from the research was an important consideration for scholars interviewing people less privileged than they. Joan Sangster explains that even when historians interview people because they value their insights and lives, they still approach interviewees in the role of professional scholars. Although a political commitment to ending inequality often shapes research programs involving oral history, historians must still concede that they use gathered personal memories in order to publish materials that ultimately advance their own careers. Thus, historians benefit more directly from oral histories than those who share their personal life stories.[13]

An acknowledgment that oral history did not level the power imbalance between the researcher and the interviewee was related to other issues about subject-centred research. How much control should interviewees have in the interpretation of their life stories? What agendas do research participants bring to the interview? How reliable is memory, and how does collective historical consciousness affect what we remember?

The interpretations of historians are often at odds with interviewees' understandings of their own past. This issue is especially clear to feminist historians writing about women who do not share the researcher's analysis of the impact of patriarchal relations on their choices and actions. Historians note that when women talk about their lives, they tend to understate their role in past events and to organize their memories around family rather than themselves.[14] Contradictions between women's understanding of their past and historians' analysis of their lives have led to histories that capture the complexities of women's perceptions of changing patriarchal relations and gender roles.[15] Yet such conflicting explanations also raise questions about interpretation. Documenting how women have understood their circumstances is a fundamental goal of women's history. But it is also the historian's job to analyze how race, class, and gender have affected women's opportunities. To do so, historians face the ethical dilemma of imposing their frameworks on their reconstruction of women's lives.[16] Rather than using oral histories as evidence of "how it was," historians now recognize that this evidence merits the same critical and reflective analysis as written records.

How, then, could oral history be a methodology that produces subject-centred research? Historians have been helped to work through this ethical dilemma by a growing understanding of how people remember. Memory is fragile. What we remember and how we make sense of it depends on how we understand our current situation.[17] Michael Frisch explains that in order to use oral history effectively, historians must consider "what happens to experience on the way to becoming a memory."[18] There is a relationship between culture and individuality that transforms personal experiences into collective memory, which then needs to be interrogated to make sense of the discrepancies between personal recollections and written records.

Discrepancies between oral and written evidence are commonly found in relation to events that research participants choose not to discuss. People tend to exclude unpleasant experiences from their recollections. For example, women often deny incidences of violence and gender-based harassment in their lives or are reluctant to talk about these experiences. Yet women's recollections of such difficult memories are crucial for understanding individual agency and for documenting changes in women's consciousness of their right to resist violence. When women are reluctant to talk about such events, historians find themselves in the uncomfortable position of deciding whether or not to push them to talk about things they would rather forget. Interviewers face a difficult choice between respecting the interviewee's privacy and perpetuating the silences and taboos that keep women from speaking out about violence and abuse.

To summarize: oral historians have been engaged in ethics discussions since the field gained credibility thirty years ago. Ethics debates among practitioners arise from tensions between fieldwork and the need to meet the standards of the discipline. The emphasis on privacy and confidentiality has been a key point of contention between REBs and oral historians. The original *TCPS* did not reflect historians' ethics and professional concerns. It presented new dilemmas and criteria based on the policy's emphasis on reducing harm, which had little to do with the moral issues that historians face in the field. REBs' strict interpretations of the policy made it difficult to pursue projects on sensitive issues and often ignored the methods that are practised by oral historians and which are proven measures for balancing the reputations of their informants with the requirements of the discipline.

In the following sections, I expand on these issues by discussing privacy and confidentiality, free and informed consent, and research involving First Nations, Inuit, and Métis peoples and assess how *TCPS2* responds to oral historians' criticisms of the original policy.

PRIVACY AND CONFIDENTIALITY

Alessandro Portelli describes oral history as "the science and art of the individual."[19] It is a methodology that helps us understand the relationship between culture and individuality. Personal narratives give social historians insight into how individuals have made sense of their world and how they perceived the impact of social, political, and cultural change in their everyday lives. When interviews are compared, patterns may emerge, but unique responses to historical events offer important insights about tensions within communities and the way social location influences individual recollections of an event. The original *TCPS* policy, however, demanded anonymity, with a few exceptions accorded to qualitative researchers. Oral historians often had to resist REBs that insisted on anonymity because safeguarding anonymity does not adhere to the professional standards of their discipline. Traditionally, the discipline of history has not deemed anonymous sources to be credible evidence; all sources should be accessible to other scholars so that they can verify the accuracy of the research and develop the historiography.[20] The revised policy concedes that oral historians need not protect privacy. *TCPS2* states, "In oral history, anonymity is the exception."[21] Yet the policy's increased emphasis on privacy legislation could nevertheless put restrictions on the secondary use of data.

Anonymity is not a new ethical issue for social historians. Researchers who use archived medical records and court cases to understand sensitive issues such as family conflict and sexual identity have also grappled with issues of confidentiality. Public archives require researchers examining sensitive records to sign research agreements that oblige them to use pseudonyms or initials, or to code the records so that individuals cannot be traced through footnotes. These measures are in place because the producers and subjects of the files did not anticipate that they would enter the public domain, and because the records discuss experiences that people usually keep private. Since historians cannot gain the informed consent of the people they encounter in records, and the process of acquiring consent could invade their privacy, maintaining anonymity is preferred. Nevertheless, it is worth asking what is lost by these protective measures. As Franca Iacovetta and Wendy Mitchinson explain, "our legal obligations as researchers to protect the privacy of individuals in the past can lead us to write the marginal into history by writing their names and faces out of it."[22]

Historians conducting oral histories can give research participants the choice to reveal their identity or to protect their privacy. It is common practice to ask a participant for consent to reveal his or her identity before conducting an interview. When I did interviews for *No Place to Go*, a study of the history of women's organizing against spousal assault in small cities and rural communities, I decided to let the research participants decide whether or not they wanted to remain anonymous.[23] REBs and colleagues in other disciplines challenged my decision, arguing that the research participants might not be fully aware of how others in the community would react to their statements once they were in print. They advised me not to leave this decision to the research participants because residents of small cities do not have the same degree of anonymity as residents of larger cities, and would not be aware of the negative implications of having their opinions published in my work. I maintained that these women were known in their communities because of their social activism. While they were key players in their communities, many of them were less well known in the broader women's movement. I wanted to acknowledge them as political figures, and did so by identifying them with their consent.

Only three of the thirty women I interviewed for *No Place to Go* requested that I not identify them in the research. They asked for confidentiality either because they did not think they had been key players in the organization of a women's shelter or because they wanted to protect the privacy of family members. One woman requested confidentiality to protect her mother's privacy. Her experience in a violent family had informed her advocacy for battered women, as well as her analysis of services provided to battered women. It was important to her and for my analysis, to make the connection between her personal life and political activism. The women who refused anonymity have struggled to ensure that women's political work is recognized and shared my view that activists should be acknowledged. When I explained to Doreen Worden, a lesbian activist who has worked to maintain lesbian visibility in her community, why university ethics policy prefers that researchers guarantee confidentiality and why she might prefer that I use a pseudonym, she replied, "I like my name."[24] Her conviction made me realize that ethics policies and practices that assume that research participants cannot make this decision are condescending.

There are also situations when concealing identity may offend the religious convictions and cultural customs of research participants. When Janis Thiessen was applying for ethics approval to interview Mennonite business leaders and intellectuals in Winnipeg, for instance, she had to convince the university REB that her informants should be given the choice to reveal their identity because "many of them saw their participation as a witness to the work of God in their lives."[25] These informants also requested that the tapes and transcripts using their real names be donated to the church conference archives as a "legacy for their descendants."[26] Imposing anonymity would have offended the human dignity of these research participants.

Under the original policy, concern about privacy and confidentiality also sparked debates between oral historians and REBs about the secondary use of data. To protect the confidentiality of human subjects, the *TCPS* required researchers to place limits on the use of the data, and to identify any anticipated secondary uses of the data. More significantly, the policy advised researchers to destroy their data upon completion of the research as a means of ensuring confidentiality. Among historians, however, it is not common practice to destroy tapes and transcripts of interviews. As mentioned above, professional standards require researchers to make oral evidence available to other scholars for verification. Moreover, preserving the past is an important element of oral history. Destroying evidence conflicts with what historians do. Oral history creates historical evidence. Researchers rarely use all of the data in an interview, and expect that the tapes will be useful to future historians. Under the previous policy, REBs had compelled some historians to include in their consent forms the option to destroy recordings.

An unexpected implication of the debates about secondary use of data is that it has become more difficult to deposit recordings of interviews into public archives. Researchers are now careful to include in their consent forms a statement that the recordings will be donated to a public archive upon completion of the project. Interviewees can thus place restrictions, such as guaranteeing confidentiality or closing the records for thirty to fifty years, on the recordings before they are in the public domain. However, historians who conducted oral histories prior to the implementation of the federal ethics policy are worried that the rich evidence in their research will not be released for future scholarship. One historian who had donated interviews with war veterans to the Canadian Department of Veterans Affairs was surprised when they contacted him for release forms. The interviews had been conducted in the 1970s, prior to the requirement to obtain written consent. The chilling climate created by the ethics policy threatens to make oral histories conducted in the 1970s and 1980s inaccessible to future researchers.

TCPS2 discusses the benefits of secondary use of data, especially in historical research, and provides guidelines for safeguarding privacy and confidentiality, including a discussion of secondary use of data. Researchers must ask for consent for the secondary use of data before they conduct the interview. They must ensure that identifiable information will not be disclosed without the consent of the individual and that subsequent research does not lead to harm. REBs must also consider privacy laws that place restrictions on contacting people about the secondary use of data.[27] Historians should monitor carefully the implementation of this policy because the need to balance privacy laws with consent for secondary use of data places a serious burden on future historical research.

The revised policy puts greater emphasis on privacy legislation. Its guidelines recommend that researchers seek legal counsel to ensure that they comply with Canadian laws, and that those doing research abroad ensure that they are in compliance with multi-jurisdictional legislative regimes. One graduate student faced delays in the approval of his application because the REB insisted that he contact the government or an equivalent university-based ethics board of the country in which he was doing research. The student was not able to fulfill this requirement because he was not affiliated with a university abroad and because there was no equivalent to the REBs in that country. Ultimately, the REB approved his application, but the delays were frustrating and time-consuming.[28]

Historians have been critical of privacy legislation. Two recent examples that illustrate how overprotection of individual privacy is an impediment to historical research should make oral historians wary of the continued emphasis on privacy and confidentiality in ethics policy. In 2005, the government amended the Statistics Act to restrict access to census micro-data only to those who consented to the release of information. Only 56 percent of Canadians consented, and consequently a significant proportion of data will not be transferred to Library and Archives Canada. More damaging to future historical research is the cancellation of the long-form census in 2010, purportedly to protect Canadians from invasive questioning. In the current climate, which prioritizes privacy over historical research, oral historians need to be attentive to ethics protocols that may put unnecessary restrictions on the secondary use of oral histories in the interests of protecting privacy.

I am not arguing that historians do not need to give due consideration to the protection of confidentiality. Indeed, they do need to ask when and why it may be appropriate to conceal an informant's identity. Pragmatically, for instance, offering confidentiality may facilitate recruitment of participants for research on sensitive issues. Decisions about granting anonymity rest on the historian's assessment of the potential harms and risks that the publication of information may have for the research participants. Informants may disclose information that disrupts familial or employment relationships or community harmony, in which cases it would be preferable to protect the anonymity of research participants. This is a decision that scholars may make in collaboration with interviewees in their discussions about free and informed consent.

In our submission to the Panel, Peter Twohig recommended the following options, which give research participants the choice to determine the degree of privacy they want:

1 Open consent, which permits secondary data analyses: Research participants agree to an interview and sign a consent that would allow the participant to be identified and authorize the transcript and recording to be deposited in an archive for future research.
2 Open consent with no secondary data analyses: Research participants agree to an interview and sign a consent that would allow the participant to be identified but would permit the researcher alone to make use of that interview and transcript.
3 Limited consent with no secondary data analyses: Research participants agree to an interview and sign a consent form that would require the researcher to anonymize the interview and transcript in

any analysis and destroy the recording and transcript after a specified period of time.

4 Limited consent with secondary data analyses: Research participants agree to an interview and sign a consent that would require the interviewer to remove any personal descriptors from the tape and transcript but would allow these materials to be deposited in an archive for future research.[29]

These options balance individual privacy with historians' obligation to preserve the past. They also remind researchers of their ongoing ethical responsibilities to research participants. In chapter 1 of this volume, Brian Calliou argues that researchers who interview Elders have an ethical obligation to Aboriginal communities to make the oral histories accessible to others and to ensure that local authorities have control over how this knowledge is used in future studies.[30]

Many Aboriginal communities have established their own protocols for researchers. Scholars should also consider their ongoing obligations to other cultural, social, and religious communities. In research involving a community with a strong collective identity, historians should seek to donate the oral histories to an archive that is available to members of that community.

FREE AND INFORMED CONSENT

Successful oral histories rely on the participation of individuals who are interested in a proposed project and are therefore willing to share their memories. In addition, interviewees' comfort with the process depends on the researcher's genuine respect for the person who is sharing his or her life story. Reciprocal respect and trust, which are prerequisites of a good interview, can be upset if the relationship between the informant and the researcher is bureaucratized, by consent forms, for instance. Dealing with consent forms can break down the friendly rapport established before the interview begins. Raising the issue of potential risks and harms casts a particular chill on an interview and adds an air of formality that makes an interview less open and tends to make the interviewee nervous.[31] Historians' frustrations with signed consent forms echo those expressed by researchers in other social sciences. Researchers working with privately held records must also apply for ethics approval for their research projects and obtain consent in writing in order to use the documents. This requirement complicates the fieldwork because informants often provide researchers with sources considered to be private records only during the interview and researchers must ask informants to sign another set of documents to use the materials.

TCPS2 contains some measures to minimize the effect of this bureaucratic requirement on the interviewing relationship, especially in research where it is culturally inappropriate or with vulnerable research participants. But it still insists on the need to document consent and to "ensure that researchers are not exposed to unnecessary risks."[32] These risks are supposed to be listed in the consent forms. Describing potential harms and benefits of the research in the consent form seems superficial because it is difficult to predict what interviewees will discuss. REBs try to determine the impact that the interview will have on the informant by reviewing the prepared interview questionnaire. However, following an interview schedule is a practice that is based on the researcher's ability to know what results they anticipate before they begin their research. Historians do not hypothesize about research outcomes because looking for evidence to prove a predetermined hypothesis may deter them from analyzing the evidence that does not support the hypothesis. Researchers bring to the interview a list of questions based on their archival research. In practice, however, research participants often raise interesting issues that take an interview in a different direction. A good oral historian listens to the informant and follows his or her lead. Following a fixed research schedule approved by an REB does not work in the field.

The purpose of reviewing interview schedules is to ensure that research participants will not be harmed during the study. Historians researching sensitive issues or community conflicts expect that they will bring up unpleasant memories, but overly cautious REBs equate upsetting research participants with doing harm. At times it may indeed be morally responsible to exclude oral histories from studies so that people who have suffered violence and abuse do not have to relive these experiences. In his study of residential schools, for instance, John Milloy decided that it would be unethical to conduct interviews with former students because he did not have adequate resources to provide counselling for them.[33] However, this caveat should not be applied to all research on private matters because talking to people about painful memories provides invaluable insights into individual agency that are rarely found in the written record. *TCPS2* states that one of the significant ethical dilemmas that researchers and REBs face arises in seeking the balance between overprotection and the imposition of an undue burden on particular individuals and groups. While researchers need to be aware of the harm that their questions may

potentially cause, erecting barriers to their involvement in research undermines the policy's core principle of justice. The policy instructs REBs not
to intervene in order to protect people it deems to be vulnerable.[34]

Oral historians have developed methods to reduce harm and potential
embarrassment to informants. Personal ethics guide what historians use
in their publications. In research involving people who are not public figures, responsible historians are careful not to publish material that will
potentially make interviewees uncomfortable. Follow-up with informants to ensure that they will not be embarrassed by the published work
is an established practice. Researchers often allow interviewees to review
transcripts in order to make corrections or to delete portions of their
interview; or they may ask informants to review the pages where they are
quoted to ensure that they are not misrepresented in the final analysis. In
addition to addressing ethical concerns, these procedures ensure accuracy because reading the narrative can sharpen an informant's memory.

RESEARCH INVOLVING FIRST NATIONS, INUIT, AND MÉTIS PEOPLE

Relationships between historians and First Nations, Inuit, and Métis communities raise contentious issues. Questions about the role of historians
on policy issues and as expert witnesses in court cases involving First
Nations land claims have led to heated debates about the responsibilities
of non-Native scholars to the Aboriginal communities they study.[35] And
historians also disagree about methodology and the interpretation of archival and oral evidence. Postcolonial theories have informed recent research, in order to allow historians to counter historical writing that has
marginalized indigenous peoples in political, economic, and social life.
Oral sources have been central to the process of reclaiming indigenous
voices in reassessments of colonial contact and historical examinations of
their experiences in the twentieth century.

Oral tradition is respected as a valid interpretation of relations between
indigenous peoples and colonizers. Though the terms are often used
interchangeably, oral history and oral tradition are not the same thing.
Oral history is a research method based on Western epistemological paradigms; the evidence of oral history is subject to critical assessment and
its validity is tested against the written record.[36] Oral tradition is a far
more complex process of transmitting political and cultural traditions as
well as preserving the past.[37] As Julie Cruikshank argues in chapter 8 of
this *Reader*, "local voices from North American indigenous communities provide more than grist for conventional disciplinary paradigms and

have the power to contribute to our understanding of historiography."[38] Oral traditions are accounts of the past that are mediated by the context and social position of the person narrating the events. Historians struggle with how to integrate oral tradition into their discipline in a manner that meets historical criteria and respects the legitimate demands of First Nations peoples for control over their stories.[39] Story ownership is a key issue for historians who use oral sources. Researchers working in collaboration with indigenous communities were critical of the TCPS because it did not adequately address the reciprocal relationships between Aboriginal research participants and scholars.

When drafting the original TCPS, the three councils decided not to establish policies on research with Aboriginal communities because they realized that they had not sufficiently consulted with researchers and with those communities. They did, however, include a short section to initiate discussion about the practices and protocols that should be included in ethics policy.[40] This policy vacuum made it virtually impossible to undertake controversial research projects with groups and individuals who held dissenting views within their community. Under the TCPS, researchers working with Aboriginal peoples had to acquire written approval from Band Councils in order to interview members of their community. This practice followed measures recommended by First Nations, Inuit, and Métis leaders to prevent researchers from exploiting members of their community, and in recognition of the role of indigenous peoples as guardians of their culture and knowledge systems.[41] The policy did not adequately consider the ethical dilemmas arising from interactions with leaders who acted as gatekeepers. Historical examination of divisive issues – especially women's issues – was difficult because of the requirement to obtain approval from the Band Council. For instance, one graduate student who was examining Aboriginal women's experiences of the war dependants' allowance policy during the Second World War did not conduct interviews because the REB at her university expected her to send a letter to all Band Councils and Indian Friendship Centres asking permission to talk to community members. By the time her application was approved, she had insufficient time to build the relationships required to secure interviews with indigenous women.[42] By giving control of research to Aboriginal leaders, the TCPS had sought to prevent the appropriation of indigenous knowledge. But it did not adequately consider that giving exclusive control of research participants to elected Aboriginal leaders could exclude dissenting voices. Under the original policy, research on divisive issues in indigenous communities could potentially further alienate individuals, such as women who had lost their status and had not benefited equally from the advancements in Aboriginal rights and entitlements. *TCPS2* addresses these limitations by recommending that Aboriginal women's groups and other community-based indigenous organizations might be better research partners for projects that involved vulnerable individuals.

TCPS2 definitively states that the interpretation of the policy must not impede research on controversial subjects in First Nations, Inuit, and Métis communities. Researchers should seek to include research participants who are not part of the formal leadership, but must also be aware that "groups or individuals whose circumstances make them vulnerable may need or desire special measures to ensure their safety in the context of a specific research project."[43] When I first wrote on this issue, I argued that the *TCPS* could exacerbate the political exclusion of Aboriginal women in their communities and in Canadian society by limiting research on the specific problems that women faced. The original policy perpetuated the artificial distinction between individual and collective rights. Aboriginal women's groups have been critical of this distinction because those who opposed their political goals argued that they were more concerned with their own rights than with the collective rights of the group.[44] *TCPS2* advises researchers to be aware of how patriarchal government policies have undermined women's leadership roles in indigenous communities and continue to limit women's full participation in society. Moreover, it recognizes that Aboriginal people are individuals with specific obligations to community, but "also respects the autonomy of individuals to decide whether they will participate in research."[45]

The policy insists that these guidelines must be implemented in accordance with ethical policies developed by First Nations, Inuit, and Métis communities and groups. The guiding principle of the policy is to ensure that non-Aboriginal researchers develop reciprocal relationships with Aboriginal groups and leaders in order to produce research that is beneficial to the community. Most important, *TCPS2* begins from the premise that this is an evolving document that must change to reflect the new strategies adopted by First Nations, Inuit, and Métis people to manage their respective knowledge systems.

HISTORICAL RESEARCH UNDER *TCPS2*

Reflecting on the ethics of oral history, Portelli cautions that we must not allow the institutional requirements of professional ethical research to "bureaucratize our attitude."[46] Unfortunately, after the implementation of the *TCPS*, historians were compelled to focus on bureaucracy; and since the introduction of *TCPS2* this situation has not changed. Discussions among historians often turn to sharing strategies to ensure a successful application to the REB rather than examine deeper questions about balancing academic honesty with ethical considerations. Even though the revised policy incorporates many of the ethical issues that inform oral history practice, procedural questions continue to dominate historians' conversations about ethics and research. There is reason for concern. In informal conversations at conferences some graduate students have admitted that they avoid oral history because they are concerned that ethics administrators will delay their research and make it impossible for them to complete their graduate work in a timely manner. At a workshop on oral history practice that I attended at Concordia University in 2011, which dealt with the ongoing ethical negotiations that influence relationships between scholars and research participants, graduate students spoke about difficulties with REBs.[47] This was an international conference. The similarities among the graduate students, who were working under ethics policies in different countries, underscore the continued need to monitor the implementation of ethics policy at the institutional level.

Despite improvements in the policy, the apprehensive climate created by *TCPS* continues to inform how we think about ethics policy and how REBs implement the policy. It is the implementation of *TCPS2* at the institutional level, rather than the policy itself, that creates barriers to research. Researchers should be able to use the policy to defend themselves from obstructive REBs and university administrations that are more concerned with legal liability than ethical responsibility. The *TCPS2* clearly states that REBs "need independence in the decision-making process to ... properly apply the core principles of [*TCPS2*] ... to their ethics review of research projects."[48] It advises against overprotection of research participants because it impedes justice, a core principle of the document. Academics should use the document to defend ethical research strategies. We need to be especially vigilant in defending graduate students whose research is scrutinized by research boards and advise them to use the policy to defend their research principles. Teaching ethics policy and practice is essential to mentorship in the field.

The regulatory power of federal ethics policies remains a vital cause for concern among researchers who have promised confidentiality to research participants. In contentious cases, university administrators and researchers sometimes disagree on how these federal policies govern the institution's legal obligations to researchers and research participants.

Two recent cases of court subpoenas for the identities of research participants demonstrate the disparate interpretations of the extent to which university-based researchers are able to guarantee confidentiality to their research participants. In the United States, the subpoenas of interviews conducted by Boston College researchers with former Irish Republican Army operatives pitted university administrators against researchers.[49] The researchers guaranteed research participants confidentiality and insisted that the university's primary ethical obligation was to the welfare of interviewees. University administrators, on the other hand, rejected unmitigated protection of confidentiality and insisted that the university should put limits on confidentiality if research participants discuss activities that violate the law. Ted Palys and John Lowman conclude that the case has made clear that university administrators and researchers do not always share the same ethics.[50]

The Boston College subpoena raises the important issue of balancing researchers' ethical obligations to protect confidentiality with legal requirements to disclose information. The revised Canadian policy stresses the "ethical duty of confidentiality" and guarantees that "institutions shall support their researchers in maintaining promises of confidentiality."[51] When researchers are compelled by legal authorities to disclose confidential research materials, the policy instructs them to "maintain their promise of confidentiality to participants within the extent permitted by ethical principles and/or law."[52] This is determined on a case-by-case basis. But who pays for the legal expenses incurred by researchers who fight against what they deem to be unwarranted disclosure of confidential information? This was a key issue in the recent dispute between University of Ottawa administrators and criminologists Chris Bruckert and Collette Parent. Bruckert and Parent filed a motion before the Superior Court of Quebec to prevent the release of their confidential records. The police had seized the recording and transcript of "Jimmy," a pseudonym for Luka Magnotta, who had agreed in 2007 to participate in Bruckert and Parent's SSHRC-funded study on sex escorts and their clients. Magnotta was subsequently charged with the brutal murder of Lin Jun in 2012. Bruckert and Parent insisted that the information in the transcript should not be released because it was not pertinent to the murder case. More significantly, as a result of the seizure of the records, one of the research participants informed Bruckert that she had failed to maintain her promise of confidentiality. Because the University of Ottawa administration refused to cover the criminologists' legal expenses (a decision criticized by five members of the institution's REB), CAUT agreed to fund the case.[53] In

February 2014, the court quashed the search warrant, arguing that in this case the value of the evidence in the confidential interview to the murder case did not outweigh the public interest in protecting the promise of confidentiality.[54]

This case illustrates that legal liability remains a primary concern of cautious university administrators. Even if they acknowledge the importance of their role in supporting researchers to protect confidential material, university administrators may not agree that it is their responsibility to pay the legal fees of researchers when they challenge the seizure of confidential research materials under subpoena for criminal cases. Ted Palys filed a complaint against the University of Ottawa to the Secretariat on Responsible Conduct for Research (SRCR), arguing that failure to support its faculty members is a violation of the university's obligations under *TCPS2*.[55] In its decision, the SRCR stated: "institutional support consists of providing researchers with financial and other support to obtain the independent legal advice which makes that resistance possible or ensuring that such support is provided."[56] To ensure that institutions are able to provide such support, Palys recommends that granting agencies require that universities contribute to a defence fund or subscribe to insurance to enable them to provide support for researchers.

CONCLUSION

Oral history is a deeply political, moral, and ethical practice. In the 1970s, social historians were excited by the potential of oral history as a way to bring to light those "hidden from history." Oral history has challenged traditional historical narratives by focusing on the everyday lives of ordinary people rather than the extraordinary acts of great men. Since then, practitioners have debated how the unequal power relationship between the professional historian and participants in oral history projects influence oral history. Some scholars, including Joy Parr in chapter 16 of this *Reader*, have been critical of the assumption that oral history is inherently radical, and have called for a deeper exploration of how social consciousness influences personal memory. In the final section of this *Reader*, Winona Wheeler, Pamela Sugiman, and Claudia Malacrida reflect on how their commitment to advocacy and empowerment of less powerful people propels critical reassessments of the assumption that oral history democratizes the production of history.

Oral historians have developed methodologies that promote the dignity of the people they interview and protect them from harm that might arise from the research. These practices balance ethical concerns with methodological requirements of the field. In attempting to harmonize the ethics review process, the first *TCPS* imposed research paradigms on historians that did not suit historical methodologies and research goals; the methods that university REBs urged scholars to use contradicted what social historians want to accomplish and what the discipline expects them to do. More seriously, ethics governance hampered historical enquiry into private life and controversies in the past. The introduction of federal guidelines resulted in conflicting interpretations of the policy on the part of university administrators concerned with REBs and researchers who sought to protect the research participants or to acknowledge their contributions in their published work.

The *TCPS* thus inadvertently created combative relationships between REBs and researchers, especially those working in the social sciences and humanities who did not see their ethical values reflected in the federal policy. The Canadian case is not unique. The adoption of ethics policies to govern university-based research instigated an international dialogue among qualitative researchers opposed to the intervention of institutional ethical review in their own research. Knowledge of the history of these policies would be useful in order to develop a better understanding of disparate interpretations of the policy. Zachary Schrag's history of ethics policy and the development of Institutional Review Boards (IRBs) in the United States demonstrates how well-intentioned policy makers, in search of a universal policy that drew primarily on medical models of research, created barriers to social science researchers. Just as significantly, social scientists did not have the political power to shape the development of ethics policy and IRBs.[57] There may be parallels in the origins of the Canadian policy that deserve historical investigation. But more recently, Canadian scholars in the social sciences and humanities were able to successfully lobby for important amendments to the policy.

The revised policy incorporated many of the ideas that researchers brought to the Panel during its three-year consultation with academics in the social scientists and humanities. Unfortunately, the contentious relationship between researchers and REBs that had resulted from the original policy continues, even though the current policy has made accommodations for methodologies from these fields. Institutional REBs tend to be overly cautious despite the policy's directive that they should not obstruct research. Contradictory interpretations of ethics policies have led some researchers to the conclusion that ethics policy is ultimately a needless level of bureaucracy that researchers should fight to dismantle. I do not, however, think that we should abandon federal ethics policy. *TCPS2* is a good document that is attentive to diverse research strategies and ethical dilemmas that occur in the field. Even though it is time-consuming and often frustrating, documenting how our research strategies reflect ethical practices in the field is a useful process. We in the social sciences and the humanities should focus our energies on ensuring that the document will have the regulatory power to protect both research participants and the scholars who work with them.

The ethical practices that oral historians use have evolved over time, according to experiences in the field and in response to developments in historical methodologies and questions. Similarly, ethics policies must have room to grow and to change. And we should expect new ethical dilemmas to emerge as new historiographical and political debates are waged. The most positive change in the revised policy is its endorsement of ethics regulation that is "committed to the continued evolution of [the] document."[58] *TCPS2* anticipates changes in our understating of ethical responsibility, but rather than entering into fruitful discussions on these important matters, researchers still assume that the ethics bureaucracy is in place to hinder research and to protect universities rather than vulnerable research participants. Recent examples demonstrate that these beliefs are not unfounded. This is not the intent of *TCPS2*, a policy that seeks at the federal level to open an ongoing dialogue among community stakeholders, researchers, and universities about ethical research involving humans. We need to ensure that these discussions also occur at the level of our institutions.

NOTES

1 My thinking about the disjunct between ethics policy and oral history has been sharpened in conversations with Emily Arrowsmith, Margaret Conrad, Marc Milner, Janis Thiessen, R. Steven Turner, Sharon Weaver, and Jennifer Whiteside. All errors or omissions are my responsibility.

2 Canadian Institutes of Health Research, the Natural Sciences and Engineering Council of Canada, and the Social Sciences and Humanities Research Council of Canada.

3 Nancy Janovicek, Sarah Carter, and Peter Twohig, "Submission to the Interagency Advisory Panel on Research Ethics Consultation," November 2003. Copy with author.

4 Zachary Schrag, *Ethical Imperialism: Institutional Review Boards and the Social Sciences, 1965–2007* (Baltimore: Johns Hopkins University Press, 2010).

5 Sarah Dyer and David Demeritt, "Un-Ethical Review? Why It Is Wrong to Apply the Medical Model of Research Governance to Human Geography," *Progress in Human Geography* 33, no. 46 (2009): 46–64.

6 Will C. van den Hoonaard, ed., *Walking the Tightrope: Ethical Issues for Qualitative Researchers* (Toronto: University of Toronto Press, 2002).

7 Canadian Institutes of Health Research, the Natural Sciences and Engineering Council of Canada, and the Social Sciences and Humanities Research Council of Canada, *Tri-Council Policy Statement: Ethical Conduct for Research Involving Humans* (December 2010), 7.

8 Ibid.

9 Medical Research Council, the Natural Sciences and Engineering Council of Canada, and the Social Sciences and Humanities Research Council of Canada, *Tri-Council Policy Statement on Ethical Conduct for Research Involving Humans* (Ottawa: Public Works and Government Services Canada, 1998), i.6.

10 CIHR et al., *Tri-Council Policy Statement*, 8.

11 Paul Thompson, *The Voice of the Past: Oral History*, 2nd edition (New York: Oxford University Press, 1988).

12 Robert Perks and Alistair Thompson, eds., *The Oral History Reader*, 1st edition (London: Routledge, 1998); Sherna Berner Gluck and Daphne Patai, eds., *Women's Words: The Feminist Practice of Oral History* (New York: Routledge, 1991).

13 Joan Sangster, "Telling Our Stories: Feminist Debates and the Use of Oral History," *Women's Review of History* 3, no. 1 (1994): 5–27.

14 Gluck and Patai, *Women's Words*.

15 Karen Dubinsky, "'Who Do You Think Did the Cooking?' Baba in the Classroom," in *Changing Lives: Women in Northern Ontario*, edited by Margaret Kechnie and Marge Reitsma-Street (Toronto: Dundurn, 1996), 193–7.

16 Sangster, "Telling Our Stories."

17 Neil Sutherland, "When You Listen to the Winds of Childhood, How Much Can You Believe?" *Curriculum Inquiry* 22, no. 3 (1992): 235–56.

18 Michael Frisch, "Oral History and *Hard Times*: A Review Essay," in *The Oral History Reader*, edited by Robert Perks and Alistair Thompson (London: Routledge, 1998), 33.

19 Alessandro Portelli, *The Battle of Valle Giulia: Oral History and the Art of Dialogue* (Madison: University of Wisconsin Press, 1997), 57.

20 Linda Shopes, "Oral History Interviewing, Institutional Review Boards, and Human Subjects" (presented at the Organization of American Historians Meeting, Washington, DC, 2002).

21 CIHR et al., *Tri-Council Policy Statement*, 143.

22 Franca Iacovetta and Wendy Mitchinson, "Introduction: Social History and Case Files Research," in *On the Case: Explorations in Social History*, edited

by Franca Iacovetta and Wendy Mitchinson (Toronto: University of Toronto Press, 1998), 6.

23 Nancy Janovicek, *No Place to Go: Local Histories of the Battered Women's Shelter Movement* (Vancouver: UBC Press, 2007).

24 This chapter stems from a previously published article on the *TCPS*. Nancy Janovicek, "Oral History and Ethical Practice: Towards Effective Policies and Procedures," *Journal of Academic Ethics* 4 (2006): 147–74. In my original article on this topic, I did not identify Worden. In his review of my article, Zachary Schrag made the astute observation that "[t]his point would have resonated better had Janovicek named the activist in this article." Writing under the original policy (and as a less confident postdoctoral fellow), I was concerned that identifying her would not comply with the policy's guidelines for secondary use of data. Schrag's review is available at: http://www.institutionalreviewblog.com/2007/01/nancy-janovicek-offers-canadian.html (accessed 12 July 2013).

25 Janis Thiessen, personal email correspondence with author, 27 January 2004.

26 Ibid. These interviews were conducted for her book *Manufacturing Mennonites: Work and Religion in Post-War Manitoba* (Toronto: University of Toronto Press, 2013).

27 CIHR et al., *Tri-Council Policy Statement*, 62–4.

28 Personal email correspondence with author, 14 July 2013.

29 Janovicek, "Submission."

30 Brian Calliou, "Methodology for Recording Oral Histories in the Aboriginal Community," chapter 1 in this *Reader*.

31 Van den Hoonaard, *Walking the Tightrope*.

32 CIHR et al., *Tri-Council Policy Statement*, 10.

33 John S. Milloy, *A National Crime: The Canadian Government and the Residential School System* (Winnipeg: University of Manitoba Press, 1999).

34 CIHR et al., *Tri-Council Policy Statement*, 47.

35 John Reid, "History, Native Issues, and the Courts: A Forum. Introduction," *Acadiensis* 27, no. 1 (autumn 1998): 3–7; Stephen E. Patterson, "History, Native Issues, and the Courts: A Forum. Historians and the Courts," *Acadiensis* 28, no. 1 (autumn 1998): 18–23.

36 Julie Cruikshank, "Oral Tradition and Oral History: Reviewing Some Issues," *Canadian Historical Review* 75, no. 3 (fall 1994): 403–18.

37 Linda Tuhiwai Smith, *Decolonizing Methodologies: Research and Indigenous Peoples* (London: Zed, 1999).

38 Julie Cruikshank, "Oral History, Narrative Strategies, and Native American Historiography: Perspectives from the Yukon Territory, Canada," 265, chapter 8 in this *Reader*.

39 Cruikshank, "Oral Tradition and Oral History: Reviewing Some Issues"; Jo-Anne Fiske, "By, For, or About?: Shifting Directions in the Representations of Aboriginal Women," *Atlantis* 25, no. 1 (fall 2000): 11–27.

40 MRC et al., *Tri-Council Policy Statement*, 91–114.
41 Mi'kmaq Ethics Watch, "Principles and Guidelines for Researchers Con-ducting Research with and/or Among Mi'kmaq People," available at: http://mrc.uccb.mc.ca/prinpro/html (accessed 29 January, 2004); Royal Commission on Aboriginal Peoples, *Ethical Guidelines for Research: Appendix B* (Ottawa: Royal Commission on Aboriginal Peoples, 1996).
42 Emily Arrowsmith, "Fair Enough? How Notions of Race, Gender, and Sol-diers' Rights Affected Dependents' Allowances Policies Towards Canadian Aboriginal Families During World War II" (PhD dissertation, Carleton Uni-versity, 2006).
43 CIHR et al., *Tri-Council Policy Statement*, 116.
44 Janet Silman, *Enough Is Enough: Aboriginal Women Speak Out* (Toronto: Women's Press, 1987); Sharon Weaver, "First Nations Women and Govern-ment Policy, 1970–92: Discrimination and Conflict," in *Changing Patterns: Women in Canada,* 2nd edition, edited by Sandra Burt, Lorraine Code, and Lindsay Dorney (Toronto: McClelland & Stewart, 1993), 92–150; Audrey Huntley and Faye Blaney, *Bill C-31: Its Impact, Implications, and Recommen-dations for Change in British Columbia: Final Report* (Vancouver: Aborig-inal Women's Action Network, 1999); Sharon D. McIvor, "Self-Government and Aboriginal Women," in *Scratching the Surface: Canadian Anti-Racist Thought,* edited by Enakshi Dua and Angela Robertson (Toronto: Women's Press, 1999), 167–86; Janovicek, "Oral History and Ethical Practice," 168.
45 CIHR et al., *Tri-Council Policy Statement*, 107.
46 Portelli, *The Battle of Valle Giulia*, 56.
47 The papers presented at this conference are published in Anna Sheftel and Stacey Zembrzycki, eds., *Oral History Off the Record: Toward an Ethnography of Practice* (New York: Palgrave MacMillan, 2013).
48 CIHR et al., *Tri-Council Policy Statement*, 67.
49 For background on the case see *Boston College Subpoena News.* Available at: http://bostoncollegesubpoena.wordpress.com/ (accessed 13 May 2014).
50 Ted Palys and John Lowman, "Defending Research Confidentiality 'To the Extent the Law Allows': Lessons from the Boston College Subpoenas," *Jour-nal of Academic Ethics* 10, no. 4 (fall 2012): 271–97. These interviews were used as evidence in the arrest of Gerry Adams in April 2014 for the 1972 murder of Jean McConville. Ed Molony, "The real threat to peace in North-ern Ireland," *Globe and Mail,* 10 May 2014.
51 CIHR et al., *Tri-Council Policy Statement*, 58.
52 Ibid.
53 "uOttawa criminologists go to court to protect research confidentiality," *CAUT/ACPPR Bulletin* 60, no. 1 (January 2013): 1; "REB members deplore uOttawa's refusal to defend confidentiality," *CAUT/ACPPR Bulletin* 60, no. 4 (April 2013): 1. The University of Ottawa offered to contribute $150,000 to the CAUT's legal expenses in this case. "Court upholds researchers' right to

protect confidential information," *CAUT/ACPPR Bulletin* 61, no. 2 (February 2014): 1 and 7.

54 Parent c. R., 2014 QCCS 132 (CanLII), http://canlii.ca/t/g2sq6 (accessed 13 May 2014).

55 "Complaint targets uOttawa for failure to defend confidentiality," *CAUT/ACPPR Bulletin* 60, no. 6 (June 2013): 1 and 2.

56 Ted Palys, "Who Do You Trust? Protecting Research Confidentiality to the Extent Permitted by the Law," Keynote presentation to the annual meeting of the Canadian Association of Research Ethics Boards. Montreal, Quebec, 25–26 April 2014. Slides for the presentation available at: http://www.sfu.ca/~palys/Palys-CAREB2014.pdf (accessed 13 May 2014). Thanks to Ted Palys for providing more background on his complaint to the SRCR. Email correspondence with Ted Palys, 13 May 2014.

57 Schrag, *Ethical Imperialism*.

58 CIHR et al., *Tri-Council Policy Statement*, 6.

4

Legal Issues Regarding Oral Histories

Jill Jarvis-Tonus

When asked to consider legal issues relevant to oral histories, I thought the topic would be straightforward. In fact, the subject turned out to be quite complex. In this chapter, I touch briefly on various rights that may arise from the creation of oral histories, with a focus on copyright. I will also briefly discuss other claims that may be available to those providing the oral histories, referred to as orators, such as breach of confidence, breach of contract, slander and libel, and invasion of privacy. The extent to which copyright or any other rights may be available to oral historians or to orators, particularly in the increasingly digital world, remains uncertain. As with most legal issues, each case will be governed by its facts. However, knowledge of the general legal principles that apply should assist oral historians to develop with orators agreements that recognize each party's rights and limit historians' liability for third-party misuse.

GENERAL COPYRIGHT PRINCIPLES

Turning first to copyright protection: there has been little Canadian case law that addresses the subsistence of copyright in a work like an oral history. A brief discussion of this case law is set out below. Applying general principles set out in our Canadian Copyright Act (the "Act") indicates that one or more copyrights should arise when an oral history is created.

By way of background, the Act grants creators of original dramatic, literary, musical and artistic works, and owners of sound recordings (that is, CDs, DVDs, and other audio/digital works) the right to control (1) the works' reproduction in any material form, (2) their telecommunication to the public, and (3) their first publication; and it grants creators the right to authorize others to do any of those things. The owners of a copyright-protected work, other than a sound recording, also have the right to convert or adapt it into another type of work (e.g. a novel into a film), to perform the work in public, or to authorize third parties to do these acts.

Dramatic and literary works are categorized broadly and include, respectively, recitation pieces, choreography, scenic arrangements or acting forms, and speeches, compilations of information, tables, and computer programs.

Copyright arises automatically in Canada at the time the work is set in a fixed form, such as a manuscript or a DVD, or uploaded onto a website. At this point, the work becomes a tangible form of expression, capable of protection, rather than an abstract idea on which no one can claim a monopoly. The fixed work must also meet a minimum level of originality to be considered a work of authorship. In Canada, the required level of originality is relatively low, in that the work must constitute a small degree of intellectual labour, skill, and judgment by the author and not be copied from another's work. For example, instruction sheets, text for packaging, and a schedule of horse races have all been accorded copyright protection, although of limited originality.

Generally, the author of the work owns the copyright, although there are exceptions; most notably, employers own copyright in works created by employees within the scope of their employment.

COPYRIGHT AND ORAL HISTORIES

How do these principles apply to an oral history? The questions to ask are: (1) Does the history qualify as a "work" because it constitutes an original work of authorship and has been sufficiently fixed? (2) If so, who can claim the copyright?

Works of Original Authorship

To answer these questions, we have to examine the nature of oral histories. They are to a great extent a spontaneous and free-form telling of events and anecdotes by the orator in response to the questions of the historian. Some structure is likely imposed on the direction of the history by the historian, who may have prepared a series of written questions in advance. In many cases, though, the historian will ask additional spontaneous questions during the course of the interview on the basis of the orator's answers. The finished product, then, is a combination of spontaneous and random responses arising from a loosely arranged written structure.

The history itself can be preserved on a CD or DVD, or in a digital file from which a printed transcript may then be produced. Does this final form qualify as a work?

Canadian courts have recognized that a dramatic work that contains a certain degree of improvisation in its performance remains protectable.[1] However, if the random or unpredictable nature of the material departs too substantially from the structure of a work, copyright may be denied.[2] Compilations of facts and examination questions are clearly protectable as literary works, and recitations are similarly protected as dramatic works. Therefore, to the extent that an overall structure for the oral history exists (that is, the interview questions), it is reasonable to argue that the resulting material, fixed on a recording storage medium, could qualify either as a literary or dramatic work.

Copyright would also subsist in the sound recording embodying the history. This constitutes a second layer of copyright, separate from that arising in the material contained on the sound recording. The copyright in the recording gives the owner the right to control any copying or rental of the recording and to make the recording available to the public by telecommunication through online demand services such as iTunes.

Fixation of the Work

The next question is whether the oral history is sufficiently fixed as a medium of expression to attract protection. The interview by the oral historian will be fixed to some extent on paper when a list of questions is compiled. A second fixation of the questions occurs when the interview is recorded on whatever media. This is the only form of fixation, however, for the orator's responses.

Under our present Act, it is unclear whether fixation on media of a spontaneous utterance creates a copyright in those words. Even if the words of the speaker are sufficiently original to be considered a work, as will be discussed below, they must be fixed in a manner recognized by the Act. For example, dramatic works under the statute must be fixed "in writing or otherwise."[3] Literary works are traditionally fixed in writing as well, although in the digital age these writings can be electronic.

However, as recently affirmed by the Supreme Court of Canada,[4] the Act should be interpreted in a technologically neutral manner to reflect our age of rapidly changing technology. For example, several years ago, the Act was amended to provide that live television programs that are recorded on videotape simultaneously with their broadcast will be sufficiently fixed to qualify as a work for which cable retransmission royalties may be claimed.[5] There are numerous other examples of non-traditional methods of "fixing" a work. For example, books, speeches, and essays are composed at computer terminals with the text being preserved on disks, or directly online (digital files and blogs, for example), so that the text can be downloaded and converted into print. Although it is possible to produce a paper copy of the work, in practice, several drafts of a manuscript may be edited on the terminal screen and never reduced to paper. Each draft will attract its own layer of copyright. Choreography is now being created without traditional paper notation by videotaping the dancers in rehearsal with the choreographer.

It is also interesting to note that in 1988 the United Kingdom Copyright Act (an earlier version of which served as the model for the Canadian Act), was amended to state that "literary work" means "any work, other than a dramatic or musical work, which is written, spoken or sung"[6] and that "copyright does not subsist in a literary work unless and until it is recorded, in writing or otherwise."[7] Copyright experts have interpreted these UK changes to mean that copyright will subsist in extemporaneous speeches, if they are original and recorded at the time they are made.

With the ever-expanding methods of recording content, and the focus on interpreting the Act in a technology-neutral manner, it is possible that the Act could be interpreted or may be amended in such a way as to protect verbal storytelling fixed in non-traditional ways.

COPYRIGHT OWNERSHIP

The History Content

Assuming, then, that an oral history is a work that has been sufficiently fixed, who would own the rights? Copyright in the interview questions and the recording of them would be owned by the oral historian or the historian's employer. As author of the interview format, the interviewer would clearly own copyright, unless an employee of another, in which case the employer would own the copyright. In Canada it is less likely that the orator providing answers to the interview questions would hold a copyright.

Two cases from the mid-1990s confirm that the historian would own copyright in interviews embodied on a recording medium. In the case of *Gould Estate* v. *Stoddart Publishing Co.*,[8] the estate of the famous pianist Glenn Gould attempted to prevent a freelance reporter, Jock Carroll, and his publisher, Stoddart, from publishing a book on Mr Gould which included various photographs of him and the text of interviews Mr Carroll had conducted with Mr Gould years earlier for an article in *Weekend Magazine*. Although the case revolved principally around an action for misappropriation of Mr Gould's personality rights and the question of whether there were any implied restrictions on the use Mr Carroll could make of the photos and interviews obtained with Mr Gould's consent, the estate also argued that Mr Gould had a copyright in his responses in the interviews as a form of literary work, akin to a lecture, address, speech, or sermon.

The court disagreed on the basis that Mr Gould's spontaneous responses to Mr Carroll's questions were not expressed in a material form that had a more or less permanent endurance. Unlike a speech or recitation that has been composed in writing prior to its delivery, Mr Gould's responses to questions came in a spontaneous manner and not from a carefully prepared text or even from notes. Offhand and spontaneous answers to questions were deemed not to be "the kind of discourse which the Copyright Act intended to protect."[9]

However, the court, both at the trial and the appellate level,[10] indicated that the historian, as the interviewer, would hold a copyright in the finished work. The trial judge noted that a "person who makes notes or report of the speech is the author of the report and obtains copyright in the report."[11]

The appellate court judge on the same point stated: "It is evident from this record that Gould did not have a copyright with respect to his oral utterances or in the 'transcriptions' of them. To the contrary, Carroll as the author of the text in the book was the owner of the copyright in the very written material the appellants are attempting to suppress."[12]

The second case of note is *Hager* v. ECW *Press Ltd. et al.*,[13] in which Hager had written a book about famous aboriginal people which contained a chapter on Shania Twain. The chapter was based primarily on several interviews Hager had conducted with Ms Twain. The defendants, a writer, Michael Holmes, and the publisher, ECW Press, published a complete biography of Ms Twain, in which Holmes included sixteen passages from Hager's chapter. The quotations attributed to Ms Twain were copied exactly and Ms Hager's original text was paraphrased, using similar concepts, thought sequences, and sentence structures. Hager sued for copyright infringement.

One of the defences raised by the defendants was that there was not sufficient creativity or originality on Hager's part in recounting the words used by Shania Twain during the interview to attract copyright protection. Again the court disagreed, relying on the above-noted Gould case as well as other older UK case law: "These cases demonstrate that under

Anglo-Canadian law in so far as private interviews are concerned, it is the person who reduces the oral statements to a fixed form that acquires copyright therein. That individual is considered to be the originator of the work."[14]

In the end, Holmes and ECW Press were found to have infringed Hager's copyright in her chapter and ordered to pay damages.

Sound Recordings/Transcriptions

In addition, there would be an owner of copyright in the sound recording on which the history is fixed. The Act provides that the owner of copyright in a recording is the person "by whom the arrangements necessary for the first fixation of the sounds are undertaken."[15] This could be the oral historian or the historian's employer. In unusual cases, it could be the orator, if he or she commissions the creation of the oral history and arranges and pays for the recording media, and the recording engineer's time.

Finally, if the historian makes a paper transcription of the recording, which entails editing and correcting the interview, copyright may arise in the transcript as a derivative work and be claimable by the historian or the historian's employer.

Term of Copyright Protection

In Canada the terms of these copyrights differ. Copyright in the interview and the transcripts would subsist for the life of the author(s) plus fifty years from the end of the calendar year in which the last author dies, whereas copyright in the recording subsists for fifty years from the end of the calendar year in which it is made, if unpublished; or, if published within that fifty-year term, for fifty years from the end of the calendar year in which it was first published. During these terms, any unauthorized copying of the recording, in whole or substantial part, would infringe both copyrights, for which the historian, if he or she owns both copyrights, could claim damages and an injunction. It is important to note that ownership as determined by the Act can always be changed by written assignment.

Summary of Canadian Law

To summarize, oral historians likely expend sufficient labour in preparing their questions and recording the resulting interviews to claim copyright in the underlying interview material, as well as any edited transcriptions derived from the recorded interview. If they arrange for the recording to be made, they would also own copyright in the recording.

The more difficult issue is whether the orator could also claim copyright in his or her words which could be exercised against both the historian and third parties. The relatively limited case law, discussed above, and Canadian copyright policy to date, indicates that protection should not extend this far, because the orator's words, being primarily spontaneous and random, constitute ideas rather than a "work" of intellectual labour and skill. However, given the right set of facts, it is not outside the realm of possibility that an orator could still bring such a claim to prevent subsequent reproduction of his or her words either by the historian or by researchers using the historian's materials, particularly if the structure/nature of the questions was known by the orator prior to the interview.

The orator would have to prove that his or her comments were sufficiently original and fixed to overcome the holdings in the Gould and Hager cases and attract protection. If an interview questionnaire has been forwarded to the orator prior to the interview he or she might rely on preparatory notes or comments created before responding at the interview, as a way of arguing there is an underlying literary work of responses, fixed on paper or electronically, and elaborated upon at the interview.

The hurdle would be to show that the orator is not just providing spontaneous conversation, but pre-created commentary that is a work of authorship and not just random thoughts in which no monopoly should be granted. The potential existence and strength of copyright in the orator's contribution to the history will be dependent on the surrounding facts in each case.

The United Kingdom

As mentioned, the UK Act, as amended, infers that spontaneous spoken words, if recorded, attract copyright protection. Not only has the definition of a literary work been expanded to include spoken words, but a statutory exemption from infringement has been included in the 1988 UK Act.[16] The exemption permits third parties to use a person's spoken words once recorded for specific purposes without infringing copyright. Surely, this section would not have been necessary unless it was possible that spontaneous speech could constitute a copyrightable work under British law.

The exemption provides that where a record of spoken words is made, in writing or otherwise, for the purpose of reporting current events or communicating to the public the whole or part of the work, it is not an infringement of any copyright in the words as a literary work to use the record or material taken from it, or to copy the record, or any such material, and use the copy for that purpose. The intent of this section seems to be to prevent an orator from restraining further use by others of his or her words, recorded as part of either a report of a current event or a telecommunication, for these same purposes. However, by inference, unauthorized use of the words for any other purpose, such as inclusion in a commercially published book, would constitute infringement of the orator's copyright.

The exemption also specifies that the record of the words may not be used if the orator, prior to his or her words being recorded, specifically prohibited either the making of the recording or further use of the recording by third parties.[17]

Although not citing specific case law, the pre-eminent UK text *Copinger and Skone James on Copyright* at 3-15, describes copyright as residing with the person who spoke the words regardless of who "fixes" them in a recording.

Applying this exemption to oral histories, it would appear that under UK law, an orator does hold a copyright in his or her spoken words, but if the orator grants an interview as part of a broadcast or a report on a newsworthy topic, without stipulating any restrictions as to its use, he or she cannot enforce that copyright in the responses to prevent further uses of his or her works for those specific purposes. The historian who makes the recording would have the right to authorize reproduction of the recording by third parties.

The United States

The United States courts have dealt with the protection of recorded words in two interesting decisions. Caution must be used, however, in directly applying their reasoning to Canadian law, as there are significant differences between each country's copyright statutes. However, on the issue of what constitutes authorship of a work, the following cases may be of value.

In the first case,[18] the writer Ernest Hemingway had a friendship with a less well known writer, A.E. Hotchner. Over the years, Hemingway had many conversations with Hotchner about life and writing which Hotchner carefully documented. During Hemingway's lifetime Hotchner wrote many articles that incorporated these conversations, and Hemingway made no objection. After Hemingway's death, Hotchner wrote a full biography entitled *Papa Hemingway: A Personal Memoir*, which extensively used portions of their conversations.

Hemingway's widow brought an action against Hotchner on a number of grounds, including that use of the conversations infringed Hemingway's common law copyright.

A preliminary injunction restraining publication of the book was denied by the New York Supreme Court. It held that common law copyright could not exist in spontaneous oral conversations on a number of grounds, including that to provide such protection would unduly impinge on the constitutional right to free speech, and that a conversational exchange was the creation of more than one participant, and therefore could not be solely the work of one individual.

The trial court agreed, holding that conversations were the product of interaction between parties and were not individual intellectual works. Therefore, the Court stated, any one participant should have the right to publish the conversation, verbatim or otherwise.

Hemingway's widow appealed the decision to the New York Court of Appeal. This court concurred with the Trial Division in the result by not granting relief. However, their reasoning left it open for another court to find copyright in conversations.

The Appellate Court did not determine whether copyright existed because, even if it did, they felt the evidence showed that Hemingway had consented to publication of his conversations by not objecting during his lifetime. The court, however, did not preclude the possibility of protection for conversations, provided such right would not unduly fetter freedom of speech. Mr Justice Fuld stated:

> The essential thrust of the First Amendment is to prohibit improper restraints on the voluntary public expression of ideas; it shields the man who wants to speak or publish when others wish him to be quiet. There is necessarily, and within suitably defined areas, a concomitant freedom not to speak publicly, one which serves the same ultimate end as freedom of speech in its affirmative aspect. The rules of common law copyright assure this freedom in the case of written material. However, speech is now easily captured by electronic devices and consequently, we should be wary about excluding all possibility of protecting a speaker's right to decide when his words, uttered in private dialogue, may or may not be published at large. *Conceivably, there may be limited and special situations in which an interlocutor brings forth oral statements from another party which both understand to be the unique intellectual product of the principal speaker, a product which would qualify for common law copyright if such statements were in writing* [emphasis added].

Concerning such problems, we express no opinion; we do no more than raise the questions, leaving them open for future consideration in cases which may present them more sharply than this one does.[19]

Under this case, copyright in the orator's words conceivably could attract copyright protection in appropriate circumstances; for instance, if the orator was the primary participant in an interview situation, and not just one of two or more having a conversation, and if the orator had not consented to further uses of his or her comments or anecdotes.

The same issue arose in the United States in the case of *Jerry Falwell* v. *Penthouse International Limited*.[20] The evangelist Jerry Falwell brought an action against *Penthouse* magazine and its reporters, claiming that *Penthouse*'s publication of an interview with him infringed common law copyright in his conversation.

The court rejected that any common law copyright existed in spoken words, stating that the existence of such a right had never been established by a court. Mr Justice Turk stressed that recognizing such a right would run contrary to freedom of speech. He stated:

> However different or unique plaintiff's thoughts or opinions may be, the expression of those opinions or thoughts is too general or abstract to rise to the level of a literary or intellectual creation that may enjoy the protection of copyright. Although the general subject matter of the interview may have been outlined in the reporters' minds prior to their meeting with the plaintiff, the actual dialogue, including the unprepared responses of plaintiff, was spontaneous and proceeded in a question and answer format.[21]

On balance, then, US courts have been reluctant to recognize copyright in spontaneous conversations. The *Hemingway* case suggests that rights in a conversation might arise in specific circumstances, but does not delineate what those circumstances would be. On the other hand, the *Falwell* case seems to totally deny protection for spontaneous conversations.

SUMMARY OF THE LAW

It remains doubtful that in Canada an orator has an enforceable copyright in his or her words, but the historian should own copyright in the oral history structure of the questions and, typically, the recording of the oral history by virtue of making the arrangements necessary for the recording to be made.

The UK law seems to favour copyrights for orators; the US law does not. Both countries' copyright laws would recognize copyright in the recording embodying the oral history. Generally speaking, to the extent that the orator can show that the taped conversation was not totally spontaneous, but resulted from prepared answers or notes, it may be possible for him or her to lay some claim to rights in the interview as a literary work.

In addition, if the oral history includes a recitation of a traditional story or legend which may have been communicated verbally from one generation to another in a set form, it could be argued, that once fixed on the recording, a copyright arises because the story is not random but a structured series of words never before fixed on paper or other medium. As author of that particular "telling" of the story, the orator could perhaps claim a limited copyright. A policy consideration against granting a copyright would be an undue restriction on freedom of speech.

Slander and Libel

I turn now to a brief discussion of other possible claims available to an orator, beginning with the law of slander and libel. Slander and libel originated as common-law tort actions designed to protect a person's reputation. In most provinces, including Ontario, there are now statutes that set out the parameters of the claim.

A complainant must establish that a statement has been made which was defamatory, that it referred to the complainant, and that it was published.

A statement will be defamatory if it is a false statement about a person that discredits that person in the eyes of right-thinking members of society generally. In applying this definition, an objective standard is used. In other words, would the statement put the person in disrepute in the eyes of the average, reasonable reader?

The words are given their ordinary, natural meaning in determining whether they are defamatory, although the concept of innuendo can be applied. Under this concept, even if the words in their ordinary and natural meaning are not damaging to the complainant, if they are published and the publisher knows certain extraneous facts about the complainant's life which colour the ordinary meaning of the published words, such words may be defamatory by innuendo.

In order to prove that there has been a publication, it must be shown that there has been a communication of the statement to one person other than the complainant. The breadth of the publication only affects the measure of damages.

Generally speaking, written statements are categorized as libel and oral statements as slander. The action is personal, which means that only the person defamed has a right, and this right is extinguished upon that person's death.

Proper defendants are those persons who contributed or participated in publication of the defamatory statement. In some instances there will be more than one participant, including an interviewer, a reporter, an editor, and a publisher. In some cases, secondary players such as distributors or lenders of publications may also be liable, but only if they actually knew of the libel or could, with reasonable care, have discovered it.

Certain defences are available such as justification (if the statement is true it is not libelous, no matter how damaging); and "fair comment" (if the published statement constitutes a comment honestly made on true facts concerning a matter of public interest). If actual malice by the publisher can be shown, a fair comment defence will not succeed.

Libel claims could arise out of the use of oral histories in at least a couple of ways. First, the orator could complain if a researcher uses the oral history as part of another publication that is defamatory. In this situation, the historian may not be liable because he or she has not participated in the defamatory publication. Presumably, the original oral history was given voluntarily by the orator for research purposes. The mere supply of the tape to a third party who then uses it without the historian's knowledge as part of a defamatory publication may be too indirect a link to make the oral historian a participant in the tort. Applying the test for secondary participants discussed above, a historian might become liable if he or she actually knew the subsequent publication would be libelous, or could with reasonable care have discovered the libel.

Perhaps a greater risk exists that, in the course of an interview, an orator may make an untrue and defamatory statement about another party. In such case, if the tape is then circulated to researchers, the other party may sue not only the original orator, but also the oral historian, alleging that, by making the tape and circulating it, the historian has participated in a defamatory publication.

Breach of Confidence

An orator might also claim that use of the oral history by third parties constitutes a breach of confidentiality between the orator and the historian. The law of confidence protects not only information concerning marketable ideas or inventions, but also personal information which would embarrass the discloser if it was publicly circulated.

The orator would have to show that the information was disclosed within the bounds of a confidential relationship. If the interview was granted voluntarily for research purposes, this point may be difficult to establish unless the orator can show that the research was to be private and not for subsequent public circulation. Therefore, the orator should be made aware before the interview is conducted of the potential uses for the recorded material and be given an opportunity to stipulate any restrictions that should apply to its use.

If the agreement with the orator stipulates that a confidential relationship does not exist between the parties, and that the history may be given to third parties, a breach of confidence action would fail.

Alternatively, the agreement could permit the orator to specify a time period within which the information would be kept confidential. Once such period expires, the obligation of confidentiality would no longer exist. This may be an appropriate restriction where the orator disclosing sensitive information about others does not want that information publically disclosed until such other people have died.

Invasion of Privacy

Finally, an orator might complain that use of the oral history by third parties invades his or her privacy.

Invasion of privacy has been recognized in Canada as a common-law tort called "misappropriation of personality." In some provinces, the action has been codified in privacy statutes. The tort has two aspects: (1) it is an offence to invade a person's privacy or solitude, causing mental suffering; and (2) it is unlawful to make an unauthorized use of a person's (usually a famous person's) likeness or name for commercial purposes.

The first aspect, an invasion of one's solitude, would seem more applicable to the use of oral histories. For example, in the case of *Dowell et al.* v. *Mengen Institute et al.*, the plaintiffs were participants in a conference about unemployment. The Mengen Institute, one of the defendants, was preparing a documentary on the subject, and the participants, before being filmed, signed a waiver stating that they granted the institute the right to "portray me, *use my words*, name or likeness in a documentary."[22]

The conference became an encounter session with psychiatrists, in which the plaintiffs became quite emotional on camera. They then wished to revoke their consent and restrain publication of the film on the basis that it made them appear seditious and unbalanced. The court expressly recognized the right to so protect one's privacy, but held that in this instance the plaintiffs were restrained from bringing an action because of their consents.

Therefore, if an agreement with an orator stipulates that the oral historian and any researchers authorized by him or her has a right to use that person's words and name, a privacy claim would likely be defeated. In addition, some of the provincial privacy statutes recognize defences similar to that raised in defamation actions. Therefore, if the orator claiming the invasion of privacy is a public figure, and if the history concerns issues of public interest, fair comment may be permissible and preclude a privacy claim.

Finally, an invasion of privacy action, such as that in the Dowell case, is personal, and extinguishes upon the death of the person whose privacy has allegedly been invaded.

TERMS TO INCLUDE IN WRITTEN AGREEMENTS

Oral historians should take steps to protect themselves against potential claims based on these areas of law. Well-drafted agreements between the oral historian and the orator should be signed before the interview takes place. Ideally, from the historian's perspective, the agreement should include the following:

1 An acknowledgment that all rights, including all copyright, worldwide, in the interview are to be owned by the historian or the historian's employer;
2 An assignment clause from the orator to the historian or the historian's employer of all these rights;
3 A further assurances clause in which the orator agrees, for no further payment, to sign any further assignments, waivers or other documents as the historian or the historian's employer may request in future to ensure that all rights are properly owned by the historian or the historian's employer;
4 A waiver throughout the world of any moral rights that may have been automatically given to the orator under the law (on the assumption that the orator owns a copyright in his or her contribution to the oral history). Under the Act, authors are given moral rights in their copyright-protected works, in addition to and separate from the copyright.[23] Moral rights enable authors to require that they be credited as the author, where reasonable in the circumstances, and to prevent unauthorized changes to their works or uses

of their works in association with an institution, product, or service where such changes or uses can be shown to be detrimental to the author's professional reputation. Moral rights last for the same length of time as the copyright in the work and cannot be assigned to anyone else but can be waived by the author. Including these waivers in the agreement will protect the historian from any claims later that the manner in which the historian edited or transcribed the history was detrimental to an orator's professional reputation;

5 A warranty from the orator that any statements he or she will make will be true, and not deceptive, defamatory, obscene, or otherwise unlawful;

6 An indemnity from the orator that he or she will cover all the historian and/or the historian's employer's costs in the event there is a breach of the above warranties in the form of a legal complaint against the historian or his or her employer by a third party;

7 A waiver of any invasion of privacy or misappropriation of per-sonality rights or claims from the orator in respect of the use of the orator's name or picture in association with the history;

8 Either an acknowledgement that there is no duty of confidentiality on the historian and/or the historian's employer concerning the content of the history or a clear outline of any terms of confidenti-ality that the orator is imposing on the use of the history and how long these confidentiality terms are to last.

RECENT LEGISLATIVE CHANGES: THE COPYRIGHT MODERNIZATION ACT

The focus of this paper has been specifically on the creation and owner-ship of rights in oral histories, but the reader should be aware that recent updates to the Canadian copyright law through the Copyright Moderniz-ation Act may affect how oral historians research and write oral histories and how others can access and use oral histories. Some of the most rel-evant provisions for oral historians are summarized below.

(1) One of the fair dealing sections of the Act[24] has been expanded to allow fair dealings of copyrighted works for the additional purpose of "education." "Education" is not defined, so we will need to wait for case law to develop the scope of educational fair dealing. The Canadian gov-ernment has, however, indicated that the educational purpose should be within a structured context, in a manner that takes into consideration the legitimate interests of the copyright owner.[25] Therefore, there likely needs

to be a connection between the use and an educational institution, such as a high school or university, or at least, to a private commercial company that offers structured courses of study. However, it would appear (provided the manner in which the work is copied meets the second requirement for fair dealing, namely, it would be considered "fair" under six factors developed by the Supreme Court of Canada[26]) that oral historians attached to such structured educational entities could make reasonable use of third-party works in writing an oral history. Conversely, other academics could likely rely on this new purpose as well when using oral histories owned by the oral historian.

In general, the courts have been expanding the concept of "fair dealing" under the Act for the last decade into a "user's right" as opposed to just a defence against infringement claims. Addressing itself specifically to fair dealing for the cited purpose of "research," the Supreme Court of Canada has held that research should be interpreted broadly and liberally and need not be restricted solely to non-commercial activities but could in appropriate cases include commercial research.[27] Furthermore, fair dealings with works for another enumerated purpose of "private study" need not, as was previously believed, be restricted to one student making copies for his or her own review but can apply to a classroom setting where an instructor makes copies for all the students in the class.[28]

(2) Oral historians conducting research at libraries, archives, and museums[29] may now have the staff at those institutions make them copies of materials from their collections, including articles from newspapers and periodicals,[30] and such copying will be permissible as fair dealing, although it is not the staff but the historian who is engaged in the permitted purpose of research or private study.[31] However, the staff person making the copy can provide only a single copy and must inform the requesting party that the copy can only be used for research or private study and that any other use may require the authorization of the copyright owner.[32] It is also now permissible to ask staff at one such institution to obtain digital[33] copies of works from another library, archive, or museum through a digital transmission and still rely on the fair dealing provisions for education, research, and private study.[34] However, the institution that obtains the digital copy from another institution must "take measures" to prevent the historian who ultimately uses the requested copy from further copying it, except for making a single print copy, transmitting the copy to anyone else, or using the digital copy after five business days from its first use.[35]

(3) There are also new provisions enabling archivists to make copies of unpublished works deposited in the archives for the purposes of private

study and research,[36] provided (a) that the person who deposited the unpublished work was made aware that copies would be provided to researchers for these purposes[37] and (b) that no prohibitions against such copying have been set by the person depositing the work and/or the copyright owner.[38] Finally, the archive can only provide one copy of the unpublished work and must inform the party requesting the copy that it can only be used for private study or research without obtaining the copyright owner's permission.[39]

(4) Performers have certain copyrights in their performances of which oral historians should be aware. A "performer's performance" is defined broadly enough in the Act to likely include persons delivering oral histories, in some circumstances.[40]

Since 1997, a performer's copyright in his or her performance includes giving the performer the sole right: (a) in respect of live performances, to control the public performance and/or communication of his or her performance by telecommunication systems other than conventional television/radio signals; (b) to fix or authorize the fixation of his or her performance in any recording medium; (c) if fixed on a sound recording, to make copies of that sound recording; (d) to rent that sound recording; (e) to prevent any bootleg recordings of his or her performance made without his or her authorization;[41] and (f) to receive equitable remuneration regarding published sound recordings, for their public performance or telecommunication to the public.[42] The Copyright Modernization Act expanded these copyrights to also give a performer: (a) the exclusive right to make a sound recording of his or her performance available online through an on-demand service: and (b) to control or authorize the first sale or transfer of such a sound recording where it is embodied in tangible object (for example, a CD or DVD).[43]

(5) Finally, despite the broadening of fair dealing with the anticipated effect of making research and private study materials more readily available for fair use by oral historians, it should be noted that the Copyright Modernization Act also brought in new causes of actions for copyright holders which prohibit users to override or otherwise tamper with technological protection measures, such as encryption programs placed on works by copyright owners, in order to get access to and/or use a copyrighted work.[44] How these new sections interrelate with users' rights under the fair-dealing sections is not clear as yet, but, for now, caution must be used by oral historians not to interfere or break any technological "locks" on copyrighted works, even when conducting research and/or private study for an oral history.

In conclusion, an oral historian should be fully aware of the rights that he or she may exercise over the works created, as well as those claimable by orators. If potential complaints can be anticipated and dealt with in appropriate agreements, disputes can hopefully be avoided.

NOTES

1 *Kantel* v. *Grant, Nisbet & Auld Ltd.*, [1933] Ex. C.R. p. 84.
2 FWS *Joint Sports Claimants* v. *Canada* (Copyright Board) (1999), 36 CPR (3rd) 483, (Fed. C.H.).
3 *Canadian Copyright Act R.S.C. 1985*, v. C-42, s. 2 (Butterworth Canada Ltd.'s Office Consolidation).
4 *Entertainment Software Association* v. SOCAN [2012] 2 S.C.R., 326.
5 Supra. at n.3, s.3(1.1).
6 United Kingdom Copyright, Designs and Patents Act, 1988, s.3(1).
7 United Kingdom Copyright, Designs and Patents Act, 1988, s.3(2).
8 74 CPR (3rd), 206.
9 Ibid., at p. 217.
10 *Glenn Gould Estate* v. *Stoddard Publishing Co. Ltd.* 80 CPR (3rd), 161.
11 Supra, at n.8, p. 216.
12 Supra, at n.10, p. 169–70.
13 [1998] 85 CPR (3rd), 289.
14 Ibid., at p. 301.
15 Supra at n.3, s.2.
16 Supra at n.6, s.58(1).
17 Supra at n.6, s.58(2).
18 *Estate of Ernest Hemingway, et al.* v. *Random House, Inc. et al.*, 53 Misc. 2d 462, 279 N.Y. s.2d 51 (S.C.), affirm'd 29 A.D. 2d 633, 285 N.Y.S. 2d, 568, (S.C. Appellate Division), affirm'd 296 N.Y.S. 2d, 771 (CA).
19 Ibid. at p. 778.
20 *Jerry Falwell* v. *Penthouse International Limited* 521 F. Supp. 1204 (1981) (U.S. District CT).
21 Ibid. at p. 1208.
22 (1983) 72 CPR (2nd), p. 239 (Ont. High Ct.).
23 Supra at n.3, ss.14.1, 14.2, 28.1, 28.2.
24 Supra at n.3, s.29. Fair dealing for the purpose of research, private study, education, parody, or satire does not infringe copyright.
25 Government of Canada, "Balanced Copyright," Copyright Modernization Act – Backgrounder. http://www.ic.gc.ca/eic/site/crp-prda.nsf/eng/h_rp01237.html (accessed 30 June 2014).
26 *CCH Canada Ltd.* v. *Law Society of Upper Canada* [2004] 1 SCR 339 at para 53. "… the following factors be considered in assessing whether a dealing was

fair: (1) the purpose of the dealing; (2) the character of the dealing; (3) the amount of the dealing; (4) alternatives to the dealing; (5) the nature of the work; (6) the effect of the dealing on the work."

27 Ibid. at n.26; *Society of Composers, Authors and Music Publishers of Canada* v. *Bell Canada*, [2012] 2. SCR 326.

28 *Alberta (Education)* v. *Canada Copyright Licensing Agency* (Access Copyright), [2012] 2. SCR, 345.

29 Supra at n.3, s.2: "library, archive or museum" means (a) an institution, whether or not incorporated, that is not established or conducted for profit or that does not form a part of, or is not administered or directly or indirectly controlled by, a body that is established or conducted for profit, in which is held and maintained a collection of documents and other materials that is open to the public or to researchers, or (b) any other non-profit institution prescribed by regulation.

30 Supra at n.3, s.30.2(2).

31 Supra at n.3, s.30.2(1).

32 Supra at n.2, s.30.2(4).

33 Supra at n.3, s.30.2(5.01).

34 Supra at n.3, s.30.2(5).

35 Supra at n.3, s.30.2 (5.02).

36 Supra at n.3, s.30.21(1).

37 Supra at n.3, s.30.21(2).

38 Supra at n.3, s.30.21(3).

39 Supra at n.3, s.30.21(3.1).

40 Supra at n.3, s.2: performer's performance means any of the following when done by a performer: (a) a performance of an artistic work, dramatic work or musical work, whether or not the work was previously fixed in any material form, and whether or not the work's term of copyright protection under this Act has expired; (b) a recitation or reading of a literary work, whether or not the work's term of copyright protection under this Act has expired; or (c) an improvisation of a dramatic work, musical work or literary work, whether or not the improvised work is based on pre-existing work; replaced by SC 1997, c. 24, s.1(2); added by SC 1997, c.47, s.56(3).

41 Supra at n.3, s.15(1).

42 Supra at n.3, s.19(1).

43 Supra at n.3, s.15(1.1).

44 Supra at n.3, ss.41 to 41.21(2).

SECTION TWO

Interpretation

Reflections on the Politics and Praxis of Working-Class Oral Histories

Joan Sangster

Oral history theory and practice are inescapably intertwined, and both are moulded by international currents of thought as well as by more specific national and regional intellectual and social influences. Our theoretical discussions are also implicitly political, whether we acknowledge it or not: like oral history more generally, women's and working-class oral history – indeed all varieties of history – are intrinsically processes of political explication, in the same way that "all political argument in some way involves a construction of the past as well as the future."[1] While recognizing a general shift over the past thirty years in oral history writing from social science to cultural approaches,[2] from an emphasis on experience to one on subjectivity, my reflections on the creation of working-class histories in Canada suggest that we cannot characterize this shift as a simple linear trajectory. In oral history research, ideas from earlier and later periods have overlapped and informed each other, and there have been continuities as well as discontinuities over time. Our current moment offers us an opportunity to reflect on our previous work, to develop a critical praxis that incorporates both the insights and the oversights of past work: this is preferable to a Whig historiography that suggests an onward and upward story in which each new academic orientation theoretically trumps the previous one. Not only does such a perspective diminish the importance of situating our oral history praxis within the changing academic, political, and social context that shaped our research, but it also discourages us from identifying the acuity of previous work or the limitations of current work, both of which may be useful in our future practice of oral history.[3]

Periodizing oral history as an academic and political practice is not an easy task. It is difficult to establish exact "origins," since there are inevitably antecedents to consider: folklorists, anthropologists, and popular writers were all using oral history long before the 1960s, sometimes with the expressed purpose of preserving the voices of "ordinary" working people. Eyewitness recollections have long been a historical source; however, the increased emphasis put on archives and documents as history professionalized in the late nineteenth century did marginalize oral accounts.[4] Nevertheless, by the late 1960s there was a new openness toward oral history in the Canadian historical profession, as growing numbers of practitioners embraced a method previously associated with journalism and the social sciences, especially anthropology. This turn to oral history was shaped profoundly by the "new social history," the political climate, and movements of social transformation that emerged in the 1960s and 1970s. Historians intent on challenging the scholarly status quo, particularly the reigning emphasis on history "from above," and who wished to revive class analysis as a means of exploring the experiences of marginalized groups, welcomed a method that might feature historical actors who had left fewer written records created by their own hands, or in their own voices. Feminist historians also saw oral history as a potential counterbalance or additive to predominantly text-based archives, which had tended to reinforce the prevailing inattention to women's lives.

While some social and political historians expressed concerns about the reliability and fallibility of memory associated with oral history, we should not go as far as to imply a general rejection of oral history. Steven High's suggestions that oral history was initially "greeted with anger and sarcasm" by the profession and that the "New Social History" framing oral history practice "did not change our relationship to the past or the public" but made us "more inward-looking than ever" both seem rather dubious.[5] Early issues of the Canadian Oral History Association Journal (later *Oral History Forum d'histoire orale*) confirm that oral history was welcomed by women's, working class, and immigration/ethnic historians, many of whom worked in overlapping areas.[6] This project of recovering subaltern histories was perceived not only as an alternative to the political undertaking of more mainstream historians who focused their sights on nation building and high politics, but also as a decentring of the power of the professional expert in favour of listening to the local knowledge of the working class, allowing them to interpret history *as they saw it.*

While some later reflections on the emergence of oral history have assumed a Whig narrative in which oral-history practice became more sophisticated and complex over time, as a naïve belief in the objectivity of interviews was replaced by more discerning and critical cultural analysis of oral history, the actual writing on oral history suggests a more nuanced and less linear story.[7] These early recuperative efforts were not treated simply as mere reflections of life events, or "mined for information or a bit of colour."[8] The knowledge interviewees offered was not necessarily seen as unmediated, pure, and objective because it came from the mouths of the marginalized groups; nor was it relayed in a singularly celebratory tone. Certainly, recuperation and preservation were strong themes in the early flush of enthusiasm about oral history. Many of those initially drawn to the practice of oral history acknowledged a general political commitment to revaluing working-class history and culture, and to understanding the complex history of gender and class relations. However, their project was not characterized by an unquestioning faith in realism or objectivity. Indeed, many working-class and women's historians challenged claims to objectivity in the dominant historiography, arguing that such claims masked a political investment in existing class and gender relations; they wanted to present a *different set of truths* drawn from social history, contesting what one famous British historian polemically referred to as "the propaganda of the victors."[9] Many North American oral history projects were imagined as *political* projects of recovery: they were intended to democratize history, challenge its silences and omissions, and take issue with the reigning definitions of historical significance. A form of historical "reparation," they were examples of "movement history"; that is "academics and activists engaged in the study of social protest [with] moral and political as well as intellectual" goals in mind.[10] Questioning the reality of working-class memory may not have had a prominent place in some of the initial forays into interviewing because, for practitioners dedicated to labour history as a political project, turning a skeptical eye on such interviews, portraying them as constructed narratives, would likely have been seen as a deliberate undermining, if not dismissal of workers' voices.

Interest in oral history was incubated not only within academe but also by ad hoc political groups, state-funded historical projects, new alternative presses, and vibrant social movements. Journals in feminist and labour studies were key sites for publishing the work of oral historians, as were book series and collections dedicated to the publication of auto/biographies of workers, and oral histories created collaboratively by workers and academic interviewers, in the tradition of "plural authorship."[11] Trade union organizations and labour studies programs within universities also encouraged the collection of oral histories of the labour movement, and while some were celebratory in tone, others addressed controversial issues relating to politics, anti-communism, and the exclusion of women from the union movement.[12] In the United States, projects intersected with the civil rights movement,[13] while in Canada, youth involved in state-funded community groups collected oral testimonies from indigenous peoples as part of their project of political mobilization of First Nations peoples.[14] In one Canadian project, graduate students interested in working-class history interviewed men and women who had lived through the First World War: their "viewpoints," they argued, had been silenced in the mainstream heroic histories of war centred on the battlefront, not the home front.[15] This interviewing collective drew from Raymond Williams's theoretical writing on oral tradition, dialect, and the culture of language, adapting it to their own project.[16]

In many of these grass-roots endeavours, oral history was seen as an alternative source that might uncover "authentic" renditions of popular experience; yet researchers also discussed the "active participation of the interviewer" in the interview, dissonances between written and oral sources, and the way in which oral testimony could bring to light aspects of social and cultural history "embedded in the spoken language."[17] Recovery, in other words, was not conceived of as a pure, simple, and unmediated process. However, oral history efforts tied to social movements might be more decentralized, uncoordinated, and reliant on disappearing funds; while some interview material was donated to archives, the tangible products of such activism were more difficult to preserve, particularly before the current academic requirements of research proposals, consent forms, and monitoring through ethics boards.[18]

In the 1970s, the presence of an active Left and a revitalized women's movement spurred feminist labour historians to turn to oral history in order to understand both the politics of women's resistance and the gendering of class formation.[19] Both labour and women's historians using oral history were interested in uncovering a "hidden history" that encompassed the "everyday" and the "personal,"[20] from working conditions on the factory floor to leisure and domestic family life. The latter theme elicited questions of unpaid as well as paid labour, the former largely obscured to date, not only in historical writing, but also in contemporary economic and social science measures of work. Feminist critiques of a male-centred scholarship on class, along with the emphasis of the new social history on working-class life, community, and culture, brought gender analysis more clearly into focus for oral historians of the working class who were interested in exploring the exercise of power relations, including women's negotiations, accommodations, and resistance to power. They were often motivated by a belief in the potentially empowering nature of oral history, both in the sense of countering the prevailing elite picture of the past and also in the sense of empowering individuals as they remembered and reinterpreted their pasts. While some writing was intentionally popular and journalistic, reaching out to a general audience, other pieces engaged in scholarly theoretical and conceptual debates in both disciplinary and interdisciplinary contexts. Social scientists were undertaking similar projects of interviewing, using oral histories as a means of understanding women's domestic labour, their family lives, and their subjective views about everyday life.[21]

My own interest in oral history grew out of precisely this zeitgeist of the new social history and 1970s movements for social transformation; I was caught up in debates that crossed the activist/academic spectrum concerning the creation of hybrid Marxist-feminism and in a concurrent political praxis of socialist-feminist organizing. Our political interests and activities raised significant questions about the history of women workers and women on the Left, underlining the importance of linking the past and present in a critical dialogue: what theoretical positions had fostered women's demands for equality? Around what concerns did working-class women mobilize in the past? How was the sexual division of labour reproduced in political parties? How did one ensure that questions of gender, sexual, and reproductive freedom were not obscured by social-ist economism? By interviewing women both in the Communist Party of Canada (CPC) and in the democratic socialist Co-operative Common-wealth Federation (CCF) from 1920 to 1960, I could compare the two leftist traditions, considering contemporary feminist questions about the efficacy of vanguard parties and the value of separate feminist organizing within socialist parties. Focusing on women on the Left also implicitly challenged the prevailing "two wave" categorization of feminism, which had obscured the history of socialist and communist women's activities from the 1920s to the 1960s, relegating them to a forty-year "trough" of supposed political somnolence.

My questions for social democratic and communist women were prompted by the politics of the period; the interviews were likely also shaped by my age, ethnicity, and class background, as well as by the ideological similarity or distance that women felt in relation to me. The prevailing Thompsonian emphasis in social history at the time – on ex-perience, human agency, and the active "making of class" – also influ-enced my research; these themes seemed especially resonant with regard to oral history, with its promise of people "making" their own history by recovering memories of working-class life. Although more critical pieces were emerging, warning us against a facile equation of oral history with "democratization,"[22] retrieving women's recollections and contextualizing them were still key priorities. Most historians of the working class did not see interviews as a simple panacea for the paucity of written sources; nor did they believe that eyewitness accounts were the be-all-and-end-all for research. Interviews were understood to be variable sources, not simply "truth," and unpacking the meaning that events had for workers was not completely absent from the agenda. Women's posture, silences, language, and justifications were sometimes noted, but to concentrate on these issues in our writing might have undermined the voices of women who had already been historically silenced; to focus on the fluidity or distortions of memory might have resurrected a privileging of written sources. Moreover, it might have seemed somewhat self-preoccupied to reflect in writing on my role in the interview. After all, I was not that interesting; these women were.

Despite the fact that I felt a sympathetic connection to some of the women I interviewed, in most instances there were boundaries between us. I was assuming a role as an academic investigator; they were acting as informants. As social scientists later argued, to deny the fact that we are implicitly "trading on" our professional identities in the process of collecting oral histories can deny or mask our authorial power.[23] I was also wary of imposing post-sixties feminist priorities on working-class lives that had unfolded in a different era; for example, if my politics assumed that reproductive and sexual choice were important political goals, I knew this was not necessarily true for my interviewees. One needed to pose questions that allowed their priorities to become visible, analyzing those in the context of their own times. Yet, as historians relaying our interviewees' views, we cannot avoid all retrospective judgments about their politics, since judgment is inherent to all historical writing. Moreover, it was not just what women said, but also the feeling they conveyed that was important to my analysis. The strongly held belief of left-wing women that motherhood inevitably defined women's lives more than men's, their investment in an ideology of care, came through as so genuine that I could hardly characterize both parties' relegation of women to home-centred issues as mere manipulation, as it might appear from written sources, and indeed, as other historians had argued.[24] The dominant cultural scripts of the time were internalized, though I could also see some subversion of those scripts as women rejected a vision of privatized mothering in favour of a more public, political, and "militant" version of social mothering.[25]

Women's failure to remember key events, I realized when doing the interviews, was not necessary accidental; after all, "memory is what we forget with."[26] It was obvious that women interpreted their political past in light of their subsequent political lives and loyalties. This was not so much "an organized structure of forgetting"[27] as individuals coping with a subsequent history that may have become puzzling, painful, or discomforting. Some women were still deeply invested in social democratic or communist politics; others were not, and their understanding of the past was shaped by their entire political evolution. However, integrating such background thoughts about why women remembered the way they did into our scholarly writing, making these issues an integral part of our historical commentary, was not usually part of our praxis. Nor was discussing what we did not ask women about, or what they would not reveal. I have since asked how I might have engaged more directly with interviewees on difficult and uncomfortable topics. By never questioning women when they misremembered, altered, or romanticized (in my view) I closed down an opportunity to understand why they misremembered or romanticized, and how they came to justify – in some cases – the unjustifiable, such as (in the case of communist women) the Stalinist show trials of the 1930s or Stalinism more generally. If we fail to question our interviewees, we can censor others by censoring ourselves. In retrospect, I think the notion that oral historians should avoid challenging and contradicting our interviewees – a shared problem across the field of oral history – can be condescending, especially if, like these women, they lived lives of engaged, political, public activism.

My analysis of these early "recuperative" efforts in working-class oral history has emphasized the imperative that working-class historians saw in situating all texts in their historical context, thereby analyzing oral history as historical evidence, rather than as "text." Did this emergent generation of oral historians see the project as one of simple recovery and "uncritical celebration"?[28] I am not so sure that we can divide working-class oral history into moments of celebratory recovery, and later, moments of deeper investigation of meaning and subjectivity. The project of recuperation did not disappear after the 1990s, and the seeds of studying memory and subjectivity were already apparent in the 1970s. Michael Frisch and Ronald Grele, for instance, were both writing in the 1970s about the need to focus our discussion on how memory was created, by whom, and why.[29] Nonetheless, in social history more generally, by the 1990s one can trace a new degree of attention to subjectivity, identity, narrativity, and memory that was reflected in both women's and working-class oral history.

By the 1990s and into the new millennium, debates and priorities in oral history had shifted course, a direction described by two scholars, in unnecessarily polarized language, as a move from "realism to narrativity."[30]

A more intensively self-critical analysis of our process of interviewing came to the fore. One could see a shift from the third to the first person voice, from the erasure of the historian's presence in the interview to a discussion of it, from a concern with objectivity to a greater focus on subjectivity, from an emphasis on "events" to understanding the "meaning" those events held for workers. Taking Alessandro Portelli as a guide, we looked to "oral sources to tell us not just what people did, but what they wanted to do, what they believed they were doing, and what they now think they did." "Subjectivity," as Portelli argued, "is as much the business of history as are the more visible facts."[31] There was increased discussion of Michael Frisch's concept of "shared authority,"[32] the relationship between oral historians and the communities with which they collaborated, our obligations to our interviewees, as well as to conceptual paradigms emphasizing language, discourse, and narrativity. Attention to "memory" replaced "individual memories" as the relationship between memory and oral history – for some distinct and contentious, but for many others intertwined – was explored.[33]

A changing international political and academic context framed these shifts. In working-class history more generally, Thompsonian notions of experience, an emphasis on conscious working-class agency, and an interest in ideology were less salient as historical materialism came under critique and the Left was in decline and disarray across the globe. Historians defending the theoretical suppositions of the "new" (now older) social history were challenged by those who decried what they saw as an ideological generation supposedly "patrolling the boundaries"[34] of working-class history, not letting the light of post-structuralist theory shine in. In feminist scholarship, the academic "turn to culture"[35] and post-structuralist theory was perhaps more noticeable as interest shifted from "consciousness to language, from the denotive to the performative."[36] Nevertheless, the influence of cultural historians who questioned the boundaries between "history and literature" and saw the "context itself as a text" had some effect on the entire discipline.[37] The continuing influence of feminism also encouraged attention to the operation of multiple axes of power, both in the research process *and* as a historical theme emerging from the interview itself. An increased attention to identity and subjectivity reinforced the project of integrating race, gender, and sexuality into working-class history, an interest that paralleled, in some countries, new attention to indigenous history and oral tradition, particularly as indigenous groups used oral histories in their courtroom battles over land and other rights.[38]

Post-structuralist theory, ascendant by the 1990s, took on divergent permutations across disciplines, and was differentially received and criticized across the globe, in relation to divergent political contexts and intellectual traditions. Working-class history was arguably more resistant than other academic areas to the demolition of materialist ways of seeing; however, the mantras of deconstruction, contingency, and fluidity were transnational constants in social history scholarship. Fragmentation, pastiche, indeterminacy, and above all, the linguistic and cultural constructions of oral narratives were stressed: life histories, as one anthropologist wrote, may "provide us with a conventionalized gloss on a social reality that ... we cannot know ... we may be discussing the dynamics of narration rather the dynamics of society."[39]

Oral historians, influenced by such theoretical writing, challenged notions of the subject, shifted their interpretive accent from the structural to the discursive, and reflected more openly on the interview as its own unique process of knowledge creation. Analysis of the interview as a cultural text and reflection about the interview as a process of social exchange became increasingly apparent in working-class and women's oral-history praxis. The interview was seen as a personal and social happening: reflexivity became integral to discussions of oral history, rather than an a priori contemplation of our sources before we wrote our monographs and articles. Increased emphasis was placed on the provenance, meaning, and textuality of the interview, along with non-textual forms of communication, including silences, hesitations, and avoidance.

Although such reflection intensified under the influence of post-structuralist appraisals of knowledge production, it is important to remember that critiques of objectivity, skepticism concerning agency, forms of cultural relativism, and "incredulity concerning metanarratives" already had a place within the discipline.[40] So too did discussions of the making of working-class memory, which, as we have seen, emerged almost simultaneously with working-class oral history in the 1970s. Moreover, critical reflections on post-structuralist historical writing justifiably warned of its tendency to veer toward discursive determinism, and the danger of obscuring key questions about the social contexts that frame discourse, the social location of those who are speaking.[41] An academic emphasis on subjectivity can become subjectivism, and textuality slip into textualism to the detriment of an analysis of the structures and ideologies shaping working-class lives. Analyzing our own role in the interview also runs the risk of placing the researcher in the limelight, rather than the voices of our interviewees. At what point does this become autobiography, not history?

Suggesting a Whig historiography of ever-increasing sophistication, then, problematically ignores some of the shortcomings and challenges posed by a culturally inflected, post-structuralist oral history theory.

The increased emphasis on the construction of memory and augmented attention to the interview as process did give us permission to reflect in print on why and how working-class people remembered the way they did, as well as dissecting the power dynamics shaping interviews. When I undertook research on the lives of wage-earning women in a small manufacturing city in the 1990s, international interdisciplinary debates in oral history stimulated my analysis of the interplay between women's narratives and the dominant ideological norms of the time; they encouraged me to explore in greater depth how workers' accommodation and resistance to power relations operated in the workplace.[42] Theoretical debates of the time were questioning oral history as a positivist methodology that automatically yielded "better" access to women's experiences; this writing questioned the "authenticity" of oral history as a more direct means of understanding women's lives, and called for a decentring of the power of the interviewer in the interview process.

Using five women's rather different recollections of one strike in a textile factory, I explored why and how working women remembered this significant event in quite different ways, some downplaying the violence, others stressing it, some stressing the justice of the workers' cause, others presenting a more management-sympathetic view. Oral history, in other words, could be pressed into answering the question: why do workers remember the way they do? How do we account for a working-class political consciousness that is fragmented and contradictory?

While the theoretical debates of the time offered me new ideas about the construction of women's memories, I did not see this construction as infinitely variable; nor were women's recollections made "inauthentic" because they were shaped by their own individual histories. Also, to concentrate only on specific, individual stories can be misleading; some atypical aspects of women's lives may inevitably be suppressed in our writing if we are analyzing the more common, shared experience of class relations. Women's memories, I argued, were a product not only of their individual stories but also of the dominant ideologies of the time and the productive and reproductive relations framing their lives as workers and family members. In the case of both the earlier left-wing women and these working women, it was important to shed light on how and why certain discourses came to dominate, while others remained alternative and marginal. To do this, an understanding the social location of the interviewees and the social context framing their lives remained critical. If we accept that "subjectivity is not a romantic fiction of the self prior to socialization but rather bears marks of the person's interaction with the world,"[43] then the powerful influence of social context can never be ignored. While academic discussions concerning narrativity and identity in oral history may have encouraged me to add interpretive threads to my analysis, the importance of placing texts in context, and assessing interviews as evidence remained as great as in the initial moment of oral history recuperation.

Moreover, the notion, embraced by some feminists, that one could really "share authority" with an interviewee seemed problematic, an idealization that ran the risk of masking our inevitable control over how the interview was relayed in print, and our academic investment in it. Certainly, the interview has its own dynamic which distinguishes it from textual sources; the personal encounter may have inhibited women's discussions of violence, conflict, or divisions between women or within the working class.[44] Our questions will also change over time. Were I to interview the same women now, I would likely pose some different questions, perhaps probing more concertedly into ethnic and cultural identity, and asking about the religious divisions of Catholic and Protestant, which they were reluctant to discuss. This openness to modification simply reinforces the axiom that oral history, like all historical practice, is shaped in part by the frames, questions, and ideas circulating at the time of its creation.

While writing on memory and subjectivity has had an effect on scholarship, the recuperation of events, experiences, and beliefs is to this day a key purpose of working-class oral history.[45] Oral history remains appealing precisely because it offers a window into the everyday experiences and feelings obscured in written sources, and because it suggests a story of working-class agency distinct from the history of those exerting class and political power. Despite the influence of theories stressing the fragmented and discursively produced subject, and concerted challenges to the concept of experience, some elements of the earlier recuperative project, including the notion that one can locate a "knowable" working-class experience, have had staying power. The rich and diverse use of oral history in Canadian working-class history makes this point emphatically. Well into the 1990s and the new millennium, many historians remain committed to a method that allows women to become historians of their own lives, challenging, changing, altering, or building on existing written histories. Feminist historians interested in the lives of working-class women continue to ask questions about longstanding themes of interest – paid and unpaid work, family relations, union activity, ethnic identity, and experiences of racism and cultural resilience. Rather than concentrate on the "constructedness" of memory, these historians treat their interviewees' statements as generally reliable renditions of the past; they grant their words a significant measure of realism and veracity. As in the earlier period, historians of labour, gender, and immigration/ethnicity especially continue to use oral history as a means of exploring women's productive and reproductive labour, sense of identity, and political and union roles, as well as the interconnected experiences of class, gender, and "race."[46] The interviews used in these scholarly studies are generally assumed to have a measure of "authenticity," and there is minimal reflection on the subjective nature of the interview process, though I am sure that these authors processed many of these questions in their a priori assessment of their sources.

In Ruth Frager's *Sweatshop Strife: Class, Ethnicity, and Gender in the Jewish Labour Movement of Toronto, 1900–1939*, to take only one example, interviews are used to explore working conditions, the family economy, union growth, and forms of resistance pursued by Eastern European Jewish immigrants. Frager uses her interviews to make a strong scholarly argument about the distinctive political and labour consciousness of these immigrants, which was shaped by their interconnected sense of class and ethnic identity. She generally accepts her interviewees' statements as reliable renditions of the past, and does not discuss the interview as a dialogue shaped by history and ideology, including her history as a younger socialist feminist drawing on the memories of older communists.[47] Similarly, a straightforward acceptance of subaltern stories characterizes Margaret Little's account of the history of Mothers' Allowance, in which oral histories are used to show single mothers' resistance to state practices of welfare surveillance and their dislike of the system for its invasiveness, sexism, and parsimony.[48] This is not to criticize, but rather to emphasize strong continuities with earlier scholarship and suggest that to characterize this writing as naïvely positivist misses the authors' a priori assessment of the veracity and meaning of all their sources, their weighing of how they use and relay oral history material.

During the initial turn to oral history as a valued process for historians of the working class, our sense that workers' stories, not ours, should be showcased had some merit; it was a valuable element of movement history. The theoretical insights of Raymond Williams, who was concerned with "the relationship between inherited culture and the individual," offered us a way of seeing oral histories as dynamic "works in progress" as individuals "grappled with the contradictions and complexities of their lives."[49] Elements of the earlier project of recovery, I have argued, have had some staying power in historians' actual practice of working-class oral history. While acknowledging these continuities, the theoretical debates shaping the field have also changed over time, and we must also recognize divergent views and debates within the field of working-class oral history. There are differences, for instance, between a post-structuralist informed, discursively constituted subject on the one hand, and a reflective subject who is an agent of history on the other hand; between a post-structuralist accent on the determining power of language and a materialist emphasis on the importance of social determination – the latter a characteristic of the earlier moment of social history scholarship. A distinction can be made between the post-structuralist emphasis on the constitutive influence of cultural scripts on individual memory and an earlier understanding of the individual as a social being, shaped, but not determined by cultural and ideological forces. For some scholars with post-structuralist inclinations, recovering the experience of women or the working class through oral histories may now seem a "seductive" but ultimately impossible, perhaps hazardous goal, opening the door to nostalgia and the "naturalization" of class."[50] To others, including myself, still grounded in more materialist analyses, it remains a valid analytic project, particularly in the historian's quest for subaltern voices.

Is there a way forward that integrates the insights and oversights of such different approaches to oral history? Divergent theoretical assumptions, with different epistemological starting points, cannot be simply collapsed, integrated, or absorbed into each other. However, we might attend to some of the issues raised by post-structuralist theories as a means of fine-tuning a materialist approach in which "the social" still figures most prominently. Paying attention to subjectivity, narrativity, and memory does not necessarily obscure the critical importance of historical context if we see subjectivity as being embedded within social life. Both Marxist and feminist discussions of standpoint, historical materialism, and the relations of ruling may be useful in this regard. Discussions about oral history practice have often involved debates over questions of voice, ethics, collaboration, and "who speaks for whom." However, feminist theory can provide other critical insights into the social landscape in which our interviews unfold, keeping us focused on two sides of the same coin: the perspective of the interviewee and the realm of "the social."

Dorothy Smith's suggestion that the standpoint of the interviewee should be the starting point for our inquiry is a case in point. This admonition does not assume that the interviewee offers an essentialized, superior, unmediated point of view, but rather that we need to think about the actualities of her everyday experiences, her relations with others, her working, thinking, everyday life. Both the interviewer's and the interviewee's "location in the social order" matter, for the cumulative effects of our experiences shape our understandings of the world, a knowable world always "brought into being by human activity."[51] Taking this maxim to heart may help us understand the "social relations pervading [our interviewees'] world, but perhaps invisible to it," exploring the way in which their experiences are bound up with prevailing ideologies and the relations of ruling.[52] Thinking about the standpoint of the interviewee does not assume that those on the margins – like the working class – always speak from an oppositional standpoint; there is no direct, determinate line from experience to political consciousness, for the views "from below" are multiple and contradictory, sometimes critical of, but also "vulnerable to the dominant culture."[53] Indeed, as feminist theorists have argued, alternative perspectives are arrived at, or "achieved" through human reflection, and the latter could become a part of telling a life history, as it elicits or reveals "counter-memories"[54] – those that are an uncomfortable fit with ruling ideas of the social order. This is not to say oral histories are either "therapeutic"[55] or automatically revelatory or radicalizing; simply that listening to the voices of the working class, the poor, and the marginalized, and understanding the contexts that shape their voices remain important to oral history practice.

Second, we can pay close attention to subjectivity and narrativity by "reading" working-class interviews through theories of language that are historical, social, and materialist – but not determinist. As V.N. Volosinov argues, language is always "reciprocal, the product of the relationship between speaker and listener, addressee and addressor."[56] Meaning does not reside in "words," but rather words take on meaning through social interaction and human relations.[57] Attentiveness to language and narrativity need not obscure the importance of "the social" in the lives of our interviewees, for subjectivity is always embedded in social life: material context, coercion and consent, and power and ideology profoundly shape our lives, as well as the way we understand and recount them.

Similarly, drawing on Bakhtin, Smith stresses the social and interactive nature of communication: "Active, relational, dialogic" language involves social communication, not merely "texts, statements, categories."[58] The way we tell our life history may embody certain themes, accents, and meanings. These will shift according to who is speaking, why, and the context, but the "life of language" resides in the "nexus of social relations, and in human relations of social conflict."[59] Not only does this approach prevent our captivity in the endless circuit of discourse, but the emphasis on interaction and conflict may help us understand the nature of working-class consciousness without making it unitary, homogenous, and unchanging. A worker's recollections, for example, may reveal both oppositional discourses and a language of accommodation to the social order. As she makes sense of her life, she may help us understand under what conditions, in what moments, in what ideological spaces alternative views come to the fore, how they are developed, or perhaps silenced, pushed to the back recesses of memory.

Finally, our attempts to theorize oral history might benefit from continuous dialogue with broader debates about historical interpretation, particularly those concerning the subject and human agency. Literature on oral history often stresses how fundamentally different it is from other sources; yet written texts are not simply "mute and frozen"[60] as some might suggest. Some of the challenges portrayed as particular to oral history have resonances across historical methodologies: asking "hard critical questions"[61] of one's sources and connecting the "horizontal linkages" in workers' experiences are challenges many working class historians wrestle with. Written records are not static, nor are they without feeling; they convey affect, elicit emotional responses, sometimes different ones depending on the reader and the context of the reading. As Linda Gordon noted that when she examined the case files of battered women, she often felt the women themselves were "speaking to" her.[62] The case files of criminalized women that I read were similarly interpreted in a subjective, interactive manner, coloured by my own politics, emotions, and assumptions. Women's words in these files might be collected – in contrast to oral sources – *against the will* of the informant, with transcriptions of their conversations then becoming public documents, raising ethical issues (as in oral history) ranging from the protection of one's sources to how we use them and convey them to others. They also elicit questions about how memory is shaped by the different context in which the subject is speaking. An incarcerated woman, whose words may appear to be recorded verbatim in textual form, may change her story, according to who she is speaking to, and yet each utterance may incorporate certain truths. While we should not discount the methodological differences between our use of oral and textual sources, a theoretical dialogue that crosses these boundaries may still enrich our understanding of both oral and written histories.

Reflecting on more than four decades of a rich tradition of working-class oral history, we need not, then, overemphasize a linear shift from the "objective observer to the subjective interaction,"[63] from mere commemorative writing to critical analysis. When working-class oral history was increasingly embraced as a methodology in the 1970s, many practitioners were guided by their political investment in a project they hoped would reveal a different truth about history, and re-animate marginalized voices in history. For some historians, these remain important goals. However, focusing too intently on recovery, we were subsequently warned, could become an illusory, "facile democratization" if we did not concurrently query "subjective reality,"[64] including the complex interaction between ideology and history, past and present. Queries about the construction of memory were introduced in some early scholarly pieces, but this conversation proliferated and intensified considerably as the method of oral history was interrogated through a new theoretical lens.[65] As a consequence, historians put more emphasis on exploring the way in which personal narratives were shaped by historically changing cultural norms and conventions, and reflected more openly on their own, as well as their interviewees' subjective construction of memory.

However, subjectivity and recovery, culture and context, may be inseparable, different sides of this coin, with heads or tails dominant at different times in our practice of oral history. Many historians continue to see oral history as a method that is distinct because of the nature of human interaction involved – a method that draws out new, often marginalized perspectives of working-class knowledge holders, reveals themes hidden from other kinds of textual sources, and is animated by political questions. While the enriching impact of increased attention to cultural scripts, memory, and subjectivity in oral history writing is evident in much current scholarship, the recuperation of working-class experience has proven a resilient theme for some labour historians. Political questions still animate our scholarship: How do social being and social consciousness interact? What stimulates changes in collective consciousness? What makes systems of inequality, oppression, and exploitation "tick," and what renders them untenable? Those questions, I believe, cannot be satisfactorily explored by focusing only on the discursive and subjective, at the expense of recognizing also the social context of class relations in which workers live their lives as well as the difficult experiences of disparity and struggle that have permeated their lives, and indeed continue to shape how they interpret their past and the present.

NOTES

1 Popular Memory Group, "Popular Memory: Theory, Politics, Method," in *The Oral History Reader*, 2nd edition, edited by Robert Perks and Alistair Thomson (London: Routledge, 1998), 47.

2 Lyn Abrams, *Oral History Theory* (London: Routledge, 2010), 7.

3 This chapter draws on ideas explored in two previous articles on oral history: "The Politics and Praxis of Canadian Working-Class Oral History," in *Oral History Off the Record*, edited by Stacey Zembrzycki and Anna Sheftel (New York: Palgrave Macmillan, 2013) and Joan Sangster, "Oral History and Working Class History: A Rewarding Alliance," *Oral History Forum d'histoire orale* 33 (2010): 1–15.

4 Paul Thompson, "Historians and Oral History," in *The Voice of the Past: Oral History* 2nd edition (Oxford: Oxford University Press, 1988), chapter 2.

5 The tendency to exaggerate the "anger and sarcasm" that greeted oral history is found in Steven High, "Sharing Authority in the Writing of Canadian History: The Case of Oral History," in *Contesting Clio's Craft: New Directions and Debates in Canadian History*, edited by Christopher Dummitt and Michael Dawson (London: Institute for the Study of the Americas, 2009), 23. The evidence High cites from popular reviews in the *Globe and Mail* suggests a less categorical rejection; indeed, one review by Ramsay Cook praises some oral history, but criticizes the book he is reviewing for using oral sources badly and not comparing them to written evidence. Also, social historians' enthusiastic involvement of women, ethnicity, and labour is evident in the early issues of the *Canadian Oral History Association Journal*.

6 For example, *Oral History Forum d'histoire orale* 4, no. 2 (1980). Not all projects evolved from social history; for example, one explored mainstream politicians. See Peter Oliver, "One Oral Historian's View," *Canadian Oral History Association Journal* 1 (1975–76): 13–19.

7 There are many historiographical treatments of the field of oral history: for one excellent overview, see Abrams, *Oral History Theory*.

8 High, "Sharing Authority," 46.

9 E.P. Thompson, interview in *Visions of History* (New York: Pantheon Books, 1976), 8. This view reflected a generation of American New Left scholars described by Jim Green, *Taking History to Heart: The Power of the Past in Building Social Movements* (Amherst: University of Massachusetts Press, 2000), 2.

10 Green, *Taking History to Heart*, 2.

11 Alessandro Portelli, quoted in Green, *Taking History to Heart*, 3. For example, trade unionist Gil Levine edited *Patrick Lenihan: From Irish Rebel to Founder of Canadian Public Sector Unionism* (St John's, Newfoundland: CCLH, 1998) while an academic and trade unionist, both leftists, talked "across their differences" to create a life history of Jack Scott: Bryan Palmer, ed., *Jack Scott: A Communist Life* (St John's, Newfoundland: CCLH, 1988).

12 For examples, see Wayne Roberts: *Where Angels Fear to Tread: Eileen Tall-man and the Labour Movement* (Hamilton: McMaster University Labour Studies, 1979); *A Miner's Life: Bob Miner and Union Organizing in Timmins, Kirkland Lake and Sudbury* (Hamilton: McMaster University Labour Studies Program, 1979); *Organizing Westinghouse: Alf Ready's Story* (Hamilton: McMaster University Labour Studies, 1979).

13 From 1967 to 1973, Howard University ran a project documenting the civil rights movement. Rebecca Sharpless, "The History of Oral History," in *The History of Oral History: Foundations and Methodologies*, edited by Thomas Charlton, Lois Myers, and Rebecca Sharpless (Lanham, MD: AltaMira Press, 2007), 18.

14 Kelly Pineault, "Shifting the Balance: Indigenous and Non-Indigenous Activism in the Company of Young Canadians, 1957–73" (Master's thesis, Trent University, 2011).

15 Daphne Read and Russell Hann, eds., *The Great War and Canadian Society: An Oral History* (Toronto: New Hogtown Press, 1978), 7.

16 Russell Hann, "Introduction," *The Great War and Canadian Society*.

17 Ibid., 10, 24, 30.

18 There were exceptions: see Sara Diamond, *Chambermaids and Whistlepunks: An Oral History of Women in B.C. Labour, 1930–55* (Vancouver: Press Gang, 1983). This collection of interviews was later put in the Simon Fraser University Archives. The current role of ethics boards varies across nations, but in some cases, historians have argued that the kind of oversight demanded has a "chilling" effect on oral history. For the American case, see Linda Shopes, "Legal and Ethical Issues in Oral History," in *The History of Oral History*, edited by Charlton et al., 139. See also chapter 3 by Janovicek in this *Reader*.

19 Gail Cuthbert Brandt, "Weaving It Together: Life Cycle and the Industrial Experience of Female Cotton Workers in Quebec, 1910–1950," *Labour/Le Travail* 7 (1981): 113–26; Joan Sangster "Women of the New Era: Women in the Early CCF," and Georgina Taylor, "The Women ... Shall Help to Lead the Way: Saskatchewan CCF-NDP Women Candidates in Provincial and Federal Elections, 1934–65," in *Building the Cooperative Commonwealth: Essays on the Democratic Socialist Tradition in Canada*, edited by W. Brennan (Regina: University of Regina, 1985): 69–97 and 141–60; Elizabeth Roberts, *A Woman's Place: An Oral History of Working-Class Women, 1890–1940* (London: Basil Blackwell, 1984); Vicki Ruiz, *Cannery Women, Cannery Lives: Mexican Women, Unionization, and the California Food Processing Industry, 1930–50* (Albuquerque, NM: University of New Mexico Press, 1987).

20 Sherna Berger Gluck, "From First Generation Oral Historians to Fourth and Beyond," *Oral History Review* 26, no. 2 (summer 1999): 3.

21 Meg Luxton, *More Than a Labour of Love: Three Generations of Work in the Home* (Toronto: Women's Educational Press, 1980); Lillian Rubin, *Worlds of*

Pain: Life in the Working-Class Family (New York: Basic Books, 1976). These include reflection on method: Anne Oakley, "Interviewing Women: A Contradiction in Terms," in *Doing Feminist Research*, edited by Dorothy Roberts (London: Routledge and Kegan Paul, 1981), 30–61.

22 Luisa Passerini, "Work Ideology and Consensus under Italian Fascism," *History Workshop Journal* 8 (1979): 82–108.

23 Janet Finch, "It's Great to Have Someone to Talk to: The Ethics and Politics of Interviewing Women," in *Social Researching: Politics, Problems, Practice*, edited by C. Bell and H. Roberts (London: Routledge and Kegan Paul, 1984), 78; Judith Stacey, "Can There Be a Feminist Ethnography?" in *Women's Words: The Feminist Practice of Oral History*, edited by Sherna Berger Gluck and Daphne Patai (New York: Routledge, 1997), 111–20.

24 Elsa Dixler, "The Woman Question: Women and the American Communist Party, 1929–41" (PhD dissertation, Yale University, 1974).

25 Joan Sangster, *Dreams of Equality: Women on the Canadian Left, 1920s–1950s* (Toronto: McClelland & Stewart, 1989), 237.

26 Aldous Huxley, quoted in Bernard Ostry, "The Illusion of Understanding: Making the Ambiguous Intelligible," *Oral History Review* 5 (1977): 7.

27 Paula Hamilton, "Edge: Debates about Memory and History," in *Memory and History in Twentieth-Century Australia*, edited by Kate Darion-Smith and Paula Hamilton (Melbourne: Oxford University Press, 1994), 13. Of course, memory was also recast as party histories reinterpreted the past over time.

28 Gluck, "From First Generation," 5.

29 For example, Ronald Grele, *Envelopes of Sound: The Art of Oral History* (Chicago: Precedent Publishing, 1975); Michael Frisch, "Oral History and *Hard Times*: A Review Essay," *Oral History Review* 7, no. 1 (1979): 70–9.

30 George Rosenwald and Richard Ochberg, "Introduction: Life Stories, Cultural Politics, and Self-Understanding," in *Storied Lives: The Cultural Politics of Self-Understanding*, edited by Rosenwald and Ochberg (New Haven: Yale University Press, 1992), 2.

31 Alessandro Portelli, "What Makes Oral History Different?" in *The Death of Luigi Trastulli and Other Stories* (Albany: SUNY Press, 1991), 50.

32 Michael Frisch, *A Shared Authority: Essays on the Craft and Meaning of Oral and Public Histories* (Albany: SUNY Press, 1990); Linda Shopes, "Oral History and the Study of Communities: Problems, Paradoxes, and Possibilities," *The Journal of American History*, 89, no. 2 (September 2002): 588–98.

33 Kerwin Lee Klein, "On the Emergence of Memory in Historical Discourse," *Representations* 69 (winter 2000): 127–50.

34 John Vernon, "Who's Afraid of the Linguistic Turn: The Politics of Social History and Its Discontents," *Social History* 19 (1994): 81–98.

35 Michèle Barrett, "Words and Things: Materialism and Method in Contemporary Feminist Analysis," in *Destabilizing Feminist Theory: Contemporary*

Feminist Debates, edited by Michèle Barrett and Anne Phillips (Cambridge: Polity Press, 1992), 204.

36 Seyla Benhabib, "Epistemologies of Postmodernism: A Rejoinder to Jean-François Lyotard," in *Feminism/Postmodernism*, edited by Linda Nicolson (New York: Routledge, 1990), 125.

37 Lloyd Kramer, "Literature, Criticism and Historical Imagination: The Literary Challenge of Hayden White and Dominick LaCapra," in *The New Cultural History*, edited by Lynn Hunt (Berkeley: University of California Press, 1989), 100–14. For another discussion of the post-structuralist, cultural turn and feminist oral histories see Kristina Llewellyn, chapter 6 in this *Reader*: "Productive Tensions: Feminist Readings of Women Teachers' Oral Histories."

38 There are some interesting differences between the way in which Indigenous voices and working-class ones are discussed in the academic literature. The different engagement is likely shaped by the peoples and social movements we are working with. On Indigenous oral history see Julie Cruikshank, *Life Lived Like a Story: Life Stories of Three Yukon Native Elders* (Vancouver: UBC Press, 1990); Nancy Wachowich, with Apphia Agalakti Awa, Rhoda Kaukjak Katsak, and Sandra Pikujak Katsak, *Saqiyuq: Stories from the Lives of Three Inuit Women* (Montreal: McGill-Queen's University Press, 1999); Julie Cruikshank, "Oral Tradition and Oral History," *Canadian Historical Review* 75, no. 3 (1994): 403–18. On courtroom battles: Dara Culhane, *The Pleasure of the Crown: Anthropology, Law and First Nations* (Burnaby: Talon Books, 1998).

39 Vincent Crapanzano, "Life Histories," *American Anthropologist* 86, no. 4 (1984): 955.

40 Perez Zagorin, "History, the Referent, and Narrative Reflections on Postmodernism Now," *History and Theory* 38, no. 1 (February 1999): 6.

41 Paula Moya and Michael Hames-Garcia, eds., *Reclaiming Identity: Realist Theory and the Predicament of Postmodernism* (Berkeley: University of California Press, 2000).

42 Joan Sangster, "Telling Our Stories: Feminist Debates and the Use of Oral History," *Women's History Review* 3, no. 1 (1994): 5–28; "The Softball Solution: Women Workers and Male Managers in a Peterborough Clock Factory," *Labour/Le Travail* 32 (1993): 167–99; *Earning Respect: The Lives of Working Women in Small-Town Ontario, 1920–50* (Toronto: University of Toronto Press, 1995).

43 Rosenwald and Ochberg, "Introduction," in *Storied Lives*, 8.

44 Although I found women reluctant to talk about this, other historians have sensitively uncovered the history of violence in other contexts: e.g., Marlene Epp, "The Memory of Violence: Soviet and Eastern European Refugees and Rape in the Second World War," *Journal of Women's History* 9, no. 1 (1997): 58–88.

45 Katrina Srigley, *Breadwinning Daughters: Young Working Women in a Depression-Era City, 1929–39* (Toronto: University of Toronto Press, 2010), 6.

46 Franca Iacovetta, *Such Hard-Working People: Italian Immigrants in Postwar Toronto* (Montreal: McGill-Queen's University Press, 1990); Ruth Frager, *Sweatshop Strife: Class, Ethnicity, and Gender in the Jewish Labour Movement of Toronto, 1900–1939* (Toronto: University of Toronto Press, 1992); Carmela Patrias, *Relief Strike: Immigrant Workers and the Great Depression in Crowland, Ontario* (Toronto: New Hogtown Press, 1990); Varpu Linstrom-Best, *Defiant Sisters: A Social History of Finish Immigrant Women in Canada* (Toronto: Multicultural History Society, 1992); Dionne Brand, *No Burden to Carry: Narratives of Black Working Women in Ontario, 1920–1950s* (Toronto: Women's Press, 1991); Pamela Sugiman, *Labour's Dilemma: The Gender Politics of Auto Workers in Canada, 1937–1979* (Toronto: University of Toronto Press, 1994).

47 Like my earlier work on the Left, Frager's study does not interrogate in print how communists' reflections may have been shaped by their position in a post-Holocaust period, post-1956 world. Yet, in one case where our research overlaps, on fur unions, more recent research has helped me see how much some participants in those battles did retell the history differently over time based on their changing political loyalties. Joan Sangster, "Canada's Cold War in Fur," *Left History* 13, no. 2 (2009): 10–36.

48 Margaret Little, *No Car, No Radio, No Liquor Permit: The Moral Regulation of Single Mothers in Ontario, 1920–1997* (Toronto: Oxford University Press, 1998).

49 Anna Green, "Individual Remembering," 41.

50 Craig Ireland, "The Appeal to Experience and Its Constituencies: Variations on a Persistent Thompsonian Theme," *Cultural Critique* 52 (autumn 2002): 92, 97.

51 Dorothy Smith, *Texts, Facts and Femininity: Exploring the Relations of Ruling* (London: Routledge, 1990), 90.

52 Ibid. See also Marie Campbell and Ann Manicom, "Introduction," in *Knowledge, Experience, and Ruling Relations*, edited by Marie Campbell and Ann Manicom (Toronto: University of Toronto Press, 1995), 9.

53 Nancy Hartstock, "Postmodernism and Political Change: Issues for Feminist Theory," *Cultural Critique* 14 (1989/90): 24, 27.

54 Natalie Zemon Davis and Randolph Starn, "Introduction," *Representations* 26 (spring 1989): 5.

55 Paula Hamilton, "The Oral Historian as Memorist," *Oral History Review* 32, no. 1 (spring 2005): 13.

56 V.N. Volosinov, *Marxism and the Philosophy of Language* (New York: Seminar Press, 1973), 86.

57 Ibid., 106.

58 Dorothy Smith, *Writing the Social: Critique, Theory, and Investigations* (Toronto: University of Toronto Press, 2004), 120.

59 David McNally, "Language, History and Class Struggle," in *In Defense of History: Marxism and the Postmodern Agenda*, edited by Ellen Meiksins Wood and John Bellamy Foster (New York: Monthly Review Press, 1997), 29.

60 Michael Frisch and Dorothy Larson, "Oral History and the Presentation of Class Consciousness: *The New York Times* v the Buffalo Unemployed," in Frisch, *A Shared Authority*, 61.

61 Linda Shopes, "Oral History and the Study of Communities," 597. As Shopes notes in another piece, "oral history material must be used in much the same way as intellectual historians use their documents – as clues into the mind of a person or group." Linda Shopes, "Oral History and Community Development," in *Presenting the Past: Essays on History and the Public*, edited by Susan Porter Benson, Stephen Brier, and Roy Rosenzweig (Philadelphia: Temple University Press, 1986), 256. The second quotation is from Roger Horowitz and Rick Halpern, "Work, Race and Identity; Self-Representation in the Narratives of Black Packinghouse Workers," *Oral History Review* 26, no. 1 (winter/spring 1999): 26. Similarly, distinguishing public history as an approach that is "reflective" while the "traditional" history degree provides "enrichment study" sets up an exaggerated dichotomy. Noel Stowe, "Public History Curriculum: Illustrating Reflective Practice," *The Public Historian* 28, no. 1 (winter 2006): 40.

62 Linda Gordon, "Comments on That Noble Dream," *American Historical Review* 96, no. 3 (June 1991): 684.

63 Ronald Grele, ed., "Introduction," in *International Annual of Oral History 1990* (New York: Greenwood, 1990), 2.

64 Passerini, "Work Ideology and Consensus under Italian Fascism," 57.

65 For an early positive article on oral history from a Canadian political historian, see Ostry, "The Illusion of Understanding," 7–16. Issues of power imbalances and power sharing were especially evident in the feminist literature by the 1990s. Susan Geiger, "What's So Feminist About Oral History?" *Journal of Women's History* 2, no. 1 (1990): 175 and articles in Gluck and Patai, *Women's Words*.

6

Productive Tensions: Feminist Readings of Women Teachers' Oral Histories[1]

Kristina R. Llewellyn

The best feminist work ensures that research is grounded in women's experiences, considers the power relations between researchers and researched, and works towards the elimination of patriarchal oppression.[2] While these ideals are evident in most feminist studies, for more than three decades now scholars have also debated what the "linguistic turn" means for exploring the past lives of women. Oral historians of women have welcomed but also wrestled with post-structuralist assertions that gender is a question of language to be subjectively deconstructed within local contexts.[3] Feminists working from a materialist position – pioneers of women's oral history – have challenged many aspects of this "turn" in scholarship. Many of them insist that an examination of economic conditions, both domestic and industrial, that uncover definable and generalizable principles of gender hierarchy must be the foundation of historical inquiry, including work stemming from oral sources.[4] While these are crude depictions of what are diverse theoretical camps, feminist oral historians must deal with the inherent tensions produced between post-structuralism and materialism.[5]

As I began my doctoral research on Canadian women teachers in post–Second World War schools in 2002 – a project that relied heavily on oral histories – I was fully immersed in postmodern questions of narrative deconstruction, subjectivity, and identity politics. And then I read Joan Sangster's work in which she warns oral historians about the dangers of post-structuralism's practice of emphasizing "form over context, of stressing deconstruction of individual narratives over analysis of social patterns, of disclaiming our duty as historians to analyze and interpret women's stories."[6] While I heeded her concerns, I wondered if materialism was not equally dangerous for interpreting women's narratives, given the propensity to impose narratives that define power as objective, economic, and unified. As I began the interviewing process, I needed to answer the question of how each of these frameworks might shape my readings of women teachers' oral histories. Would a feminist reading of oral histories benefit from a post-structuralist *or* materialist analysis? In this chapter I argue that an analysis of oral histories benefits from engaging with the productive tensions between feminist post-structuralism and materialism. In this, I join feminist scholars, many outside of oral history, who have explicitly countered the fragmentation of these theories.[7] I demonstrate how feminists working in the field of oral history may reconcile concerns for structural equality with questions of discursive power and may examine women's political agency within hierarchies of identification. It is this interpretive lens, as Marjorie Theobald explains, that will encourage feminist oral historians to work within layers of narrative, rather than beyond them,[8] thereby sharing in the goal of de-normalizing patriarchal representations of the past.

Drawing upon examples from my research on women teachers' oral histories, I explore three key interpretive concepts for oral historians: knowledge, discourse, and identity.[9] While these terms are interrelated, I treat them separately here for the sake of clarity. The first section addresses knowledge, or the assertions of "truth" that oral historians can draw from women teachers' representations of the past. Many post-structuralist feminists assert that oral historians can reveal multiple truths about intersectional oppressions in history by paying close attention to how interviewees organize their narratives. Materialist feminists have questioned the political efficacy of seeking such truths and instead encourage oral historians to examine the gendered structures of power that are evident from narratives. The second concept is discourse, which in this case refers to teachers' use of language to explain their occupational identities. While feminist post-structuralists exploring oral histories tend to focus on the power of language, materialist feminists stress that discourse is fashioned by the structural parameters of a given time and place. My third section addresses women teachers' identity constructions. Post-structuralist feminists are attentive to women's individual narratives in order to reject the imposition of "Woman." In contrast, materialist feminists emphasize efforts to understand women as a group, defined according to social patterns of patriarchy and informed by class relations. The tensions between these feminist frameworks should not be – nor can they be – simply combined by scholars.[10] Rather, the potential of women's oral history is found between these theoretical traditions, where truths are located within the structural limits of their construction, language as a path to historical experience is understood in relation to material life, and questions about the self are inextricable from social and political life.

THE TRUTHS OF WOMEN'S STORIES

As Luisa Passerini argues, oral histories are revelations of truths, but "it is up to the interpreter to discover in which sense, where, for what purpose."[11] When considering what historical evidence oral histories reveal, post-structuralist feminists focus on knowledge production, or the process through which interviewees make sense of their lives. Narratives are treated as linguistic constructions which, being open to multiple interpretations, provide evidence of how people conceptualize their past experiences. Life as text, as argued by Jacques Derrida, emphasizes that there is no clear window into the inner life of a person, because the view is always filtered through the glaze of language and processes of signification.[12] Post-structuralists emphasize that the knowledge gained from oral histories is thus always a fluctuating truth that exists within the layers of life as it happens, life as it is told by the subject, and life as narrative interpreted by the historian.[13] The role of the oral historian is not to provide the facts of the past, even if this were possible; rather it is to analyze the way historical knowledge is created through people's discourses and informed by subject locations.

Approaching oral histories as such a text has led to the re-conceptualization of many fields of study, including my work on women teachers. Educational historians have traditionally written about the conditions of women's work requiring factory-like labour, constrained by such factors as prescriptive curricula and authoritarian administrators. My own research examines the costs for women of seemingly "democratic" reforms in Toronto and Vancouver secondary schools in the years following the Second World War.[14] Although schools widened access, increased social services, and decentralized decision-making, these initiatives conformed to a conservative ideal of citizenship – white, Judeo-Christian, middle-class, and heterosexual – in an effort to restore a sense of "normality" following war. Women teachers were welcomed in schools to fill a labour shortage, but were included only insofar as they represented motherly guardians of a traditional social order. Women taught while men were given the power to manage.[15] The women I interviewed brought forward an abundance of stories to illustrate the gender hierarchy of schools. For example, many women recalled that male veterans were quickly promoted to positions as principals, and school officials insisted that all men who had been in service be called by their ranks. The women characterized these men as "benevolent dictators," or as "military-like, who ran a tight ship."[16] Yet, when I asked explicitly about gender discrimination, almost all of the women denied its existence. How, I wondered, could they deny their oppression while detailing events to the contrary? Were they misremembering?

While I wanted to hear about the ways in which gender oppression resulted from postwar education reforms, interviewees provided a more complex tale of the power relations that shaped their work. Kate Rousmaniere contends that a richer picture of the history of teaching emerges from oral histories by looking "sideways into the picture presented ... in order to identify teachers' motivations, feelings, and reactions."[17] As I listened for a multiplicity of truths rather than for a single story, it became apparent that one of the reasons the women in my study did not name sexism was that they were able to work within patriarchal structures to assume a measure of authority. Many of the women told me that a postwar militaristic rank provided a clarity of work conditions that was quietly negotiable. They argued, for example, that a firm pecking order let them know where they stood and often translated into greater control over their own students; they were the commanders of their classrooms and thus determined curriculum content, even finding ways to teach subversive lessons about Communism and use "blacklisted" textbooks.[18] Some also added, as Donna Weber said in a hushed tone, "we just laughed – 'squadron leader what's his name.'"[19]

I began to recognize more of women's informal authority when I read their oral histories for clues, patterns, and themes, embracing conflicting truths about how teachers understood and acted upon their surroundings. Such a conceptual stance, influenced by post-structuralism, rejects an empiricist view of the past as objectively fixable through the scientific pursuit of facts.[20] This approach is crucial for feminist scholars because it undermines traditionally male-based scientific claims to knowledge or knowing, including biological determinism of gender disparities. At the same time, however, this framework rejects attempts by feminist empiricists to re-inscribe objectivist notions of "Woman."[21] And here is where materialist feminists provide an important note of caution. Acceptance, or in some case suspicion, of all truth claims is politically untenable for a feminist agenda that seeks political reform. Roberta Spalter-Roth and Heidi Hartmann, for instance, are critical of any feminist epistemological position that does not claim scientific credibility and generalizability. Without such evidence, they argue, feminists would be discredited in policy debates and unable to actualize their goals for political reform.[22]

If considering materialists' calls for a strong political agenda *and* post-structuralists' calls to respect women's many truths, the seduction for some oral historians could be to write a descriptive story that privileges the seemingly transparent knowledge of women – a "let the stories speak for themselves" approach.[23] To take this approach is to misinterpret the idea, articulated by Paul Thompson, that "transforming the 'objects' of study into 'subjects,' makes for a history which is not just richer, more vivid and heartrending, but truer."[24] If I were to valorize women teachers by letting them tell their stories unmediated, then their oral histories would be reduced to reminiscences or personal anecdotes. More problematic, I could unwittingly depict these women's narratives as a form of constrained consciousness that confirms conservative rhetoric of teachers' apolitical subjectivities. Instead, I needed to privilege the truths provided by women teachers' oral histories – evidence unavailable in archival sources – but still treat memory as an unstable basis for knowledge about the past. [25] Only through respectful skepticism of narratives may I explore the ways in which these women teachers' oral histories might destabilize patriarchal tropes about schooling.

Donna Haraway argues that relativism is the "perfect mirror twin of totalization in the ideologies of objectivity; both deny the stakes of location, embodiment, and partial perspective; both make it impossible to see well."[26] To escape the respective traps of relativism (associated with post-structuralism) and totalization (associated with materialism), Haraway re-articulates feminists' conception of objectivity as situated knowledge. She argues that embedded, active, partial visions of the world, rather than transcendence, make up our individual knowledge. This, she asserts, is the legitimate way of seeing. By embracing situated knowing, such objectivity enables feminist researchers to communicate generalizable, yet complex, evidence that could lead to real change for women.[27] For oral historians to see partial perspectives as substantive evidence, as Haraway encourages, it is imperative to acknowledge that oral histories are productions. Leslie Bloom argues that feminist researchers provide the most illuminating illustration of meaning making in history when they show a genuine respect for a subject's right to define her own history, but simultaneously recognize the explicit role of the researcher in the history constructed.[28]

This is not a simple task. Oral historians wrestle with the power inequalities inherent in the interviewer-interviewee relationship, from the question-answer format to the interpretive process. Feminist oral historians across theoretical traditions have been at the forefront of the effort to redistribute power over meaning making, developing what Michael

Frisch calls a shared authority between interviewer and interviewee.[29] Such strategies include treating the interview as a conversation, asking subjects to review transcripts, and collaborating in publications.[30] My interviews were admittedly research-centred, based on a predefined interpretive framework, and without formative consultation. This was, in part, due to a graduate student timeline and the hamstrings of university ethics requirements.[31] According to Kathryn Anderson and Dana Jack, such an approach means that "I am already appropriating what she says to an existing schema, and therefore I am no longer really listening to *her*."[32] This was evident from two interviews I conducted with Hazel Chong. Hazel repeatedly expressed a desire to know if she was *the first* Chinese-Canadian to teach in a public secondary school. Whether she was the first was less important to me than tracing the manifestations of Anglo-Canadian racism and gender in postwar schools. But Hazel was not interested in being remembered as a trail-blazing *minority* educator; she presented what seemed like rehearsed stories of her successful home economics teaching in which she was able to, as she put it, "white herself" for a June Cleaver–like image.[33] Why did Hazel actively seek to be remembered as a pioneer in teaching yet recount a narrative of accommodation to Anglo-Celtic, patriarchal ideals of postwar citizenship? Was this life narrative shaped by my status as a white, Anglo-Celtic, female? Was this a happy ending to a difficult life story, informed with insights of second-wave feminism and official multiculturalism?

While my role and the context in which this oral history was produced cannot be ignored, Karen Olsen and Linda Shopes argue that academics may actually overestimate their importance in the interview process. They write: "If we define the terms of inquiry by asking the questions, they [interviewees] also define it by answering the questions as they wish."[34] In the act of oral history telling, participants perform stories for their own purposes.[35] After rereading interview transcripts, it became clearer that Hazel had her own agenda that her carefully selected pictures, rehearsed stories, and silences would not let me ignore. As a local-born Chinese or *tusheng* woman, assimilating was a pioneering story. She was part of a generation that welcomed opportunities in an era that espoused racial "egalitarianism."[36] These were opportunities not free from discrimination, but free to perform normative citizenship – the white, Christian, nuclear family ideal – in newly opened spaces, including schools.[37]

The process of interpreting Hazel's story, and those of other women, reveals the false duality of imposing a research agenda on oral histories *or* letting oral histories speak for themselves; and, likewise, of accepting all women's truth claims *or* treating all oral histories with excessive skepticism. Historical knowledge produced through oral histories is a reported discourse created by interviewees in particular contexts and analyzed within scholars' own location and research frameworks. By laying bare their "objective" research lens, inseparable from the ways interviewees seek to construct their own life histories, oral historians of women can make significant claims to political truths about the gendered past.

DISCURSIVE MEANINGS OF WOMEN'S NARRATIVES

Feminist analysis of the knowledge created through oral history is directly related to debates about language versus structure. Post-structuralism privileges the role of signs and discourses to explain gender oppression. From this perspective, the literary devices that women teachers use to construct their oral histories provide a window into what may have happened in the past. Michèle Barrett notes that post-structuralism challenges the ability of materialist feminism's concentration on structural explanations, particularly economic conditions, to understand gender oppression.[38] But materialist feminists provide a challenge of their own. They react against works, associated with post-structuralism, which describe women's lives as floating above their contexts, rather than being embedded within them.[39] An analysis of women teachers' linguistic patterns provides historical meaning only if they are contextualized by additional evidence about the women's working conditions. Given the *orality* of oral history, few scholars in the field ignore the implications of language. The question that persists is: how does discourse relate to the material lives of women?

An analysis of discourse, suggests Kathleen Casey, is an examination of the systems of "controlling metaphors, notions, categories and norms which develop and delimit the subjects' conceptions and expressions of personal, work and social relations."[40] Seen this way, discourse is a way of perceiving women's experiences as deeply embedded within competing forces in society. Mikhail Bakhtin argues that voices create structures through which the reality of a multitude of concrete worlds might be perceived or discussed.[41] The form and context of oral histories are thus inseparable. Language is not synonymous with life, but language choices are grounded by and speak to lived experiences. In order to read women teachers' oral histories effectively, then, I needed to be attentive to discourses and the material world of these texts. Oral historians in all fields must read both for structure, or the experiences of the material world and the workings of it, and for culture, or the ways memories of events and experiences are organized through language.[42]

My study of women's oral histories applied these simultaneous readings. Particularly illustrative of this approach is my interpretation of women's perceptions of postwar professionalism.[43] I was initially surprised that women did not use words like nurturing or caring to describe the qualities of a good teacher; after all, postwar edicts required that they replicate the nuclear family model, inclusive of demure, motherly behaviours. Other studies on women teachers, notably the work of Richard Quantz, note, on the contrary, that interviewees draw upon familial metaphors to describe school life, including mother-student relationships and father-figures for administrators.[44] Not only were such familial references missing from the women's oral histories in my study, but the interviewees actively rejected any imposition of such characterizations in my line of questioning. Instead, the women chose words that portrayed their professional selves as disengaged scholars and technicians for student achievement. Fran Thompson, for example, said that women, like all high school teachers, "loved their subject ... [it] never occurred to them that they had to know anything about their students."[45] Archival research helped to explain these women's discursive constructions: educational officials accused women of lacking professional commitment as a result of their supposed sociable and irrational dispositions, and espoused misgivings about their capabilities for the scientific knowledge necessary in this space-race era. Women teachers' narratives reflect their efforts to cast themselves as much-admired rational, detached professionals and thus claim legitimacy within the public world of postwar secondary schools – an entitlement bestowed on men by virtue of their sex.

Materialist feminists could rightfully question whether such discursive authority merely affected the subjective worlds of these women without any change to their material realities. Admittedly, the extent to which each woman was able to reject familial metaphors, or adopted the language of masculinist professionalism, directly related to her material reality. Women who held graduate degrees, taught in male-dominated subject areas, and/or were heads of departments fiercely refused the language of traditional femininity and made strong claims to rationality. For other women, who did not hold a degree, took crash summer courses to become teachers, and/or returned to teaching after children, claims to a masculinist image of professionalism were hard put. The narratives of those women were dominated rather by a language of survival. Phoebe

McKenzie stated, "There was a strain on me. I knew I had to prove myself," and Muriel Fraser described her career as "managing to survive."[46] Interviewees were fully aware that major social movements against gender discrimination took place after the post–Second World War era.

It would be a mistake, however, to dismiss women's expressions of empowerment as lacking concrete effects on their work. For example, Sophie Canning, a lesbian who was not out during this period in her life, described her teaching self, in terms similar to those of many of the other interviewees, as emotionally detached from students. But for Sophie, unlike the other women, the implication of displaying affection for her female physical education students was ominous. Women who "refused to organize their private lives and sexuality around a man" were considered by postwar psychologists to be mentally unstable, a danger to the nation, and certainly unfit to teach.[47] When asked about her sexual identity, she stated: "I would not tolerate it; [homosexuality] was a terrible word."[48] Sophie's construction of her professionalism was "real" both discursively and materially; it enabled her to keep her job and claim a successful career in her life history.

These examples demonstrate that attention to discourse assists oral historians to understand not only how women construct themselves but also how dominant discourses, shaped by institutional structures, define women's narratives. While this is evident from what interviewees said (metaphors, analogies, word choices), equally revelatory is what was not said. Even after some sixty years from the period under study, some aspects of women's histories needed to go unspoken. Sophie would not use the word homosexuality when referring to her teaching days. Catherine Darby whispered a cryptic story to me about threats during an anonymous late night phone call because men felt "women were pushing for too much."[49] And when I asked Beverley Hurst if she had more decision-making powers than principals, she simply gave me a wry smile and pointed a finger at her own chest.[50] Attention to silences, tone, pauses, and body language reveals as much about the culture of women's work in postwar education as their choice of words. These devices speak directly to the vulnerabilities and difficult knowledge women remember from that era; postwar "democratic" reforms were founded upon a distinction between public and private spheres that made women, and those who did not prescribe to normative citizenship, a sideshow in the public world. Oral historians perpetuate the privatization of women's words if discourse analysis is not an integral part of the transcription process. In an effort to ensure that interviews are intelligible and that interviewees are depicted as intelligent, transcriptions – often by third parties – regularly remove or overlook devices such as digressions, pauses, and body language.[51] It is warranted to eliminate "elements (such as repetitive false starts and mis-statement of names and locations) that are part and parcel to any conversation."[52] But transcription must include "various symbols and codes to represent inflection, intonation, pauses and other aspects of communication not represented by typing out the spoken word alone."[53]

As my research demonstrates, a study founded on an analysis of discourse *or* materialism could not possibly provide the fullest historical explanation of women's teaching lives, since the meaning of these concepts is defined in their relation to one another. Women's narratives are embedded within the historical and contemporary context of their lives. As such, their oral histories reveal the societal imperatives by which they organized their narratives as effective teachers, as well as the ways women manipulated discourses to shape the structural parameters of their working lives. Women teachers' literary devices – the spoken and the unspoken – are neither powerless nor all-powerful. Rather, their language is an active site of negotiation for researchers to explore women teachers' subjectivities and material worlds (that is, factors such as gender, class, race, region, and workplace).

UNDERSTANDING WOMEN'S IDENTITY CONSTRUCTIONS

The question that remains is: what do women teachers' oral histories, which are based on multiple truths and discourses, say about the women's identities? How should feminist oral historians express women as historical subjects? Post-structuralist feminists contend that scholars must give particular attention to individual narratives because each person has a unique identity composed of different social locations. Given the multiple subjectivities of each woman I interviewed – including sexuality, race, socio-economic status, and much more – it would be impossible to present one picture of the "Woman" teacher in postwar Canada. Feminist materialists raise concerns, however, that if the historical record is reduced to a series of individual life histories then larger commentaries on social patterns of women's oppression may go silent. While feminist materialists acknowledge the intersectionality of oppression, they emphasize an understanding of women's solidarity. As a result of searching for similarities among interviewees' narratives, I am able to speak to broader cultural and political agendas that have historically marginalized women teachers.

Standpoint theorists offer feminist oral historians a rationale for generalizing findings from interviewees. Nancy Harstock contends that women as an oppressed group have a vision of society that is distinct from that of men.[54] She argues that this vision, struggled for by women over time, needs to be privileged by researchers. Dorothy Smith refers to standpoint theory as a strategic research method that enables scholars to understand the ruling apparatuses that shape each woman's everyday life.[55] Smith and Harstock turn to a Marxist framework to escape what they see as post-structuralists' endless categories, which ignore the "co-ordering of actual activities," or the patterns of women's experiences and changes in women's lives.[56] My work privileges the unique commentary of women. And this commentary reveals many points of unity among their respective life histories. For example, all interviewees commented on the surveillance of women's morality by postwar school officials.[57] Karen Phillips recalled an inspector telling "the French teacher that she hadn't powdered her nose; she should pay more attention to her appearance," and Grace Logan remembered having to read for students "the little bit from the Bible ... [about] what values there are to be expected in a woman."[58] What emerged across oral histories was a "Woman" teacher who was positioned by officials as the angel, not a political agent, for citizenship.

Locating such solidarity among women's life stories once again provides evidence of much-needed political efficacy for feminist researchers. But such solidarity has not been historically liberating for *all* women. Postcolonial feminists raise concerns that an "authentic womanhood" perpetuates imperialism.[59] Who gets to stand for "Woman"? While the woman teacher was confined by the angel image, the effects of this image depended on her multiple subjectivities. Alma Erickson, a white, middle-class, heterosexual teacher, described with ease looking "neat and smart," which was important because students "from the Indian reserve and those people down there didn't have much money."[60] As a Chinese-Canadian, Hazel Chong had a more precarious status. She remembered a racist attack in which a student yelled "I'm not gonna take anything from a goddamn Chinaman anymore!"[61] If considering race alone then Hazel, unlike Alma, failed to embody ideal citizenship – the white, Woman teacher. This conclusion ignores, however, the intersectionality of a woman's identity. Chandra Mohanty argues that a fixed identity continues to colonize the "Third World Woman" or the "Black Woman" according to White Western images of their powerlessness.[62] She asserts that feminist researchers must be cautious that the "Woman" they identify does not simply reproduce the researchers' vision of non-Western women's cultures as statically "other."

Hazel certainly was not powerless. Hazel drew upon her middle-class, heterosexual status to construct a racialized identity that, as noted earlier, was exemplary of postwar femininity; students praised Hazel for her colour-matched outfits and fine sewing skills. In order to see the hierarchies of identification that define women, it is necessary to be attentive to the individuality *and* collectivity of women's narratives.

Mikhail Bakhtin would argue that it is impossible to interpret oral histories otherwise, since individuals are relational beings. He contends that the notion of private, powerful selves separate from social selves is a myth. The self is defined in its encounter with the other; self-identity is a product of social forces.[63] Each oral history is not an individual narrative *or* a social story. Each oral history in my study is about a teaching self that is free and structured, personal and public, as well as internally and externally shaped. These relational dimensions became clear as I delved further into interviewees' physical representation. I was surprised initially with how much women spoke about their choice of dress during their teaching days.[64] They offered detailed accounts of shopping excursions with colleagues, and their favourite skirts. These choices were important to affirm the nuclear family ideal – in fact tight sweaters were deemed "disturbing for male students" and sheer nylon blouses were banned.[65] By recognizing what Julie Cruikshank terms "the social life of stories,"[66] it became evident how nationalist agendas were embodied by women's presentation of self. What was revealed, as Michel Foucault writes, is "the point where power reaches into the very grain of individuals, touches their bodies and inserts itself into their actions, attitudes, their discourses, and everyday lives."[67]

Yet, within their stories of dress, women presented themselves as autonomous individuals, making personal choices about appearance. How could they recount stories of gender conformity and still claim professional autonomy? What seem like misnomers or contradictory depictions of self are what Kathleen Weiler refers to as "bad fits."[68] "Bad fits" are the very point at which a subject actively negotiates her concept of self in relation to past and present society. While women often represented themselves as accommodating postwar edicts, "bad fits" in their narratives also showed how women crafted oppositional identities. Some women used their oral histories as a way to disclose or remake their identity. Melanie Kilburn, for example, recounted what seemed like a rather generic tale of a girl fixated on a broken nail during a basketball game. She admonished the student, saying: "How could you give a darn about your fingernail?"[69] Whether this event occurred as remembered is unclear but Melanie is representing her "self" as a woman with contemporary feminist critiques of beauty standards. Sophie Canning's narrative disclosed her lesbian identity in ways that seem impossible in postwar years. Sophie characterized herself as having a "dress problem." Unlike other women who wore a tunic to teach physical education, she wore pants: "long blue pants, fairly tight." She framed her decision to wear pants as an act of resistance, immediately commenting that she encouraged same-sex square dancing in her classes. Although she feared being "outed" at this time, she refused to have her historical identity as a teacher defined by hetero-social conformity.

Women do not have a coherent self that moves through history with a single identity. Rather, the self is an unstable identity created through accommodation and resistance to the social systems in which it is embedded both past and present. Women have the power to articulate a coherent identity, but it is for the oral historian to explain the formation of that identity as an ideological struggle for agency. Identity formation, then, needs to be deconstructed to understand common frameworks of women's differentiated experiences. What it meant to be a woman teacher, and how that was defined according to each subject's material needs and available languages, was the focus of my oral history research. In exploring that meaning, I read women teachers' oral histories as individual and social stories and for differentiation and solidarity.

Feminist scholars of oral history must wrestle with the theoretical challenges posed by both feminist post-structuralism and feminist materialism. Post-structural analysis encourages oral historians to deconstruct narrative form and from that to locate the multiplicity and individuality of women's life experiences. Feminist materialist insights are needed to focus oral historians on the way relations of power shape women's histories and thus provide a place of solidarity from which to speak about gender.[70] Approached as complementary rather than fragmenting, these theoretical frameworks provide oral historians with the tools to interpret richer meanings from women's narratives. A dual reading of women teachers' oral histories enabled me to explore how national agendas and school structures limited women teachers' claims to professionalism, while also demonstrating the ways in which women invoked or rejected cultural discourses, from motherhood to morality, to assert their authority. Although these approaches are often contested within feminist theory, together their productive tensions provide a framework for "good" feminist research in oral history – research that voices women's historical experiences in an effort to unsettle oppression.

NOTES

1 This chapter draws from my book *Democracy's Angels: The Work of Women Teachers* (Montreal and Kingston: McGill-Queen's University Press, 2012). I wish to thank the anonymous reviewers for *Democracy's Angels* and this *Reader* for their helpful feedback. I am most grateful to the women teachers who shared their life histories, which pushed me to reconsider my feminist approach to oral history. This work was made possible thanks to the support of the Social Sciences and Humanities Research Council of Canada.

2 Sandra Harding, "Introduction," in *Feminism and Methodology*, edited by S. Harding (Bloomington: Indiana University Press, 1987), 8–9.

3 Barbara Johnson, *A World of Difference* (Baltimore: Johns Hopkins University Press, 1987), 37.

4 Jennifer Wicke, "Celebrity Material: Materialist Feminism and the Culture of Celebrity," *The South Atlantic Quarterly* (fall 1994): 741.

5 Joan Sangster notes in chapter 5 of this *Reader* that women's historians had been addressing issues of narrative construction and identity politics long before the "linguistic turn." These issues have, however, become much more subject to theoretical consideration among oral historians in the last twenty years.

6 Joan Sangster, "Telling Our Stories: Feminist Debates and the Use of Oral History," in *Rethinking Canada: The Promise of Women's History*, 3rd edition, edited by V. Strong-Boag and A. Fellman (Toronto: Oxford University Press, 1997), 317.

7 See, for example, Heidi Gottfried, ed., *Feminism and Social Change: Bridging Theory and Practice* (Champaign, IL: University of Illinois Press, 1996).

8 Marjorie Theobald, "Teachers, Memory and Oral History," in *Telling Women's Lives: Narrative Inquiries in the History of Women's Education*, edited by K. Weiler and S. Middleton (Philadelphia: Open University Press, 1999), 21.

9 Kathleen Weiler, "Reflections on Writing a History of Women Teachers," in *Telling Women's Lives*, 44.

10 In chapter 5 of this *Reader*, Joan Sangster similarly argues that these theoretical approaches cannot simply be collapsed.

11 Luisa Passerini, "Women's Personal Narratives: Myths, Experiences, and Emotions," in *Interpreting Women's Lives: Feminist Theory and Personal Narratives*, edited by Personal Narratives Group (Bloomington: Indiana University Press, 1989), 197.

12 Jacques Derrida, *Of Grammatology* (Baltimore: Johns Hopkins University Press, 1976).

13 Joan Scott, "Experience," in *Feminists Theorize the Political*, edited by J. Butler and J.W. Scott (New York: Routledge, 1992).

14 Llewellyn, *Democracy's Angels*. For this research, I conducted twenty oral histories from 2001 to 2005 with women who had taught in Vancouver or Toronto for at least two years between 1945 and 1960.

15 For example, from 1930 until 1970 in Toronto, there were only two female principals, and that number would not double to four until 1980. Cecilia Reynolds, "Hegemony and Hierarchy: Becoming a Teacher in Toronto, 1930–1980," *Historical Studies in Education* 2, no. 1 (1990): 111, 115.

16 Ibid., 128. See, for example, interviews with June West, Karen Phillips, Ellen Stewart, Grace Logan, and Donna Weber in *Democracy's Angels*. Pseudonyms were provided for interviewees in my study, except in the case of Hazel Chong, who provided subsequent permission to use her real name.

17 Kate Rousmanière, *City Teachers: Teaching and School Reform in Historical Perspective* (New York: Teachers College Press, 1997), 1–2.

18 Llewellyn, *Democracy's Angels*, 118–20.

19 Interview with Donna Weber (pseudonym), conducted with Kristina Llewellyn (Vancouver, BC, 22 May 2005). Interview copy with the author.

20 Sandra Harding, "Conclusion," in *Feminism and Methodology*, 182–4; Spalter-Roth and Hartmann, "Small Happiness: The Feminist Struggle to Integrate Social Research with Social Activism," in *Feminist Approaches to Theory and Methodology*, edited by S. Hesse-Biber, C. Gilmartin, and R. Lydenberg (New York: Oxford, 1999), 334–6.

21 Harding, "Conclusion," 184.

22 Spalter-Roth and Hartmann, "Small Happiness," 340–1.

23 See, for example, Alice Duffy Rinehart, *Mortal in the Immortal Profession: An Oral History of Teaching* (New York: Irvington Publishers, 1983).

24 Paul Thompson, *Voice of the Past: Oral History* (Oxford: University of Oxford Press, 1978), 90.

25 Kathleen Weiler, "Remembering and Representing Life Choices: A Critical Perspective on Teachers' Oral History Narratives," *Qualitative Studies in Education* 5, no. 1 (1992): 40.

26 Donna Haraway, *Simians, Cyborgs, and Women: The Reinvention of Nature* (New York: Routledge, 1991), 191.

27 Haraway, *Simians, Cyborgs, and Women*, 187; see also, Donna Haraway, "Situated Knowledges: The Science Question in Feminism and the Privilege of Partial Perspective," *Feminist Studies* 14, no. 3 (1988): 583.

28 Leslie Rebecca Bloom, "Stories of One's Own: Nonunitary Subjectivity in Narrative Representation," *Qualitative Inquiry* 2, no. 2 (1996): 176–88.

29 Lynn Abrams, *Oral History Theory* (New York: Routledge, 2010); Michael Frisch, *A Shared Authority: Essays on the Craft and Meaning of Oral and Public History* (New York: SUNY Press, 1990). See also, Sherna Berger Gluck and Daphne Patai, eds., *Women's Words: The Feminist Practice of Oral History* (New York: Routledge, 1991).

30 Abrams, *Oral History Theory*, 71.

31 For more information on the limitations posed by the Tri-Council Policy Statement, especially for graduate students, see Nancy Janovicek's chapter (chapter 3) in this *Reader*.

32 Kathryn Anderson and Dana C. Jack, "Learning to Listen: Interview Techniques and Analyses," in *Women's Words: The Feminist Practice of Oral History*, edited by Gluck and Patai (New York: Routledge, 1991), 11–26.

33 Hazel Chong, interview with Kristina Llewellyn (Vancouver, BC, June 2008). Interview copy with the author. See also Sadie Chow (pseudonym initially given to Hazel Chong), interview with Kristina Llewellyn (Vancouver, BC, 16 September 2005). Interview copy with the author.

34 Karen Olsen and Linda Shopes, "Crossing Boundaries, Building Bridges: Doing Oral History among Working-Class Women and Men," in *Women's Words: The Feminist Practice of Oral History*, edited by Gluck and Patai (New York: Routledge, 1991), 196–7. See also Pamela Sugiman's chapter (chapter 14) in this *Reader*.

35 Abrams, *Oral History Theory*, 136–7.

36 Wing Chung Ng, *The Chinese in Vancouver, 1945–80: The Pursuit of Identity and Power* (Vancouver: UBC Press, 1999), 40–1. See also David T.H. Lee, *A History of Chinese in Canada* (Taipei: Canada Free Press, 1967).

37 Kristina Llewellyn, "Teaching June Cleaver, Being Hazel Chong: An Oral History of Gender, Race, and National 'Character,'" in *Writing Feminist History: Productive Pasts and New Directions*, edited by C. Carstairs and N. Janovicek (Vancouver: UBC Press, 2013), 178–99.

38 Michèle Barrett, "Words and Things: Materialism and Method in Contemporary Feminist Analysis," in *Destabilizing Theory: Contemporary Feminist Debates*, edited by M. Barrett and A. Phillips (Cambridge: Polity Press, 1992), 202–3.

39 For example, Judith Butler, *Gender Troubles: Feminism and the Subversion of Identity* (New York: Routledge, 1990).

40 Kathleen Casey, *I Answer with My Life: Life Histories of Women Teachers Working for Social Change* (New York: Routledge, 1993), 31.

41 Mikhail Bakhtin, *The Dialogic Imagination* (Austin: University of Texas Press, 1981), as quoted by Casey, *I Answer with My Life*, 20–1. See also, Joy Parr, "Gender History and Historical Practice," in *Gender and History in Canada*, edited by J. Parr and M. Rosenfeld (Toronto: Copp Clark Limited, 1996), 15. Parr argues: "Experiences are not made by discourses, but discourses are the medium through which experiences are comprehensible … a way to understand how power works."

42 Popular Memory Group, "Popular Memory: Theory, Politics, Method," in *Making Histories*, edited by R. Johnson, G. McLennan, B. Schwartz, and D. Sutton (London: Hutchinson, 1982), 228–34. See also Petra Munro, *Subject to Fiction: Women Teachers' Life History Narratives and the Cultural Politics of Resistance* (Philadelphia: Open University Press, 1998).

43 Llewellyn, *Democracy's Angels*, 50–77.

44 See, for example, Richard Quantz, "The Complex Vision of Female Teachers and the Failure of Unionization in the 1930s: An Oral History," in *The Teacher's Voice: A Social History of Teaching in Twentieth Century America*, edited by R.J. Altenbaugh (London: Falmer Press, 1992).

45 Fran Thompson (pseudonym), interview with Kristina Llewellyn (Toronto, ON, 20 November 2001). Interview copy with the author.

46 Llewellyn, *Democracy's Angels*, 58–60.

47 Sheila L. Cavanagh, "The Heterosexualization of the Ontario Woman Teacher in the Postwar Period," *Canadian Women Studies* 18, no. 1 (1998): 66; Madiha Didi Khayatt, *Lesbian Teachers: An Invisible Presence* (Albany: SUNY Press, 1992), 21–6.

48 Sophie Canning (pseudonym), interview with Kristina Llewellyn (Salt Spring Island, BC, 19 September 2005). Interview copy with the author.

49 Catharine Darby, (pseudonym), interview with Kristina Llewellyn (Vancouver, BC, 19 May 2005). Interview copy with the author.

50 Beverley Hurst (pseudonym), interview with Kristina Llewellyn (Toronto, ON, 14 December 2001). Interview copy with the author.

51 See, for example, Sue Middleton and Helen May, *Teachers Talk Teaching, 1915–1995: Early Childhood Schools and Teachers' Colleges* (New Zealand: Dunmore Press, 1997).

52 James Fogerty, "Oral History and Archives: Documenting Context," in *History of Oral History: Foundations and Methodology*, edited by T.L. Charlton, L.E. Myers, and R. Sharpless (Lanham, MD: AltaMira Press, 2007), 207.

53 Elinor A. Mazé, "The Uneasy Page: Transcribing and Editing Oral History," in *Handbook of Oral History*, edited by T.L. Charlton, L.E. Myers, and R. Sharpless (Lanham, MD: AltaMira Press, 2006), 244.

54 Nancy Harstock, "The Feminist Standpoint," in *Feminism and Methodology*, edited by S. Harding (Bloomington: Indiana University Press, 1987), 159–60. See also, Patricia Hill Collins, "Learning from the Outsider Within: The Sociological Significance of Black Feminist Thought," in *Feminist Approaches to Theory and Methodology*, edited by S. Hesse-Biber, C. Gilmartin, and R. Lydenberg (New York: Oxford, 1999).

55 Dorothy Smith, *The Everyday World as Problematic* (Toronto: University of Toronto Press, 1987), 111.

56 Ibid., 141.

57 For more on women teachers' embodiment of citizenship, see Kristina Llewellyn, "'Better Teachers, Biologically Speaking': The Authority of the 'Marrying-Kind' of Teacher in Postwar Schools," in *Contesting Bodies and Nation in Canadian History*, edited by P. Gentile and J. Nicholas (Toronto: University of Toronto Press, 2013).

58 Karen Phillips (pseudonym), interview with Kristina Llewellyn (Toronto, ON, 26 November 2001). Interview copy with the author; Grace Logan

(pseudonym), interview with Kristina Llewellyn (Vancouver, BC, 19 September 2005). Interview copy with the author.

59 Barrett, "Words and Things," 210.

60 Interview with Karen Phillips; Alma Erickson (pseudonym), interview with Kristina Llewellyn (Vancouver, BC, 15 September 2005). Interview copy with the author.

61 Interviews with Hazel Chong, 2005 and 2008. Hazel recounted the same story during both interviews.

62 Chandra Talpade Mohanty, "Under Western Eyes: Feminist Scholarship and Colonial Discourses," in *Third World Women and the Politics of Feminism*, edited by C. Mohanty, A. Russo, and L. Torres (Bloomington: Indiana University Press, 1991), 54.

63 Mikhail Bakhtin, *The Dialogic Imagination* (Austin: University of Texas Press, 1981), as paraphrased by Casey, *I Answer with My Life*, 20–6.

64 Llewellyn, *Democracy's Angels*, 90.

65 *The Province*, "Tight Clothes in Dirty Thirties Never Raised Teachers' Eyebrows," 9 September 1958; *The Province*, "'Naughty Nylon' Problem Invades City Schools," 28 May 1952.

66 Julie Cruikshank, *The Social Life of Stories: Narrative and Knowledge in the Yukon Territory* (Vancouver: UBC Press, 2000). See also Cruikshank's chapter (chapter 8) in this *Reader*.

67 Michel Foucault, "Prison Talk," in *Power/Knowledge: Selected Interviews and Other Writings, 1972–1977*, edited by C. Gordon (New York: Pantheon Books, 1980), 39.

68 Weiler, "Remembering and Representing Life Histories," 43.

69 Melanie Kilburn (pseudonym), interview with Kristina Llewellyn (Toronto, ON, 21 January 2002). Interview copy with the author.

70 Sangster, "Telling Our Stories," 317.

7

A Canadian Family Talks about Oma's Life in Nazi Germany: Three-Generational Interviews and Communicative Memory

Alexander Freund

On 25 May 2006, Irma Hiebert sat down at the large, wooden dining room table in her daughter's turn-of-the century house in Winnipeg's Wolseley neighbourhood to talk about her life in Nazi Germany. Around the table sat her daughter Nancy Pauls, her granddaughter Karla Schulz, and I, a stranger to the family. All four participants came to this oral history interview from a specific vantage point of experience: Hiebert, born in Germany in 1919, had lived through the Third Reich and was the only "contemporary witness" in the group. Pauls, born in 1959, and Schulz, born in 1985, grew up in Canada. I was born in Germany in 1969 and immigrated to Canada in 2002. Although we were separated by space, generation, and experience, oral history – the practice of "actively making memories" – brought us together.[1] In particular, I was interested in finding out how this Canadian family "made memories" out of a difficult German past.

Less than half an hour into our conversation, the following discussion about Nazis and German-Canadian identity developed:

PAULS: I've heard the stories about the war, and your [Hiebert's] brother, and the Nazis. I've heard them all my life. Then I heard them in school. Then it was different. Then it felt like [...] these are parts of history [...] And I didn't realize the rest of the world knew about it [...] Then I was a little embarrassed, about being German.
HIEBERT: Oh, I see.
PAULS: I don't – I didn't feel embarrassed, even though I had a sense that you had a sense of shame about what your country did, and those kinds of things.

HIEBERT: Yes, I do.

PAULS: I didn't feel that way but all of a sudden I felt like, I don't think I want everybody to know I'm German [laughs].

SCHULZ: Well, and see, I had the opposite reaction, immediately of being like, "No, I'm German. German people aren't like that. My grandmother was there, she wasn't like that."[2]

This brief exchange hints at the complex ways in which families make memories, negotiate history, and construct family stories. It is not characterized by the pattern of the old handing preserved memories down to the young. Rather, these family memories are constructed through communicative interaction. Family lore, memory, and school knowledge interact with one another; often-told stories and convictions provide a scaffold for asking uncomfortable questions, testing new interpretations, and premièring secret feelings. Together, family members ever so subtly rearrange their own roles and those of their relatives, much like a group of playwrights meeting over coffee and cake to work on a play. Such redrafting is informed by individual experiences and collective memories. It is also shaped by the communicative situation, in this case the oral history interview. At stake, for all *four* participants in this casual yet formal "table talk,"[3] was the need to make sense of a troubling past, to understand one's own relationship to this past, and to find and secure one's place in society through the sharing of stories.

This article explores the use and usefulness of the three-generational interview method and the concept of communicative memory for studies of family memory. I begin by describing and explaining the three-generational interview method and the concept of collective memory. After introducing the three interviewees, I outline two of the "foundational family stories" that family members told during our interviews. I then analyze some of the communicative structures shaping the dynamics of the interview and the construction of family memory. I conclude with an assessment of the usefulness of the interview method and the concept of communicative memory for oral history practice. Both the method and the concept, I argue throughout this article, are invaluable for the study of family memory. The stories generated in the group interview do more than simply reveal additional information not generated in the one-on-one interviews. They show the family's communicative interaction in creating and negotiating family memories – memories that constituted and were constituted by communicative memory.

THREE-GENERATIONAL INTERVIEW AND COMMUNICATIVE MEMORY

My use of the three-generational interview method is inspired in particular by the work of German social psychologists who interviewed German families in order to understand how they (re-)constructed the Nazi past through storytelling about personal or relatives' experiences in the Third Reich.[4] Family interviews attempt to recreate the casual family talks around the kitchen table in which family members construct – often *en passant* – family memories and oral traditions.[5]

Family interviews show us how comfortable or uncomfortable families are when talking about the past. They document families' repertoires of anecdotes and well-rehearsed stories. They shed light on silences, myths, and taboos and on the willingness of families to engage with new and perhaps troubling questions. If families are perceptive and reflective, they may be able to develop a meta-narrative about remembering and storytelling, describing in some detail how they learned family anecdotes and what these anecdotes meant to them. Family interviewing seeks to understand how members of different generations are involved in memory construction – an interactive construction beyond the unidirectional "handing down" and "receiving" between the old and the young.

Family interviews are usually preceded by extensive life story interviews with members of different generations in one family. Members of at least two generations are then brought together in the family interview, to talk about the experiences of the oldest generation. Interviewers may ask for emotional feedback ("What is it like to participate in this family discussion?" "Can you imagine what your mother may be feeling right now?"), for elaboration, examples, and clarification ("Do you know how many people your father employed in the factory?" "What do you know about your great-grandfather?") as well as reflections ("Your grandmother lived through some very difficult years in Germany, in the Nazi period. So, how did that affect your visits to Germany or how you felt about the places?"). Next to storytelling, interviewers may use photographs, film sequences, or other memory techniques to stimulate intergenerational remembering and dialogue. The three-generational interview method is closely linked to the concept of "communicative memory" developed by Jan Assmann and Harald Welzer. We have long left behind the idea of individual memory as a computer-like system of storage and retrieval, and instead view memory as a process. Cognitive psychology and neurosciences have helped us better understand how memory works through interactive communication.[6] Assmann differentiates collective memory by distinguishing "cultural memory" and "communicative memory."[7] Cultural memory is defined as a society's long-term memory. Communicative memory is the short-term memory that is maintained by the living three to four generations, stretching over a span of some eighty years and continually moving forward in time. Communicative memory "includes those varieties of collective memory that are based exclusively on everyday communications. These varieties, which M[aurice] Halbwachs gathered and analyzed under the concept of collective memory, constitute the field of oral history."[8] Communicative memory is based on the fleeting, unstable, disorganized, unspecialized communication between people who may alternate between the roles of storyteller and listener. Communication among students on the schoolyard, within the family around the kitchen table, among colleagues at the water cooler, or among strangers in the supermarket are examples of such everyday communication. "Through this manner of communication, each individual composes a memory which, as Halbwachs has shown, is (a) socially mediated and (b) relates to a group."[9] People do not communicate with just anyone, but are connected through group membership, be it the family, a neighbourhood group, a political party, or a nation: "Every individual belongs to numerous such groups and therefore entertains numerous collective self-images and memories."[10] Welzer applies the concept of communicative memory to the individual and the family, asking how memory is continually negotiated and constructed, often through stories about the past that engender historical interpretations *en passant*.[11]

In their book *Opa war kein Nazi* [Opa was not a Nazi], Welzer and his colleagues described communicative structures that help explain how families construct memory. Two of those, "interpretive patterns" and "empty speaking" (*leeres Sprechen*) are central to the analysis in this chapter.[12] I have added the notion of "foundational family stories" and "loss of detail" as two other narrative structures. I explain these concepts later on.

The purpose, then, of my group interview with the Hiebert family was to see communicative memory in action. As in all interviewing, however, I could not be just an outside observer. As I will note throughout my analysis, I was a participant in this communicative activity, albeit not as a member of the family group.

INTERVIEWS AND PARTICIPANTS

Three members of the Hiebert family are at the centre of this study: Irma Hiebert; her daughter Nancy Pauls; and her granddaughter Karla Schulz.

Irma Hiebert (née Busch) was born in Hamburg in 1919 into a middle-class family. Her mother, Helene (née Broders, b. 1892), was a housewife; her father, Wilhelm (b. 1895), owned a tool-making factory and a store that sold second-hand hardware. After tenth grade, in 1936, Hiebert worked for seventeen years in her father's office. The family lived in a large, six-room rented apartment and employed domestic servants. Hiebert explained that she was too old to be in the Hitler Youth, unlike her sister, Leni (b. 1920), and her brother, Willy (b. 1925). Willy died in 1943. Later that year, in July 1943, Allied bombs destroyed the store. The family evacuated its apartment and moved into the grandmother's mansion on the outskirts of Hamburg. After the war, the father rebuilt the store and helped the Allies dismantle machinery. Hiebert's mother died in 1947, and when her father remarried shortly thereafter, Irma's relationship with him soured. She decided to leave Hamburg. At the age of thirty-four, in 1953, she im-migrated to Canada, where she worked as a domestic servant for a Jewish family in Winnipeg until she married a Mennonite man from Winkler, Manitoba, in 1954. He had served in the Canadian Air Force in England during the war and entered the Netherlands and Germany as part of the occupation force. From 1958 to 1962, they lived at a military base in Ger-many. Hiebert's husband died in 2000. They had two daughters, a son, eight grandchildren, and three great-grandchildren. Hiebert died in 2012.

Hiebert was among a quarter of a million German immigrants to come to postwar Canada. She was one of twenty-five thousand single German women who intended to work as maids in a Canadian household. Her experience of working for a Jewish family right after the war was not un-common for postwar German immigrants. Neither was her experience of marrying shortly after her arrival in Canada.

Nancy Pauls was born in Germany in 1959. After the family's return to Winnipeg, she completed school and became interested in religion. At the age of eighteen, she married a Mennonite man, and they had a son and a daughter. They separated in 1999. Since high school, Pauls has had various jobs in a daycare, a small business, and a retail setting. In 1980, she was among the founding members of an independent church. She has made her house on Home Street into a home not only for her mother and her children, but also for her extended family and friends. While there have been several studies of postwar German immigrants, we know vir-tually nothing about their children or grandchildren, and they themselves have produced few textual sources about their experiences of growing up German in Canada.

Karla Schulz was born in Winnipeg in 1985. Her mother is Irma Hie-bert's daughter Jackie; her father, Theodore, is a Mennonite who worked for a credit union. From the age of six to ten, she lived in New Brunswick, where Hiebert visited her three times. When she was fourteen, she moved to Roblin, a small town in southern Manitoba, where "there was a lot of racism and just general hatred for people who thought they were different. I was already old enough that that really bothered me in a way I wanted to do something about." Her mother told her stories of being called "Kraut" at school, but she herself never experienced anything negative related to her German background. By the time she was eleven, she knew that she was gay and that she could not tell her parents. She confided in her older sister and brother. Eventually, she broke with her parents and after graduating from high school in 2003, she moved in with Hiebert and Pauls's family. Shortly before, Hiebert had taken Schulz on a trip to Germany with Pauls and a number of other family members. Hiebert took all of her children and grandchildren to Germany at some point in their lives. Schulz was twenty years old at the time of the interview and a student at the University of Winnipeg. The three women are among 2.7 million Canadians (and 109,000 Winnipeggers) who, according to Statistics Canada, in 2001 identified as German or part-German.

All three women were interviewed individually in 2005 by my research assistant, Angela Thiessen, a German-speaking Mennonite from Winnipeg and then an undergraduate student at the University of Winnipeg. I chose to interview all three women as a group in 2006 because they encompassed three generations, including a member of the first generation who had lived through the Third Reich as an adult. Furthermore, they seemed to be willing to speak about the Nazi past. I spent three hours at their home, two of which were recorded. There was immediate rapport, in part because Thiessen had developed a trusting relationship and in part because I am from Irma Hiebert's hometown of Hamburg. This rapport did not diminish even when I asked difficult questions about the family's involvement in the Nazi state. During the group interview, I let the family reminisce together. If needed, I intervened by directly asking family members for a response to the topic that we were discussing at the moment.

FOUNDATIONAL FAMILY STORIES

"From countless incidents, families choose a few stories to pass on, the funniest or perhaps the most telling," S.J. Zeitlin et al. state in *A Celebration of American Family Folklore*.[13] Indeed, in the course of the interviews, several stories about Hiebert's life in the Third Reich and the postwar period emerged as central in the family's communicative memory. I call these "foundational family stories," because they are the foundation on which other stories are built and they act as a foundation for the family unit. The three foundational family stories about the Third Reich were about Hiebert's brother, Willy; the fate of Hiebert's homosexual co-worker, Mr Erjardt; and the bombing of Hamburg. The foundational family stories about the postwar period and Hiebert's migration centred on Hiebert's decision to emigrate; her getting a job as a maid in a Jewish Canadian home with the help of Jewish German friends; and her marriage to a Mennonite man of peasant background. Thus, all foundational family stories emerged from Hiebert's experiences rather than those of Pauls or Schulz. Yet, all three participated in selecting and highlighting certain stories. And while all family members believed they were telling the same story, there were a number of significant differences between those stories. Here I focus on the first two of the Third Reich stories.

As Ruth Finnegan points out, "[the] explicit crystallization of a family's shared memories also results from a family history or individual auto-biography being written or recorded."[14] Thus, family memories are not simply formed and frozen at one moment in time and then "performed" over and over again. Rather, their crystallization is always shaped by the communicative situation. This can be the writing of a family history or autobiography, as Finnegan notes, but also a family interview. It is there-fore important to remember that these foundational family stories were created in the context of interviews. We heard family stories that were selected from the family's repertoire of anecdotes and rearranged by the narrators. These family stories were, in other words, "crystallizing" as we recorded them.

During the interviews, Pauls and Schulz also spoke of how they had learned the stories. Hence, a meta-narrative about intergenerational storytelling was told.[15]

Oma's Brother's Death

Irma Hiebert began her life story with her brother's death: "I came over to Canada in 1953, because [...] we had a death in our family; my brother died very suddenly. My mother died twelve [sic] years later and then my father married again after ten months. I was working for my father. We just did not get along after that."[16] Hiebert repeated this sequence of events several times throughout the interviews. The brother's death was tightly interwoven with the bombing of Hamburg, the mother's death, the father's remarriage, and her own emigration. The decade 1943–1954 is at the centre of her life story and constituted the major turning point of her life.

In the course of the interview, she revealed further details about the nature and circumstances of Willy's death. The second time she mentioned it, she explained that he had died of a brain haemorrhage. Later, she elaborated:

> It was a very severe haemorrhage. But he was arrested by the Nazis. My children tell me sometimes, there was a movie, it is called *Swing Kids*.[17] He had friends, he was still in school, he was sixteen I guess and they liked American music and they had maybe sort of a group, I do not know. I do not remember much of that but they arrested him, maybe some of the other friends too, I guess. Then for three weekends he had to go to jail on the weekend. That was in 1942. And he died in 1943.

Swing Kids were apolitical bourgeois teenagers, mostly in Hamburg, but also in other German cities, during the Nazi period. They enjoyed listening to Jazz, wearing long hair, dressing loudly, and dancing wildly. They were harassed by the Gestapo and Hitler Youth for being so different from the Nazi ideal of youth.[18] Irma Hiebert continued:

> I do not know what they [Nazis] did to him in those three weekends that he was there but maybe they told him: "Do not tell anybody what we did or what happened to you." Maybe that happened. It must be a year after when he had this brain haemorrhage. My oldest daughter Jackie was saying – we talked about it not too long ago – if it had anything to do with it, that they hit him over the head. I do not know why he had the haemorrhage [...] I do not know if it had anything to do with it but sometimes you just wonder.

In the family interview, Hiebert added: "That was probably a medical reason, you know, I talked to my doctor at that time – maybe his veins were too thin or maybe that was the reason, you know."

Much of Hiebert's story is corroborated by documents in the Hamburg State Archives. In mid-October 1942, Hiebert's brother, Wilhelm Busch, served two weekends in jail for illegally purchasing a revolver. He was sentenced along with twelve other teenagers who had participated in "disseminating obscene literature," theft, illegal trade, and sale of coffee, stationery, and firearms. While investigating these offences, the Gestapo also collected information about Swing youth of the groups "Bismarckclub" and "Kaffee-Hag." Busch died from a brain haemorrhage on 30 May 1943 in the Altona Children's Hospital.[19]

How did the next two generations speak about Hiebert's memory? In her individual interview, Pauls had not mentioned the story.[20] Schulz had mentioned it a few times without giving much detail beyond the points that he had been sick, in prison, and in the Hitler Youth, and that he had died.[21] It is only through the family interview that we get a better sense of how they remembered this story. In the group interview, Pauls and Schulz explained that they had "always known" the story. Schulz said: "You're a kid and your parents, your mom is talking to your grandmother and you put it together. No one ever sat me down and told me about this, but just over the years I knew he was in jail and I knew that he had been taken in that manner and then that he had died." Pauls added: "I remember growing up and you hear little pieces and you hear a little bit more of the picture." Referring to a photograph of Willy that Hiebert kept in her bedroom, the family discussion quoted in the introduction developed.

After Hiebert mentioned that her brother and sister "both had to join that Hitler Youth," Schulz commented that she always felt "like my family were also victims in this. And the German people were also victims of what happened." Schulz explained that she did not want to excuse people who ignored what was happening, but that for Hiebert it must have seemed hopeless to do anything against the Nazis. She went on to state that her Oma felt guilty about this: "I didn't feel like she had carelessly stood by and knew what was happening but just couldn't be bothered. It wasn't that way at all. It was just this futile feeling of wanting to change it and wanting it to not be happening." Pauls then brought up the idea of "balance": "I feel like the stories you've told, Mama, are about trying to balance not saying the wrong thing at the wrong time. You've talked about how teachers in school would say to kids, 'if you hear your parents saying something bad about the Nazis or against Hitler, you have to report your parents.' That was always kind of a freaky thing."

Hiebert and Pauls also recounted that the family had received Willy's military draft papers half a year after his death. Hiebert commented: "My sister and I, we always thought, why did he have to die? And at that point we said, 'Now we know why he died. He didn't have to fight for the Nazis.' I don't know, it was something we thought. Maybe God thought he's not going to do that. I don't know [laughs]. You find something, you think about things like that." "Well, you do, Mama," Pauls agreed, "because I mean, I don't know your parents well enough to say how they behaved with you children or what they taught you. But I know your sister and I know you. And I cannot conceive that your brother, coming from the same family, would have wanted to fight for the Nazis."

When I asked her why she was certain about this, Pauls elaborated: "The two most amazing women on the planet, as far I am concerned, would be my mother and my Tante [aunt] Leni. And I mean, she was the same, in that she had incredibly strong, passionate, very articulate feelings about the rights of others and how you respect people no matter where they are from and who they are. This is what God wants us to be doing." Together with Hiebert, Pauls then described one of her aunt's visits to Winnipeg. One day, they came across an Aboriginal demonstration downtown. Her sister, Hiebert recalls, "wanted to join" the protest. "And then I went into an argument with her in German." Pauls then vividly described the scene of the two women arguing in German in front of the protest about the situation of Aboriginals in Canada.

At the end of the interview, Schulz summarized Willy's story: "He died, he was not killed by the Nazis but that idea – and that was a familiar story that they felt, her and her sister, almost that there was a reason that he died and this was the reason. And that they were like almost grateful for the death of their brother because it saved him from that."

The three women agreed on the basic facts of Willy's death but ascribed different meanings to it, and used it in different ways. Despite the importance of her brother's death to her own life, Hiebert's factual recounting is sparse. Yet, if her memory is failing and if she had given more details in earlier years, they are not provided by Pauls and Schulz, who tell the story in their own ways. Hiebert offered a detached description of Willy's death, which could not be clearly ascribed to a medical problem, Nazi brutality, or God's intervention. Throughout the interviews, Hiebert emphasized, "I hate the Nazis until I die," but if her brother's death was any motivation for this hate, it is invisible in her story. Pauls and Schulz used this episode to explain how they had learned family stories, how they were confronted with different interpretations at school, and to offer their own interpretations, depicting their family members as victims of war and Nazi terror and as heroes who fight for tolerance and freedom.

The "Gay Man" in Oma's Office

The story of Herr Erjardt, the "gay man" in Oma's office, played an important role in Schulz's life story. Hiebert had not mentioned the story in her individual interview. Pauls had referred to the story to explain why she believed her grandfather had not supported the Nazis or believed in Nazi ideology: "The fact that there was a man who was a homosexual who worked in my grandfather's factory [sic], and they took him away, and just the horror of that, and just the … there is nothing that you can do. Obviously, my grandfather had no problem with him working there, and him as a person." She described the situation as a "struggle" for her grand-father. While for Pauls, this story was about her grandfather, for Schulz, it was about Oma's values and her own struggles. Schulz had been rejected by her parents because of her homosexuality. Her Oma was "upset" about "how my mom could not handle it and how my mom was horrible about it. Oma, she gets really passionate about this because of the Nazis. There was a gay man in their office and he got taken and that sort of thing – hor-rible, horrible that it happened to her and I would probably prefer if she was a little bit intolerant and had not had to have those experiences."

In the group interview, Schulz introduced this story. When describing their visit to Hamburg in 2003, the story "came up," Schulz said, as they were looking for the location of the family store. Later in the interview, Pauls referred to the story to explain how her grandfather had balanced the need to survive and his rejection of the Nazis. Hiebert added further details: "The secret police phoned and wanted to talk to my father and then they did and then they came over. And this young man, he was with us a long time. They believed he was gay. Paragraph 75 [sic], and they remember. Anyway, they came and picked him up and I don't know what happened later to him."

The Nazi state prosecuted male homosexuals under the constitution's paragraph 175, which had been on the books before the Nazi seizure of power, but was made more severe in 1935. Even before then, gay men had been arrested, imprisoned, put in concentration camps, and forcibly castrated. Erjardt may have been one of the fifty thousand men sen-tenced for "unnatural sex" and identified in concentration camps with a pink triangle. There is, however, no record of him in the Hamburg State Archives.[22]

Schulz and Pauls explained how this experience made Hiebert, and consequently her children and grandchildren, tolerant:

SCHULZ: Going through that experience made Oma such a person who cared about minorities and who cared about rights for every-one … That was always this really important lesson that she would teach us … That always made me really proud. How much Oma cared about those things and how angry she would still feel and how she always stood up and was not quiet, like, ever in my growing up about issues like that. And didn't let the fact that she was an old grandmother stop her from wanting to go in the gay pride parade … If she has something she believes in, not being able to stand up for what she believed in, in that time, I think really caused her to teach all of us that we have to treasure our freedom in Canada … PAULS: It has translated to all of your grandchildren, that sense of tolerance and acceptance of other people, and in a way that you are willing to stand up and fight for.

When asked how they would explain why the Nazis persecuted gays, Schulz and Pauls began a dialogue about different interpretations. Schulz had taken a university course on the politics of racism and drew on this knowledge to argue that "it wasn't just the Jewish people, it was mentally handicapped people and gypsies and gay people … anyone who wasn't a part of this new race that Hitler was trying to create" was persecuted. Pauls interjected to say, "there is an insanity level to it … bottom line for me it has to do with [Hitler] being utterly insane. But also there is this sort of mob mentality or where you – everybody kind of gets on this bandwagon that says, we are better than they are and we can make ourselves better somehow, the more we step on them. Which makes me ashamed not so much to be German as to be human." Schulz explained that she had studied "the roots of fascism" at university, "all the theories, of like, how can you explain this apparently very insane thing. And I don't think you can just say it was because German people hated Jewish people, it had always been so. Or it was just a mob mentality. I think there is pretty calculated planning and pretty rationalized evil there. I believe there are traces in modernity and all that kind of thing of – just reading about the factory and how it got turned into, you know, we are going to create profit or we are going to create death." Pauls then drew the connection to the family and ethnic group experience: "It is something we will all at different points look at differently and perhaps more specifically because it's a part of our history through Oma. In a way that, if we were Ukrainian or if we were Serbian or something, we would look at the historical things differently. We look at the German things differently." Schulz agreed: "It has always been really important for me to understand that situation as well as possible because of my own family's involvement in that."

As with the story about Willy's death, the three women agreed on the basic facts of Erjardt's story, which were scarce and provided solely by

Irma Hiebert. Only Pauls and Schulz told the story in different ways and used it for different purposes. For Pauls, it explained her grandfather's "balancing act" during the Nazi period, whereas Schulz drew on the story to talk about both, homosexuality – an issue of great personal importance to her – and her grandmother's values – values that she but (and this is only implied) not her parents shared.

The two wartime stories described here were paramount in the family interview but played different roles in the individual interviews. The death of Hiebert's brother was important to Hiebert, because it was the beginning of a major turning point in her life that ended with her migration to Canada. It played a very minor role in Pauls's and Schulz's life stories. Erjardt's story was important to Schulz but not to Hiebert or Pauls. In the family interview, however, the three women showed that they were well acquainted with the stories (if not necessarily the details) and had interpreted them in certain ways. Hiebert's interpretation was "factual" and "objective." She provided details, albeit sparse. Her descriptions were "thin" rather than "thick." Pauls's and Schulz's telling had few details and a lot of evaluation.

During the interviews, both Pauls and Schulz admitted that they did not ask the very hard questions because they were afraid of the answers. Pauls explained, "You want to ask the questions but sometimes you do not want to know"; Schulz said that she would not ask Oma questions like: "Did you know more than maybe even you allow yourself to remember?" Despite these hesitations, they were open to considering difficult and troubling questions during the interviews.

INTERPRETIVE PATTERNS, "EMPTY SPEAKING," AND LOSS OF DETAIL

The Hiebert family's memories about Oma's life in Nazi Germany were not a random sample of stories recalled from a repertoire of anecdotes. These stories had "crystallized" over the years through repeated reminiscing and telling in ever-changing circumstances. Yet, they were not simply routine performances of fixed stories. Family memories and stories are in constant flux; crystallization is an ongoing process, which continues both inside and outside of the interview space. When we interview a family, we are not simply recording their "finished" stories. Rather, their stories are changed in the course of the interviews. The particular setting of the interview leads both to a new arrangement of stories and to variations in them; certain facts may be withheld for instance. The Hiebert family's stories were told in a specific and unusual manner, in a context in which members decided to share stories with a wider audience, and in which a historian elicited further details and reflections. In this situation, the stories were open to changes and diverse interpretations.

Despite this unique communicative situation, some of the underlying narrative structures were not specific to the situation. "Interpretive patterns" and "empty speaking" are two such structures that Welzer and his colleagues identified in interviews with German families.[23] I would add "loss of detail," a phenomenon described but not theorized by Welzer et al., as another structure that seems pertinent when trying to explain how families work on their communicative memories.

These narrative structures are functions of "implicit memory."[24] While explicit memory is the conscious attempt to recall episodes from the past, implicit memory encompasses what we unconsciously remember. Explicit and implicit memories are closely interconnected, because implicit memories "frame" and constitute explicit memories. Statements emerging from implicit memory are formulated "not as memories, but as convictions."[25] Implicit memory includes "images" (*topoi*) and contextual arguments (*Deutungsmuster*, or interpretive patterns[26]). When German families talk about the Nazi past, Welzer et al. argue, their explicit memories are often framed or guided by images or stereotypes of "the (bad) Russian," "the (good) American," "the (rich) Jew," or "the Germans." Interpretive patterns are complex arguments such as "Germans and Jews are definitely two different groups of people," or there was little resistance to the Nazis because "human beings" are easily manipulated, or "one was forced to join the National Socialist German Workers' Party (Nationalsozialistische Deutsche Arbeiterpartei); one could not act otherwise because of one's economic situation or because *everyone* was doing it."[27] Images and interpretive patterns, even when they are not explicitly mentioned, serve as intergenerational points of reference for family stories. They allow different generations to unconsciously and tacitly agree on some basic assumptions about the past that they traverse in their conversations.[28]

Such tacit assumptions structured the Hiebert family's discussions about the Nazi past. In the story about her father's factory supplying the war industry, Hiebert explained that "he did not work for the Nazis ... This is some kind of a thing to stay alive." Pauls agreed: "That's the kind of thing that would have been expected." While Hiebert referred to this explanation a few times, for Pauls it was the main interpretive pattern for telling her grandfather's story. The tacit assumptions guiding this discussion correspond to those that Welzer et al. found among German families: "Nazis" and "Germans" were different from each other, and because "the Nazis" were so powerful, "the Germans" could not do anything to stop them.[29]

Hiebert's and Pauls's statements are also examples of "empty speaking." Empty speaking is a means of transferring "inconsistent, contradictory, and nebulous stories" from one generation to the next; this allows listeners to fill them with meaning. This transfer is carried by words such as "they" or "it" (leaving it up to listeners to fill "they" or "it" with concrete images of actors, actions, or events).

Complementary with empty speaking is a loss of detail in the generational transfer of memory. Hiebert's stories contained historical details that did not surface in the stories told by subsequent generations. In the story about "the gay man in Oma's office," Hiebert knew Mr Erjardt's name, remembered the law under which he was prosecuted (and persecuted), and recalled the Gestapo phoning them before making the arrest. This detail was lost in Pauls's and Schulz's recounting. This loss of detail, like empty speaking, makes room for new interpretations. Pauls saw the causes of Erjardt's arrest in Hitler's insanity and a "mob mentality." Such views were shaped both by what Jerome Bruner calls folk psychology, popular adaptations of major psychological theories, and by other forms of folk knowledge, in this case early popular historical explanations of the Third Reich as an aberration from the normal course of German history and a catastrophe brought on by a madman.[30] In the telling of the story, Pauls constructed her grandfather, *en passant*, as a helpless victim who despite his "struggle" – another example of empty speaking – could not do anything against the Nazis. And she portrayed him as a hero. He was a good German who was tolerant of homosexuals and successfully saved his family and business without caving in to Nazi demands, at least not too much.

Schulz offered a more advanced interpretation that drew on recent structural explanations of Nazism: it was "calculated planning and pretty rationalized evil" that was a result of modernity rather than some eternal German anti-Semitism. This was perhaps a reference to historians' rejection of the "Goldhagen thesis" – in his book *Hitler's Willing Executioners*, Daniel Goldhagen argues that Germans' "eliminationist anti-Semitism" was an enduring part of the German character. Despite Schulz's school knowledge that the German population at large was implicated in the Nazi atrocities, she exempted her Oma and portrayed her as a victim who suffered through the experience of her co-worker's arrest, and as a hero who came out of the experience as a fighter for tolerance and freedom, teaching her family "that we have to treasure our freedom in Canada."

In the telling of such stories, framed as they are by implicit memories, a silent consensus emerges; in the case of interviews, this consensus includes the interviewer. This consensus often prevents people from asking difficult questions. For instance, the fact that the Gestapo called Hiebert's father before making the arrest did not irritate the listeners, including myself. All simply assumed that first of all, this was a historically plausible scenario and second, that Hiebert's father could not do anything to help his employee without risking his life or job. Thus, the question of whether Hiebert's father could have warned Erjardt of the impending arrest is left unasked.[31]

The study by Welzer et al. demonstrated how children and grandchildren made their parents and grandparents into heroes of resistance and victims of Nazi terror. This was particularly true for children with higher education. They had good school knowledge of what had happened in the Third Reich, but they did not connect this with their own families. Surveys conducted by Welzer et al. support these results.[32] We see similar dynamics in the German-Canadian case. Pauls portrayed her mother (and aunt) as a fighter for tolerance and was "amazed" at her grandfather's ability to maintain a "balance" between objecting to Nazism and saving his family and business. Schulz similarly portrayed her Oma not only as a victim of war and of the inability to resist Nazism, but also as the person who taught them to be tolerant and to cherish freedom.

The story of Willy's death is a good example of how the family crafted victim and hero stories through stereotypes, interpretive patterns, and loss of detail. Hiebert offered three explanations for her brother's death. Pauls and Schulz did not consider the medical explanation (thin veins, according to the doctor). Pauls embraced the religious explanation (God spared Willy from fighting for the Nazis). It intimates that Willy's death was that of a martyr. The political explanation (the Gestapo's beating killed Willy) was mentioned only indirectly but throughout all of the interviews. Schulz (and, according to Hiebert, her mother, Jackie) was most convinced: "He died, he was not killed by the Nazis but that idea."

To argue that the children and grandchildren of postwar German immigrants, like their cousins in Germany, made the first generation into victims and heroes is not to say that they set out to whitewash their parents' or grandparents' biographies. Remembering and storytelling are means of crafting coherent identities that make sense to oneself and to others. Thus, Pauls, who knew her mother's and aunt's strong anti-Nazi feelings, simply could not conceive of questioning her grandfather's and uncle's image as anti-Nazis.

CONCLUSION

Alexander von Plato argues that the family interview method creates artificial family harmony and in turn, leads to systematic misinterpretations.[33] The interview with the Hiebert family proves von Plato right; the family worked towards harmonizing their stories. Empty speaking and loss of detail helped them gloss over irritating details and agree on the best version of the story. Yet, the family interview is not a unique communicative situation in family lives. Balancing diverse and even contradictory memories of the same events is an integral part of creating family stability and secure identities. Thus, the family interview sheds light on family dynamics that revolve around the important act of harmonizing family relations. The interview also demonstrates the usefulness of the method if it is used in addition to, rather than instead of, the one-on-one interviews. The family interview added further stories, details, and interpretations and, most important, it illuminated the process of communicative memory.

The Hiebert family's foundational stories could be read as family myths: the brother-martyr, the father-hero, the mother/grandmother-victim. Oral historians have used the concept of myth to undermine master narratives and deconstruct basic assumptions of positivist historiography. The concept of myth, however, can only describe a story as myth. The concept of communicative memory, on the other hand, seems to be a powerful alternative that explains how stories become myths in intergenerational communication about the past. Communicative memory seems well suited to locate and analyze "the displacements, omissions, and reinterpretations through which myths in personal and collective memory take shape."[34] Again, the method of family interviewing helps us gain insight into processes of communicative remembering that facilitate the construction of family myths.

Communicative structures like empty speaking and loss of detail are not a panacea. They have limited explanatory power. They tell us a lot about what is happening when families talk about the past, but they do not tell us everything. Welzer's analysis, as von Plato argues, glosses over the more critical and reflective aspects of family's table talk and communicative memory. Family loyalty, even at the unconscious level, is not always as overpowering a force as Welzer et al. implied. Gabriele Rosenthal, for example, conducts family interviews in order to work through conflicts.[35] She carefully selects which family members to interview in a group, intending to avoid insurmountable conflicts. While there were no open conflicts in the Hiebert family, had other members such as Schulz's parents been a part of the interview, there may have been greater potential for conflict and disagreement about Erjardt's story, for instance. Welzer's analysis also glosses over the connections between school knowledge and family memory. These two are connected and play on each other. Karla Schulz used her university knowledge about Nazism to figure out what role her Oma had had in all of this. She also used it to redirect other family members' understanding of history, when she pleaded against her aunt's "insanity" argument. Yet, these concepts provide concrete analytical tools that help us move beyond vague, metaphoric descriptions of memory processes.

In summary, the three-generational family interview is a powerful tool in the oral historian's toolbox. In addition to providing greater complexity to one-on-one interviews by providing another layer of context, family and other group interviews allow us to counter the individualizing forces of one-on-one interviewing that always imply an independent individual with autonomous access to lived experiences and memory. Family interviews demonstrate that our narrators are positioned in complex webs of experiencing and remembering that undermine any notion of the autonomous individual. Similarly, the concept of communicative memory is an important notion that helps us understand how collective family memory works. Oral historians' investigations of family memory would benefit from using both of these approaches more frequently.[36]

NOTES

1 Paula Hamilton and Linda Shopes, "Introduction," in *Oral History and Public Memories*, edited by Hamilton and Shopes (Philadelphia: Temple University Press, 2008), vii–xvii, viii.

2 Irma Hiebert, Nancy Pauls, and Karla Schulz, interview by Alexander Freund, Winnipeg, 25 May 2006. All interview recordings and transcripts cited in this article are in the author's possession.

3 Angela Keppler, *Tischgespräche. Über Formen kommunikativer Vergemeinschaftung am Beispiel der Konversation in Familien* (Frankfurt: Suhrkamp, 1994).

4 Gabriele Rosenthal, ed., *The Holocaust in Three Generations: Families of Victims and Perpetrators of the Nazi Regime* (New York: Continuum, 1998); Dan Bar-On, *Legacy of Silence: Encounters with Children of the Third Reich* (Cambridge, MA: Harvard University Press, 1989); Dan Bar-on, *Fear and Hope: Three Generations of the Holocaust* (Cambridge, MA: Harvard University Press, 1998); Harald Welzer et al., *Opa war kein Nazi: Nationalsozialismus und Holocaust im Familiengedächtnis* (Frankfurt: Fischer, 2002); Karoline Tschuggnall and Harald Welzer, "Rewriting Memories: Family Recollections of the National Socialist Past in Germany," *Culture & Psychology* 8, no. 1 (March 2002): 130–46; Harald Welzer, "Collateral Damage of History Education: National Socialism and the Holocaust in German Family Memory," *Social Research* 75, no. 1 (spring 2008): 287–314.

5 Welzer et al., *Opa war kein Nazi,* 10.

6 Jerome Bruner, *Acts of Meaning* (Cambridge, MA: Harvard University Press, 1990); Jerome Bruner, *Actual Minds, Possible Worlds* (Cambridge, MA: Harvard University Press, 1996); Donald E. Polkinghorne, *Narrative Knowing and the Human Sciences* (Albany: SUNY Press, 1988); Polkinghorne, "Narrative and Self-Concept," *Journal of Narrative and Life History* 1, nos. 2 and 3 (1991): 135–53; Harald Welzer, *Das kommunikative Gedächtnis. Eine Theorie der Erinnerung,* 2nd edition (Munich: Beck, 2008).

7 Jan Assmann, "Kollektives Gedächtnis und kulturelle Identität," in *Kultur und Gedächtnis,* edited by Jan Assmann and Tonio Hölscher (Frankfurt: Suhrkamp, 1988), 9–19; also see the very literal and thus at times difficult to understand English translation by John Czaplicka, "Collective Memory and Cultural Identity," *New German Critique* 65 (spring/summer 1995): 125–33.

8 Assmann, "Collective Memory," 126.

9 Ibid., 127.

10 Ibid.

11 Welzer, *Das kommunikative Gedächtnis.*

12 Welzer et al., *Opa war kein Nazi.*

13 S.J. Zeitlin, A.J. Kotkin, and H.C. Baker, eds., *A Celebration of American Family Folklore* (New York: Pantheon Books, 1982), 2.

14 Ruth Finnegan, "Family Myths, Memories and Interviewing," in *Studying Family and Community History: 19th and 20th Centuries. Volume 1: From Family Tree to Family History,* edited by Ruth Finnegan and Michael Drake (Cambridge: Cambridge University Press, 1994), 117–22.

15 I have edited the quotations from the transcripts for clarity, omitting broken-off words and sentences, reformulations, hesitations, and repetitions unless they add additional meaning for the purpose of this analysis.

16 Irma Hiebert, interview by Angela Thiessen, Winnipeg, 14 July 2005.

17 This is probably a reference to the movie *Swingkids,* dir. Thomas Carter, USA, 1993. The way films affect memory is discussed by Welzer et al., *Opa war kein Nazi,* chapter 5.

18 Michael H. Kater, *Different Drummers: Jazz in the Culture of Nazi Germany* (Oxford: Oxford University Press, 2003), esp. 153–62; "German Swing Youth," http://www.return2style.de/amiswhei.htm (accessed 13 March 2010).

19 State Archives of Hamburg, 213–11 Staatsanwaltschaft Landgericht – Strafsachen, 1663/45; Ulf Bollmann, State Archives of Hamburg, email to author, 17 February 2009.

20 Nancy Pauls, interview by Angela Thiessen, Winnipeg, 18 August 2005.

21 Karla Schulz, interview by Angela Thiessen, Winnipeg, 19 August 2005.

22 After the war, neither the Allies nor the two German governments recognized homosexuals as victims of the Nazis. In fact, Paragraph 175 in its 1935 version continued to be in effect in West Germany until 1969 and in its pre-1935 "milder" form in East Germany until 1968. Michael Burleigh and Wolfgang Wippermann, *The Racial State: Germany 1933–1945* (Cambridge: Cambridge University Press, 1991), 183, 197. See the monument for homosexual victims of Nazi persecution at http://www.lsvd.de/gedenk-ort/eng-chronicle.htm (accessed 18 June 2014).

23 Welzer et al., *Opa war kein Nazi*.

24 This discussion is based on Welzer et al., *Opa war kein Nazi*, 135. Welzer et al.'s argument rests on the description of implicit memory discussed by Peter Graf and Daniel L. Schacter, "Implicit and Explicit Memory for New Associations in Normal Subjects and Amnesic Patients," *Journal of Experimental Psychology: Learning, Memory, and Cognition* 11 (1985), 501–18; Daniel L. Schacter, *Searching For Memory: The Brain, the Mind, and the Past* (New York: Basic Books, 1996).

25 Welzer et al., *Opa war kein Nazi*, 136.

26 On *Deutungsmuster* in discourse analysis, see Reiner Keller, "Analysing Discourse: An Approach from the Sociology of Knowledge," *Historical Social Research-Historische Sozialforschung* 31, no. 2 (2006): 223–42.

27 Welzer et al., *Opa war kein Nazi*, 137, 155.

28 Ibid., 136–7.

29 Ibid., 150–6.

30 Bruner, *Acts of Meaning*; Bruner, *Actual Minds*; Friedrich Meinecke, *The German Catastrophe* (Cambridge, MA: Harvard University Press, 1950).

31 Welzer et al. found, in many family talks, that "contradictory evidence" seldom led to listener "irritations," including interviewers. *Opa war kein Nazi*, 151.

32 Ibid.

33 Alexander Freund, "Interview with Alexander von Plato, Grabow, Germany, 8 April 2009," *Oral History Forum d'histoire orale* 29 (2009): part 12, 5:40–13:00.

34 Paul Thompson and Raphael Samuelson, eds., *The Myths We Live By* (London: Routledge, 1990), 5.

35 Rosenthal, ed., *The Holocaust in Three Generations*.

36 I thank Irma Hiebert, Nancy Pauls, and Karla Schulz for giving generously of their time and for their courage to talk about a difficult past that many people still find troubling to discuss in their own families, let alone with a stranger and for a public audience. I also thank my research assistant Angela Thiessen for her excellent work.

8

Oral History, Narrative Strategies, and Native American Historiography

Julie Cruikshank

The question of the place and meaning of stories and their contribution to the way we think about the past is receiving fresh attention in the humanities and human sciences.[1] In North America, as elsewhere, this renewed focus has consequences for oral histories, once evaluated by historians and anthropologists primarily with reference to questions about accuracy, objectivity, reliability and verifiability.[2] A rich vein concerns how oral narratives intersect with social practice, how they continue to provide a framework for understanding contemporary issues, and how stories are inevitably part of larger social, historical, and political processes. Viewed from this perspective, narrative authorizes ways of seeing and interpreting the world;[3] invokes a social system;[4] and provides a moral education.[5] It also frequently depicts states of vulnerability and unreasonable relationships that accompany colonial encounters.[6] Oral transmission of stories is a pan-human activity, probably the oldest form of history-making, and in many parts of the world has a continuing role in the production and reproduction of history.

Theoretical attention to the work accomplished by oral narrative destabilizes any simple idea that stories passed on as oral tradition transparently "speak for themselves" or that there is one prescriptive, cross-culturally valid method for evaluating their historical value. Facts, as Eric Wolf points out, cannot find their voice without some theoretical assistance.[7] The notion that oral traditions from the North American continent can be viewed as broadly homogeneous data from which facts about "what really happened" can be extruded ignores substantial research on memory and forgetting that has emerged from such diverse settings as post-Stalinist Russia, Africa, Kentucky coal mining communities, Europe, and Asia.[8] Oral histories from indigenous North America are too frequently evaluated with reference only to one another; yet encapsulating them within a continental tradition sometimes partitions these narratives from international debates to which they might contribute.

Storytelling may be a universal human activity but the concepts communicated in stories depend on close attention to local metaphor and local narrative conventions. Author Michael Dorris pointed out years ago that national literatures come from coherent aggregations of people who share identifiable languages and world views; terms like American Indian or Native American, he argued, homogenize one of the most linguistically and culturally plural areas the world has ever known.[9] With growing awareness that oral spoken performances are always situated, approaches to analysis of oral tradition are converging. Anthropological attention to cultural categories, cosmologies, and symbols is merging with archaeologists' grasp of the material record and historians' critical evaluation of written documents. Linguists working with indigenous storytellers alert us to the variety of narrative genres grouped under the broad rubric of "Native American literature."[10] If there are broad pan–North American similarities in storytelling traditions, they probably have more to do with epistemology than with content. Indigenous peoples who grow up immersed in oral tradition point out that their narratives are better understood by absorbing the successive personal messages revealed to listeners over time than by trying to analyze and publicly explain their meanings.[11]

This chapter builds on long-term ethnographic work – talking with people about issues and questions grounded in everyday experiences – in a particular region of northwestern Canada. During the 1970s and 1980s, I had the opportunity to work with several elders from the Yukon Territory, speakers of Tagish, Tutchone, and Tlingit and English languages, who were interested in documenting memories and having me transcribe their narratives for children, grandchildren, and other family members. Framed as a collaborative project from the outset, this work initially seemed to contribute directly to a larger project of documenting social histories that are often elided in the written record. My search for theoretical guidance widened as I came to see how elders of First Nations ancestry in the Yukon Territory continue to tell stories that make meaningful connections between past and present. Stories, like good theories, make connections that may not at first glance seem straightforward.

In trying to understand issues surrounding transmission of orally narrated histories in northwestern Canada, I have been drawn to questions about narrative raised decades ago by scholars working independently in very different parts of the world – Harold Innis, Mikhail Bakhtin, and

Walter Benjamin. Each was concerned about the role of oral storytelling in human history and each deplored the consequences when oral storytelling becomes marginalized by more powerful knowledge systems. Each insisted that narrative is grounded in material circumstances of everyday life and capable of addressing large questions about the consequences of historical events. Such ideas have relevance for ongoing discussions and debates about history that are part of daily conversation among Yukon First Nations. Angela Sidney and Kitty Smith, Yukon elders whose work is discussed in this chapter, were contemporaries of Innis, Bakhtin, and Benjamin although they lived much longer and their worlds differed considerably. Their stories certainly incorporate information about the past, but more important, the act of storytelling provides ways of making historical changes understandable.

Approaches to the analysis of oral narrative have become embroiled in broad methodological and theoretical debates in the social sciences. Time-worn arguments about the reliability of oral history are familiar enough, but there are deeper issues. To begin with, oral tradition is frequently situated at one pole of century-long discussions opposing universalist and particularist explanations, now usually framed in terms of global *vs.* local distinctions. My contention is that to relegate them only to the local and the particular is to oversimplify the very real *work* that stories do. Second, oral narrative is frequently positioned on the "mentalist" side of a philosophical divide that distinguishes materialist from idealist approaches to understanding power; again, I think this distinction is misplaced. Third, approaches stressing narrative understanding may seem superficially to strand oral tradition on the shores of post-modern relativism when they actually address hierarchies of power in very precise ways. Such troublesome dualisms have a long history, but insights from Bakhtin, Benjamin, and Innis may guide us through this thicket and back to a broader understanding of narrative's role in exploring intersections among knowledge, power, and ideology.

I begin this chapter by introducing writings that raised questions about the potential of local oral narratives to engage with global issues long before such concerns were taken seriously. I go on to discuss how the shifting power relations described by Innis, Bakhtin, and Benjamin speak to conditions in the Yukon during the late nineteenth and early twentieth centuries. I draw on work by Angela Sidney and Kitty Smith, briefly summarizing basic understandings about local social organization that each would expect of an intelligent listener, and then illustrate with two stories *about* their stories. I identify where I see convergence among the approaches of these five writers and storytellers. I argue that local voices from North American indigenous communities provide more than grist for conventional disciplinary paradigms and have the power to contribute to our understanding of historiography.

Late in life, the Canadian economic historian Harold Innis developed an enduring interest in oral tradition. Investigating how Empire manages the awkward problem of administering far-flung territories, Innis was drawn to the history of communication. He pointed to overweening imperial ambition to assert power during periods of territorial expansion by monopolizing and categorizing information and by routinely silencing local traditions that do not fit official categories. A crucial feature of administration in the hinterland is the process of classification and control of activities, and the authorization of official observations, categories and statistics in written texts. While this process is conventionally rationalized as both producing knowledge and serving the interests of those administered, it invariably occurs at the expense of existing regional traditions. Innis came to see colonialism as simultaneously economic and intellectual.[12]

Innis admired the structural characteristics of oral tradition and saw it as having potential to counterbalance mechanical segmentation of time and space by insisting on the importance of qualitative time in human affairs. Oral tradition, he argued, permits continuous revision of history by actively reinterpreting events and then incorporating such interpretations into the next generation of narrative. Its flexibility allows a gifted storyteller to adapt a given narrative to make sense of a confusing situation.[13]

Innis's views about the creative potential of oral tradition mirrored those of his contemporary Mikhail Bakhtin, also writing during the 1930s and 1940s, though from more constrained circumstances in Stalinist Russia. They wrote in different languages and neither ever encountered the other's work, but their approaches were similarly eclectic. Bakhtin, like Innis, was drawn to the open-ended possibilities he saw in oral dialogue and the thoroughness with which totalitarian regimes worked to suppress those possibilities. Observing the chilling transformations occurring in 1930s post-revolutionary Russia, Bakhtin concluded that there must be forms of resistance more effective than the violent replacement of one set of leaders by another, and he looked to everyday spoken language for inspiration. He sought out cases where narrative successfully resists such domestication, marginalization, and erasure and was eventually drawn to processes set in motion by conversational forms of oral storytelling. He interpreted what he called its "dialogic" relational possibilities (especially when laced with disruptive humour) as a model inherently opposing authoritarian speech.[14]

In the same decade but in another country, Walter Benjamin grappled with similar issues engulfing Europe during early years of Hitler's ascendancy. He, too, noted the insidious consequences of deteriorating dialogue in modern society, attributing this at least partly to the diminishing role of the storyteller. As communications technology proliferates, he argued, information becomes fragmented and detached from the moral philosophical guidance we think of as knowledge and might once even have called wisdom. Benjamin believed that orally transmitted narratives develop in their hearers a capacity to listen, a deteriorating skill in an age of ever-fragmenting information. The power of narrative storytelling, in his view, lies in its capacity to interweave drama and practical experience with moral content. Storytelling is open-ended rather than didactic, allowing listeners to draw independent conclusions from what they hear. By the very act of telling stories, narrators explore how their meanings work; by listening, audiences can think about how those meanings apply to their own lives. Stories allow listeners to embellish events, to reinterpret them, to mull over what they hear and to learn something new each time, providing raw material for a developing philosophy.[15] Once interactive storytelling is replaced by mechanical communication, he alleged, human experience becomes devalued.

What relevance have these ideas to understanding Native North American oral histories from the northwestern part of the continent? Bakhtin's reference point was Russian peasant culture and his target the increasingly authoritarian Soviet state in which he lived, but he drew his examples from the way medieval French peasants used ribald, satirical humour to challenge authority through carnivals.[16] Yet he never, in any of his translated writings, directly discusses everyday storytelling from his own times. Likewise, Innis carried out his economic studies in northern Canada and his historical investigation of classical oral tradition without ever seeming to connect the two. Despite a prodigious appetite for labour-intensive research that took him across northern Canada and an open admiration for the work of his colleague Edward Sapir on indigenous languages, Innis never seemed to encounter living oral traditions in his own country reporting, regretfully, that "(W)e have no history of (oral tradition) except as ... revealed darkly through the written or printed word."[17] Had he been aware of the intensity with which indigenous residents were drawing on long-standing oral traditions to interpret the same events he was analyzing near the Klondike goldfields, he might have observed dynamics similar to those that so intrigued him in ancient Greece – the processes set in motion when writing began first to overwhelm narrative traditions and then to actively domesticate or suppress them.

Forces bearing down on northwestern North America during the late nineteenth and early twentieth centuries were precisely those discussed by Innis in his account of the Klondike gold rush, by Bakhtin as he observed the mechanics of aggressive state expansion, and by Benjamin, whose writings documented the forces mobilizing Nazi Germany. Here, I outline briefly key events experienced by the generation of indigenous men and women born near the upper Yukon River at the end of the nineteenth century. "Events" are indeed a mainstay of history, but the processes that underlie and shape those events may be even more revealing. The Klondike gold rush in 1896–98 and the construction of the Alaska Highway during the Second World War are significant because they advanced forces already contributing to a globalizing world during the early twentieth century. Despite their widely differing life experiences, Kitty Smith (b. 1890), Walter Benjamin (b. 1892), Harold Innis (b. 1894), Mikhail Bakhtin (b. 1895), and Angela Sidney (b. 1902) were all contemporaries, and each experienced the early years of the twentieth century as formative.

In North America, the British empire reached its northwesterly extension through the fur trade, but as Europe spiralled into a depression in the 1870s and fashion tastes changed, furs were replaced by the more lucrative and liquid commodity, gold, as the staple of choice. The Klondike gold rush in the closing years of the nineteenth century attracted more than thirty thousand immigrants from North America and Europe to one tributary of the Yukon River within a few years, making Dawson City an instant, sprawling metropolis. Local men and women along the Yukon River, speakers of Athapaskan languages, became involved in packing, guiding, and providing food for prospectors. A few years later, some worked on sternwheelers built to navigate the Yukon River from its headwaters to Dawson City. Consequences of this gold rush included disruption of indigenous trade networks; introduction of epidemics; influx of missionaries; opening of residential schools; and the establishment of a federal and territorial government infrastructure to administer the new Yukon Territory as a northern colony of Canada. Following the non-Native exodus after the turn of the century, the population plummeted from 27,000 in 1900 to 4,000 in 1921.[18]

What some older people referred to as the "second rush" advanced during the Second World War. Hastily constructed in 1942–43, the Alaska Highway was built to deflect an anticipated invasion of North America by

Japan. Again, more than thirty thousand men, this time American soldiers and Canadian civilians, arrived to participate in the construction phase, and then left as quickly as they had come. Once again, epidemics tore through Yukon communities.[19] The new road replaced the Yukon River as the administrative axis of the territory, subjecting indigenous peoples to ever greater bureaucratic surveillance as the "opening of the north" proceeded. The highway acted as a kind of gravel magnet attracting people in search of short-term jobs away from distant settlements.[20] Its short- and long-term consequences affected both long-standing social institutions associated with kinship and the relationship between indigenous peoples and their lands and livelihoods.

By the mid-1970s, I had been living in the Yukon Territory for five years and was working closely with senior women engaged in the project of recording their life stories. They and their families wanted to see accounts written in their own words describing memories and experiences spanning almost a century. The stories we hear from two of these women, Angela Sidney and Kitty Smith, shift the focus from well-known events to their everyday consequences. Mrs Sidney's paternal uncles and her aunt were involved in the official discovery of Klondike gold. Four of Mrs Smith's maternal uncles were charged with murder following an altercation between Tagish people and prospectors and were brought to trial in Dawson City.[21] Each woman lost family members in influenza epidemics that accompanied both "rushes." Kitty Smith lost her mother who returned home in 1898 to comfort her own mother when Kitty's uncles were arrested; the young mother died after contracting influenza. Angela Sidney watched two sons go overseas during the Second World War and lost a much-loved daughter to influenza. The narratives they tell about those years provide compelling evidence of how ancient narratives provide scaffolding from which to interpret inexplicable events, allowing families to carry on. The metaphors central to historical narratives told by Angela Sidney and Kitty Smith are culturally distinctive, highly gendered and rooted in mid-nineteenth century matrilineages. These stories demonstrate how global forces driving human history are always experienced in locally significant ways. Familiar narratives provide ways to engage with historical events and expand our understanding of the social *work* that stories accomplish.

In telling their life stories, these women make generous assumptions that listeners or readers have a basic understanding of local concepts surrounding kinship. Anthropologists use the term "moiety" (from the French, *moitié*, "half") to describe a broad organizational principle found in many parts of the world whereby everyone belongs to one of two inter-marrying "sides." In the Yukon, membership in moieties named Crow (Kajìt) and Wolf (Ägunda) is transmitted through matrilineal descent so that everyone inherits his or her mother's affiliation. Moieties are exog-amous, and well-understood rules prescribe that one must always marry a member of the opposite moiety. During these women's lifetimes, moiety and clan relationships were expected to guide behaviour at birth, at the onset of puberty, marriage, death, and other less formal occasions. This principle profoundly influenced their interpretations of historical changes that have occurred during this century.

By the time Mrs Sidney and Mrs Smith were born, some inland Atha-paskan families were incorporating coastal Tlingit-named clans within moieties: for example, Deisheetaan (a Crow clan) and Dakl'aweidí (a Wolf clan). The most important clan property – songs, stories, and ceremonial crests – passed from generation to generation through the maternal line. Appreciating the significance of this convention clarifies the way stories and songs are performed, transmitted, and interpreted by local audiences. Shared assumptions about family and clan property underscore the broad utility of Pierre Bourdieu's concept of social capital embedded in social institutions. Social capital, Bourdieu argues, accumulates along with the practical competence that eventually determines who is entitled to speak and to be heard.[22]

The life histories these women tell are also grounded in enduring nar-ratives learned in childhood and told as adults. As we worked, my under-standing of our objectives shifted significantly. Initially, I expected that by recording life histories we would be documenting events, and compiling accounts that could be stored, like archival documents, for later analysis. I was interested in hearing these women talk about events chronicled in written documents and tried to steer our conversations in that direction. I always brought questions to our sessions, but as I began to take increasing direction from the narrators, these questions changed. In the beginning I asked about what would be called secular history – stories they might have heard about the gold rush and the early twentieth–century fur trade, and about their experiences as children and young adults. I wanted to know about the changes brought by the construction of the Alaska High-way and the subsequent interventions and control over women's lives that followed as government programs extended northward.

Although the older women responded patiently to my line of inquiry for a while, they soon quite firmly shifted their emphasis to the "more important" accounts they wanted me to record. They would give brief answers to my questions and then suggest that I write down a particular story they wanted to tell me. Usually these were narratives they had learned as youngsters and had heard and told many times, but for an untrained listener they inevitably involved a bewildering series of characters and episodes. At their insistence, I continued on their terms, and it was only later when I came to see how they were using these narratives as reference points to talk *about* their life experiences that I came to appreciate what they were doing. Narratives about a boy who went to live in the world of salmon, about a girl who married a bear, of men who travelled to the "other world" in search of a lost sister, or of women who journeyed to live with stars provided pivotal philosophical, literary, and social frameworks essential for guiding young and not-so-young people, framing ways of thinking about how to live life appropriately. These narratives erased any distinction between "story" and "history." They were embedded in social life and in the words of Angela Sidney, provided guidance about how to "live life like a story."[23] Gradually I came to see oral tradition less as historical evidence than as a window on the ways the past is culturally constituted and discussed. In other words, stories were not merely *about* the past, they also provide guidelines for understanding unexpected changes.

As an anthropologist, I think that theoretical discussions need to be grounded in everyday life, and so I turn to two instructive ways of history-making demonstrated by these women. In one series of stories, Angela Sidney shows how a single story can do many different things. In the other, Kitty Smith shows how apparently different stories can convey a unifying message about the importance of matrilineal, matrilocal, marital arrangements in maintaining social continuity. Both women test the boundaries of narrative conventions even within their own culture in ways that might have appealed to Bakhtin and Benjamin.

ANGELA SIDNEY'S GIFT

Angela Sidney was born in 1902 in the southern Yukon to a Tlingit mother and a Tagish father. Like their mother, Angela and her siblings were members of the Deisheetaan clan. As the eldest daughter, she had many opportunities to hear about her bi-cultural Tagish and Tlingit ancestry and her Deisheetaan clan history when, as a young woman, she took on the responsibility of caring for her mother, La.oosTláa (Maria), who was plagued with ill health. A measles epidemic associated with the gold rush had robbed La.oosTláa of her four eldest children, who all died before Angela was born. La.oosTláa never fully recovered and eventually lost her eyesight. When Mrs Sidney and I met in the early 1970s, she was eager to work on the project of recording her life history for family members, and mirroring Bourdieu's formulation of social capital she remarked one afternoon, "Well, I have no money to leave to my grandchildren; my stories are my wealth."[24]

I was delighted to have the opportunity to work with Mrs Sidney on this project. However, after we had collaborated closely for several months and finally produced a 120-page booklet, typed and edited under her supervision, I was somewhat disconcerted by the fact that only ten to fifteen pages had anything to do with what I then would have called life "history." The rest seemed to fall into genres of oral literature that I felt ill-equipped to understand, involving fabulous characters whose dazzling exploits often eluded my comprehension, complex lists of toponyms, songs, and lengthy genealogical sequences interwoven with references to historical events. As I continued to listen to and learn from Mrs Sidney, it became clear to me that she was using these larger narratives as reference points to reflect on her own life experiences, as models both for choices she had made and for explaining those choices to others.[25] Here I summarize just one story that encapsulates how she earned her reputation as a community historian.

One of the stories she asked me to record in 1974 depicted a heroic ancestor remembered by the name of Kaax̱'achgóok.[26] Briefly, Kaax̱'achgóok was a famous Tlingit ancestor of the Kiks.ádi clan, one of several Tlingit clans. One autumn, he went hunting sea mammals with his nephews but almost immediately received a sign that this was an inauspicious time for hunting and that he should return home. Reluctantly, he destroyed his spears and returned to his winter village, but eventually he could no longer bear the humiliation of having to send his wives to beg for food and hearing about the disrespectful treatment they were receiving. Setting out to sea once again with his nephews, he was blown off course and marooned on a small island. Kaax̱'achgóok spent the following months devising ways to feed himself and his nephews, and perfecting a way to plot the sun's trajectory as it moved north to reach its zenith at the summer solstice. He chose that moment to set sail for home, using the sun as a navigational guide to chart his direction. "I gave up hope, and then I dreamed that I was home," he sang in his account of his travels. Despite his successful return, he faced the difficult business of acknowledging how much had changed during his absence.

Mrs Sidney told me this story first in 1974 when we were both primarily interested in transcribing it for publication in a form that she considered accurate. More than a decade later in 1985, when I was visiting her one day, her son, Peter, and his wife arrived. The conversation turned to Peter's experiences as a veteran of the Second World War. He had been stationed overseas for a period and Mrs Sidney began to speak about how she and her husband had bought their first radio "to hear where they're moving the troops so we would know where he is," and her joy when the war ended and they received a telegram announcing his return. The remainder of her story concerned the plans she made to welcome him back when he returned home after the war, hosting a community feast and publicly giving him the most precious gift she could think of – the song sung by Kaax̲'achgóok – on his return, a song she subsequently referred to for the rest of her life as "Pete's song." As a member of his mother's Deisheetaan clan, her son was entitled to receive the song as a gift from her, she pointed out, and she saw it as accurately reflecting the feelings of a man forced to spend an indefinite period away from home and ultimately able to return. Songs constitute some of the most important property of Tlingit-named clans, and she was clearly pleased when her husband complimented her on thinking of such a culturally appropriate gift.

But she then went on to tell a third story about this story – concerning social processes set in motion by her gift. No sooner had she publicly given Peter this gift in 1945 than she was formally challenged by elders from her father's Dakl'aweidí clan, who disputed her right to sing it much less give it to a member of her own clan. They argued that this song was the property of the Kiks.ádi clan and that her Deisheetaan clan had no right to use it. The remainder of her account is the story of how she proceeded with her own ethnographic research to prove that she had acted correctly and had not appropriated another clan's property. She travelled down to the coast to Skagway, Alaska, on the same train that had brought her son home. There, she interviewed Tlingit elders about an incident that had occurred many years earlier, sometime during the nineteenth century. They agreed with her that a dispute had broken out between the Kiks.ádi clan and her own Deisheetaan clan, resolved only when Kiks.ádi agreed to give this "Kaax̲'achgóok song" to the Deisheetaan. Her story *about* the story confirmed, to the satisfaction of her uncles, that she had acted appropriately. Being able to tell this story forty years later in the presence of her son (who knew the story well after all and was by now a character in it) and to his non-Tlingit wife and to me reconfirmed her competence in using stories in socially significant ways. By demonstrating the connections among a narrative, a song, and this gift, she was also able to extend her abilities to juxtapose discrete historical events – an ancient clan dispute and a contemporary international war.

A fourth telling was performed for a very different audience, most of them familiar with Mrs Sidney and her role as a well-known storyteller but few knowledgeable about this particular story. When Yukon College opened in Whitehorse in 1988, Mrs Sidney was asked to participate in the ceremonies. This was an important event for Yukoners because the college allows students to enroll in university courses without having to leave the north. For the ceremony, Mrs Sidney decided to tell the story of Kaax̱'achgóok, explaining, in her own words: "The reason I sang that song is because that Yukon College is going to be like the Sun for the students. Instead of going to Vancouver or Victoria they're going to be able to stay here and go to school here. We're not going to lose our kids anymore. It's going to be just like the Sun for them, just like for that Kaax̱'achgóok."[27]

Very carefully, then, Angela Sidney was able to show how a single story can *do* several different things. She constructed an important link between an ancient narrative and historical events from different time periods – clan ties that connected coast and interior during the nineteenth century; a war that caused painful separations ameliorated by the successful return of her own son in the 1940s; the opening of a college in the 1980s – with continuity provided by a gift that weaves these events together. The story also tracks her emerging stature as a person of significance in her community, one who repeatedly demonstrated during her lifetime that a single story, well told, can transform commonsense meanings that "everyone knows" and add significance to everyday life.

KITTY SMITH'S CARVINGS

Kitty Smith was born in approximately 1890, at least twelve years earlier than Angela Sidney. She, too, was born into a bi-cultural family with a Tagish mother and a Tlingit father. Orphaned as a youngster, she was raised by her Tlingit father's mother – unusual in a society where obligations of clan and kinship are traced through one's maternal line. We also began working together in 1974 and, like Mrs Sidney, Mrs Smith insisted that I record many stories that initially seemed distant from my understanding of "history." She began with detailed genealogical information and only later introduced critical events from her own life – her mother's disappearance and subsequent death in an influenza epidemic when Kitty was seven or eight years old; her own arranged marriage as a young woman; her decision to leave this marriage some years later (a courageous but unconventional choice during the early 1900s); and her eventual reunion with her "mother's people," members of her own Tagish maternal kin group. In describing these events she, too, drew heavily on foundational narratives she had learned as a child to provide explanations for decisions she made during her own life.[28] In the life story that emerged during our conversations over the years, this reunion with her matrilineage becomes pivotal. Narratives about dangers of distance from matrilineal kin and loyalty of clan members to one another dominate her account. In trying to learn more about her mother's early death she was led to the tragic story about the circumstances surrounding the arrest, trial, and subsequent execution of her mother's brother, convicted in the death of a prospector in 1898.[29]

During the years we worked together, Mrs Smith sometimes referred to carvings that she had made years earlier. Whenever I actually asked her about them, though, she would shrug off my queries about where they might now be – she had sold them or given them away, she said – and would then move on to tell the stories that she had carved. Shortly before she passed away in 1989, some carvings in the local MacBride Museum were identified as possibly hers. Her granddaughter and another friend made arrangements with the museum's director to bring Mrs Smith to visit, and when the carvings were brought out she readily indicated the ones she had made. But nearly a century old by then, she was more amused than surprised by this discovery and not at all inclined to provide an elaborate explication of what they "meant." Instead, she examined her favourite carving, renaming it *Azänzhaya*, "it got lost," and enjoying the irony of her own joke.

A few years later, in 1992, I asked her daughter, May Hume Smith, now an elder herself, whether she had ever seen her mother's carvings in the museum. Their continuing existence was a surprise for her but May recalled childhood memories of her mother carving and agreed to visit the museum with me. With encouragement from museum staff, we spent two afternoons examining carvings and recording May's commentary. She immediately singled out those made by her mother and settled in to talk about them. Then, like her mother, she retold the stories embodied in the carvings. What struck me immediately was that these were recognizably the same narratives that Mrs Smith herself had told, several years earlier, to describe critical turning points in her own life.[30]

One carving and story concerns Dukt'ootl', an orphan whose marginal status is vindicated when he is able to perform a task no one else in the community can accomplish, saving both his own life and the lives of others. The narrative reflects both the despair and the optimism that Mrs Smith often expressed about her own childhood as an orphan cut off from maternal kin. A second is the story of Naatsilanéi, "the man who made killer whales," a story she told me several times as she reflected on the dangers of distance from one's maternal relatives when one is compelled to live with affines. In this narrative, a man is abandoned by his opposite moiety brothers-in-law and left to die on an island. He saves himself through the transformative power of carving, fashioning killer whales that carry him back to safety. A third is a carving of the man who abandoned his wife to co-habit with Bear woman, reflecting Mrs Smith's distress when her first husband announced that he was taking a second wife. Her carving shows the man moving toward his bear wife while the human wife carries away her child, leaving the lovers behind.[31]

NARRATIVE AND HISTORICAL MEMORY

What do these narratives convey about the place and meaning of stories for our understanding of First Nation histories? Sentient bears and whales who encompass personhood and take on roles as non-human actors in historical dramas are more likely to be classified as "myth" than as historical evidence by listeners raised in a Western tradition. But the historical accuracy of Homeric poems, Icelandic sagas, Tlingit oratory, or Tagish life stories is probably beside the point if we understand their contribution as assisting social memory. In the context of oral history in Canada, the narratives Angela Sidney and Kitty Smith tell make more precise contributions. They directly confront familiar, common sense categories that take for granted clear distinctions between "nature" and "culture," but they also challenge Euro-American myths that portray official Yukon history as a narrative of frontier individualism.

Raymond Fogelson coined the term "epitomizing" to characterize dramatic incidents that condense complex cultural forces and make them easy to grasp in an icon or symbol.[32] The discovery of Klondike gold in August 1896 and the construction of the Alaska Highway in 1943 have both served as key epitomizing events in official Yukon history. "Discovery Day," 17 August, has long been enshrined as a statutory holiday in the Territory. Both events were commemorated in anniversary celebrations during the 1990s: the fiftieth anniversary of the highway, and the centennial of the gold rush. Individualism remains a cherished self-characterization in Yukon settler society. Yet, as symbols, the gold rush and Alaska

Highway construction convey quite different messages for indigenous people raised hearing about these events from elders who experienced them. The kinds of "freedom" embodied in frontier narratives that portray humans in mortal combat with nature or as shedding social connections in pursuit of individualism surely appeared to Angela Sidney, Kitty Smith, and their contemporaries as the freedom of ghosts – humans approaching the vanishing point.[33]

Angela Sidney's masterful account of how narrative sustains human connections across clan, gender, and generation in the face of enormous external pressures demonstrates Walter Benjamin's thesis that a story can do many things and convey many messages. Her gift links events spanning more than a century – the settlement of a conflict between clans through the exchange of a narrative; the use of that narrative to welcome a returning son; her public address late in life expressing hopes for the futures of generations of grandchildren. Her story also addresses an international war in the middle of this century that brought a highway, epidemics, and took away young men from the Yukon, some of whom did not return. It demonstrates the complex process by which oral history is publicly verified in communities where it is told: her own uncles were prepared to denounce her until she proved to them that she had the right to tell this story and to make it a gift to her son. It speaks to late-twentieth-century attempts to rebuild Tlingit and Athapaskan relationships now severed by an international boundary but still critical to many families in the southern Yukon Territory.

Mrs Sidney's account chronicles her expanding reputation in her own community as she persisted in using and reusing one powerful story to make people understand a variety of larger issues. To live life "like a story," in her words, is to confront modernist global narratives with deeply held local ones embedded in a social order in which human and non-human persons are deeply interconnected.

Kitty Smith, too, has much to say about the well-lived life. While she knows and tells stories about model lives, where everything proceeds as it should, her own experience taught her that things seldom work so smoothly. Real life, she might say, is full of contradictions. Narrative gives us ways to think about this. Rather than being clear-cut reflections of ideal life, oral narratives may very well invert social behaviour, because one purpose is to resolve symbolically those areas that cannot easily be worked out in the sphere of human activity. Orphaned as a child, raised by her father's clan, unhappy in her first marriage, she was drawn to stories that dramatize contradictions, and she found them, in Levi-Strauss's terms, "good to think with." Stories of Dukt'ootl', Kaats', and Naatsilanéi began as ancient narratives. They brought their explanatory power to dilemmas she experienced early in life; later she began to carve images from those stories in poplar, then sold them or gave them away. Eventually, years on, some were discovered in the collections of the MacBride Museum. Mrs Smith was pleased to see them again, but only to a point: in her view, they had already accomplished their work long ago. Yet for young people from her community who continue to see her carvings exhibited, they commemorate a life, contribute to social memory, and reinforce a consistent message: ties of kinship must not be torn apart by external pressures.

Stories like those Mrs Sidney and Mrs Smith tell are not simply elaborate mental constructions. They are as grounded in everyday, material conditions as they are in local ideas and practices. Nor are oral traditions in any way natural products. They have social histories and they acquire meanings in the situations in which they emerge, in situations where they are used, and in interactions between narrators and listeners. They have their roots in ancient narratives, but contemporary tellings emerge in settings where powerful forces impinge directly on local experience.

Ethnography presents us with ways in which humans construct continuity and integration in the face of disorder. One compelling question is how people enmeshed in this disorderly world create an identity that has continuity, especially when there is no script. We do this by working with those strands of tradition we have at our disposal to produce and reproduce the idea that the world is still continuous, and to go on to create those continuities, often by weeding out the really incongruent portions. Culture does not produce itself; rather, images like those of Kaax'achgóok, Kaats', Dukt'ootl', and Naatsilanéi resonate because they become translation devices to explain new experiences that do not seem to have cultural roots. The ways in which Mrs Sidney and Mrs Smith use these images demonstrate their determination to achieve consistency between old values and changing circumstances.

NOTES

1 See the following for overviews: William Cronon, "A Place for Stories: Nature, History and Narrative," *Journal of American History* 78, no. 4 (1992): 1347–76; David Cohen, "The Production of History," in *The Combing of History* (Chicago: University of Chicago Press, 1994), 1–23; Karin Barber, *Anthropology of Texts, Persons and Publics* (Cambridge: Cambridge University Press, 2007);

Keith Carlson, Kristina Fagan, and Natalia Khanenko-Friesen, eds., *Orality and Literacy: Reflections across Disciplines* (Toronto: University of Toronto Press, 2011).

2 Comparing Jan Vansina, *Oral Tradition as History* (Madison: University of Wisconsin Press, 1985) with Bruce Granville Miller, *Oral History on Trial* (Vancouver: UBC Press, 2011), 67–86, provides one instance of how approaches to analysis of oral tradition have changed in recent decades.

3 See Michel de Certeau, *The Practice of Everyday Life,* translated by Stephen Randall (Berkeley: University of California Press, 1984), 123.

4 Hayden White, *Content of the Form: Narrative Discourse and Historical Representation* (Baltimore: Johns Hopkins University Press, 1987), 14.

5 Alasdair McIntyre, *After Virtue: A Study in Moral Theory* (Notre Dame, IN: University of Notre Dame Press, 1981), 114.

6 Luise White, *Speaking with Vampires: Rumor and History in Colonial Africa* (Berkeley: University of California Press, 2000).

7 Eric R. Wolf, *Envisioning Power: Ideologies of Dominance and Crisis* (Berkeley: University of California Press, 1999), 16.

8 Daria Khubova, Andrei Ivankiev, and Tonia Sharova, "After Glasnost: Oral History in the Soviet Union," in *Memory and Totalitarianism,* edited by Luisa Passerini (Oxford: Oxford University Press, 1992), 89–101; Luise White, Stephan Miescher, and David Cohen. *African Words, African Voices* (Bloomington: Indiana University Press, 2001); Isabel Hofmeyer, *We Spend Our Years As a Tale That Is Told: Oral Historical Narrative in a South African Chiefdom* (Johannesburg: Witwatersund University Press, 1993); Alessandro Portelli, *They Say in Harlan County: An Oral History* (Oxford: Oxford University Press, 2010); Luisa Passerini, *Memory and Totalitarianism, 1992* (New York: Oxford University Press, 1992); Selma Leydesdorff, Luisa Passerini, and Paul Thompson, *Gender and Memory* (Oxford: Oxford University Press, 1996); and Rubie Watson, ed. *Memory, History, and Opposition: Under State Socialism* (Sante Fe: School of American Research, 1994).

9 Michael Dorris, "Native American Literature in an Ethnohistorical Context," *College English* 41, no. 2 (1979): 147.

10 Del Hymes, *In Vain I Tried to Tell You* (Philadelphia: University of Pennsylvania Press, 1981); Richard Dauenhauer and Nora Dauenhauer, *Haa Shuká: Our Ancestors: Tlingit Oral Narratives* (Seattle: University of Washington Press; Juneau: Sealaska Press, 1987); Keith Basso, *Wisdom Sits in Places: Landscape and Language among the Western Apache* (Albuquerque, NM: University of New Mexico Press, 1996).

11 Phyllis Morrow, "On Shaky Ground: Folklore, Collaboration, and Problematic Outcomes," in *When Our Words Return: Writing, Hearing and Remembering Oral Traditions of Alaska and the Yukon,* edited by Phyllis Morrow and William Schneider (Logan: Utah State University Press, 1995), 29.

12 Harold Adams Innis, *Empire and Communications* (Oxford: Clarendon, 1950); *The Bias of Communication* (Toronto: University of Toronto Press, 1951).

13 Innis, *Bias,* 64–100; see also Judith Stamps, *Unthinking Modernity: Innis, McLuhan, and the Frankfurt School* (Montreal: McGill-Queen's University Press, 1995), 48–51.

14 Mikhail Bakhtin, *The Dialogic Imagination* (Austin: University of Texas Press, 1984); *Rabelais and His World,* translated by Helene Iswolsky (Bloomington: Indiana University Press, 1984).

15 Walter Benjamin, "The Storyteller," in *Illuminations,* edited by Hannah Arendt (New York: Schocken, 1969), 83–109; see also Stamps, *Unthinking Modernity,* 23–40.

16 Bakhtin, *Rabelais.*

17 Innis, *Bias,* 8–9.

18 M.C. Urquhart, ed., *Historical Statistics of Canada* (Toronto: Macmillan, 1965), 14.

19 John Marchand, "Tribal Epidemics in the Yukon," *Journal of the American Medical Association* 123 (1974): 1019–20.

20 Julie Cruikshank, "The Gravel Magnet: Some Social Impacts of the Alaskan Highway on Yukon Indians," in *The Alaska Highway: Papers of the Fortieth Anniversary Symposium,* edited by Kenneth Coates (Vancouver: UBC Press, 1998), 172–87.

21 Julie Cruikshank, *The Social Life of Stories: Narrative and Knowledge in the Yukon Territory* (Lincoln: University of Nebraska Press; Vancouver: UBC Press, 1998), 71–97.

22 Pierre Bourdieu, *Language and Symbolic Power,* edited by John B. Thomson (Cambridge: Polity, 1991), 7–8.

23 Julie Cruikshank, in collaboration with Angela Sidney, Kitty Smith, and Annie Ned, *Life Lived Like a Story: Life Stories of Three Yukon Elders* (Lincoln: University of Nebraska Press; Vancouver: UBC Press, 1990).

24 Angela Sidney, Kitty Smith, and Rachel Dawson, *My Stories are My Wealth,* recorded by Julie Cruikshank (Whitehorse: Council for Yukon Indians, 1977).

25 Sidney in Cruikshank et al., *Life Lived,* 37–158.

26 Cruikshank et al., *Life Lived,* 139–45. This narrative was also recorded more than a century ago by J.R. Swanton, "Tlingit Myths and Texts," *Bureau of American Ethnology Bulletin* 39 (1909): nos. 67 and 101, p. 225–7 and 321–3; and more recently by Dauenhauer and Dauenhauer, in *Haa Shuká,* 82–107 and in notes, p. 323–33.

27 Sidney, "Story of Kaax'achgóok," *Northern Review* 2 (1988): 9–16.

28 Smith in Cruikshank et al., *Life Lived,* 175–262.

29 Cruikshank, *Social Life,* 71–97.

30 Tapes and transcripts of these interviews are filed with the MacBride Museum in Whitehorse, Yukon.

31 Photographs of Mrs Smith's carvings appear in Cruikshank, "Imperfect Translations: Rethinking Objects of Ethnographic Collections," *Museum Anthropology* 19, no. 1 (1995): 25–38. The story of Dukt'ootl' has been recorded in many versions, including Swanton, "Tlingit Myths," No. 93, and Dauenhauer and Dauenhauer, *Haa Shuká*, 138–51 and notes p. 348–59. Versions of Naatsilanéi's story can be found in Swanton, "Tlingit Myths," Nos. 4 and 71 and in Dauenhauer and Dauenhauer, *Haa Shuká*, 108–37 and notes p. 334–47. The narrative about Kaats' is inscribed on totem poles from Wrangell to Yakutat and recorded by Swanton, *Tlingit Myths*, Nos. 19 and 69 and in Dauenhauer and Dauenhauer, *Haa Shuká*, 218–43 and notes p. 390–406.

32 Raymond Fogelson, "Ethnohistory of Events and Nonevents," *Ethnohistory* 36 (1989): 133–47.

33 McIntyre, *After Virtue*, 118–19.

SECTION THREE

Preservation and Presentation

9

Hidden from Historians: Preserving Lesbian Oral History in Canada[1]

Elise Chenier

In their 1989 collection, editors Martin Duberman, Martha Vicinus, and George Chauncey point out that the twenty-nine essays gathered in their book represent the "first phase of historical reclamation"[2] of the lesbian and gay past. At that time, the history of sexuality was still a curious new field. Its practitioners had to go hunting for publishers, and their chance of landing a job in an academic institution was slim to none. Since then, the field of lesbian, gay, and queer studies has come to enjoy mainstream respectability in some quarters, and a small but significant number of faculty and graduate students are being rewarded for research in this once controversial field.[3] Today, lesbian, gay, and queer history is far from hidden.

Yet much of the research undertaken by Canadian historians of the lesbian past remains out of public view and is at risk of being lost. The late 1980s and early 1990s witnessed a surge of research activity undertaken by grassroots organizations such as Lesbians Making History, by filmmakers Aerlyn Weissman and Lynne Fernie, and by historians such as Becki Ross and Cameron Duder. These researchers undertook extensive oral history interviews with lesbian and gay women who came of age in the 1950s, 1960s, and 1970s, yet only some have donated their materials to archives. Moreover, those interviews were recorded on analogue cassettes that degrade over time. To date, only one set of these interviews has been digitized; most of this valuable research material remains in the possession of the interviewers, who have little time and few material resources that would allow them to take the necessary steps toward preservation. Hours of research material about a relatively hidden area of Canadian historical experience are at risk of being lost forever, and because many of the narrators have died, there is little possibility of reclaiming these stories a second time.

In the postwar period most lesbians and gay men worked hard to hide, not preserve a record of, their private lives. Much of what we know about this era results from the efforts of lesbians and gays who in the 1970s, 1980s, and 1990s initiated and sustained local oral history projects and built community archives to hold their records. In Canada, however, no single institution or archives actively supports and promotes the production and preservation of oral histories of lesbians, gays, or members of any other sexual minority group. Though existing archives are today often delighted to receive such material, none is taking steps to encourage its production or to adequately preserve the material they already possess. My findings suggest that one of the main reasons why Canadian lesbian oral history collections are in danger of disappearing is the absence of an active archival collection and preservation program. The other is an absence of training in oral history methods that teaches community and academic researchers to think beyond the completion of their own projects and develop a preservation plan.

This chapter reports on the fate of lesbian oral history interview material collected in Canada since the mid-1980s. The first section provides a brief introduction to lesbian and gay oral history. Key research projects undertaken in Canada since the late 1980s are summarized and findings from a questionnaire distributed to researchers for the purpose of this study are presented. Contrary to what many historians might suspect, homophobia has not been a significant barrier to archival preservation of lesbian oral history. Rather, a lack of training in oral history methodology and the absence of a dedicated grassroots movement to collect and preserve a lesbian (or gay) "people's history" are the main reasons why very few lesbian oral histories have been archived. This chapter also describes the Archives of Lesbian Oral Testimony (ALOT). Currently in the collection and digitization stage, it will eventually store and make accessible the tremendously rich resource material about lesbian experience produced by researchers in Canada and around the world. Finally, recommendations are offered that will help to address some of the main problems that exist in the collection, preservation, and future use of oral history.

Findings presented here are based on thirteen questionnaire responses received from academics, public historians, and community activists about their lesbian oral history projects. Most of the respondents I know personally and contacted directly. I also posted a query to the Canadian Committee on Women's History and the Canadian Committee on the

History of Sexuality discussion lists. This generated two additional responses. I corresponded with three archivists: one from the Canadian
Lesbian and Gay Archives (CLGA) in Toronto, one who operates a gay
and lesbian archives out of his home in Vancouver, British Columbia, and
another from the University of Ottawa's Canadian Women's Movement
Archives, which holds a large lesbian oral history collection. I also gathered information from the past project leader of the Vancouver-based
Queer History Project.

The thirteen respondents collected oral testimonies from women who
lived most of their lives in British Columbia, Manitoba, Ontario, and/or
Quebec. Two undertook their research as public or community historians;
eleven were graduate students or held a tenure-track position at a university at the time they conducted their interviews. Consequently, this chapter summarizes the work of one community-based lesbian history group
(Lesbians Making History), one public historian (Michael Riordan), and
eleven university-based scholars. It is not an exhaustive account of lesbian
oral history projects in Canada, but the findings presented here shed light
on key collection and preservation issues plaguing lesbian oral history in
Canada.

This discussion is limited to research projects that either focused exclusively on lesbians or which included lesbians or gay women. The
reasons are partly pragmatic. My interest in this topic evolves from my
own work in the field of lesbian history, but it also reflects the current
state of affairs in the lesbian and gay research and collections community. In the second half of the twentieth century the lives of gay men and
women often overlapped and were sometimes complementary. Lesbians,
gay men, and transpeople faced similar sets of life challenges. As "queers"
living during a time of tremendous pressure to conform to heteronorma-
tive imperatives, they were all subject to various forms of oppression, exclusion, and trauma. They responded by forming private social networks
and socializing in half-hidden spaces that they often shared. Gay men,
lesbians, and transpeople sometimes went to the same bars, beaches, and
house parties. They occasionally joined forces to fight assailants on the
streets and at other times provided "heterosexual cover" for each other
by attending work and family functions together as "normal" couples. But
their lives were also quite distinct. Men who remained closeted at work
could usually support themselves comfortably on a male wage whereas
women, whose wages were generally much lower, had to make do with
much less. For transpeople, finding any kind of job at all could prove impossible. Moreover, lesbians, gay men, and transpeople did not always

consider themselves natural allies. For example, the gay male community could be extremely sexist toward lesbians. Toronto's St Charles Tavern, a popular 1960s and 1970s gay male bar, effectively barred butch (masculine) women by imposing a skirts- and dresses-only policy for women. Men were not required to gender-conform in their style of dress. This complex past partly explains why few oral testimony-based studies include lesbians and men in equal measure, and even fewer include gay men, lesbians, *and* transpeople.

Oral historians' commitment to dismantle traditional relations of power led them to seek out ways to share authority with narrators. They hoped to enable their informants to tell their own stories, gave informants more control over the interview, and invited them to challenge their interpretations of their testimony. Collecting and telling history was about much more than expanding the historical record to include the experiences of those who were "hidden" from traditional historical narratives; it was a means to empower people perceived to have a common set of interests. These projects were typically community- not university-based. As one early advocate explained, oral history was a means to "[break] through the barriers between the chroniclers and their audience; between the educational institution and the outside world."[4] Working-class, women's, immigrant, Aboriginal, and, especially in the United States, African-American history, and the communities from which narrators came were enormously enriched by this project.

Lesbian and gay community activists and historians were equally turned on to oral history as a liberating practice. It was a way to write gay and lesbian experience into existence, to challenge heterosexism and traditional history, and to engender pride within a community long forced to live on the social, economic, and political margins of society. Lesbian and gay community history "builds lives and identities, and provides both knowledge of the world and knowledge of the self. It is work that makes lesbian and gay living possible."[5] The connections between history, storytelling, and life make clear the passion of these early oral historians' commitment to an ambitious political project.

In 1973 educator and archivist Joan Nestle founded the Lesbian Herstory Archives (LHA) in her home in Brooklyn. That she called it the "Herstory" Archives marks the way feminist theory and activism was part of the foundation upon which lesbian history was built. Nestle was rescuing lesbian *and* women's history. For a variety of reasons, including the fact that men held leadership positions in most early gay organizations, lesbian and gay archives are typically dominated by material related to, and produced by, men. Only by making lesbian material a priority, and by having lesbians on staff to build relationships with lesbian community members, does a meaningful repository of women's material emerge.[6] Gay male sexism and lesbian separatism were two determinants in establishing an archives dedicated exclusively to the lesbian experience. "But the strongest reason," Nestle explains, "was to end the silence of patriarchal history about us – women who loved women."[7]

History and politics are mutually reinforcing practices aimed at building and strengthening community. Like other activist historians, Nestle viewed the archives as an "answer [to] the challenge of exclusion." And since lesbians are excluded as women and as homosexuals, it is little wonder she considered the LHA "the work of a lifetime."[8] She also shared with Jonathan Ned Katz, Esther Newton, Cherrie Moraga, and others a belief that it was essential to bring history to the public rather than expect the public to come to them.[9] Furthermore, she understood that women needed extra encouragement to see that the ephemeral from their lives was worthy of its own file folder in an archives cabinet.[10] She travelled to large and small communities to tell women about their lesbian past and to encourage them "to record their experiences in order to formulate our living Herstory." LHA was not a hallowed institution meant solely for academics; it was "for everyone, for surviving, a place to create a family album."[11]

Nestle's path-breaking work inspired others to start historical reclamation projects of their own. The most important was the Buffalo Women's Oral History Project, founded in 1978 by Madeline Davis and Elizabeth Kennedy. The model they established – to produce a written history of an urban lesbian community, to create an archives of oral history materials, and to give the history back to the community from which it came – was reproduced in cities across the United States and elsewhere.

By the time Davis and Kennedy fulfilled their first objective in 1993, oral history was firmly established as an important method and source for historians of modern and marginalized sexualities. Both John D'Emilio and Allan Bérubé used oral history to document the ways in which people experienced, resisted, and organized against oppression.[12] The second wave of scholarship worked from this foundation to pose different questions, cover new social and geographic terrain, and introduce new conceptual and theoretical directions. George Chauncey showed that the pre–Second World War era was still within reach for oral historians; Marc Stein demonstrated that it was possible to study both women and men, and argued that it was necessary to do so; John Howard revealed that second-hand stories can be used to document the histories of those whose experiences are not readily captured by "gay" history; and Nan Alamilla Boyd established how, when combined with traditional archival sources, oral testimony can be used to further elaborate, and complicate, what we already know about cities, social movements, and the queer past.[13]

The work of Nestle and Davis and Kennedy has had a global impact in the field of lesbian history and was the inspiration for the first lesbian oral history project in Canada. The Lesbians Making History (LMH) collective was a Toronto-based lesbian group of feminist women who set out to collect local stories from women who had been "out" in the public lesbian community in the 1950s, 1960s, and 1970s. They collected extraordinary testimonies, some of which formed part of the background research for Lynne Fernie and Aerlyn Weissman's documentary film *Forbidden Love: The Unashamed Stories of Lesbian Lives*.[14]

University-based scholars have also benefitted from the LMH interviews. Though initially committed to keeping this grassroots project out of the hands of academics (even though some of the group's members were academics themselves), by the early 1990s LMH changed its position and shared the transcripts with graduate students, and later scholars with university positions. I was the first beneficiary of this policy change. The LMH interviews formed the bulk of the oral history material I used for my Master's thesis. Cameron Duder also used the collection in his PhD research. Most recently, some of the interview material was included in Gary Kinsman and Patrizia Gentile's book *The Canadian War on Queers*.[15]

One might think that the natural place for this important collection would be the Canadian Lesbian and Gay Archives (CLGA). Founded in Toronto in 1973 as the Canadian Gay Liberation Movement Archives and later renamed the Canadian Gay Archives, the collection was a community-based effort that grew out of the records of *The Body Politic* (TBP), the most important gay liberation magazine in the English-speaking world. Though the TBP collective included feminists, male volunteers dominated the archives. As Nestle intuited in 1973, largely gay, male-run, volunteer organizations make little effort to collect or promote material relating to women. According to Ron Dutton, a Vancouver-based archivist of western Canada's gay and lesbian past, lesbian separatism was also a factor. When he began building his collection in the mid-1970s, lesbians seemed uninterested in working collaboratively with men, and the separatist environment made him feel uncomfortable about approaching them to request items such as meeting minutes.[16] Indeed, in 1986 separatism inspired lesbians to establish the Archives lesbiennes de Montréal–Traces, an archives independent of the Archives Gaies du Québec and "*accessibles à toutes les lesbiennes et aux femmes intéressées.*"[17]

Perhaps it is for these reasons that the CLGA does not have a strong profile in the lesbian community. Long dominated by male volunteers, in 1993 the Board signalled a desire to become more inclusive by changing its name from the Canadian Gay Archives to the Canadian Lesbian and Gay Archives. In the early 2000s Mary MacDonald, a lesbian, historian, and heritage expert, served a successful term as its President and led the archives through half a decade of tremendous growth. However, none of these advances has translated into substantive increase in lesbian content. The CLGA is greatly limited by a lack of stable funding and remains dependent upon the efforts and interests of its mostly male volunteers. It has not played a leadership role in the collection or preservation of Canada's lesbian past.

LESBIAN ORAL HISTORY RESEARCH IN CANADA

Over the last three decades, Canadians have been actively collecting lesbian oral testimony. To find out more about the fate of this research material, I sent questionnaires to sixteen people who undertook oral history research with lesbians and gay women. I received thirteen responses. Two respondents were leaders of community projects; eight were graduate students at the time they undertook their projects (four of those have published or intend to publish the results of their research); three began their projects as tenure-track or tenured professors and are working toward monographs.

Despite the fact that trained historians dominate the field of lesbian oral history in Canada, Canadians are in danger of losing the source material researchers have worked so hard to collect. Among the respondents, only Karen Duder has preserved the interviews in accessible archives.[18] Valerie Korinek is in the process of gathering oral history research material for her study of the prairies and has made arrangements to donate her interviews to the Saskatchewan Archives Board. Gary Kinsman and Patrizia Gentile plan to donate their recordings to the CLGA.[19] Despite their intention to do so, four others – including Michael Riordan whose book *The Unauthorized Biography of the World* contains an entire chapter on the importance of preservation[20] – have never pulled their material together to place in archives. Other scholars and grassroots activists have been more successful: Becki Ross, the author of a major study of the Lesbian Organization of Toronto, donated many of her tapes to the Women's

Movement Archives, and Tom Warner, author of a comprehensive study of queer activism in Canada, donated his to the CLGA.[21]

One might wonder if archives themselves pose a barrier to preservation. Audiotapes are not easy to store and Canadian archives are often ill equipped to handle them, and not everyone is convinced that queer experience has historical value.[22] However, none of the researchers reported any difficulty piquing the interest of archivists and those who have not yet donated their collections do not anticipate that an archives would reject their research material. While I have not undertaken a study of the collection policies or practices of mainstream archives, the evidence suggests this material is of interest to some of the major Canadian archives. Indeed, in 1975 the Archives of Ontario offered to house *TBP*'s Gay Liberation Archives collection. Today major collections of lesbian and gay material can be found in city, provincial, and university archives.[23]

Archives are not barriers to the preservation of lesbian oral testimonies. Funding, however, is. Becki Ross, for example, donated her analogue tapes to the Women's Movement Archives but insufficient staffing means that preservation of her tapes consists of playing them once a year.[24] There are government funds available for such projects. Currently the University of Victoria Archives holds a grant from Library and Archives Canada's National Archival Development Program, Heritage Canada, to digitize Cameron Duder's analogue tapes. Applying for grant money, however, is a time-consuming process that requires skilled staff dedicated to the task. Though part of the University of Ottawa, the Canadian Women's Movement Archives employs only one archivist. Without more staff, preservation efforts will be minimal at best.

Another significant barrier is an increasing fear of legal action on the part of narrators. Consent forms rarely provide the necessary permission to allow other researchers to use the material.[25] Even though Ross's tapes are archived, for example, permission to use the material was granted to Ross only. Unfortunately, most researchers, myself included, failed to think beyond their own research projects and did not acquire narrators' consent to allow third parties to use the interview material. This is true even for the LMH collective, whose project was to collect oral histories for the benefit of the community. Because their process was often informal, and because they did not explicitly ask narrators to permit others to listen to the tapes, it is not clear what legal constraints there may be on future use.

Interviewing vulnerable populations creates unique problems concerning formal consent. Line Chamberland's narrators were uneasy about signing forms related to a project on lesbian experience because the mere act of putting their name to paper risked exposure that could negatively affect their personal and professional lives. Chamberland borrowed a technique from lesbian researcher Didi Khayatt.[26] She gave narrators a form outlining how she would protect their identity in her research reports. Chamberland signed the form, not the narrators. This way, narrators were provided with a legal document outlining how the interview data would be used, stored, and protected, without having to put their name to paper. At that time, universities did not require the kind of elaborate consent forms they do today; consequently, such arrangements were easy to make and met everyone's needs. Such arrangements, however, create problems with respect to preservation and future usage. How can we protect the interests of the narrators and still preserve this valuable material for the future?

When writer and community activist Michael Riordan began his research on lesbian and gay life in Canada, he did not acquire signed permission from his narrators and now fears that without them, the tapes are useless to archives. Like Lesbians Making History, his projects are community-based endeavours that imagined giving history back to the people that gave it to him. Neither he nor the LMH collective imagined a world in which a research ethics regime would make "telling our stories" risky business. The regulation of oral history projects by university ethics boards is a complex and vexing issue that cannot be fully explored here. Suffice it to say that forms composed just ten years ago do not provide sufficiently clear consent for the continued use of those interviews because they fail to meet the increasingly elaborate and legalistic requirements of archivists, and even of publishers.[27] A lack of training in oral history methodology is also a major problem. Better training could eliminate such problems and could teach researchers to think beyond the project at hand. Remarkably, not one of the thirteen questionnaire respondents had any training in the practice of oral history.

"Trained" academics have not fared any better. It never occurred to me to include permission to donate the interviews to an archives in my own consent forms, and it appears not to have occurred to others, either. Those researchers who did (Duder, Gentile and Kinsman, Llewellyn) found that some of their narrators were hesitant to allow others access to their interviews. Interviews about sexuality and sexual identity typically include at least some discussion of private sexual matters and can also include discussion of painful and embarrassing memories. Moreover, as Valerie Korinek found, women are much more reluctant than men to consent to granting others access to their interviews. Interviews about lesbian life typically explore some of the most intimate aspects of narrators' life experiences. Understandably, these narrators have heightened concerns about privacy. In some cases, narrators have reason to be concerned that their testimony could compromise their personal safety and security in the present day.

That some of us have not thought beyond our own project confirms the suspicions of early oral history activists. They predicted that the institutionalization of lesbian and gay history would only benefit scholars, not the communities they studied. These early suspicions seem to have some merit. Respondents to my questionnaire confirmed that once projects are completed, most academics move on to other things, leaving the interview material untouched and unused.

Failing to preserve research material may be a generational issue as well. With the professionalization of the history of sexuality and the waning of the gay liberation movement, young scholars may not feel that their projects are important for community building and may not recognize the full value of their own work. We need to make sure that they do.

VANCOUVER'S QUEER HISTORY PROJECT

The categories we use to write the history of the queer past have changed, but scholars and community members remain as interested in oral history as ever. In Canada, one of the most recent developments on this front is Out on Screen's Queer History Project (QHP). An initiative of the Vancouver Queer Film Festival, QHP began as a film-commissioning project and has grown into an innovative, on-line space where queer Vancouverites are invited to contribute stories and read about and listen to the stories of others.[28] Similar to early gay liberation projects, it seeks to document "our history beyond the medium of film, and to give other people the chance to join the conversation." Now in the building stage, the QHP runs workshops to entice people to come out and record their histories. Their long-term goal is to create a permanent, on-line repository of Vancouver's queer history.

The project is run by a student of archival studies, and while she is keen to have academics act as advisors, "we don't want the tone of the site to be too academic in its content and presentation; it's meant to be more informal and accessible."[29] With funding from the Canadian Council for the Arts, the City of Vancouver, and Imperial Tobacco, among others, the project has resources to build a visually pleasing website, hire staff to run the workshops, advertise to the community, and equip interviewers with needed technological support. It is a perfect example of how projects get done, and preserved, when grassroots passion is supported by a stable source of funding.

That the QHP has grown out of the film community may seem odd, but film has been the most successful medium for meeting the objectives laid out by early oral historians. Canadian filmmakers Lynne Fernie and Aerlyn Weissman created the award-winning documentary *Forbidden Love: The Unashamed Stories of Lesbian Lives*, an outstanding exploration of butch/fem culture and lesbian experience in postwar Canada. They conducted extensive oral history research before selecting the nine narrators who appear in the final version. Unlike scholarly books and articles, which are not always read outside the academic community, *Forbidden Love* has been seen by hundreds of thousands of people, and has had just the kind of effect that Nestle hoped the Lesbian Herstory Archives would: it helped women survive.[30] Fernie and Weissman went on to make a documentary about Jane Rule, a well-known lesbian author, activist, and early contributor to *The Body Politic*. Nancy Nichol, another Toronto-based filmmaker, has also produced a number of documentaries on the gay liberation and rights movements in Canada.[31] All of these films rely on narrators' first-person accounts.

Activists and academic scholars have recently launched new oral history projects that sidestep traditional identity categories such as "lesbian" and "gay." Day Wong's Hong Kong–based oral history group uses "7-Eleven" as a metaphor for women who have sex with women, as in "there must be one near you."[32] Vancouver's QHP strives to escape some of the homogenizing tendencies of "identity" as an organizing principle and strategy of recognition by framing its project as the history of a community. This strategy is also being used successfully by another on-line archives, the ACTUP Oral History Project.[33] QHP and the ACTUP Oral History Project were initiated in the digital age. Their testimonies are preserved in sustainable formats and made accessible on websites. But what of all those analogue tapes still languishing in basements across Canada?

ARCHIVES OF LESBIAN ORAL TESTIMONIES (ALOT)

While I was undertaking research for this chapter, it became obvious that a permanent digital archives was necessary if lesbian oral history was to be preserved for future use. With a secure institutional position in hand and the support of Simon Fraser University's Special Collections archivist,

I find myself in a good position to take steps toward preserving unarchived lesbian oral history collections. My long-standing friendship with Maureen Fitzgerald, who currently has the LMH collection in her custody, and Fernie, who has kept the research tapes she and co-director Weissman produced in their research for *Forbidden Love*, made it easier to convince them to donate their material to this project. I have added my own interviews and recently received a donation of VHS tapes of a lesbian and gay community television program produced in Alberta. We are currently working to gather material produced by scholars, community activists, public historians, and lesbians themselves, across Canada. The next phase is to extend the archival reach beyond Canada.

ALOT will exist as a digital archives housed on the Simon Fraser University server and managed by the library's Special Collections unit. This may be too removed from the community to whom these testimonies belong, but some narrators' concerns about the protection of their privacy make administrative oversight necessary. Special Collections has a staff able to manage requests to access the material through a password-protected site. Narrators who request limits on access can be assured that their instructions will be carefully followed.

By naming this collection the Archives of Lesbian Oral Testimony, I am not ignoring the fact that "lesbian" is a problematic identifier. Oral history has played a major role in advancing lesbian identity politics, politics that many people now reject. Post-structuralist critiques of identity show that the term "lesbian" homogenizes populations and emphasizes sameness over difference.[34] Moreover, many of the women whom lesbian historians identify as "butch" might better be understood as transgender.[35] The term "lesbian" has never worked well in my own historical work. Most of the women I interviewed came out in the 1950s and 1960s and uniformly loathed the word "lesbian." To them it signifies mental illness. They called themselves "gay." I have always been uneasy about using "lesbian" to describe them, but since contemporary audiences generally assume the word "gay" refers to a male subject and do not equate "lesbian" with mental disease, I have made it my practice to use "lesbian" in titles of papers and articles and provide explanations in the text. At ALOT we hope to collect testimonies from women who experienced same-sex desire, regardless of what, if any, word they used to identify themselves. People can avoid labels, but archival collections cannot. Since at this historical moment the word "lesbian" has a clear meaning that researchers and an interested general audience will understand, it seems the most suitable name to use.

This collection, however, is not just about the narrators. It is also about the researchers and their projects. ALOT not only houses lesbian history but also will be an archives of the late-twentieth-century movement to reclaim lesbian history itself. Thus, by ascribing the name "lesbian" to this collection, we do not mean to close off the possibility of rethinking the lesbian subject. The intention is to capture the rich body of material produced by those research projects that set out to record and examine what was called "lesbian existence" or "experience."[36] Consequently, ALOT is also an archives of the emergence of lesbian history as a tool for social change and oral history as a method and practice.

RECOMMENDATIONS

Early lesbian and gay historians argued that we are all members of communities and that only through the help of communities do we accomplish great things. In Canada, oral history is currently undergoing a period of revival. The Canadian Oral History Association (COHA) is in the process of rebuilding itself into a professional organization for the promotion of oral history, and there are at least two Canada Research Chairs, Mary Ellen Kelm and Steven High, whose area of expertise is oral history. Steven High has built an extraordinary oral history laboratory and training program at Concordia University, and five oral historians at Simon Fraser University launched their own oral history training program in the 2009–10 academic year. This is all good news for the future of oral history in Canada. There are some concrete steps that must be taken, however, to ensure the future of the queer (and not-so-queer) past. On the basis of my research findings, I offer the following recommendations:

1 More training needs to be made available for community and scholarly oral history in Canada. It would be a major step forward if academics provided training for their students and for local communities by offering courses in oral history in their departments, through continuing education, or by volunteering their time and expertise in the wider community.
2 Researchers need to make themselves aware of consent issues beyond research ethics boards at their own institutions, and to consult with archives and publishers when composing consent forms to ensure that they will be of value to future scholars, and to researchers themselves, should they decide to publish their results.

3 COHA should act as a clearing house for up-to-date information concerning legal issues of consent as they are defined, and as they evolve, in universities, archives, and the publishing industry.

4 Archives should make scholars, artists, activists, and other researchers aware of the need to preserve their research material once their projects are completed and should aid them in making plans for their preservation.

5 Greater availability of federal and provincial funding for the digitization of research material must be provided to ensure that existing analogue tapes do not deteriorate to the point that recorded testimony is lost. Once digitized, these recordings can be made more accessible by being made available on-line. However, for digitized or born-digital materials, long-term preservation is an ongoing process that must respond to changes in technologies and standards, and an enduring digital preservation management project relies equally on organizational frameworks, technologies, and financial and staffing resources.

6 When applying for grants, researchers should include requests for funds to aid in the preparation of research material for archival donation.

7 Community research groups should be encouraged to apply for funding to enable them to consider preservation of their material.

8 COHA should consider actively courting the lesbian, gay, and queer communities to collaborate in developing oral history projects.

9 The Canadian Lesbian and Gay Archives should be encouraged to play a more active role in collecting and preserving lesbian material, and promoting and preserving lesbian, gay, and queer oral history.

Canada's lesbian past is richer than most of us can imagine. It has been the subject of outstanding scholarly books and wildly popular films, and still we have only skimmed its surface. Lesbian history challenges assumptions about what "counts" as proper history and complicates what we think we know about the past. It has been a source of fascination for those who would otherwise take no interest in Canada's past at all. More profoundly, as Will Roscoe and Joan Nestle proclaimed, history saves lives by validating lesbian, gay, and queer people's right to live a full and rich life free from oppression and censure. The oral history collections I have described took tremendous effort to build. They are an essential part of our heritage and must be preserved. Governments, granting agencies, and universities need to provide the necessary funding; archives need to play a more activist role in promoting and preserving the collection of this material; researchers must plan for the future; and teachers must show them how to do it. Only in this way will the history of our marginal communities not be marginalized once again.

NOTES

1 This chapter is the result of deep and abiding commitment by Canadian activists, archivists, and scholars to documenting our history. I am grateful for the input provided by the respondents to the research questionnaire, to Harold Averill, Nicole Maunsell, and Lucie Desjardins, and to Carolyn Anderson, who reminded me of the Red Deer Museum debacle of 1997. Any errors and omissions are my own.

2 Martin Duberman, Martha Vicinus, and George Chauncey, eds., *Hidden from History: Reclaiming the Gay and Lesbian Past* (New York: New American Library, 1989), 2.

3 Marc Stein, "Committee on Lesbian and Gay History Survey on LGBTQ History Careers," *Perspectives* 39, no. 5 (2001): 29–31.

4 Paul Thompson, "The Voice of the Past," in *The Oral History Reader*, 2nd edition, edited by Robert Perks and Alistair Thomson (New York: Routledge, 1998), 26.

5 Will Roscoe, "History's Future: Reflections on Lesbian and Gay History in the Community," in *Gay and Lesbian Studies*, edited by Henry L. Minton (New York: Haworth, 1991), 176.

6 Karen Martin, "Lesbian Biography and Oral History in the Gay and Lesbian Archives of South Africa," *South Africa Archives Journal* 40 (1998): 33–6.

7 Joan Nestle, "The Will to Remember: The Lesbian Herstory Archives of New York," *Feminist Review* 34 (spring 1990): 87. Other examples include the Archives lesbiennes de Montréal–Traces in Montreal, Quebec; the June Mazer Lesbian Archives in California; the Ohio Lesbian Archives; the Pacific Northwest Lesbian Archives in Seattle, Washington; and Glasgow Women's Library's Lesbian Archive.

8 Cited in Roscoe, "History's Future," 176.

9 For a fuller list of early historians and community lecturers, see Roscoe, "History's Future," 163.

10 See Sherna Berger Gluck and Daphne Patai, eds., *Women's Words: The Feminist Practice of Oral History* (London: Routledge, 1991).

11 Nestle, "The Will to Remember," 87–8.

12 John D'Emilio, *Sexual Politics, Sexual Communities: The Making of a Homosexual Minority in the United States, 1940–1970* (Chicago: University of Chicago Press, 1983); Allan Bérubé, *Coming Out under Fire: The History of Gay Men and Women in World War Two* (New York: Free Press, 1990).

13 George Chauncey, *Gay New York: Gender, Urban Culture, and the Making of the Gay Male World, 1890–1940* (New York: Basic Books, 1994); Mark Stein, *City of Sisterly and Brotherly Loves: Lesbian and Gay Philadelphia, 1945–1972* (Chicago: University of Chicago Press, 2000); John Howard, *Men Like That: A Southern Queer History* (Chicago: University of Chicago Press, 1999); Nan Alamilla Boyd, *Wide-Open Town: A History of Queer San Francisco to 1965* (Berkeley: University of California Press, 2003).

14 *Forbidden Love: The Unashamed Stories of Lesbian Lives*, directed by Lynne Fernie and Aerlyn Weissman, National Film Board of Canada, 1992. For different reasons, this award-winning film is also in the process of becoming "hidden." The National Film Board purchased the music rights for ten years. The film has not been available for purchase since these rights expired in 2004. Since the film was never released on DVD, only those VHS tapes currently in circulation at university and public libraries, and in private collections, are available to us. Those, however, will soon lose colour, image, and sound. Unless the NFB issues a re-release, *Forbidden Love* will also become "hidden from history." Lynne Fernie, personal correspondence, December 2008. The film was finally reissued in 2014.

15 Gary Kinsman and Patrizia Gentile, *The Canadian War on Queers: National Security as Sexual Regulation* (Vancouver: UBC Press, 2009).

16 Ron Dutton, personal correspondence, March 2009.

17 "Archives lesbiennes de Montréal–Traces (Montréal): répertoire sommaire, correspondance et autres documents, 1986–1990," X10-1 Series 1: Main files, box 3, Canadian Women's Movement Archives, Archives and Special Collections, University of Ottawa Library.

18 University of Victoria, "Browsing Women's Studies by Author: 'Duder, Karen,'" https://dspace.library.uvic.ca:8443/handle/1828/3700/browse?value= Duder%2C+Karen&type=author (accessed 19 June 2014).

19 Patrizia Gentile, personal correspondence, April 2009.

20 Michael Riordan, *The Unauthorized Biography of the World: Oral History on the Front Lines* (Toronto: Between the Lines, 2004). When contacted about this study, Riordan pointed out his failure to take his own advice.

21 See Becki Ross, *The House that Jill Built: A Lesbian Nation in Formation* (Toronto: University of Toronto Press, 1995); Tom Warner, *Never Going Back: A History of Queer Activism in Canada* (Toronto: University of Toronto Press, 2002), ix. See http://www.biblio.uottawa.ca/content-page.php?g=en&s= archives&c=src-fondscoll#cwma (accessed on 2 October 2009).

22 In this study I am concerned exclusively with the preservation of analogue tapes, but digital recordings pose unique preservation challenges as well. See John Paul K. Anbu and Marion L.N. Chibambo, "Digital Preservation: Issues and Challenges," *Trends in Information Management* 5, no. 1 (January–June 2009): 42–58. For a very useful discussion of oral history in Canada in general, see Alexander Freund, "Oral History in Canada: A Paradox," in *Canada*

in *Grainau/Le Canada à Grainau: A Multidisciplinary Survey of Canadian Studies after 30 Years/Tour d'horizon multidisciplinaire d'Études canadiennes, 30 ans après*, edited by Klaus-Dieter Ertler and Hartmut Lutz (New York, Hamburg: Peter Lang, 2009), 305–35; on the preservation of oral history materials in Canada see Riordan, *An Unauthorized Biography of the World*, 136–49. On homophobia, see Roscoe, "History's Future," 176.

23 See, for example, the Martin Crane Collection in the Vancouver City Archives.

24 Lucie Desjardins, Archivist: Archives and Special Collections, University of Ottawa, personal communication, April 2009.

25 See Nancy Janovicek's chapter "Oral History and Ethical Practice after TCPS2," chapter 3 in this *Reader*.

26 Madiha Didi Khayatt, *Lesbian Teachers: An Invisible Presence* (Albany: SUNY Press, 1992).

27 Publishers often require that living narrators give their consent to the publication of any findings related to their testimony. If permission to publish interview testimony was not obtained at time of the interview, researchers must go back to the narrators who, after the passage of time, are not always willing to allow their testimony to appear in book form.

28 Nicole Maunsell, Co-ordinator: Queer History Project (QHP), personal correspondence, April 2009.

29 Ibid.

30 One woman I interviewed explained to me how she finally understood who she was after watching the film. She was in her late seventies, and at that point began actively looking for a female partner. Helen Carscallen, interviewed by Elise Chenier, 1996.

31 Nancy Nichol, *Proud Lives: Chris Bearchell* (Montreal: Intervention Video, 2007); *Pride and Resistance* (Montreal: Intervention Video, 2007); *Politics of the Heart/La politique du coeur* (Toronto: V Tape, 2005); *Stand Together* (Toronto: V Tape, 2002). Though not a work of history, see also Laurie Colbert and Dominique Cardona, *Thank God I'm a Lesbian* (Toronto: Women Make Movies, 1992).

32 Day Wong, "Beyond Identity Politics: The Making of an Oral History of Hong Kong Women Who Love Women," *Journal of Lesbian Studies* 10, no. 3–4 (2006): 42.

33 http://www.actuporalhistory.org (accessed on 2 October 2009).

34 Day Wong, "Beyond Identity Politics," 29–48; Nan Alamilla Boyd, "Who Is the Subject? Queer Theory Meets Oral History," *Journal of the History of Sexuality* 17, no. 2 (May 2008): 177–89.

35 Judith Halberstam, *Female Masculinity* (Durham: Duke University Press, 1998).

36 Roscoe, "History's Future," 177.

10

Oral History as Process-Generated Data

Alexander Freund

PROCESS-GENERATED ORAL HISTORY

Oral history has developed as both an archival and a project-centred practice. While the main objective of archival projects has been to complement an archive's extant textual government and private documentation, that of oral history projects has been to answer a specific research question. Whether they are collected for a specific project or an archive, what makes interviews into oral histories – and what distinguishes oral history from qualitative interviews conducted in other disciplines – is that oral histories are made accessible to other researchers through their deposition in public repositories.[1] Thus there exists now a vast global archive of previously produced oral histories that researchers may use for addressing their own research questions.[2] These interviews, conducted by other researchers, may be considered process-generated data similar to data produced for purposes other than that of the researcher at hand. For the purpose of this chapter, I refer to such extant oral history collections as Process-Generated Oral History (PGOH), but let me make clear that this terminology is not used in the field of oral history.

The trick – and this is the main point of this chapter – is to find ways to tease information out of these data for one's own purposes. Knowing about the nature of oral history sources as well as the method of and theoretical discourse about oral history offers a path to a more efficient and effective use of extant oral history collections. In order to make full use of this process-generated resource, it is fruitful to understand oral histories not simply as sources to be mined for facts (data), but rather as complex social constructs that are inherently subjective and thus offer multiple layers of meaning. Alessandro Portelli, one of the most renowned oral historians, expressed it perhaps best when he said that oral histories "tell us not just what people did, but what they wanted to do, what they believed they were doing, and what they now think they did."[3]

Despite a large global archive of oral histories dating back at least to the 1930s, researchers have been reluctant to use other people's interviews.[4] They are often eager to rush out and conduct their own interviews, even though oral history is an extremely labour-intensive research method. If researchers use other researchers' oral histories at all, they often only use the transcripts (as is the case, for example, at Columbia University) or even only the summaries (as is sometimes the case at the Multicultural History Society of Ontario). Seldom do they go to the lengths of listening to (or watching) the interviews. Time and technology, however, are changing these dynamics. There is now a wealth of oral history material for time periods for which conducting new interviews is impossible, because eyewitnesses are no longer alive. All former slaves in the United States are now dead, as are all pioneers of the American and Canadian West and all veterans of the First World War. We now have to rely on interviews conducted by earlier generations of researchers.

In order to demonstrate the usefulness of PGOH, let me introduce a case study. One of my projects has been to study the ways in which German immigrants to North America have been confronted and are dealing with the Nazi past, both in mediated and personal encounters with veterans, Jews, and other European immigrants who arrived after the Second World War. In my search for sources, I conducted a lot of oral history interviews with German immigrants and their children, but I also used extant collections of interviews with German immigrants and their descendants. One collection I came across consisted of sixty-five interviews with German immigrants in Winnipeg, Manitoba, that German-Canadian historian Arthur Grenke had conducted in 1971. He had wanted to find out about their community between the founding of Winnipeg in the early 1870s and the First World War. Grenke had located the interviewees with the help of German churches and clubs and through other interviewees. He had also contacted prominent Germans mentioned in newspapers. Grenke recorded the interviews on reel-to-reel tapes and deposited them at the Manitoba Museum in Winnipeg. The interviews were not transcribed, but topical indexes were created and cassette tape copies were available for listening onsite or for purchase. Grenke used the interviews for his dissertation about the formation and early development of Winnipeg's German community between 1872 and 1919.[5]

While my own research focuses on German post–Second World War immigrants and their children and grandchildren, I wanted to include pre-war immigrants in my research in order to look for differences and similarities and thus to better contextualize and understand the postwar immigrants' perceptions and experiences. My assumption was that even though I knew the interviews had been for a project about the time before 1920, interviewees – at least if given the opportunity by a skilled interviewer – would nevertheless talk about the postwar years because that was the time in which the interviews were conducted. Another reason I was interested in Grenke's interviews was that they were conducted before public discourse in Canada shifted from the Second World War to the Holocaust.[6] These early interviews provided an unusual opportunity to gain insight into German-Canadians' perception from that time period. Thus, Grenke's interviews gave me access to a generation of immigrants that was no longer alive. And it gave me insight into a time period (the 1960s and early 1970s) that I could no longer research by conducting my own interviews. PGOH provide insights into the times of their production. In the coming years, an increasing number of historians and other researchers will turn to such sources to answer their questions.

There is another reason why researchers will increasingly turn to PGOH – and why they will increasingly listen to them rather than rely solely on transcripts or summaries. That reason is digital technology. By 2018, the National Library of Australia plans to have all of its then nearly 45,000 hours of sound materials online.[7] The Shoah Foundation already has all of its 52,000 interviews digitized and indexed and made available at research centres around the world,[8] and watching the interviews is the only means by which this massive collection can be used – there are no summaries or transcripts. The Library of Congress has made available online thousands of hours of interviews dating back to 1932.[9] The Regional Oral History Office at the University of California (Berkeley) makes parts of its collection available via iTunes and the university's own YouTube site. Around the world, private and public foundations invest in digitizing oral history collections. These efforts make oral history interviews more accessible. Researchers in the past avoided listening to cassette tapes or reel-to-reel tapes not only because it was more time-consuming than going through transcripts or summaries, but also because repositories often had only limited means of making such tapes accessible, thereby discouraging their use.[10] Access via computers – be it via the Internet or at secure offline work stations at libraries – is becoming easier and more convenient and thus invites the researcher to listen to interviews, or at least to quickly "listen in" on some interviews.

Nevertheless, despite digitization, using oral histories conducted by other researchers remains a time-consuming research process. For social scientists interested in using PGOH, knowing something about the oral history research method helps them to more effectively and efficiently use oral histories as sources. Oral historians have developed specific methodological procedures and standards that affect the nature and quality of the oral history interview. These include: the project design and actual interview process, technology and recording media, the interviewer-interviewee relationship, the ethical and legal dimensions of oral history, and interview forms and strategies. Knowing these procedures and standards helps social scientists to evaluate other researchers' projects and decide whether and how to use PGOH.

Project Conceptualization

Oral history projects – whether conducted for a specific research project or to expand an archival collection – are produced in several stages: the pre-production stage, the production stage, and the post-production stage. The pre-production stage includes the steps of conceptualization, research, and interview-preparation. The production stage consists of the actual interview. The post-production stage includes ongoing contact with the interviewees, processing of the interview for archival deposition, and, in the case of specific research projects, analysis and interpretation as well as various forms of dissemination, including publications, documentaries, exhibits, and artistic productions. According to the American Oral History Association, projects should always follow a basic principle: "Regardless of the purpose of the interviews, oral history should be conducted in the spirit of critical inquiry and social responsibility and with a recognition of the interactive and subjective nature of the enterprise."[11] If all these steps are completed as suggested by various guides and introductions to oral history, the oral history project is ready to be used by other researchers as well.

Unfortunately, in many cases reality differs from the handbook ideal. Time, money, and skills limit what can be accomplished in an oral history project, which sometimes happens to be overly ambitious. At times, first-time oral historians want to conduct as many interviews as possible and leave too little time and money for the pre- and post-production phases. The end results are often poorly conceptualized, poorly recorded, poorly conducted, and poorly documented oral histories that are of limited if any use for other researchers. It all seems so easy: you buy a recorder at the electronics shop next door, find some interesting people, and ask them a lot of questions. When researchers hear that experienced oral historians usually budget at least $1,000 (US) for *one* hour of audio-recorded interview, they are incredulous. But this is simply a reflection of the time, technology, and skill one needs to invest in a good oral history project. And if this is not done, it shows in the results.

Big oral history centres and institutions are more likely than others to produce first-class oral histories, but this is not always the case. For instance, some of the transcripts of interviews with German and Austrian Jewish émigrés at Columbia University, for which the original recordings were destroyed, often show blank spaces – words, sentences, even paragraphs not understood by the interviewer and transcriber, perhaps because of a heavy German accent or the use of the German language. Many of the interviews the Multicultural Historical Society of Ontario conducted in the 1970s and 1980s are of poor quality in every respect, because delayed government funding prevented the institution from training the interviewers. In general, interviewers' field notes and research notes were rarely kept.[12] For smaller projects, often conducted by one person for an academic project or by a small group of people interested in a specific history, documentation about the project's conceptualization may be incomplete or inaccessible. Publications based on the research, such as theses and dissertations, may then be helpful sources to better understand the oral history interviews. Thus, while the Manitoba Museum has some information about the interviews that Grenke conducted with German immigrants in Winnipeg, his dissertation provides not only further contextual information (for example, how he located and selected the interviewees) but also short biographies of twenty of his sixty-five interviewees.[13] Thus, before listening to the interviews (or reading their transcripts), the researcher should find out as much as possible about the provenance of the collection. A useful tool in evaluating an oral history project is provided by the American Oral History Association's Principles and Best Practices.[14]

Technology and Recording Media

The vast majority of extant oral history interviews were conducted on cassette tape and, to a lesser extent, open reel-to-reel recorders from the 1950s to the 2000s.[15] The use of such recorders has been decreasing steadily since 2000. The majority of the analog tapes have not been stored and cared for properly and are therefore deteriorating. Many tapes have not been transcribed, often have only minimal summaries, and have not been digitized. A huge resource is slowly but surely vanishing.

Increasingly, oral historians record interviews on video instead of audio, which has created a variety of challenges, ranging from production quality and storage to the influence of the video camera on the interview, ethical and legal implications, and questions researchers need to address regarding the analysis and interpretation of visual images. At the same time, not all oral histories are recorded on video or audio media. Sometimes, interviewees do not agree to being recorded and the researcher has to either take notes during the interview or create notes from memory after the interview. This question does not need to be addressed here, because such notes are rarely made accessible. Similarly, oral historians have explored the use of email as a form of interviewing, but have been reluctant to include email correspondence in the definition of their discipline. This medium too, then, will be excluded from consideration.

Faced then mostly with analog audio recordings, the researcher using archived oral histories must first of all establish that machines are still available that can play the tapes. This is already a substantial problem when it comes to reel-to-reel tapes because of the diversity of format and recording speeds, but even for cassette tapes it is becoming difficult to purchase high-quality tape decks for playback (which are needed to compensate for the poor audio quality).

The researcher may consider purchasing and digitizing copies of the tapes he or she is interested in. For smaller numbers of interviews, this can easily be done with free software such as Audacity and a computer with a soundcard. For example, I have the nine Grenke interviews I selected from his sixty-five as digital files on my computer and various mobile devices. With these digital files, I do not have to worry about deteriorating or breaking tape and they are easily portable. Furthermore, digital files are much more easily searchable than cassette tapes: fast forwarding and rewinding are faster than with cassette tapes and unlike cassette tapes, media player software allows one to skip back and forth and go to precise time points in the interview. Lastly, new qualitative data analysis software such as ATLAS.ti allows researchers to import and index digital audio files.

When obtaining copies from archives, and even when listening to tapes, a researcher will hardly ever be allowed to listen to the original tapes. I did not have the opportunity to listen to Grenke's original reel-to-reel tapes, but was given a cassette tape copy. Archives do this to preserve the original. The problem is that it is difficult to know whether the copy is exact or missing or mixed up. It is in some ways similar to using a Xerox or microfilm copy of an original document. In Grenke's case, for example, several times the last words spoken on Side A of the tape are repeated at the beginning of Side B, so I know there is nothing missing from the original recording. There are also many times when the recording is stopped in the middle of a sentence. It is unclear whether this was done: at the time of the interview, the time of the dubbing from the original, or the time of the dubbing from the master cassette tape (the original reel-to-reel tape is not used to produce copies, again in order to preserve it). On two tapes, there are unidentified interviews next to those that are identified to be on the tapes I received from the Manitoba Museum. It is not clear how these different interviews ended up on the same tape. Without being able to listen to the original tape, I cannot say for sure whether the recordings I have are complete.

Further, I am working with the digital files of Grenke's interviews. These digital files, produced by my research assistants, are thrice removed from the original reel-to-reel tape: the original was preserved as a master tape, which was copied to a master cassette tape from which all other copies were made. Thus, we created a digital file from a copy of a copy of the original. The recording is changed in many ways along the way. First, there is a loss of sound quality in each stage of analog dubbing. Second, the reel-to-reel tape of unknown length was broken up into 30-minute segments when it was transferred to cassette tape and then reassembled into 45-minute segments when it was copied from a 60-minute to a 90-minute tape. In the digital files, we digitized one tape (i.e., both sides) as one file, creating one digital audio file per cassette tape. Third, at each stage, there is not only a loss of sound quality, but the potential for further sound quality deterioration by changing various recording settings; for example, recording a Dolby B tape with Dolby C setting, or a non-Metal tape with a Metal setting. Fourth, over the years, recordings deteriorated because of improper storage.

The material condition of sources and the restricted access to originals complicate work with PGOH, but these limitations are not specific to PGOH. Archival textual documents often confront researchers with similar obstacles to access and use. Knowing about these limitations helps the researcher evaluate the sources at hand more critically. Even on the material level, the sources should not be taken at face value.

Interviewer-Interviewee Relationship

Oral historians reject the proposition that interviewers can be detached, objective, and uninvolved and thus without influence on the interview. Indeed, they acknowledge that the interview would not exist without them. American oral historian Ronald Grele argued as early as 1975 that the oral history interview is "a conversational narrative: conversational because of the relationship of interviewer and interviewee, and narrative because of the form of exposition – the telling of a tale."[16] This relationship between interviewer and interviewee creates one of the underlying structures of an oral history interview; this structure needs to be understood in order to make sense of the interview. Eva M. McMahan suggests conversation analysis as an approach to explaining how the dynamic between interviewer and interviewee shapes the tale that is told while feminist oral historians point to the gendered relationship of power and yet others have investigated how race, ethnicity, trauma, and other forces influence what story the narrator tells and how he or she tells it.[17]

The expectations and assumptions of both the interviewer and the interviewee shape the interview. Ritchie explains: "Interviewees take the measure of interviewers … and to some degree try to please them by telling what they want to hear." He describes one of the best-known examples of this influence: "A study of the Federal Writers Project interviews with former slaves, conducted in the 1930s, discovered that an elderly black woman was interviewed twice, once by a white woman and again by a black man. She gave starkly different accounts of her memories of slavery, painting a relatively benign account for the white woman and a much harsher account for the black man. She may well have spoken even more differently to another black woman."[18]

As a result of such findings, oral historians have increasingly taken into consideration how their social status, gender, race, ethnicity, age, sexuality, political conviction, religion, etc. shape their relationship to the interviewee.[19] Indeed, they actively seek to "share authority" with the interviewee.[20] This has added a conscious shaping of the conversational narrative to the subconscious one: oral historians have become ever more self-conscious of their status of power vis-à-vis their interviewees.[21] This development is further reinforced by university review boards, especially in the United States and Canada, that may make researchers even warier of asking questions that could upset their interviewees. At the same time, however, oral historians have also explored how any disagreements with their interviewees over interpreting their narratives can be fruitfully incorporated in the analysis.[22]

The stories told are also shaped by the interview setting. It makes a difference whether one interviews a longshoreman at home, at his workplace, or his favourite pub. Similarly, time in its many facets plays a role. Memory changes over time and with the narrator's position in her life course; thus, a fifty-year-old in the midst of her career or busy with child rearing will remember her childhood differently than a seventy-year-old retiree. Oral historians acknowledge that they cannot know what exactly these differences are. Data for comparison are almost always missing. The vast majority of oral historians do not return to their interviewees ten, twenty, or fifty years after the initial interview to compare the story of the fifty-year-old with that of the seventy-year-old.[23]

What, then, are the implications for social scientists using other researchers' oral histories? In Grele's words, next to listening to the interviewee, "it is equally important to be aware of the interviewer."[24] Researchers need to find out as much about the interviewer and the interview setting as possible. It will help them answer why an interviewer asked a certain question at a certain time, why she asked it in a specific way, and why she did not ask other questions. It will help them answer why an interviewee answered questions or told stories in certain ways and why she left out or glossed over certain topics.

In our case study, Grenke's book provides hints about his relationship with his interviewees. The book is about Winnipeg's German community before 1920. He describes himself as a "new Canadian," i.e., as an immigrant, and his interviewees as "old timers" whose "children and grandchildren were rapidly being assimilated and frequently had little interest in their backgrounds."[25] He also expresses his hope that other researchers will study other German communities. There is, however, no information about the place of the interviews and we do not know whether Grenke had any ongoing contact with his interviewees. Most of the interviews seem to have taken place in the homes of the interviewees, because they were frequently joined (or interrupted) by family members. Several interviewees used German words because they knew Grenke spoke German. This information helps us understand why Grenke focused on the period before 1920 and on the topics of culture and folk traditions such as song and rhymes next to questions about settlement and the demographic make-up of neighbourhoods, work, school and German language education, church, ethnic clubs, and politics. He did not ask questions about sexuality or gender roles, he asked few questions about the period 1920–1945, and no questions about the period after 1945. Thus, the interviews themselves are an important source of information about the interviewer and the interview setting.[26]

Ethical and Legal Aspects of Interviews

Social scientists are familiar with the stringent ethical requirements of universities and national research organizations. Such ethics policies usually require researchers to conduct interviews anonymously and confidentially, which means that the interviews are locked away until the conclusion of the project and then destroyed. These requirements are diametrically opposed to the goals of oral history: If interviewees consent – as they often do – to have their names used and published, then oral historians should use their names. The American Oral History Association argues that anonymity should be a last resort: "Because of the importance of context and identity in shaping the content of an oral history narrative, it is the practice in oral history for narrators to be identified by name. There may be some exceptional circumstances when anonymity is appropriate, and this should be negotiated in advance with the narrator as part of the informed consent process."[27] Eventually, interviews should be deposited at public archives and made accessible to other researchers.[28]

For oral historians, especially in North America, the gap between the principles of best practice that they have developed and the requirements of review boards has meant fighting battles with review boards to exempt their projects from their university's ethics policies.[29] At the same time, oral historians have had to learn about copyright as well as legal considerations regarding slander and libel.[30] It has been standard practice for oral historians to sign release forms and to have their interviewees sign release forms to confer copyright of the interviews to the archives. These release forms also identify any restrictions interviewees have placed on the interviews.

Further, in some cases, interviewees have the opportunity to edit the transcripts of their interviews and make accessible to researchers only the (sometimes quite heavily edited) transcripts; this accessibility is sometimes even extended to the original audio tapes – a form of editing much easier and less visible in digital than in analog formats. While practices vary widely, the goal is always to respect the wishes of the interviewees and to allow them to be heard (in order to become part of history).

For researchers using PGOH, it is therefore important to establish whether the interviews are restricted in part or in whole and whether permissions need to be obtained from the interviewees, their heirs, or their estates. Copyright governs the use of oral histories. Researchers cannot use them for commercial purposes, and the "fair use" rule, which prevents researchers from quoting interviews at length, applies. Copyright laws vary from country to country. Thus, researchers should ask the archivist or librarian how exactly they may use the oral histories under the applicable copyright laws.

Interview Strategies and Interviewer Training

Historically, the skills and training of oral historians has varied widely. Similarly, there is a great variety of interview strategies, which often vary by country or region. For example, in Canada and the United States, oral histories created for archives often employ a life story approach that structures the interview chronologically through the order of questions asked, beginning with: "Where and when were you born?" Folklorists, anthropologists, and continental European oral historians often use a more open life story approach that asks interviewees to tell their life story, leaving it up to the interviewee where to begin and end the story, and then add a phase of follow up questions to the life story.[31] Because of a lack of training facilities, oral history more often than not varies from researcher to researcher more so than from country to country. In most countries, oral history continues to be practiced outside of academia, and even in the United States, the number of oral history courses offered to undergraduate and graduate students is small, albeit increasing steadily in number. More recently, universities have even added degrees in oral and public history at both the graduate and undergraduate levels. Oral history is often not part of required historical methods courses. Thus, the typical experience of many first-time oral historians is that they conduct their interviews with very little or no training, thereby producing interviews that suffer from poor audio or video quality, poor questions, or a lack of conceptualization.

Grenke conducted his interviews at a time when oral history was not well known at Canadian universities and hardly accepted as a valid historical research method. It is therefore unlikely that Grenke had any kind of formal training in oral history. That may be the reason why the interviews are not properly introduced: Grenke did not identify himself, the interviewee, or the interview setting (date, place, project). He also did not ask for vital data such as birthplace and birth date. Other people participating in the interview are also not identified. Grenke did, however, have formal training in history, and he had a well-conceptualized research project, namely his PhD dissertation. Before conducting the interviews, Grenke had done extensive archival research, which helped him to ask specific questions of his interviewees.

The interviews were semi-structured, and Grenke began interviews by asking interviewees to talk about their lives in Europe and their migration to Winnipeg. Although he focused his questions on the period before 1920, Grenke was open to letting his interviewees go off on tangents, and several times these tangents went into the time of the Second World War. He seldom asked follow up questions and as soon as narrators had finished their stories, he reeled them back to the time before 1920. Such patience and listening skills make for valuable interviews, because they allow interviewees to tell the stories they want to share. Throughout the history of oral history, there have been interviewers who have not had the same skills. Several interviewers for the Multicultural History Society of Ontario during the late 1970s and 1980s, for example, either deleted from the tapes what they considered "tangents," cut off interviewees in mid-sentence, or dominated the interviewing by talking more than the interviewee. Thus, Grenke's openness to letting interviewees tell their stories was useful for me, because those were the times when interviewees talked about the Second World War (or had an opportunity to talk about it if they wished but chose not to). A narrative interview approach probably would have yielded even more stories.

Summaries and Transcriptions, or: The Importance (and Sometimes Inevitability) of Listening to the Interviews

Archivists have found that researchers using oral histories often consult only the transcripts and sometimes only the summaries. Seldom do they listen to the interviews. That is a major problem, because researchers miss a great amount of information and are prone to misunderstand and thus to misinterpret. They forgo basic methodological practice, which they would not do in the case of written sources: if at all possible, they would always go to the original source in order to exclude any mistakes generated by transcription, translation, and so on. They would never think of using only an archivist's summary of, for example, Canadian government administrative instructions or an immigrant's diary. While it is indeed faster to skim a printed text (that is, the transcript) than to listen to an audio recording, no researcher would rely solely on a typescript of an accessible handwritten original only because the fading ink and the author's idiosyncratic handwriting makes for difficult and time-consuming reading.

Summaries, logs, or indexes of interviews are often produced by the interviewers themselves, who will focus on the topics they are interested in. For an interview with Fred Martin, who was born in Dresden around 1895 and emigrated to Winnipeg in 1913, Grenke created an index that included entries focusing mostly on the period before 1920, but it also contained the following entries regarding the Nazi period: "World War II: Discussion of internment during W.W. II, treated very well. Bully-boys coming interns. Gaining freedom through help of lawyer." "Personalities: [...] 2. Martin Seelheim [...] Positivly [sic], Seelheim no supporter of Hitler. 3. Consul Radde came in 1937-strong supporter of Hitler. Started brewery [sic] and others remained behind to eat it." For my own project on German-Canadians' ways of dealing with the Nazi past, these somewhat cryptic notes would suggest the interview contains little if anything of use. By listening to the interview, however, I found that Martin also talked about German-Canadians' attitudes to Hitler and Nazi Germany during the war, and, most important, he developed his own explanation for Hitler's success: this was an excellent example of how one German-Canadian made sense of the Nazi past. I would have missed it had I not taken the time to listen to the interview. Similarly, Grenke's index for an interview with P. Laubenstein had no reference to the Nazi period, but Laubenstein and his wife (who is not mentioned in the index) talked about German-Canadians' and their own attitudes to Hitler, their own son's exemption from military service, and Laubenstein's joining of the German Club and his membership throughout the war. Again, valuable evidence I would have missed had I relied only on the index.

Listening to interviews unquestionably takes time – as is true of all archival research. There are few historians who have not come out of an archive after a day's work and had nothing to show for. Similarly, a day of listening to interviews may yield nothing. For example, Grenke's interviews with Mr Matthes and Anna Thiessen did not yield anything even though I had selected them from the larger group of Grenke's interviewees as having potential. But overall, with the help of a general index to Grenke's interviews, his individual interview indexes and listening to the interviews, nine interviews with a total of about seventeen hours yielded several stories that I could potentially use for my project. At the same time, I was able to mark various interview extracts for teaching purposes and for other projects I was working on.

Orality of Data

There is another reason for listening to interviews: their oral character. It is true, as British oral historian Paul Thompson points out, that the encounter between interviewer and interviewee loses some of its complexity by "freezing speech in a tape recording," but, as Thompson argues, the oral recording nevertheless "provides the most accurate document" of the original interview.[32] It is superior to the transcript, in which the nuances of emotion and the subtleties of meaning conveyed by the spoken word are often lost. The great range of oral cues – the voice's ever-changing tone, volume, velocity, pitch, and rhythm – cannot be transcribed. Neither can significant pauses, meaningful coughs, and the many forms of laughter be put down on paper. Irony and sarcasm expressed in speech may be misread or not understood at all. Indeed, researchers read the transcript in a certain tone (in their own voice) that may completely misrepresent the spoken word.

In 1981 the Italian oral historian Alessandro Portelli made a good case for listening to the oral qualities of interviews, but few oral historians followed his advice. Portelli argues that it is the orality of oral sources that make them different from written sources, because oral traits convey "essential narrative functions: they reveal the narrators' emotions, their participation in the story, and the way the story affected them. This often involves attitudes which speakers may not be able (or willing) to express otherwise, or elements which are not fully within their control."[33] But there is even more to it: a spoken story's oral traits carry the subjectivity of the interviewee and as such the most important kind of information an oral history can convey. This idea is discussed in more detail below under the heading of subjectivity. Although few researchers are willing or trained to analyze and interpret the orality of interviews, they should nevertheless listen to them to fully understand them. Eventually, it may be the increasing use of audio rather than written records that will make oral historians investigate not only the interviewer-interviewee relationship and their mutual construction of the narrative, but also the relationship between the listener and the interviewee and interviewer. Perhaps because many oral historians see the interviewer and listener as identical, this question has not yet been explored. But with the increasing secondary use of oral histories, researchers/listeners will begin to reflect on their role in the construction of the story they hear and the story they write about what they (believe they have) heard.

ORAL HISTORY AS EVIDENCE: SUBJECTIVITY, MEMORY, AND RETROSPECTIVITY

Historians traditionally explicate sources by questioning their internal and external characteristics in order to establish their authenticity and reliability.[34] Historians and oral historians have identified subjectivity and memory as major concerns related to the credibility and usefulness of oral history as evidence.[35] Although implicitly discussed in the memory debate, I add "retrospectivity" here as another characteristic of oral history that researchers should consider.

Historians understand a source's subjectivity either as bias (partiality) or as an author's specific perspective generated by his or her position in society. Traditionally, historians have viewed subjectivity as a source's weakness, because it makes it less reliable and less true. Historians have considered oral histories to be particularly subjective – suffering from the interviewees' forgetfulness, dishonesty, and reticence as well from the interviewer's intentionally or unintentionally misleading questions – and therefore to be particularly weak sources.[36] Oral historians were therefore forced to grapple with the subjectivity of their sources, perhaps more so than other historians. While they pointed out that all sources were inherently subjective, they also explored the specific nature of subjectivity in oral histories. In these discussions, oral historians extended their research into the subjectivity of their interviewees to their own subjectivity in shaping the interview. At the same time, they extended the meanings of subjectivity beyond the interviewee's or the interviewer's bias or perspective. The Italian oral historian Luisa Passerini defined subjectivity as "that area of symbolic activity which includes cognitive, cultural and psychological aspects." Rather than use similar concepts, such as "mentality, ideology, culture, world-view (*Weltanschauung*), and consciousness," she argued that "subjectivity has the advantage of being a term sufficiently elastic to include both the aspects of spontaneous subjective being ... contained and represented by attitude, behaviour and language, as well as other forms of awareness ... such as the sense of identity, consciousness of oneself, and more considered forms of intellectual activity. The importance of this term, moreover, is that it embraces not only the epistemological dimension but also that concerned with the nature and significance of the political."[37] Her colleague Alessandro Portelli argues that oral sources are subjective because they are artificially created by the historian; the interviewer shapes to some degree the content of the interview (through questions etc.); a story changes with each telling; and oral history is never complete, because "it is impossible to exhaust the *entire* historical memory of a single informant."[38]

Thus, oral historians use the term "subjectivity" as a heuristic device – Passerini even saw it as "a tool of analysis peculiarly appropriate to social history"[39] – to critically examine their sources. It is the subjectivity of oral history, according to Portelli, that reveals this source's most important information, since it "tells us less about events as such than about their meaning." Of course, interviewees often give us important factual data about the past, especially in the absence of other sources. "But the unique and precious element" of oral history "is the speaker's subjectivity: and therefore, if the research is broad and articulated enough, a cross section of the subjectivity of a social group or class."[40]

Grele points to the interviewee's own interpretation of his or her life as being of value for researchers to investigate: "In all interviews there is a tendency to impose an order on the events discussed. That is what we do as historians. In that sense, when we ask our memorists to recall events, we are asking them to be their own historians, to impose an order, an interpretation."[41] In other words, oral history can tell us how people make sense of the past, but in order to find out, we need to pay attention not only to the content (what is said) but also to the form (how it is said). Researchers interested in facts should therefore always be aware that these facts come wrapped in specific interpretations that are not simply the interviewees' interpretations, but more complex products of the interview. These interpretations, generated in the interplay of memory and performance, give us insight into people's consciousness. Oral historians agree that it is not only individual but also collective subjectivity that can be investigated. Thus, as oral historians "move[d] from issues in social history to cultural studies" during the 1980s, they explored subjectivity in its various forms, "whether it was memory, ideology, myth, consciousness, identity, desire, or any other such attributes."[42]

Subjectivity is closely linked to memory, another problem historians have identified in regard to oral history. As with subjectivity, the term "memory" has many meanings. One useful distinction is that between individual and collective memory. They are closely interlinked; I will focus here on individual memory. Skeptics of oral history argue that individual memory is not trustworthy enough to be considered a credible source; thus, oral sources are more suspicious than other sources. Since the 1970s, oral historians have pointed out the shortsightedness and bias of this argument. Thompson made the case that a lot of sources are based on oral evidence and memory, be it police reports, judicial reports, or demographic statistics, which are compiled from a multitude of interviews conducted by census takers or emigration and immigration officers at the border points of exit and entry. Thus, memory is a useful heuristic to question all sources that are based on memory.[43] As with subjectivity, oral historians turned what traditional historians saw as a weakness into a strength of the source.

Oral historians have looked to psychology and brain sciences to better understand how individual memory works. They have found that while short-term memory can be very unreliable and easily manipulated, long-term memory often is reliable. While older people may forget names and dates, the process of life review that sets in at a later stage in life allows them to remember the distant past quite clearly. A skillful interviewer will help the interviewee dig deep into his or her memory. That such memories can nevertheless not be taken at face value but must be cross-checked with other sources and for internal consistency is a given. Oral historians also keep in mind that their own research interests are not a good basis for evaluating an interviewee's memory: "People remember what they think is important, not necessarily what the interviewer thinks is most consequential."[44] And oral historians know that memories change over time and thus must always be seen in the context of the interviewee's life course. The further an experience lies in the past, the more likely it is that its memory has been smoothly integrated into the life story. Fred H. Allison compared two accounts by an American veteran of the Vietnam War about a specific firefight – one from 1968, two days after the battle, and one from 2002. The short-term memory of 1968 was full of disjointed details gathered in the context of a military exit interview. By 2002, there were fewer details, but the story had become coherent.[45] The two interviews give us different kinds of information. It is only the 2002 interview, however, that tells us what role this experience has played in the veteran's life. As Donald Ritchie explains: "People regularly reevaluate and re-explain their past decisions and actions ... [I]ndividuals use the insights gained from current events to reshape them and make new sense out of past experiences. There is nothing invalidating about this reflectivity, so long as interviewers and researchers understand what is occurring and take it into account."[46]

This point takes us to the concept of "retrospectivity." Oral history interviews are always about two different time periods, and in the case of the PGOH, researchers often have to consider three different time periods when evaluating the source. The basic idea here is simple: "Oral histories are products of the time of their creation."[47] Thus, oral histories are both about the time the interviewees reminisce about and the time in which they do the reminiscing. Why is this difference between the two times important? Historians distinguish between primary and secondary sources. Primary sources, often called the "raw material" of history, are sources created at the time under study. An article in the *Winnipeg Free Press* from 1904 about a social club of Germans is a primary source for Grenke's study of Germans in pre–First World War Winnipeg. Secondary sources, on the other hand, are sources created *after* the events we are studying. They are interpretations of the primary sources.[48] By this definition, oral histories (like autobiographies and memoirs) are secondary sources, because they are often created long after the events historians study. Thus, Grenke conducted his interviews in the 1970s, over half a century after the events he writes about. They are products of the 1970s, not the 1890s or 1920s.

Even though in practice, oral histories (like autobiographies) are considered primary sources, they are nevertheless different from other primary sources. One may argue that many sources are created after an event (police reports, newspaper accounts, diary entries, etc.) and thus all are retrospective. But oral histories, like autobiographies, are often retrospective in a way that should have become clear in the example of Allison's Vietnam veteran. Most oral histories are created not only at a different time but in a different *era* than the events they discuss. Values have changed and interviewees often judge their own actions and thoughts in this new light; hence, in the case of Allison's interview, the veteran's need in 2002 (but not in 1968) to justify his killing of Vietnamese soldiers. As Portelli and Grele say, oral histories are mostly about the meanings people ascribe to their experiences in the context of their life story. Thus, researchers using PGOH must know not only about the time they are studying, but also about the time in which the interviews were conducted. As a user of Grenke's oral histories, I must know about the 1890s–1940s to understand what the interviewees talk about and I must know about the 1960s and early 1970s to understand the context in which they recall their memories. After all, Grenke wanted his interviewees to remember their lives before a world war, a depression, another world war, a major German emigration to Winnipeg in the 1950s and the socio-economic decline of the city in the 1960s. All of these intervening events, as well as the changing social values, potentially shaped the interviewees' memories of the past. Furthermore, listening to the interviews thirty-seven years after they were conducted, I must also consider the present time in order to avoid imposing today's values on the interviewees' stories.

Oral histories as process-generated data offer a rich pool of data that can and should be analyzed and interpreted from various perspectives and with a view to uncovering interviews' multiple layers of meaning. The form of the source is as important as its content, and the two cannot be separated. If we consider the usefulness of archived interviews, it may be fruitful for social scientists to reconsider the common practice of using low-quality recording technology and destroying interviews after the conclusion of the project.

NOTES

1 Donald Ritchie, *Doing Oral History: A Practical Guide*, 2nd edition (Oxford: Oxford University Press, 2003), 24.

2 Some 1,840 collections in Canada created before 1994 are searchable in the *Guide to Oral History Collections in Canada/Guide aux collections d'histoire orale au Canada*, comp. by Normand Fortier, special issue of *Oral History Forum d'histoire orale* 13 (1993), online at http://www.oralhistorycentre.ca/

archival-records (accessed 14 Aug. 2013). The Multicultural History Society of Ontario (Canada) collected nine thousand hours of interviews with people from over sixty ethnocultural groups. International large collections include those at the National Archives of Singapore (16,000 hours), Columbia University's Oral History Center (8,000 oral histories, one million pages of transcript), and the Institute for History and Biography at the Fernuniversität Hagen, Germany (1,500 interviews). Other large collections are mentioned below.

3 Alessandro Portelli, "The Peculiarities of Oral History," *History Workshop Journal* 12, no. 1 (1981): 96–107, here 100.

4 See more recently Mike Savage, "Using Archived Qualitative Data: Researching Socio-Cultural Change," in *Understanding Social Research: Thinking Creatively About Method*, edited by Jennifer Mason and Angela Dale (London: Sage, 2011); April Gallwey, "The Rewards of Using Archived Oral Histories in Research: The Case of the Millennium Memory Bank," *Oral History* 41, no. 1 (spring 2013): 37–50. Gallwey provides further literature on "re-using qualitative data."

5 Art Grenke, "The Formation and Early Development of an Urban Ethnic Community: A Case Study of the Germans in Winnipeg, 1872–1919" (PhD dissertation, University of Manitoba, 1975).

6 Alexander Freund, "Troubling Memories in Nation-building: World War II Memories and Germans' Interethnic Encounters in Canada after 1945," *Histoire sociale/Social History* 39, no. 77 (2006): 129–55; Alexander Freund, "A German Post-1945 Diaspora? German Migrants' Encounters with the Nazi Past," in *German Diasporic Experiences: Identity, Migration, and Loss*, edited by Mathias Schulze, James Skidmore, et al. (Waterloo: Wilfrid Laurier University Press, 2008), 467–78; Peter Novick, *The Holocaust in American Life* (Boston: Houghton Mifflin, 1999).

7 Marie-Louise Ayres, Judith Pearce, et al., "Bring the Stories to the People: Online Sound at the National Library of Australia," National Library of Australia Staff Paper, 2006, online at: http://www.nla.gov.au/openpublish/index.php/nlasp/article/viewArticle/1091 (accessed 14 August 2013); National Library of Australia, Digital Collections, Audio (2008): Oral History and Folklore Collection – Preservation and Access: Digitisation of Audio Recordings, online at: http://www.nla.gov.au/digicoll/audioprogress.html (accessed 14 August 2013).

8 USC Shoah Foundation Institute for Visual History and Education (2013): Search the Archives, online at: http://sfi.usc.edu/search_the_archive (accessed 14 August 2013).

9 Library of Congress (2008): American Memory, online at http://memory.loc.gov/ammem/index.html (accessed 14 August 2013).

10 Abby Smith, David Randal Allen, and Karen Allen, "Survey of the State of Audio Collections in Academic Libraries" (Washington, DC: Council on Li-

brary and Information Resources, 2004), online at http://www.clir.org/pubs/reports/pub128/pub128.pdf (accessed 14 August 2013), 10.

11 Oral History Association, "2000 Oral History Evaluation Guidelines," Pamphlet Number 3, adopted 1989, rev. Sept. 2000 (Atlanta: Oral History Association, 2000) online at: http://www.oralhistory.org/about/principles-and-practices/oral-history-evaluation-guidelines-revised-in-2000 (accessed 14 August 2013); this document has been replaced by Oral History Association, "Principles and Best Practices of the Oral History Association" (Atlanta: Oral History Association, 2009) online at http://www.oralhistory.org/about/principles-and-practices accessed 14 August 2013.

12 Allen Nevins, "Oral History: How and Why It Was Born," in *Oral History: An Interdisciplinary Anthology*, 2nd edition, edited by David K. Dunaway and Willa K. Baum (Walnut Creek, CA: AltaMira Press, 1986), 33–5.

13 Art Grenke, *The German Community in Winnipeg, 1872 to 1919* (New York: AMS Press, 1991).

14 Oral History Association, "Principles," 2009.

15 On the history of recording technology, see David L. Morton, *Sound Recording: The Life Story of a Technology* (Baltimore: Johns Hopkins University Press, 2004).

16 Ronald J. Grele, "Movement Without Aim: Methodological and Theoretical Problems in Oral History," in Ronald J. Grele, *Envelopes of Sound. The Art of Oral History*, 2nd edition (Westport, CT: Greenwood 1985 [1975]), 135.

17 Eva M. McMahan, "A Conversation Analytic Approach to Oral History Interviewing," in *Handbook of Oral History*, edited by Thomas L. Charlton, Lois E. Myers, and Rebecca Sharpless (Lanham, MD: AltaMira Press, 2006), 336–56; Sherna Berger Gluck and Daphne Patai, eds., *Women's Words: The Feminist Practice of Oral History* (New York: Routledge, 1991); Eva M. McMahan and Kim Lacy Rogers, eds., *Interactive Oral History Interviewing* (Hillsdale: Lawrence Erlbaum, 1994).

18 Ritchie, *Doing Oral History*, 101.

19 Oral History Association, "Principles."

20 Michael Frisch, *A Shared Authority: Essays on the Craft and Meaning of Oral and Public History* (Albany: SUNY Press, 1990); see special issue of *Journal of Canadian Studies/Revue d'études canadiennes* 43, no. 1 (winter 2009) on sharing authority.

21 Valerie R. Yow, "'Do I like Them Too Much?' Effects of the Oral History Interview on the Interviewer and Vice-Versa," *Oral History Review* 24, no. 1 (1997): 55–79, here 71–2.

22 Katherine Borland, "'That's Not What I Said': Interpretive Conflict in Oral Narrative Research," in *Women's Words*, edited by Gluck and Patai, 63–75.

23 But see Gallwey, "Rewards," 2013.

24 Ronald J. Grele, "On Using Oral History Collections: An Introduction," *Journal of American History* 74, no. 2 (1987): 570–78, here 571.

25 Grenke, *German Community*, "Foreword," no page number.

26 Grele, "On Using Oral History Collections," 571.

27 Oral History Association, "Principles."

28 This practice does not negate the oral historians' responsibility to protect his or her interviewees, especially from self-incriminating statements.

29 Janovicek in this *Reader*; Robert B. Townsend, "AHA [American Historical Association] Statement on IRBs [Institutional Review Boards] and Oral History Research," *Perspectives* Online 46, no. 2 (2008), online at http://www.historians.org/perspectives/issues/2008/0802/0802aha1.cfm (accessed 14 August 2013).

30 Jarvis-Tonus in this *Reader* (chapter 4); for the United States: John A. Neuenschwander, *Oral History and the Law*, 3rd edition, revised and enlarged (Carlisle, PA: Oral History Association, 2002).

31 Almut Leh, "Ethical Problems in Research Involving Contemporary Witnesses," translated by Edith Burley, *Oral History Forum d'histoire orale* 29 (2009): 1–14; Alexander von Plato, "Contemporary Witnesses and the Historical Profession: Remembrance, Communicative Transmission, and Collective Memory in Qualitative History," translated by Edith Burley, *Oral History Forum d'histoire orale* 29 (2009): 1–27.

32 Paul Thompson, *The Voice of the Past: Oral History*, 3rd edition (Oxford: Oxford University Press, 2000 [1978]), 126, 127.

33 Portelli, "Peculiarities," 98.

34 Richard I. Schneider and Norman F. Cantor, *How to Study History* (Wheeling, IL: Harlan Davidson, 1986), chapters 2 and 3.

35 Thompson, *Voice of the Past*, chapters 4 and 5; Ronald J. Grele, "Oral History As Evidence," in *Handbook of Oral History*, edited by Charlton, Meyers et al., 43–104.

36 William Cutler III, "Accuracy in Oral History Interviewing," in *Oral History*, edited by Dunaway and Baum, 79–86; Thompson, *Voice of the Past*, 118.

37 Luisa Passerini, "Work Ideology and Consensus under Italian Fascism," *History Workshop Journal* 8, no. 1 (1979): 82–108, here 85.

38 Portelli, "Peculiarities," 104, emphasis in original.

39 Passerini, "Work Ideology," 86; Portelli, "Peculiarities," 104.

40 Portelli, "Peculiarities," 99–100.

41 Grele, "On Using Oral History Collections," 573.

42 Grele, "Oral History as Evidence," 62, 65.

43 Thompson, *Voice of the Past*, chapter 4.

44 Ritchie, *Doing Oral History*, 33.

45 Fred H. Allison, "Remembering a Vietnam War Firefight: Changing Perspectives Over Time," *Oral History Review* 31, no. 2 (2004): 69–83.

46 Ritchie, *Doing Oral History*, 33.

47 Grele, "On Using Oral History Collections," 572.

48 Schneider and Cantor, *How to Study History*, 22–3.

11

"When I Was Your Age": Bearing Witness in Holocaust Education in Montreal

Stacey Zembrzycki and Steven High[1]

For me, it was a natural progression to go from the child
survivor group, to doing interviews, to being involved in the
Holocaust centre, the Holocaust museum.
Paula Bultz, child survivor and docent, Montreal Holocaust Centre[2]

One enduring image of the Holocaust is that of the aging survivor telling his or her story to an interviewer decades later. Looking straight into
the camera, or into the distance, in accented English the survivors slowly
recount the atrocities they experienced. These eyewitness accounts have
been recorded in their tens of thousands and have since been featured in
a great many documentary films and museum exhibitions.[3] Millions have
also heard these living testimonies first hand, in their high school auditor-
iums, university classrooms, community centres, places of worship, or as
interviewers for one of the many testimony projects that emerged in the
1990s and 2000s. In addition, countless Jewish teenagers have travelled to
Poland and Israel as part of the annual international March of the Living
educational program. Still others have heard these stories directly from
their parents or grandparents.

If survivor testimony has been the subject of enormous public attention, the educational activism of survivors has been largely overlooked.
Recorded interviews, like public testimonies, have tended to focus on the
wartime experiences, and specifically the violence, endured by survivors.
Consequently, little time has been spent exploring the central role that
many have played in Holocaust education.[4] Taking survivors' work seriously allows us to view testimony from a different angle. The reasons they
bear witness and how their stories touch and inform those who listen to
them become just as significant as what is said.

Paula Bultz's deep involvement in Holocaust education in Montreal speaks to this other important dimension of testimony. Her experiential authority of "being there" and "telling it like it was" is enhanced by the fact that her childhood memories resonate with her young listeners. They can relate to another child's story. Through this shared connection, Paula believes she is making a difference. She validates her experiences as a child survivor by teaching students about the Holocaust, arguing that it "really had nothing to do with the war ... The Holocaust happened because of racism, because of hatred, because of intolerance, and because of anti-Semitism, and it happened because it was allowed to happen, because of the silence, nobody spoke up." Paula usually ends her conversations with children with an important warning: "We must never remain silent when we hear bad things happening to other people."[5]

In the postwar period, Montreal became home to the third-largest community of Holocaust survivors in the world. The city's Jewish community sought to support incoming refugees through existing and new organizations such as Jeanne Mance House, which received orphans. Most of these services were concentrated near St Laurent Boulevard, or the Main – an immigrant neighbourhood later immortalized in the novels of Mordecai Richler.[6] In the years that followed, survivors helped form their own institutions like the Montreal Holocaust Memorial Centre (MHMC). So what has been the role of survivors in Holocaust education, commemoration, and memorialization? What have they learned from their educational activism, and how have the changing demographics of Montreal classrooms affected the resulting dialogue?

In responding to these questions, this chapter draws upon the ongoing work of the Montreal Life Stories project, which has, since 2007, been interviewing survivors of war, genocide, and other human rights violations from the city's Rwandan, Cambodian, Haitian, and Jewish communities.[7] The project has interviewed almost five hundred people in multi-session interviews, using a life history approach. Unlike other testimony projects, which tend to begin and end with the violence, our approach situates it in the context of the life lived. The focus is therefore on the life remembered rather than on the historical event as such. Oral historians now find meaning in the form and structure of oral narratives, and in the silences, in what is misremembered, in the words spoken and also in the information conveyed.[8] Memory is therefore front and centre in our analysis.

Moving beyond its collection, the project has integrated these recorded stories into online digital stories, animated films, art installations, museum exhibitions, audio walks, radio programming, and live performances, and into the secondary school classroom. As a community-university research alliance, Montreal Life Stories has approached communities as partners in research rather than simply as objects of study. Survivors, exiles, and other refugees are an integral part of the project team and co-direct the project. Because everyone in the project participates in interviewing, many different kinds of conversations have unfolded. This chapter focuses on the remarkable stories told to us by a group of nineteen Ashkenazi Holocaust survivors who have served as speakers and docents at the MHMC, interviewers, and participants in the March of the Living program.

The educational activism of this group of Holocaust survivors is as much a *community of practice* as a *community of memory*. It is very much a community (of educators) within a community (of survivors) within a community (of Jewish Montrealers). Most are also child survivors. One might call this group a *community of remembering*, as their interviews reveal an active process of autobiographical memory work.[9] Group members coordinate their activities through the MHMC's speakers and docents committees, and some regularly participate in book club discussions to deepen their knowledge of the history of the Holocaust. Some survivors regard these activities almost as a form of professional development, though it was not put quite that way in our interviews. Over time, we have also come to realize that those who are active at the MHMC are generally more economically advantaged and educated than another group of survivors that is based in the Cummings Jewish Centre for Seniors. Class has shaped the narratives we have heard.[10]

In embarking on this project, we were heavily influenced by Henry Greenspan, one of the world's foremost interviewers of Holocaust survivors. Greenspan, who rejects conventional models of testimony because they tend to be a "one-way act of bestowal,"[11] argues that "a good interview is a process in which two people work hard to understand the views and experiences of one person: the interviewee."[12] Interviews must serve as spaces where trust and collaboration are nurtured so that candour and depth may develop.[13] Mindful of these considerations, we designed an interview guide that encourages reflective conversations about survivors' pre-war, wartime, and postwar experiences as well as the ways they share their stories in various settings.[14] Why did they begin to tell their story in public? What was it like the first time they did so? What can they say in forty-five minutes? What is left out and why? Have their stories evolved over time? Do the stories change according to the audience? In what way do audience expectations shape or structure what is said? Taken together, we have tried to understand how the life experiences of our interviewees affect the choices they make when bearing witness.

These sustained conversations with Holocaust survivor-educators were initiated after a 2008 conference organized by the project's Rwandan working group. Personal testimonies from Rwandan, Cambodian, and Jewish genocide survivors were an integral part of the conference program. Immediately thereafter, Steven High reflected on the political function and evolving practice of public testimony-giving in the project's online blog: "They also raised important questions that I think … our project needs to think more about (or at least I do)."[15] These testimonies "touched everyone in attendance," but to what end? Since schools are the main site of survivor testimony, it was therefore the project's education working group, rather than the Holocaust group, that initiated the interviewing of survivor-educators.

These conversations began with multi-session life history interviews that recorded up to twelve hours of remembering with each person and graduated to a variety of collaborative community-university workshops that enabled survivors to speak to each other as well as to us. In several instances, we were also able to hear their public testimonies during the MHMC's annual Holocaust Education Series or, in the case of docents, walk with them through the MHMC's permanent exhibition. These encounters allowed us to better understand how the survivors have taken their difficult, nonlinear, and even incommunicable experiences and "made them a story."[16] Over the life of the project, other storytelling spaces opened up, such as an October 2010 playback theatre performance/workshop as well as a series of workshops organized by Stacey Zembrzycki, Anna Sheftel, MHMC staff members, and a small group of survivors.

Survivors, like Paula, have been at the centre of Holocaust education in Montreal for more than thirty years. Week after week, they share their stories so that they may challenge denial and remind us of the lessons of history. These men and women are exceptional people. They are more than just survivors – they are also parents, grandparents, friends, mentors, volunteers, educators, community leaders, and activists. Hence, their work enables us to gain a deeper understanding of who they are and how the Holocaust has shaped their lives.

THE RISE OF CHILD SURVIVOR ACTIVISM

Since its creation in 1979, the MHMC has been a second home to many Montreal-area survivor-educators.[17] They have been active in every aspect imaginable and their contribution has been, and continues to be, decisive. How did this come to be? Many of our interviewees pointed to a surge in Holocaust denial in the late 1980s as having provided the spark. Some also spoke of their advancing age: their stories had to be told before it was too late. It was "now or never." Certainly, many of the interview projects that appeared in the 1990s contributed to this new sense of urgency. In Montreal alone, more than eight hundred Holocaust survivors were interviewed in a span of five or six years. The Canadian Jewish Congress (CJC), as part of its Holocaust Documentation project, conducted a number of interviews in the 1980s, and subsequent interviewing was done by the MHMC's Testimony project (480), McGill University's Living Testimonies project (120), and the Shoah Visual History Foundation (55,000 worldwide, 2,700 in Canada, and an undisclosed number in Montreal – likely several hundred).[18] The experience of being interviewed for the first time proved pivotal for many of our interviewees, leading several dozen to become speakers or docents at the MHMC soon thereafter. The legacy of these testimony projects was therefore far greater than the interview recordings themselves. These projects gave survivors, particularly those who were children during the Holocaust, the confidence needed to share their difficult narratives.[19] Child survivors formed the core of Montreal's close-knit group of survivor-speakers and docents.

When survivors trickled into Montreal in the postwar period, they faced many of the same challenges encountered by other immigrants. They also had to deal with a local population that could not yet comprehend what had happened to them. Few Canadians, Jews or Gentiles, could believe what had taken place.[20] Rather than offering sympathy, they tended to relay their own wartime struggles to survivors. Others went further. When Rena Schondorf first shared her story, her listener proceeded to comment upon her small stature before concluding that the concentration camps could not have been all that bad, otherwise a woman of her size would not have survived.[21] Ignorant comments like these effectively silenced survivors for the next thirty years. It was only in the 1980s and 1990s that they began to feel comfortable sharing their troubling memories in public. By then, as Franklin Bialystok shows so well, the Canadian Jewish community had made survivors' stories its own.

For others, and children in particular, silencing also occurred in their homes. "As a youngster," Sidney Zoltak "did not talk." "I left it to the grown-ups," he declared. "We younger people had a problem with our stories, with our experience, because we were often told, 'Well, you were only a kid, what do you remember?'"[22] If there were competing survivor narratives in a family, it was often the children's stories that were lost. In Sid's case, his mother remarried soon after coming to Canada, and his stepfather's story – a dramatic and "gory" concentration camp experience – dominated the family's narrative.[23] "We had no role," he stressed. "We were not really survivors. We were just listeners."[24] Sid credited the international child survivor conferences of the era for breaking this silence, recalling how, over time, this sort of setting, and the community that resulted, gave child survivors the confidence they needed to reveal their identities and tell their stories.[25]

For others, this realization – that they, too, were survivors – came out of other memorable experiences. In 1987, for example, Yehudi Lindeman went to a psychology conference in Israel and came back a changed man. Although he did not identify as a survivor prior to his departure, he returned as a "convert," determined to find his place in Montreal's survivor community. As a hidden child in the Netherlands, Yehudi did not experience the ghettos or death camps but was sent from safe house to safe house. The constant danger of being discovered or betrayed was his only companion. At first, he was drawn to Second Generation, a committee of the CJC–Quebec Region that was created to serve the needs of the children of survivors. Their issues were different, however, so Yehudi began to locate other child survivors in the city, and in 1989 he founded the local chapter of Child Survivors/Hidden Children, Montreal.[26] The period from 1987 to 1995 thus looms large in his narrative and that of others, like the one told by Sid, as a defining moment in their lives. Child survivors formed a community within a community within a community, and they have since developed their own particular sense of solidarity and mission.

SURVIVORS INTERVIEWING SURVIVORS

The testimonies of more than a hundred thousand Jewish survivors of the Holocaust have been collected by projects throughout the world, yet a little-known fact is that survivors acted as interviewers in many of these initiatives. They can thereby be found on both sides of the video camera. This was certainly the case in Montreal. Local survivors conducted interviews for McGill University's Living Testimonies project and the MHMC's Testimony project, and although it was an American initiative, the Shoah Visual History Foundation also employed local survivors as interviewers, including several of those involved in the Living Testimonies project. Many of the city's survivor-educators were interviewed on multiple occasions, in a very short period of time, because of this flurry of interviewing.

To better understand the emergence of a large number of "survivor-interviewers" at this historical juncture, we interviewed three of the founding members of the Living Testimonies project first together and then separately. Significantly, all three are child survivors. Living Testimonies was modelled on Yale University's Fortunoff Video Archive, which also originated within the survivor community. Fortunoff psychologist Dori Laub is a good example of the survivor-interviewer-researcher.[27] The Montreal-based team was trained by Yale, and its members adopted a similar approach: video technology, life story interviewing, single-session interviews done in a studio, and typewritten summaries in the third person.[28] Yale's life history formula asked interviewers to spend one-third of their time on life before the Holocaust, one-third on the Holocaust itself, and one-third on the postwar period. This wider lens contrasted sharply with the approaches adopted by the MHMC and the Shoah Visual History Foundation projects, which focused much more on the Holocaust itself. Nonetheless, Yehudi Lindeman, the director of Living Testimonies and a professor of literature at McGill University, recalled that there was "always a squeeze on the postwar period."[29] Time would simply run out. The group interview demonstrated that, in many respects, Living Testimonies was not a branch of the Yale tree, but had its own roots in Montreal.

When Yehudi, Paula Bultz, and "Krysia" (not her real name) spoke about the project, they stressed the fact that it came about at a time when the silence surrounding survivors' experiences was being broken. According to these three long-time friends and colleagues, survivors were speaking publicly about their wartime experiences for the first time, and one could almost feel change in the air itself. Living Testimonies came out of a committee formed by the CJC–Quebec Region that was charged with conducting interviews with survivors. Yehudi expressed a great deal of frustration with this group led by academics, because its members never felt ready to start interviewing.[30] In exasperation, he approached McGill University, where he worked, for sponsorship and found a supporter in the dean of arts, whose wife was a Holocaust survivor.

From the outset, the interview team contacted other survivors through word-of-mouth networks, and interviewed friends, friends of friends, neighbours, and relations. By the 1990s, most of Montreal's Holocaust survivors now lived in the Côte-Saint-Luc district of the city, and so the search was simplified. In one interview after another, survivors spoke about their experiences for the very first time. "All of them," insisted Krysia, "trusted me." Upon contact with her interviewees, Krysia would identify herself as a survivor, telling them a bit about her own story; on some occasions she even shared parts of her recorded testimony with interviewees, to give them the confidence they needed to go on. Building trust was a recurring theme in our two-hour group interview and in the individual interviews that followed. Another was the need to be "gentle." Like that of so many others, Krysia's activism began when she was first interviewed. Although her experiences were difficult to recount, she agreed to tell her story for her children's sake. Her daughter had asked her to participate in the project and Krysia emphasized it was "my wedding gift to my son."[31] Soon thereafter, Krysia became a Living Testimonies interviewer.

Wanting to know more about the interview process, we asked Yehudi, Paula, and Krysia to tell us what they brought to their roles as interviewers. Yehudi's response was instantaneous, emphasizing that only survivors could get the "nuances" right, which were as much emotional as they were informational. For all three, there was a sense of a shared understanding with their interviewees. Implied here was the idea that they could make a deeper connection because of their shared experience. Continuing with this point, we asked the group to comment on what went through their own minds as survivors interviewing other survivors.[32] Krysia jumped into the conversation, telling us that she was always "very professional," distancing herself from what she was hearing. "I have a job," she declared, but "I am pretty gentle." This remark led Krysia to recall her own memories of being roughly interviewed by non-survivors. Specifically, one female researcher asked her straight out if she had been raped. "I threw her out of the house," Krysia exclaimed, noting that she always did a "better job" because she is a survivor. At this point in the interview, we asked Krysia whether interviewing was hard on her. To this, she simply replied, "I'm at peace with my own story. It validates my own story."[33] Over the course of our conversation, it became clear that Paula, Yehudi, and Krysia were motivated by their own questions about the Holocaust.

This hunger for answers was perhaps most evident in Yehudi's life story. Born in 1938, he was just a young boy during the war. Because he was separated from his family, his memory of the war years is more fragmentary than most – a belt buckle, a jackboot, a house, a farm. He was hidden in one house after another during the war years – sometimes for days, and at other times for months. There were so many safe houses that their sequence was sometimes difficult for Yehudi to reconstruct, but each served as a "memory capsule" in his narrative. He has spent decades filling in the gaps in his memory – visiting the sites, tracking down host families as well as some of the other children with whom he was hidden. To this end, he recalled going to a small Dutch town with his mother in the 1980s to search for the family that shielded him for a time. They had owned a flower shop and he remembered that a train crossed the main street nearby. Seeing no train, he asked some of the old-timers on the street about it, but everyone insisted that there was no such train. Just when he and his mother were about to return to their car, an older woman came up to them and said that there had been a train owned by a company that transported goods across the street from where they were standing. Yehudi thanked her and, with this new information, he and his mother went to the spot and quickly found the flower shop just around the corner, on a side street. It was still owned by the same family. There were other such recovery missions. Eight child survivors, for example, came together for a reunion at one point. On the first day they told stories to fill in the gaps. On the second day they went to their place of hiding itself and it prompted other memories. This desire to reconnect is a powerful one in Yehudi's life story narrative, as with other survivors who were young children at the time.[34] The Living Testimonies project must therefore be understood as part of this personal search for answers.

Today, so many years later, the Montreal Life Stories project is not so much "breaking the silence" among the Holocaust survivors we are interviewing. Rather, it gives them an opportunity to assert their individuality. Our interviewees often emphasize the parts of their stories that do not easily fit into the dominant narrative. As Musia Schwartz put it, survivors deal with the remembered and lived legacies of the Holocaust in a variety of ways, and certainly we must be mindful of this.[35] Some married and some did not. Some had children; others did not. Some found faith; others lost it. Some told their children about what had happened to them and others would (or could) not. For those who did not experience the ghettos and death camps, there has been a struggle to have their stories heard at all. Children were killed quickly in the camps, so the stories of child survivors are not the same as adult memories that recall these particular places. Hidden children, like Yehudi, were secreted from one location to another, never knowing when they might be betrayed or discovered. Others were forced to live as Christians. Still others escaped the Nazi onslaught by fleeing to countries outside Germany's sphere of power. Paula and her mother, for instance, fled to Soviet-occupied Poland, only to be deported to Siberia, and since her story was so different from others, it took her a long time to identify as a Holocaust survivor. It is perhaps for this reason that she has volunteered as a docent at the MHMC rather than as a speaker.

BEARING WITNESS IN THE CLASSROOM

Many of the child survivors we interviewed are drawn to younger audiences. They prefer to speak to children who are the same age as they were during the war. If earlier generations of Holocaust survivors were integral in founding institutions like the MHMC, child survivors have directed their considerable energies to reaching out to young people through this institution. Their educational activism over the past three decades can thus be understood as a generational response to Holocaust denial and anti-Semitism on the one hand and as their unique contribution to the ongoing struggle for human rights on the other.

One of the opening questions that we often ask survivor-speakers is, "Tell us about the first time you gave your testimony in public." For some, this starting point anchors our conversation in a relatively safe place. For others, it stirs painful memories. Either way, all seem to have vivid stories about their first time bearing witness. The question serves two major functions: it gets the conversation rolling and it shifts the emphasis away from testimony. Since many of our interviewees have been interviewed before, sometimes for multiple projects, they tend to be most comfortable telling a chronological narrative that begins and ends with the violence. Our first question can therefore be surprising for some. A number of our interviewees, in fact, have responded by shifting the interview back to more familiar ground – choosing to start from "the beginning." Some clearly need to deliver their forty-minute testimony before they are ready for the dialogue we want to initiate. This alternative path works well, too, because of the project's emphasis on multi-session interviews.

In a pre-interview session, one of our interviewees, who wishes to remain anonymous, told us that he had never before been successfully interviewed. He had once agreed to be interviewed by the Shoah Visual History Foundation but had to abruptly end the conversation after only ten minutes. He could not go on. With this foreknowledge, we decided to begin our interview by focusing on his work as a speaker rather than on his raw and painful memories of the Holocaust. For him, this proved to be a good strategy: our conversation shifted back and forth between Quebec classrooms and the horrors of the Holocaust throughout our two interview sessions. His work as a speaker was a safe place for him to linger during our encounters.

By contrast, the first time that Liselotte Ivry, a child survivor from Czechoslovakia, shared her experiences in front of a classroom of children, she broke down. For her, a survivor of Theresienstadt, Auschwitz, and Bergen-Belsen, remembering and sharing proved to be "tough, but like everything else, you learn by doing." Despite this rocky beginning, Liselotte believes that speaking is an important part of who she is. It helps her come to terms with her past: "I do not have to carry the burden of surviving alone."[36]

While speaking in public remains challenging for some survivors, for others, like Ted Bolgar, it has become somewhat "routine." Over time, he has developed a unique presentation style that uses PowerPoint slides. His approach to giving testimony, quite different from the usual form, resembles that of a teacher – which he is. Ted has a clear "script" from which he rarely deviates.[37] Other survivor-speakers, however, constantly adjust to the audience to whom they are speaking. According to Batia Bettman, public testimonies have to be personal if they are going to reach their intended audience: "It is never about numbers, it's about people." Instead of shocking people, Batia engages in cooperative learning, stating that "you have to touch them," something that you can see only when looking into children's eyes. Ideas may resonate with them, but she argues that, as a teacher, she has to forge a connection with each student in a tangible way. The key to success for her is to "hook" them into the story before it even begins.[38] Despite these varied approaches, everyone we interviewed expressed a clear preference for one age group or another. Most, as stated above, favour children or youth who are approximately the same age as they were during the war years. "When I was your age" thus acts as an effective opening line for their testimonies.

Survivors also expressed their preferences about where they give their testimony, often preferring to go to non-Jewish schools. When Ted began bearing witness in the late 1990s, for example, he gave his testimony at both Jewish and non-Jewish schools. In doing so, he quickly realized that the Jewish children already knew a great deal about the Holocaust. He had to "talk to them differently" because "for them, it [was] nothing new." In scheduling speaking engagements, Ted now limits himself to non-Jewish schools because this is where he feels he can have the biggest impact.[39]

Not surprisingly, survivors also make other choices when they bear witness, determining what they will and will not reveal to their listeners. Rena Schondorf, for instance, is always concerned about the effect that her story might have on children. To this end, she refrains from telling graphic and violent parts of her story when she speaks to those under the age of twelve. Even with adolescents, Rena spends little time recounting "the different kind of hell" she experienced. A mother, grandmother, and great-grandmother, Rena always puts her listeners first.[40] When we asked

Sidney Zoltak about the parts that he leaves out of his story, he told us that he omits any memories that he knows will trigger a strong emotional reaction.[41] These are often very controlled narratives. According to Musia Schwartz, "you learn to protect yourself a bit and you objectify certain things. And you avoid this, like this acme of an emotional moment, not because you're embarrassed to shed a tear in front [of listeners] but you just … you spare yourself."[42] The survivor-speakers we interviewed have spent a great deal of time thinking about these issues. As a result, they have much to tell us about the challenges of first-person testimony in the wider context of Holocaust education.

Although each and every survivor delivers testimony differently, all seem to be asked the same kinds of questions from their youthful listeners. Many relate to religion, specifically how God could allow the Holocaust to happen. Or, alternatively, how they still believe in God after living through the horrors of the Holocaust. The questions posed may be similar, but survivors' answers always depend on their own experiences; this is one way they combat attempts to universalize what they went through.

Younger audiences ask the most concrete questions: What did you eat? What were the camps like? Even, did you meet Hitler? Through these kinds of simple questions, the children are trying to find ways into the stories that they are hearing. Older children, as you would expect, tend to ask more complex questions, making connections to Israel and to other genocides. From the outset, we wondered whether Holocaust survivors embraced or resisted these kinds of comparisons or connections. Again, it depends to some degree on the individual. There is a wide spectrum of political opinion within the survivor community. Many have, however, learned to be careful in answering questions about Israel when speaking to non-Jewish audiences. Montreal is a diverse city with hundreds of ethnicities and many religions, so when survivors go into local classrooms they are, essentially, speaking to a microcosm of the world in which we live. To wade into the explosive politics of the Israeli-Palestinian conflict, to choose an obvious example, risks entering into a heated debate and losing effectiveness. To avoid these problems, their politics are subtly embedded in their accounts of the Holocaust and in the lessons that we can learn from their experiences.[43] Audience expectations thus play a vital role in determining what can and cannot be said.

If survivors are discouraged from speaking about Israel outside of the Jewish community, at least in their public roles as MHMC speakers, they are often encouraged by their culturally diverse audiences to make connections to other twentieth-century genocides, such as those that occurred in

Armenia, Cambodia, and Rwanda. Virtually all of our interviewees told us that they are willing to make these connections but fear that in doing so the Holocaust might one day become "just another genocide."

Since bearing witness has become an important part of survivors' public lives and identities, we have been interested in finding out more about how the Holocaust is remembered, commemorated, and memorialized in their private lives, within their families and among their friends and acquaintances. When asked about telling their children about the Holocaust, Rena and Mayer Schondorf, who were married for fifty-seven years at the time of our interviews with them, simply stated that they always knew. In addition to naming their children after family members who were murdered during the Holocaust, they have a special weekly ceremony within their family. Mayer's mother was given a set of candlesticks by a young couple just before they were taken to a concentration camp and killed. Before leaving, they asked her to continue to light the candles in their memory. When Mayer's mother passed away, Rena took on this tradition, and it has since been passed on to her children and now her grandchildren. Even though Mayer also died in 2009, the family continues to light candles every Friday for Shabbat.[44]

One of the things that we found most surprising in our interviews with survivor-speakers was that a substantial number of them have chosen not to share their wartime experiences with friends and family. For some, the "telling" does not come easily in this context. There is a clear division, for instance, between Olga Sher's private life as a mother, grandmother, and wife, and her public life as a survivor. None of her children have ever seen her give testimony, and yet they have been active in Holocaust education themselves; one was the playwright for *Hana's Suitcase*.[45] She has never sat down and said, "Here it all is," although when it has come up, she has always answered their questions. When we asked Olga to explain this decision, she stressed that she has many identities, a survivor being only one of them.[46] Musia echoed this point when speaking about her children: "They know that the tape is there. If they choose to look at it only after I'm gone, then that's fine. One day they'll look at it, I'm sure. They're not ready … Your children are not your property; you're not their owner. I wouldn't try to go into their mind or heart anymore than anyone else's. Maybe less so … They have a mother, not a survivor."[47]

According to Sidney Zoltak, this perspective has a great deal to do with the desire to protect. Children and grandchildren do not want the asking to cause pain and, for their part, survivors do not want the telling to do so either. When Sid's grandchildren ask him questions and see his eyes getting red, they quickly try to stop him.[48] Sometimes it is simply easier to tell a stranger than a loved one. In the repeated telling, however, the subject has, for some, become easier to broach within families. As Ted stated, "It's farther away and I don't have to worry about spooking them because they realize that I am here and two generations away and for them, it's like history, sixty-five years." Although Ted never told his children about what he had experienced when they were growing up, he is open with his grandchildren and has even accompanied them on the March of the Living. Stories may have been withheld, but Ted noted that his children were well aware that something was not right: unlike their friends, they did not have any extended family members. Certainly, memories of the Holocaust continue to complicate the relationships that survivors form. It is for this reason, perhaps, that many married other survivors in the postwar period.

SURVIVORS AS MUSEUM INTERPRETERS

The school classroom is not the only contact zone between Holocaust survivor–speakers and their young listeners: the MHMC's permanent exhibition provides another setting in which they recount their lives. A number of our interviewees, particularly child survivors, volunteer as docents. Our exchanges with Paula Bultz and Olga Sher were particularly important in this regard, shedding light on their educational activism in this space. Their work provides an important counterpoint to museum studies, which focuses generally on exhibition creation and the close reading of the spatial arrangement of texts, images, and artifacts. The politics of memory surrounding the creation of the United States Holocaust Memorial Museum (USHMM) in Washington, DC, or memorials like the one in Berlin dedicated to the murdered Jews of Europe, have dominated the scholarship.[49] While these studies have noted the affective turn in museum interpretation, outlining how visitors' emotional experiences are consciously shaped, few have sought to understand the role of survivors in these institutions.

As its name suggests, the MHMC is part museum and part memorial. As elsewhere, the docent-led guided tour has been a key element of the museum's educational and interpretive work. While most of these visiting groups are school-based, workplace groups also visit the exhibition. A large group of Montreal firefighters, for example, were there during one of our visits. The guided tours tend to take two hours and end with a short testimony from a survivor-speaker. There is some built-in tension in this process, as tours sometimes last longer than expected – taking away from the time set aside for the speaker. Nevertheless, it is an emotionally exhausting experience for many visitors.

To understand what survivors bring to their work as museum docents, we interviewed two long-time survivor-docents about their experiences. In the first instance, we conducted a five-part interview with Olga Sher, a speaker and docent who taught child psychology at the Montreal Jewish General Hospital for twenty-five years. In our first session, Olga spoke of the ongoing shift from survivor-docents to non-survivors. There are very few active survivor-docents remaining. This changing perspective can be heard in the language used by the docents during their tours. Soon, she noted, visitors to the permanent exhibition will hear about "they" and "them" rather than "we" and "us."[50]

Like others, Olga prefers to speak to younger children, ages ten and eleven. She tries to connect to them by speaking about the experiences of children during the Holocaust. Sometimes these are her own stories and, on occasion, they are drawn from books she has read. We were both struck by how much Olga reads: she constantly referenced books in our conversations. Throughout our interviews, Olga self-consciously situated her own story in historical context. For our fourth meeting, in October 2009, we asked if she could walk us through the MHMC's permanent exhibition so that we could better understand what she does. Here is Stacey's reflection on that tour, written shortly thereafter:

> She took us into the opening room where we listened to her speak
> about life for Jews in Europe before the war. We also watched the
> first movie in the exhibit – a first for Steve and I – and Olga pointed
> out her sister in the film and photographs from their family's life
> in Poland. When we asked Olga if she does this when giving a
> tour to students, she said she does not. Olga is very clear about her
> boundaries and tries to keep her own story out of the exhibit, at
> least until her audience reaches the second floor of the museum,
> which is about the Holocaust itself. As we made our way through
> the museum, Olga spoke about the artifacts, weaving information
> from many of the books she read into her narrative. Again, she is
> hesitant about bringing her own story into the exhibit, trying to
> give her audience a sense of the larger history. She also spent a lot
> of time speaking about the images in the exhibit. As she explained
> them, she tried to give us a sense of how the people in the images
> must have been feeling and what they would have known at the

11.1 · Olga Sher discusses an exhibit at the Montreal Holocaust Memorial Centre. (Photograph by Stacey Zembrzycki)

time. Certainly, this is something that only a survivor could know. As we made our way to the second floor, we began to hear more about Olga's particular story. I think what was interesting was that she shared new memories about her experiences with us during this part of the tour. There have been some main stories in Olga's narrative, during the last three interviews, and in this case, the space brought out some new ones about her experiences before, during, and after the Holocaust.[51]

Like Olga, Paula Bultz is a gifted educator who is committed to telling the stories of children when she speaks to Montreal youth about the Holocaust; she feels that these voices have often been silenced in the past. Paula has been active as a docent since 1994. Her passion for children and their unique experiences during the Holocaust was also evident during the tour she gave us of the exhibition in May 2009.

Upon beginning a tour, Paula told us that she asks the children to cram into the museum's small lobby and look up at the words, written in four languages, that border the ceiling: To Learn; To Remember; To Feel. These words may represent the museum's mission but they also speak to Paula's purpose. She tries to teach children about the history of Judaism and the Holocaust in an informative and affective way. Like Olga, Paula weaves her own story into the exhibit's narrative, pointing out the experiences of Poles and of women and children.

Steven emphasized this in his reflection on the encounter:

Again and again, Paula picked out photos and stories (often of people she knew – as virtually all the artifacts in the museum were donated by Montreal residents) that involved children. These stories – absent from the wall panels – brought the artifacts to life. A battered baby doll in a glass case was transformed into a living object with its own story – the doll had been found in an apartment in a Polish ghetto (left behind by a family, with a child, who had been shipped off to the camps) and then brought to Canada where it continued to play its role as a child's toy, its painted nails, the result of a child's desire to have a girl doll and not a boy one. Later, we heard about the heart-shaped gift given to a young girl in the camp from her friends – who each wrote an inspirational message (in many languages) – imparting a story of resilience and resistance. Paula then told us about how the young woman was able to hide it under her arm during the death march that followed. This object was donated by a Toronto woman, again a story – it had been kept in a drawer and her children remember playing with it in child-hood, not knowing its history or significance. All of this, of course, spoke directly to the young students that she guides through time.[52]

In the downstairs section of the museum, which traces the rise of Hitler, Paula used examples from life in Canada, and politics in this country, to help explain what was going on in Germany prior to the war. She is an expert guide who tells a sophisticated story in an interesting and engaging manner. As we moved upstairs again, Paula discussed the Holocaust – the creation of the ghettos and the camps. She pointed to a map and told a part of her story, explain-ing how she and her mother were deported from eastern Poland to Siberia by the Soviets. There was a great deal of emotional power in her recounting.

The exhibition ends in the memorial room. Here, Paula spoke about one of the synagogues that was destroyed in Warsaw and how a pillar from it now stands in the centre of the room holding the ashes of some of those who were killed in Auschwitz; an eternal flame burns above the urn. On one side, written on translucent screens, are the names of five hundred towns that once had dynamic Jewish communities. On clear days, Paula told us that the sun shines through these screens, giving visitors an indication of the vibrant culture that was lost. The opposing wall, on the right side, is covered by dark slate that lists the names of many of the death, concentration, and work camps that ended Jewish life in Eastern Europe. Lastly, Paula pointed out the six lit candles that represent the six million Jews who were killed in the Holocaust. It was an affecting tour.

Our conversations with Olga, Paula, and others reveal that there is a great deal of individuality in what docents choose to say and in what parts of the exhibition they highlight. This is as it should be. For example, Paula stated that she does not show one of the museum's films to younger visitors because of its graphic nature. These guided tours led us to reflect further on the important role played by survivor-docents in Holocaust museum interpretation over the past thirty years.

Unlike speakers, docents at the MHMC comprise survivors and non-survivors. The number of survivor-docents has declined as survivors age or die, thereby widening the gap between the respective roles of speakers and docents. These differences reflect the various ways that the Holocaust may be taught. Many speakers, as the previous section made clear, reach their listeners through a personal appeal. Their authority is therefore experiential. The authority of MHMC docents is not as clearly drawn, even though all of them rely on the authority of the professionally designed exhibition itself, which teaches through text, artifact, photography, video, and commemorative space. In guiding their visitors through the exhibition space, each docent must choose what to emphasize, deciding what storyline or thread to follow and how to shape the story being told.

We have come to think that child survivors find the job of docent, rather than speaker, to be more "accessible" to them because their stories have not, until recently, fit neatly into the main narrative of the Holocaust. Survivors who were young children during the war years are also ill placed to tell their story in a linear forty-minute testimony, given that what they remember is often fragmentary or has been uncovered bit by bit in the decades that followed the war. Yet these pieces of the past are much more easily incorporated into the museum's narrative, providing vivid detail and a personal connection to the past.

ACCOMPANYING THE MARCH OF THE LIVING

Interpreting the Holocaust in a museum environment is very different from going back to where it all happened with the annual international March of the Living educational program. To accompany Jewish teenagers as they are guided through ghettos or concentration and death camps is to risk reliving the horrors. All of our interviewees spoke emotionally about the first time they returned to the countries of their birth. Others explained why they have never been able to go back. For example, postwar anti-Semitism in Poland was and, according to some, continues to be ferocious. Yet a number of survivors have travelled with large contingents of grade 10 and 11 students on the annual March of the Living to Poland and Israel. Several of our interviewees spoke of the importance of bearing witness in situ – the impact on young people can be transformative. Mayer Schondorf, who went on the March of the Living seven times with his wife Rena before his death in 2009, declared that the journey has become something of a "rite of passage" for Jewish high school students in Montreal.[53]

The March of the Living is an international educational program that brings Jewish teens from all over the world to Poland on Yom Hashoah, Holocaust Memorial Day, to march from Auschwitz to Birkenau, the largest concentration camp complex built during the Second World War, and then to Israel to observe *Yom HaZikaron*, Israel's Memorial Day, and *Yom Ha'Atzmaut*, Israel's Independence Day.[54] This two-week trip is commonly represented as a "once-in-a-lifetime experience" for the five to eight hundred Jewish-Canadian high school students who participate each year, approximately 250 of whom are from the Montreal area. According to the program's website, "Your experience on the March will be a study of contrasts. In Poland you will search for traces of a world that is no more … In Israel you will encounter a country that is striving valiantly to keep the age-old flame of Jewish nationhood alive … The Holocaust is a stark reminder of the anguish of our past – but Israel represents the hope for our future."[55] The students are accompanied by aging Holocaust survivors who travel on the buses with them. In preparation, they attend a retreat in the nearby Laurentians, a short drive north of Montreal, where they first meet the survivors and listen to their stories. The political framing of the March of the Living is thus in sharp contrast to what typifies Holocaust testimony in Montreal's public schools.[56]

The presence of Holocaust survivors on this journey is an integral part of the overall experience for these young people. According to the March of the Living Canada website, today's participants "are the last generation of Jewish youth privileged to listen to Holocaust survivors share their experiences – firsthand – in the places where their personal stories transpired." Not surprisingly, this firsthand connection is emphasized: "When you listen to a witness, you become a witness."[57]

Five of the survivor-educators whom we interviewed have accompanied these young people on the March of the Living. Whereas Batia Bettman has participated once, and Liselotte Ivry twice, Ted Bolder has gone seven times, and Rena and Mayer Schondorf have participated seven times together, with Rena going an eighth and ninth time in 2010 and 2011, after Mayer died. The trip is physically and emotionally demanding. The days begin early and end late, and the itinerary requires survivors to walk many miles on any given day. Being in these places also dredges up horrific memories that some have a difficult time relaying to students. Yet those survivors who have participated emphasized its power to teach.

When we asked Liselotte Ivry about her first March, she told us about how emotionally difficult it had been for her. She recalled approaching Birkenau, on the three-kilometre march from Auschwitz, and "literally collapsed": "[It] seemed that I heard all the voices from the past and I just fell down."[58]

Liselotte's mother died in Auschwitz-Birkenau on 4 January 1944, and her brother Jan (Hans) was sent to the gas chambers on 8 March 1944. Somehow Liselotte found the strength to pick herself up and go on, trying to "be there" for the students when they needed her. Like the others with whom we spoke, she believes that these sites of mass murder make a large impression on young people. When we asked her what it was like to see these concentration camps again, Liselotte explained that Auschwitz has become something of a museum, bearing little resemblance to the place rooted in her memory, but Majdanek "remains as it was … you see the death chambers and crematorium. You see the whole process of death right there." At this point in the interview, she asked us to turn off the recording device. She left the room and when she returned she had a piece of paper in her hand. On it was written a poem composed by a young student in 1999, outside the gas chambers of Majdanek. She asked us to read it aloud. It began:

A giant room of concrete walls
Silence now rings through the halls
The halls that once heard so many screams
The screams are now heard only in dreams

11.2 · Stacey Zembrzycki accompanied five survivors, including Ted Bolgar and Rena Schondorf, on the 2010 March of the Living, acting as a "survivor chaperone." Here Ted and a group of students talk about the past while visiting Birkenau. The remains of a crematorium, blown up by retreating Nazis, stand in the background as a testament to the destruction of this place. (Photograph by Stacey Zembrzycki)

> The dreams of people willing to care
> The people brave enough to step up and share
> And the pain of the people who all came before
> The people who came but now are no more ...

As we finished reading the last line, Liselotte, visibly shaken, declared that this is why the March is so very important. Instead of simply listening to stories, these journeys allow students to see, feel, and experience these sites.[59]

Despite the physical and emotional demands of the trip, survivors who participate in the March of the Living believe that it is their duty to do so. Like bearing witness in the classroom or guiding students through the MHMC's permanent exhibition, they see it as their responsibility to remember those who did not survive. It also has a profound effect on survivors themselves. Batia Bettman, for instance, recalled that she had mixed feelings about returning to Poland, telling us that she was not sure if she was the "right person" to go, given that the itinerary did not take participants to any of the places that were linked to her story. Nevertheless, this journey was "tiring but healing" for her: "[Being] in Poland was very comforting" and she derived a great deal of pleasure from the familiar landscape and the teenagers themselves. She appreciated their questions and helped them "[get] through the experience."[60] It is hard not to be engaged on March of the Living trips. The places and the objects elicit a strong emotional response from both survivors and students.

CONCLUSION

The wartime experiences of child survivors differ from those of adults and have often made it hard for them to identify with the word "survivor." As a hidden child, for example, Sidney Zoltak did not experience the ghettos or the death camps – this mattered within the wider survivor community. Several interviewees recalled a time when there was an entrenched idea of a hierarchy of suffering among Montreal survivors. As Sid stated, "There was a hierarchy of survivors: 'You didn't have what I had.' 'I was in Auschwitz.' 'I was in Buchenwald.' 'I was in Dachau.'" For some, Sid's experience represented only a "hiding kind of story." This particular sense of order and authority began to change when a younger generation of survivors took over the leadership of organizations charged with Holocaust education, commemoration, and memorialization. For, as Sid noted, it quickly became clear that "we were all the same." They had all been sentenced to death and in different places and in different ways, they were able to survive: "One of the things that I live with, and I do – I never deny that I'm a survivor. It's nothing to be ashamed of. It was my fate; my deck of cards."[61] Yet age did matter. If older survivors were perhaps better able to respond to Holocaust deniers by giving their eyewitness testimony of what they experienced, this chapter makes clear that the younger generation of child survivors is uniquely qualified to connect to more youthful audiences in the context of Holocaust education. The contribution of this survivor-educator *community of remembering* has been so influential and so pervasive that it is now difficult for us to imagine how to reach students once there are no survivors left to say "when I was your age."

NOTES

1 We want to thank all those who agreed to be interviewed for the Montreal Life Stories project, some of whom are quoted here. We would also like to thank the many team members who contributed to this research, as well as the Montreal Holocaust Memorial Centre.

2 Claude Lanzmann's *Shoah* and Steven Spielberg's *Schindler's List*, for instance, have played major roles in shaping societal perceptions of the Holocaust. The permanent exhibitions at the United States Holocaust Memorial Museum (USHMM) in Washington, DC, and Yad Vashem in Jerusalem have used testimony in innovative and compelling ways. See Tony Kushner, "Oral History at the Extremes of Human Experience: Holocaust Testimonial in a Museum Setting," *Oral History* 21, nos. 1–2 (autumn 2001): 83–94; Edward Tabor Linenthal, *Preserving Memory: The Struggle to Create America's Holocaust Museum* (New York: Viking, 1995); James Edward Young, *The Texture of Memory: Holocaust Memorials and Meaning* (New Haven: Yale University Press, 1993).

3 Giorgio Agamben, *Remnants of Auschwitz: The Witness and the Archive* (New York: Zone Books, 1999); Cathy Caruth, *Unclaimed Experience: Trauma, Narrative, and History* (Baltimore: Johns Hopkins University Press, 1996); Lawrence Langer, *Holocaust Testimonies: The Ruins of Memory* (New Haven: Yale University Press, 1991).

4 Paula Bultz, interview by Steven High and Stacey Zembrzycki, Montreal, 2 January 2009.

5 For more, see Anna Sheftel and Stacey Zembrzycki, "'We Started Over Again, We Were Young': Postwar Social Worlds of Child Holocaust Survivors in Montreal," *Urban History Review* 39, no. 1 (fall 2010): 20–30.

6 Montreal Life Stories (http://www.lifestoriesmontreal.ca) is funded by a Social Sciences and Humanities Research Council of Canada Community – University Research Alliance grant. For more on this project, see Steven High, "Sharing Authority: An Introduction," *Journal of Canadian Studies* 43, no. 1 (winter 2009): 12–34; and for a reflection on the interviews we have conducted with Holocaust survivors, see Anna Sheftel and Stacey Zembrzycki, "Only Human: A Reflection on the Ethical and Methodological Challenges of Working with 'Difficult' Stories," *Oral History Review* 37, no. 2 (fall 2010): 191–214.

7 See Alessandro Portelli, "What Makes Oral History Different?" in his *The Death of Luigi Trastulli and Other Stories: Form and Meaning in Oral History* (Albany: SUNY Press, 1991), 45–58.

8 The difference between an objectified "community of memory" and an active "community of remembering" was the subject of a keynote address to the Oral History Association of Australia. Identities are forged not only in moments of crisis but also in the activism that follows. See Steven High,

"Communities of Remembering in Times of Crisis: A Reflection," keynote address, Oral History Association of Australia, October 2011.

9 On reading silences in difficult narratives, see Agamben, *Remnants of Auschwitz*; Paula Draper, "Surviving Their Survival: Women, Memory, and the Holocaust," in *Sisters or Strangers? Immigrant, Ethnic, and Racialized Women in Canadian History*, edited by Marlene Epp, Franca Iacovetta, and Frances Swyripa (Toronto: University of Toronto Press, 2004), 399–414; Marlene Epp, *Women without Men: Mennonite Refugees of the Second World War* (Toronto: University of Toronto Press, 1999), 48–63; Richard S. Esbenshade, "Remembering to Forget: Memory, History, National Identity in Postwar East-Central Europe," *Representations* 49 (winter 1995): 72–96; Saul Friedlander, *Memory, History, and the Extermination of the Jews of Europe* (Bloomington: Indiana University Press, 1993); Luisa Passerini, "Memories between Silence and Oblivion," in *Memory and Totalitarianism*, edited by Luisa Passerini (Oxford: Oxford University Press, 1992), 196; Pamela Sugiman, "'These feelings that fill my heart': Japanese Canadian Women's Memories of Internment," *Oral History* 34 (autumn 2006): 78–80.

10 Henry Greenspan and Sidney Bolkosky, "When Is an Interview an Interview? Notes from Listening to Holocaust Survivors," *Poetics Today* 27 (2006): 433.

11 Henry Greenspan, *On Listening to Holocaust Survivors: Recounting and Life History* (Westport, CT: Praeger, 1998), xvii.

12 On collaboration in research, see Steven High, Lisa Ndejuru, and Kristen O'Hare, eds., "Special Issue of Sharing Authority: Community-University Collaboration in Oral History, Digital Storytelling, and Engaged Scholarship," *Journal of Canadian Studies* 43, no. 1 (winter 2009).

13 This methodological approach has also been influenced by Portelli's *Death of Luigi Trastulli*.

14 Steven High, blog, "Reflections on the Rwandan Conference," April 2008, http://www.lifestoriesmontreal.ca/en/blogs/reflections-on-the-rwandan-conference-april-2008 (accessed 3 October 2014).

15 Greenspan, *On Listening to Holocaust Survivors*; Greenspan and Bolkosky, "When Is an Interview an Interview?"

16 For a discussion of this history, see Franklin Bialystok, *Delayed Impact: The Holocaust and the Canadian Jewish Community* (Montreal and Kingston: McGill-Queen's University Press, 2000), 190–4.

17 For a survey of these projects, see Janice Rosen, "Holocaust Testimonies and Related Resources in Canadian Archival Repositories," *Canadian Jewish Studies* 4 and 5 (1996–97): 163–75.

18 In recent years, there has been an explosion of work detailing the experiences of child survivors. See, for instance, Boaz Cohen, "The Children's Voice: Postwar Collection of Testimonies from Child Survivors of the Holocaust," *Holocaust and Genocide Studies* 21, no. 1 (spring 2007): 73–95.

19 For a more thorough discussion about why survivors' voices were silenced in the postwar years, see Henry Greenspan, *The Awakening of Memory: Survivor Testimony in the First Years after the Holocaust, and Today* (Washington: United States Holocaust Memorial Museum, 2001); Zoe Vania Waxman, *Writing the Holocaust: Identity, Testimony, Representation* (Oxford: Oxford University Press, 2008).

20 Mayer Schondorf and Rena Schondorf, interview by Steven High and Stacey Zembrzycki, Montreal, 26 November 2009.

21 Sidney Zoltak, interview by Anna Sheftel and Stacey Zembrzycki, Montreal, 18 March 2009.

22 On the homogenization of survival narratives and the privileging of concentration camp experiences, see Shoshana Felman and Dori Laub, *Testimony: Crises of Witnessing in Literature, Psychoanalysis, and History* (New York: Routledge, 1992); Langer, *Holocaust Testimonies*; Dan Stone, *Constructing the Holocaust: A Study in Historiography* (London: Vallentine Mitchell, 2003).

23 Zoltak, interview.

24 Sidney Zoltak, interview by Anna Sheftel and Stacey Zembrzycki, Montreal, 11 March 2009.

25 Yehudi Lindeman, interview by Steven High and Stacey Zembrzycki, Montreal, 18 February 2009.

26 See Felman and Laub's *Testimony*. Another example of the survivor-interviewer-researcher is Yale's Geoffrey Hartman. See Hartman's "Learning from Survivors: The Yale Testimony Project," *Holocaust and Genocide Studies* 9, no. 2 (fall 1995): 192–207.

27 In addition to the archive of interviews, the project produced a book that features excerpts of twenty-five testimonies. See Yehudi Lindeman, ed., *Shards of Memory: Narratives of Holocaust Survival* (Westport, CT: Praeger, 2007).

28 Lindeman, interview.

29 Bultz, Lindeman, and "Krysia," interview.

30 Ibid.

31 There is some controversy surrounding the benefits and risks in survivors interviewing other survivors. See, for example, Michele Langfield and Pam Maclean, "Multiple Framings: Survivor and Non-Survivor Interviewers in Holocaust Video Testimony," in *Memories of Repression: Narrating Life Stories in the Aftermath of Atrocity*, edited by Nancy Adler, Selma Leydesdorff, Mary Chamberlain, and Leyla Neyzi (New Brunswick, NJ: Transaction Publishers, 2009), 199–218. The training manual of the Montreal Life Stories project notes the potential danger of "insiders" assuming they know more than they do, but we believe that, just as there is no perfect location for the oral history interviewer, there is no "wrong" location either.

32 Bultz, Lindeman, and "Krysia," interview.

33 Yehudi Lindeman, interviews by Steven High and Stacey Zembrzycki, Montreal, 12 January and 4 February 2009.

34 Musia Schwartz, interview by Stacey Zembrzycki and Anna Sheftel, Montreal, 16 June 2009.
35 Liselotte Ivry, interview by Stacey Zembrzycki and Anna Sheftel, Montreal, 9 February 2009.
36 Ted Bolgar, interview by Stacey Zembrzycki and Jessica Silva, Montreal, 12 January 2009.
37 Batia Bettman, interview by Anna Shefel and Stacey Zembrzycki, Montreal, 16 December 2008.
38 Bolgar, interview.
39 Mayer and Rena Schondorf, pre-interview by Steven High and Stacey Zembrzycki, Montreal, 17 November 2008.
40 Zoltak, interviews, 11 and 18 March 2009.
41 Schwartz, interview.
42 William Westerman, "Central American Refugee Testimony and Performed Life Histories in the Sanctuary Movement," in *The Oral History Reader*, 1st edition, edited by Robert Perks and Alistair Thomson (London: Routledge, 1998), 224–34.
43 Mayer and Rena Schondorf, interview, 26 November 2008.
44 For more on this remarkable project, see Karen Levine, *Hana's Suitcase: A True Story* (New York: Albert Whitman, 2003).
45 Olga Sher, interview by Steven High and Sandra Gasana, Montreal, 19 December 2008.
46 Schwartz, interview.
47 Zoltak, interview, 18 March 2009.
48 There is a sizeable literature on the Memorial for the Murdered Jews of Europe, the Jewish Museum of Berlin, and other sites of memory in Germany. See, for example, James Young, "The Texture of Memory: Holocaust Memorials in History," in *Cultural Memory Studies: An International and Interdisciplinary Handbook*, edited by Astrid Erll, Ansgar Nunning, and Sara B. Young (New York: Walter de Gruyter, 2008), 357–66.
49 Sher, interview.
50 Following each interview, interviewers are required to post a reflection, in the form of a blog, about their experiences on the project's internal web space. There are now well over one thousand interviewer blogs in the Life Stories project archives. Stacey Zembrzycki, blog post, 19 October 2009.
51 Steven High, blog post, 6 May 2009. This artifact has received a great deal of attention recently, as the result of a documentary created by Carl Leblanc, *The Heart of Auschwitz*, 2011.
52 Mayer and Rena Schondorf, interview by Steven High and Stacey Zembrzycki, Montreal, 28 January 2009.
53 March of the Living homepage, http://marchoftheliving.org/ (accessed 20 June 2014).

54 March of the Living Canada, http://marchoftheliving.com/mol2009/
    09intro.html (accessed 20 June 2014).

55 For relevant discussions and critiques of the March of the Living program,
    see Erica Lehrer, *Jewish Poland Revisited: Heritage Tourism in Unquiet Places*
    (Bloomington: Indiana University Press, 2013); Rona Sheramy, "From Ausch-
    witz to Jerusalem: Re-enacting Jewish History on the March of the Living,"
    Polin: Studies in Polish Jewry 19 (2007): 307–26.

56 March of the Living Canada, http://marchoftheliving.org/about/ (accessed
    20 June 2014).

57 Liselotte Ivry, "From Terezin to Montreal," http://motl.org/?p=105 (accessed
    23 June 2014).

58 Ivry, interview.

59 Bettman, interview.

60 Zoltak, interview, 18 March 2009.

61 Ibid.

12

Listening and Learning with Life Stories of Human Rights Violations

Bronwen Low and Emmanuelle Sonntag

Are you listening? Are you listening carefully? Because, sound specialist Julian Treasure argues, "We are losing our listening."[1] He differentiates listening from hearing, which is physiological, developed in utero. In contrast, listening requires one's conscious attention, so that Treasure defines it as "making meaning from sound. It's a mental process, and it's a process of extraction." While Treasure thinks there was a time when we knew how to listen, he fears we have lost this ability, having invented multiple methods of recording that mean "the premium on active and careful listening has simply disappeared."[2] All is not lost, however, for Treasure claims there are concrete ways to improve our listening skills, and he suggests teaching the skill of listening in school.

As co-directors of the Education and Life Stories working group of a large oral history project, we have been thinking a good deal about listening and pedagogy. This project is entitled Life Stories of Montrealers Displaced by War, Genocide, and other Human Rights Violations, shortened here as the Montreal Life Stories project. Housed in the Centre for Oral History and Digital Storytelling at Concordia University from 2007 to 2012 and led by principal investigator Steven High, the project was driven by the History Department's commitment to public history. The education group's principal task was to disseminate the oral histories by developing curricula for secondary schools. We took Treasure's concerns about listening seriously, working with the notion of listening as, fundamentally, the making of meaning from sound, and structured our curriculum around a set of teaching and learning principles that, borrowing from Reggio Emilia,[3] we are calling a "pedagogy of listening." In this chapter, we explore how this pedagogical stance, shaped by Jean-Luc

Nancy's theory of listening, concepts of testimony and witnessing, and notions of listening in the context of shared authority in oral history, can support the teaching of oral history. We illustrate the central principles of the pedagogy of listening with specific references to our curricular units.

Entrusted with the task of disseminating the life stories in the education system, we wondered how to best support students in carefully listening to the words, voices, meanings, and silences of people who have survived difficult or traumatic experiences. Oral history has been used in educational contexts to teach everything from popular and local history to historiography and historic methods, as students at all levels of education practise the work of historians. However, the processes of teaching and learning become complicated when these oral histories document stories of displacement, war, and genocide. These ask us to confront what Pitt and Britzman call "difficult knowledge," which is "a concept meant to signify both representations of social traumas in curriculum and the individual's encounters with them."[4] While it is impossible to predict what students (and teachers) might find difficult in their pedagogical encounters, it is much more likely that learning will be affectively charged in response to representations of social and individual crisis. This likelihood raised some important questions for us: When accounts of traumatic experience are envisioned as pedagogic, what is one hoping students will learn? What might constitute an adequate ethics of engagement? What is the place of listening in such an engagement? How might a pedagogy of listening enable the teaching of oral history?

THE CONTEXT: THE MONTREAL LIFE STORIES PROJECT

As part of the work of preserving historical memory in Quebec and Canada and of better understanding the long-term repercussions of human rights violations, a team of both university and community-based researchers video-recorded life story interviews from 2007 to 2012 with approximately five hundred Montrealers with experiences of mass violence and displacement.[5] Members of the survivor communities (Tutsi, Haitian, Cambodian, and Holocaust) were key partners in both the research and the diffusion, fundamentally shaping the project's philosophy, activities, and outcomes. Project researchers were organized into a number of working groups, four based in specific cultural communities (Rwandan, Haitian, Cambodian, and Holocaust Survivors) and three others that work across cultures using collective storytelling techniques focused on diffusion (Experiences of Refugee Youth, Oral History and Performance, and Life Stories in Education). While our working group had a number of goals, including better understanding the experiences of survivors who have been working as educators,[6] these culminated in the creation of a series of pedagogical tools, including five Learning and Evaluation Situations (LES), the curricular units in the Quebec Education Program, in French and English. They form the educational package *We Are Here* and can be accessed at www.lifestoriesmontreal.ca/curriculum. When the Education working group set itself the task of creating pedagogic materials for students, it had three principle objectives:

1 The first was to explore and promote the pedagogic possibilities of oral history in the classroom, in the context of Quebec provincial curricular guidelines and otherwise.[7]
2 The second dovetails with the recommendation from the Bouchard-Taylor Consultation Commission on Accommodation Practices Related to Cultural Diversity that Quebec should work to foster a richer and more inclusive collective cultural memory through an oral history project that would gather the stories of immigrants and refugees to Quebec.
3 The third was to offer students an understanding of the concepts and experience of human rights and of their violations, here and elsewhere. We wanted to awaken students to the social preconditions for crimes against humanity, including genocide, and their long-term effects.

These objectives meant finding entry points for this material into the Quebec Education Program, a competency-based curriculum being gradually introduced into Quebec schools as we were developing our materials. We designed the five Learning and Evaluation Situations (LES) for secondary cycle two, where the students are generally fourteen to sixteen years old. Each LES is connected to a particular subject area and develops subject-specific as well as cross-curricular competencies. The units all ask students to engage with the life stories through a close and careful viewing of and listening to the videos, to respond to them in groups and individually through different media, and to reflect on their own analytic and creative processes. In order to facilitate the use of the recordings, students mostly work with "digital stories," which are videos edited from the interviews by the subject and an editor. These tend to be under ten minutes long and bring together video, images, sound, and text.

LISTENING: BETWEEN *"AUSCULTARE"* AND CARE FOR THE OTHER

We are aware of the irony of building a new case for listening in schools. Students are commanded, daily, to "be quiet and listen to the teacher." Indeed, this listening imperative might be considered a pillar of traditional school pedagogy in which the student listens, in silence, as the teacher transmits knowledge. Listening in silence is often considered to be a prerequisite for learning; student talk is largely restricted to particular question and answer periods. Despite the long history in educational theory of critiquing this model, the student-who-listens-in-silence as opposed to the teacher-who-speaks-loudly is still regularly invoked in practice as an ideal relation in schools, as well as university classrooms. The demand for silence is in part a pragmatic response to the inherent noisiness of schools. At the same time, the listening imperative is also a key tool in the establishment of teacher authority and power, a strategy of coercion that establishes the teacher as the one who knows. This demand for silence on the part of students can also hold true in the context of listening to difficult material such as the testimonies of Holocaust survivors, where respectful listening is often assumed to require silence.

In order to develop a pedagogy of listening, we must unsettle and rework commonplace understandings of listening and learning. As curriculum designers and researchers who have been taught in traditional settings, we have had to try to move beyond our own preconceived notions about listening in classrooms. Despite the centrality of talking and listening to the communication processes that shape education, listening has been a largely neglected topic in educational theory.[8]

A pedagogy of listening requires an elaborated concept of listening. Jean-Luc Nancy offers a place to start as he begins his book-length inquiry into listening by examining the etymology of the verb écouter (to listen) in the Latin *auscultare*.[9] The first part is *aus,* the root of *auris,* which becomes the French *oreille* (ear) and *l'ouïe* (hearing). The second part of *auscultare*, according to Nancy, is marked by "une tension, une intention et une attention." While Nancy does not specify what root he refers to, Tucker suggests that the second part of *auscultare* is "akin to *clinere*, to lean, bend" (*auscultate*). Of *écouter*, Nancy says: "To listen is *tendre l'oreille* – literally, to stretch the ear – an expression that evokes a singular mobility, among the sensory apparatuses, of the pinna of the ear – it is an intensification and a concern, a curiosity or an anxiety."[10] Here the act of listening, of extending the ear, embodies a movement toward the other, establishing a relation of curiosity and attention.

Nancy also puts forward the notion that listening is inherently social by describing it as "methexic," in contrast with the visual, which is mostly mimetic.[11] The first part of the word methexis, the Greek prefix *meta*, signifies that something is with or next to something else, as in "being together." If seeing is "a making evident," suggesting a kind of distance, listening is "a making resonant."[12] Resonance implies movement and responsiveness – properties of sound that convey that sounds, if given the option, propagate and expand wherever they can, like liquid. It is this propagation that gives listening its profoundly social character.[13] Listening builds a relation to something else, and so is a mode of sharing and address.

Nancy's definition of listening as sharing through extending the ear/self toward another might be considered a foundational tenet of education itself, a process of learning to live with others, including attending to the other who is not the self. Nancy notes that this extension embodies curiosity and anxiety, two emotions arguably intensified in the context of listening to life stories of human rights violations. For many students in the Quebec schools for whom we have primarily designed our curriculum, the life stories they will be exposed to are particularly "other" – the interviewees are immigrants or refugees whose experiences of displacement and violence might be unfamiliar to them. While some students in Quebec schools might be survivors of war, genocide, or other serious human rights violation, most will not (though of course traumatic experiences are not limited to the socio-political situations documented by the Montreal Life Stories project). In thinking of how students and these stories might live and work together, we have to consider what takes place in students who listen to these difficult accounts. Might there be specificity to a pedagogy of listening in the context of the life stories of human rights violations?

THE CHAIN OF TESTIMONY

One way of thinking about the position of the student in this kind of classroom is in terms of testimony: first-person accounts of human rights violations put the speaker and listener into a relation of testifier and witness. The first witness is then charged with sharing that account, testifying to the next witness who then testifies in turn to another, initiating what Roger Simon and Claudia Eppert describe as a chain of testimony.[14] The relation is an ethical one, with witnessing held together by the bonds of an ethics forged in a relation of responsibility and respect. Testimony is thus always directed toward the other. It places the one who received it under the obligation of response to an embodied singular experience not recognizable as one's own.[15]

Two common (and understandable) responses to a story that is significantly different from one's own are either to reject it (that it is so far outside of the bounds of one's experience that it seems impossible to engage with) or to incorporate it (one thinks the story is identical to one's own experiences and so imagines knowing exactly how the other feels).[16] Neither rejection nor an incorporative/consuming response can sustain the chain of testimony, since both erase the original, either by ignoring it in its entirety or by denying its specificity, its embodied singularity. Forging an ethical response requires a listening that is neither overwhelmed by, nor disavows the uniqueness of the other. As one of the working groups focused on the dissemination of the life stories, the education working group has among its tasks to help create the conditions necessary to forge that chain of testimony. Simon and Eppert's notion of the "obligation of response" suggests that the experience of listening to a testimony makes certain demands upon the student. In our work as curriculum designers and theorists, we explore how best to support the student in meeting these demands.

In order to support the chain of testimony, Simon and Eppert call for building communities of memory in which "practices of remembrance are contested, shaped, and deepened by consideration of the shared significance of what has been heard, seen, or read."[17] It is central to the work of constructing such classroom communities to allow for students to explore and voice the "difficult and often unanswerable questions" that testimonies can invoke aloud and in "shadow-texts" that accompany their engagement with the testimonies (such as, how could this happen? Why didn't the victims protect themselves? What would I have done?).[18] The classroom must also establish the conditions for remembering in the form of retelling; in order to "re-present that story in concrete form to others," students must develop a "nuanced vocabulary of witnessing" that can take many forms, including non-verbal ones.[19] This retelling forges a link in the chain of testimony.

Prior to retelling, though, must come a close and careful listening that makes meaning from what is heard in ways that do not erase the singularity of the original. Yet if, as Treasure claims, there is a widespread loss of the ability to listen, to extend the listening self in a posture of care, what hope might we have that teachers and students will listen to testimonies that make such demands on the listener? The work of oral historians offers guidance.

LISTENING IN ORAL HISTORY

It goes without saying that listening is central to the theory and methodology of oral history.[20] The Montreal Life Stories project promoted a model of "deep listening," in which interviewers were "listening for meanings, not just facts, and listening in such a way that prompts more profound reflection from the interviewee."[21] The educational visions of relation and reciprocity through listening and dialogue resonate with a key concept in the methodology of oral history, "shared authority,"[22] or what Greenspan describes in terms of learning *with* rather than *about*.[23] Traditional power relations between researchers and interviewees are moved beyond in favour of a dual authority in which interviewees hold the authority in describing their experiences and interviewers hold the authority of critical distance and professional training. The Montreal Life Stories project has worked to expand the concept of shared authority into a more sustained process of *sharing* authority, as community and academic partners collaborate in the interpretive and meaning-making processes of constructing history prior, during, and after the interview, and play a key role in the dissemination of the stories.[24] Given that interviews can at times be very long, the project encouraged the collaborative creation of short digital stories from the longer interviews, usually edited by interviewees in partnership with digital editors. These digital stories make the life story interviews more accessible to the public, including teachers, and are the basis for our curriculum. Sharing authority in oral history takes dialogue seriously, and the perspective of the oral historian is bi-directional, envisioning both the interviewer and interviewee participating in a conversation. This contrasts with conventional notions of testimony, conceived of as a "one-way act of bestowal."[25] The focus of testimony and life story can also differ. This vision of interaction means that the act of listening transforms, in some way, the listening self. Martha Norkunas develops the idea further, in the context of teaching oral history:

> Rather than occupying an objective position, a listener should
> expect to modify her or his self-awareness and identity as a result of
> engaging with the narrator and hearing the stories. When there are
> class and power differences between listener and narrator, a listener

of conscience acknowledges them. Establishing an atmosphere of respect and equality of self in an interview means that neither the logic of the narrator nor that of the interviewer is privileged; instead the driving force of the interview lies in "the interaction and tension between the two and the ways that each is revised, reconstructed, and elaborated upon as the conversation flows back and forth."[26]

This vision of listening as negotiation reminds us that listening can have significant consequences for the listener, and that listening is shaped and limited by the socio-cultural reality of the listener. Conscious listeners understand and acknowledge that their perspectives and understandings are situated and that this reality can pose challenges for listening across differences, especially those shaped by power inequities.[27] In our pedagogy of listening, we work to develop this self-awareness in the learner. While the testimony literature helps us to understand some of the responsibility entrusted to the students who listen to the stories of survivors, as well as the potential effects of listening, the life story literature places emphasis on the ways the story changes in the interaction between teller and listener, and the ways both parties themselves can be transformed. It provides us with an account of the co-construction of meaning involved in the dynamic relation between teller, tale, and listener.

FIRST STEPS TOWARD A PEDAGOGY OF LISTENING

These various theories inform our thinking about a pedagogy of listening inspired by oral history practice; some consciously shaped the writing of the curricular materials, while others are helpful as we revisit and reflect upon what we have created. Before we speak specifically about our curricular units, we want to say something about listening in the context of the Montreal Life Stories project. The approximately five hundred life story interviews were conducted, filmed, and recorded by volunteers, most of whom are members of the partner community organizations or were students conducting intergenerational and intra-communal conversations. They are not professionals in the field of video production. The fact that the sound quality of many of the recordings is not very good heightens the commitment required by the listening students. As well, many of the speakers speak slowly or very quickly, or might have French or English accents unfamiliar to the student. This makes the close attention to listening all the more challenging and important.[28] It is also important to note that have we not yet studied any classrooms in which our curricular materials are being taught; our reflections are based on what Elliot Eisner calls the "intended" or planned rather than "operational" curriculum.[29]

All the materials begin with an activity in which students listen to one or more of the digital stories created out of the project interviews. Our first Learning and Evaluation Situation (LES) is designed for use in English Language Arts and is entitled "What a Story!: Life Stories and Digital Storytelling." In it, the students listen to and discover the narrative structure of a digital story from a Holocaust survivor (or in French, a Tutsi whose family experienced the genocide in Rwanda), analyze it, and then, in groups, create a new digital story based on a thirty-minute excerpt from an interview with another survivor. They develop editing skills, and critically reflect upon the choices made in the process. The second LES, "Dialogue Time: Interviewing and Building a Collective Timeline" (Ethics and Religious Culture curriculum), has students listen to a documentary entitled *I Was There*, featuring segments from interviews with a Haitian woman, a Cambodian woman, a Chilean woman, and a woman who survived the Holocaust. After reflecting on the practice and ethics of interviewing, the students interview people from their own communities, and then create a collective timeline based on the interviews. In the third LES, designed for the History and Citizenship curriculum, "Mapping the Elsewhere Here," students listen to a series of digital stories from the project, map these stories onto visual cartographic representations of the city which they create, and then write and map some of their own narratives, exploring ties between identity and place. In the fourth LES, "Learning about the Tutsi Genocide in Rwanda through the Graphic Novel and Interview," students read excerpts from a graphic narrative about Rwanda by Rupert Bazambanza, and watch and listen to a segment from the video interview with the artist. After doing some research, they create an additional page for the graphic narrative, where they present their position on the issue of military intervention and humanitarian assistance, a theme in the Contemporary World curriculum. In the fifth LES, "Between the Tracks: Creating an Audio Guide," designed for English Language Arts, students listen to an audio-guide whose objective is to commemorate in the streets of Montreal the genocide of the Tutsis in Rwanda. They practise listening exercises while reflecting on their abilities as listeners. They then create their own audio-guide through a writing exercise. The audio-guide is geo-tagged, situating the student production and their experiences within Montreal.

Having completed the curriculum materials, and in light of our explorations, we are now able to articulate the beginnings of a pedagogy of listening, inspired by oral history, educational theory, and a philosophy of listening, in the form of a series of interrelated objectives. This pedagogy aims to:

Promote more democratic relations. As in the notion of shared authority, the relation between student and teacher is imagined as a partnership as the class works together to co-construct knowledge and meaning from the digital stories. As students and teachers extend themselves, in the sense of Nancy, their listening contains the listening of others. Such partnership also requires facing the challenge of listening to the beliefs of others which conflict with your own. Within the Learning and Evaluation Situations, the respective listenings of teacher and students might interrupt each other as they engage with the difficult narratives of human rights violation as well as each other's beliefs; this interaction potentially creates trust among participants in a group discussion.[30]

Build a listening community. The pedagogy fosters Simon and Eppert's "community of memory" by encouraging close engagement between teacher and students, as participants listen to each other as well as to the testimonies, exploring points of connection as well as differences of opinion through dialogue. Within our LES units, students work together in listening and production groups, discussing and negotiating, through transaction, their understandings of the life stories and determining together the nature of their creative response. This community should support students through the process of grappling with stories and information that in some instances might frighten or deeply sadden them.

Develop an ethics of listening. We understand that listening can be a powerful conduit to awareness of the experiences of others, and that the listening relationship is delicate in situations in which those others have had markedly different life experiences from the listener. An ethics of listening – necessary in order for students to act as witnesses – places emphasis on self-reflexive and dialogical listening; these are the bases for a listening process that neither disavows the uniqueness of the experiences of the other nor places these experiences outside the realm of human connection and understanding. The introduction to the curricular guide includes a discussion of the ethics of doing oral history, including the concept of shared authority in the interview and in the classroom. After an initial listening exercise in "What a Story," in which students explore what they think are the central elements of a thirty-minute interview segment with a Holocaust survivor, students are asked to discuss, among other issues: "The responsibilities that accompany listening to a difficult story."[31] The LES "Dialogue Time" asks students to explore the ethics of interviewing in relation to a documentary consisting of segments from four project interviews, and then to their own work. For instance, before interviewing a senior, they do test interviews on each other. Then, as a class, they are given the following guidelines:

> Discuss the ethics of the interview. Consider appropriate questions
> to ask, and not to ask, and what is the right attitude to present? Also
> think about how to respect what the interviewee says, how to carry
> out a dialogue, how to establish a good rapport, how to maintain a
> healthy two-sided dialogue, how to listen to the person while they
> are telling their story, how to respect the interviewee's point of view,
> etc. Finally, what qualities are needed for good listening (empathy,
> confidence, etc.)?[32]

As well, before conducting their interviews at home, the students are reminded of the following ethical points: listening ethics – the importance of showing respect and tolerance; interview ethics – asking questions tactfully and establishing dialogue and interaction; the ethics of distribution – letting participants know the results will be presented to the class and the necessary timeline; the philosophy of life story interviews – they are an exchange between equals with a shared authority.[33] These ethical elements also shape the short informed consent form that the class creates together for distribution to the interviewees.

Support critical reflexive practice for students (and teacher) individually and as a collective. Students are regularly encouraged to self-reflect as they engage with the testimonies of others, exploring as they go how the stories might have changed them. Final integration activities at the end of the units ask the students to critically examine what they have learned. For instance, in "Dialogue Time," the students write a one-page text or produce an artistic work about the experience of the interview as dialogue, considering: the dialogue with the past; the dialogue of the student with the self; the dimensions of tolerance within the interview; the discovery of the other; and the implications of the interview for future relations with the person.[34] At the end of "What a Story!" students are invited to be critical of their created digital story. They discuss the significance of their choices as editors, the way that narratives have been modified, and the meaning built into the digital story vs. the meaning of the interview.[35] It is hoped that, as students seek critical distance from the story they have crafted, they will also think through the situated nature of their own perspectives and choices.

Explore the multitude of listenings. The assignments produce a range of responses to the life stories. For example, in "What a Story!" the student working groups create their own digital story versions of the same interview. This exercise makes the many possible interpretations of a story evident, and shows how different emphases can be made in the creation of a shorter text. In "Mapping the Elsewhere Here," each listening group determines what it sees as the key words or phrases to be placed on the map of Montreal, creating multiple cartographies of lived experience.

Foster a culture of close and attentive listening. The LES cultivate students' attention to their own listening processes. For instance, in "Between the Tracks," as students create the audio-guide, it is possible for them to "enter" the recording they have made; they can slow down the cadence, augment the sound, rewind or fast-forward. They cut, paste, and annotate. They are auditors who intervene in what they are listening to, and interpret their listening for potential audiences.

Foster the chain of testimony. Students are given the opportunity to narrate and then exhibit their listening through various media, giving their interviews shape and meaning in the form of digital stories, time-lines, maps, audio-guides, or a page from a graphic novel. This shaping is the precursor to exhibiting their listening, as students share their work with each other and the wider community in a spirit of methexis. In "Between the Tracks," students disseminate the audio guides they created, inspired by the one commemorating the Rwandan genocide, by connecting with the *Culture à l'écoute!* program, which promotes the creation of audio guides in Quebec schools. Students upload their guides on BaladoWeb, where they are geotagged and linked to a QR code. In "What a Story" students upload their digital story versions of the life story of a Holocaust survivor onto VoiceThread[36] and are asked to "encourage their family and friends to contribute audio, video, or text comments about the video."[37]

Support students in making connections and taking a position on current events. In the LES units, students are encouraged to make connections between what they hear and learn and their own lives. Rather than learning to think of human rights violations as existing in a separate reality, the curricula emphasise the legacy of trauma, the place of memory in everyday life, and the interconnectedness of human experience through

278 • Bronwen Low and Emmanuelle Sonntag

the co-existence of different life trajectories and stories in Montreal. For instance, in "Mapping the Elsewhere Here," the students first map the life stories they have heard onto a graphic representation of Montreal, and then insert onto the map some of their own experiences. The resulting collective map showcases the ties of identity to place and as well as potential relationships, beginning with spatial ones, between the students and the Life Story project interviewees.

Students are also supported in taking positions on contemporary issues and, in some units, moving to action. For instance, in "Learning about the Tutsi Genocide," students extensively research an element of the genocide in Rwanda in order to then "take a position on the issue of military intervention through the development of a supplementary page of the graphic narrative." Part of this process of taking a stand can involve various forms of action (without presenting a simplified notion of an adolescent's ability to intervene in violent conflicts at the international level). For instance, "Mapping the Elsewhere Here" invites discussion on how mapping can be a tool for education and citizenship. As well as representing the geographic features and landmarks of a place, maps can also "pin" the experiences of those who live there, such as refugees and immigrants who have settled in Montreal.[38] Students might also act to create a publicity campaign to promote their map within the school, or develop a promotional brochure, organize a viewing session, or present their work to other classes.

Foster students' historical imagination. The pedagogy seeks to bring historical events to life through careful attention to the life stories of others. As Julian Treasure remarks, "listening is one of the main ways in which we live the passing of time." The digital stories span the twentieth century and move into the twenty-first, animating historical events from around the globe through first-person perspectives and narrations.

LISTENING AS RELATION TO SELF AND OTHER

Crucial to the model of listening we propose here is that listening is both an individual and a shared process. While Julian Treasure seems to consider listening as an individual capacity or act, rather than as a collective one, we think that what we hear while listening is both highly personal, dependent on our social location, as well as shaped by the listenings of others and our relation to the speaking other. While this understanding shapes the oral history interview process, we argue that it should also structure teaching and learning through oral histories. Our curricular units ask students to reflect carefully and exhibit their listenings, creating occasions for exploring individual and collective meaning-making and identities. This close attention to the complex dynamics of listening can help refigure power hierarchies in educational settings as well as communities; while critiques of traditional power relations in school are certainly not new, we hope that a renewed focus on listening in classrooms might help enact more democratic visions of education. In this model, teachers and students are co-partners in a dialogic learning process, open and attentive to the perspectives and experiences of the other. This chapter is an initial articulation of what the elements of such a pedagogy might be, in relation to our curriculum but also for more general use by other researchers and teachers. We plan in the future to work with teachers to study actual uses of the Learning and Evaluation Situations in order to better understand this oral history pedagogy in practice.

NOTES

1 Julian Treasure, *5 Ways to Listen Better*, Video on TED.com http://www.ted.com/talks/julian_treasure_5_ways_to_listen_better.html (accessed 26 July 2013).

2 We recognize the limits of generalizing a (not-listening) "we," given the continued existence of predominantly oral cultures across the world, despite their marginalization by print culture.

3 Carlina Rinaldi, *In Dialogue with Reggio Emilia: Listening, Researching, and Learning* (New York: Psychology Press, 2006).

4 Alice Pitt and Deborah Britzman, "Speculations on Qualities of Difficult Knowledge in Teaching and Learning: An Experiment in Psychoanalytic Research," *International Journal of Qualitative Studies in Education* 16, no. 6 (2003): 755–76.

5 More information about this project, funded by a Community-University Research Alliance grant from the [Canadian] Social Sciences and Humanities Research Council, can be found at http://www.lifestoriesmontreal.ca (accessed 20 June 2014).

6 See Zembrzycki and High, chapter 11 in this *Reader*.

7 Glenn Whitman, *Dialogue with the Past: Engaging Students and Meeting Standards Through Oral History* (Walnut Creek, CA: AltaMira Press, 2004).

8 Michael Welton, "Listening, Conflict, and Citizenship: Towards a Pedagogy of Civil Society," *International Journal of Lifelong Education* 21, no. 3 (2002): 197–208. Significant exceptions are special issues of *Teachers College Record* (Sophie Haroutunian-Gordon and Leonard J. Waks, eds., "Special Issue on Listening" 112, no. 11 [2010]) focused mostly on the listening teacher and *Educational Theory* (Sophie Haroutunian-Gordon and Megan Laverty, eds.,

"Symposium: Philosophical Perspectives on Listening," 60, no. 2 [2011]) on listening in educational philosophy.

9   Jean-Luc Nancy, *Listening* (New York: Fordham University Press, 2007).

10 Ibid., 5.

11 Ibid., 10.

12 Ibid., 3.

13 Jean-Luc Nancy, *A l'écoute* (Paris: Galilée, 2002), 308.

14 Roger I. Simon and Claudia Eppert, "Remembering Obligation: Pedagogy and the Witnessing of Testimony of Historical Trauma," *Canadian Journal of Education/Revue canadienne de l'éducation* 22, no. 2 (1997): 175–91.

15 Ibid., 2.

16 Julie Salverson, "Change on Whose Terms? Testimony and an Erotics of Inquiry," *Theatre* 31, no. 3 (2001): 119–25.

17 "Simon and Eppert, "Remembering Obligation," 8.

18 Ibid., 7.

19 Ibid., 9.

20 Martha Norkunas, "Teaching to Listen: Listening Exercises and Self-Reflexive Journals," *Oral History Review* 38, no. 1 (2011): 63–108.

21 Anna Sheftel and Stacey Zembrzycki, "Only Human: A Reflection on the Ethical and Methodological Challenges of Working with 'Difficult' Stories," *Oral History Review* 37, no. 2 (2010): 199.

22 Michael Frisch, *A Shared Authority: Essays on the Craft and Meaning of Oral and Public History* (Albany: SUNY Press, 1990).

23 Henry Greenspan and Sidney Bolkosky, "When Is an Interview an Interview? Notes from Listening to Holocaust Survivors," *Poetics Today* 27, no. 2 (2006): 431–49.

24 Steven High, *Oral History at the Crossroads: Sharing Life Stories of Survival and Displacement* (Vancouver: UBC Press, 2014).

25 Greenspan and Bolkosky, "When Is an Interview an Interview?," 433.

26 Norkunas, "Teaching to Listen," 64.

27 Ibid., for listening exercises for oral history students which help them in the work of understanding.

28 As part of the process of selecting particular texts to be drawn upon in the curriculum, we considered their accessibility to a youthful audience in terms of audibility and visual quality, but recognize that a number of them might still pose challenges for classroom use.

29 Elliot W. Eisner, *The Educational Imagination: On the Design and Evaluation of School Programs* (New York: Macmillan, 1994).

30 Sophie Haroutunian-Gordon and Leonard J. Waks, "Listening: Challenges for Teachers," *Teachers College Record* 112, no. 11 (2010): 2811.

31 Bronwen E. Low and Emmanuelle Sonntag, *We Are Here: Life Stories of Montrealers Displaced by War, Genocide, and Other Human Rights Violations. Educational Package for Secondary Cycle Two* (Montreal, 2012), 26.

http://lifestoriesmontreal.ca/files/LES_Educational_Package_WE_ARE_
HERE_0.pdf (accessed 26 July 2013).

32 Ibid., 52.

33 Ibid., 54. For discussion of debates regarding the concept of "shared authority" see Section Four of this *Reader*.

34 Ibid., 56.

35 Ibid., 27.

36 See http://voicethread.com (accessed 23 June 2014).

37 Low and Sonntag, *We Are Here*, 28.

38 Ibid., 42.

SECTION FOUR

Advocacy

13

Narrative Wisps of the Ochēkiwi Sīpi Past: A Journey in Recovering Collective Memories[1]

Winona Wheeler

Many Indigenous communities are in the process of reconstructing their pasts, to fill the gaps caused by generations of colonial onslaught against their ways of life. Chapters are missing from community histories that were once passed down the generations through oral histories. Efforts to regain community memories pose particular challenges, especially when combining Indigenous oral history methods with European documentary evidence. This chapter explores the dynamics of collective memory loss, the complexities of combining often-disparate sources, and the need for creativity. It demonstrates that solutions can frequently be found within the community itself.

The members of the Ochēkiwi Sīpi (Fisher River) Cree First Nation live two and a half hours north of Winnipeg, Manitoba. The reserve straddles the Fisher River some five miles inland from the river's confluence with Lake Winnipeg. In many ways the community looks like many other large reserves – dirt roads, new Canadian Mortgage and Housing Corporation (CMHC) houses interspersed with older Indian Affairs houses, big trucks, dead cars, and scruffy dogs. But it also stands out for its many initiatives and developments. On either side of the bridge connecting the north and south shores of the river are the child and family services centre, the school, a state-of-the-art recreation centre, an Elder-care centre, the health clinic, the Band administration office, and new housing subdivisions. Collectively these make up an impressive community centre. A little further downriver are the Treaty grounds and the new Leigh Cochrane Memorial Visitor Centre located at the site of the old Hudson's Bay Company (HBC) post and across from the old church, formerly Methodist, now United. The panorama from the bridge yields the barren riverbank, home to new and retired fishing boats, bulrushes, flood plains, mud flats, and traces of the old river lots where the founding families made their first homes. Where the Fisher River meets Lake Winnipeg, along the sandy coastline, is Bay River Developments, a cottage development project established in partnership with the province. Fisher River Cree Nation was also instrumental in the development of the Fisher Bay Park Reserve in an effort to preserve traditional hunting, fishing, and gathering sites.

Before Treaty No. 5 in 1875 and the reserve survey in 1878, the region was a hunting, fishing, and trapping commons, a migration corridor shared by Muskego-wininiwak, *Swampy Cree Peoples*, from the north and Anishnabe or Saulteaux Peoples from the south, many of whom were related through marriage or through social and economic ties with each other and the HBC. The majority of the Cree people who settled the region came from Norway House on the northernmost tip of Lake Winnipeg. A handful of Saulteaux and Saulteaux-Cree people came from Netley Creek or St Peter's Reserve on the Red River to the south, and from the islands and eastern shores of Lake Winnipeg.

Prior to the Treaty, Norway House was the hub of the north. In the mid-1800s, as the HBC inland administrative centre, it attracted Aboriginal wage labourers (full-time and seasonal) in the HBC Home Guard Cree tradition. The Methodist mission, established in 1840 and named Rossville, encouraged further Aboriginal settlement so that by 1875 there were over eight hundred Aboriginal souls at Norway House – the Christian Crees lived around the Rossville mission, and the Pagans lived along the shores of Playgreen Lake. In the summer months the population almost doubled, as inland fur brigades and supply boats from the Bay exchanged their freight and turned around before winter froze the waterways again.

Up to the early 1870s the HBC employed an average of two hundred Aboriginal men as full-time or seasonal wage labourers. However, as trade declined and steamboats replaced flotillas, the HBC dramatically reduced its labour force. Between 130 and 140 of the two hundred Aboriginal men employed by the HBC lost their jobs on the boat brigades and another sixty to seventy lost seasonal wage labour jobs.[2] Facing starvation and in need of an alternative livelihood, the Christian Crees of Rossville petitioned the federal government for a treaty to secure land in the south for farming.[3] In the fall of 1877 a large flotilla of Muskego-wininiwak from Norway House arrived on the banks of the Fisher River, and their descendants have made this place their home ever since.

I came to Fisher River initially through kinship ties, then by discovery and work, and was drawn into this community's heritage as a member, a student, and a land claims researcher. Over the past twenty-five years land claims research has branched out well beyond its original mandate to the point that it now includes: close to a hundred hours of taped interviews with thirty-eight Old People; an Elder's genealogy project; a founding families genealogical project; a historical photograph collection consisting of over six hundred turn-of-the-century photographs of reserve life; a large collection of historical documents and secondary sources; and the Band-created Leigh Cochrane Memorial Visitor Centre. In the meantime, the specific claims case continues. Still in progress are curriculum development materials for the Sinclair School (K–12), a CD-ROM oral history project, and a book manuscript, *Kéhtéyatisak Otahchimowiniwaw Kayas kaki pé-ihikihk Ochékiwi Sīpihk, Elders' stories about the history of Fisher River.*

Of all the aspects of these projects, the writing – the textual representation of the Ochēkiwi Sīpi People's past – has proven the most challenging. The directive I received from the Elders collectively was to write their history in their own voices, to tell it the way it should be told. Although schooled in social science rather than literary methodologies, I was confident and comfortable enough working with oral traditions that the task did not seem insurmountable. But the writing just wasn't happening. When asked by a few Elders, "What's taking so long?" I whimsically replied, "writer's block." However, retrospection reveals that the problem is much deeper – more complex – than that. The problem stems from an amalgam of intersecting and paradoxical methodological contests. Simply stated, it boils down to the problem of how to write the story in the voices of the Elders, as they instructed me to, when the oral history has so many gaps that the bulk of our material comes from conventional Eurocentric primary sources.

The documentary records are plentiful. The Methodist church was thorough; records of birth, death, and marriage records as well as annual reports on the state of the church and community go back to 1840 in Norway House/Rossville.[4] Through the HBC materials I traced family migrations southward, in some cases back ten generations, and the RG10 Indian Affairs (Black Series) and Canada *Sessional Papers* provided invaluable socio-economic data for the post-treaty era. But over the course of about ten years, during which our research team interviewed thirty-eight of the oldest and most respected members living in the community, personal reminiscences and family histories, rather than oral histories of significant events, dominated their tellings.[5] We heard and recorded wonderful stories about their lives and their parents' life experiences. We also heard stories about Wesakejac, the Little People and other Lake Winnipeg mysteries, as well as descriptive accounts of traditional healing practices.

However, all but a few of the Old People were reluctant to talk about what they had heard of events that occurred during their grandparents' time or earlier.[6] Everyone could trace their ancestors back to 1875 and even earlier. Everyone knew that their ancestors had converted to Christianity back at Norway House and some knew who the baptizing ministers were. Everyone also knew when the treaty was negotiated and that they settled at Fisher River as a result of the treaty. But no one we interviewed gave us detailed stories about the Christian conversion process or what transpired at Treaty No. 5;[7] nor were there are any detailed stories about the 1877 migration from Norway House to Fisher River – a momentous event in which a fair sized flotilla consisting of three York boats (containing the women, children, dogs, and baggage), ten fishing skiffs, and twelve canoes brought 160 people, or about forty families, across Lake Winnipeg through late-autumn rain storms and unseasonable cold, on a journey that took close to two-and-a-half months.[8]

The collective memory of the community held significant events but many details were missing. For the research team, this collective memory gap among our Elders was confusing. As far as we naïvely assumed, Old People were supposed to know everything – were they purposely withholding this information, or did they really not know? How could the details of such significant events just evaporate? To a handful of Elders I finally asked directly, "why don't we know this history anymore?" Some admitted that they hadn't really listened when their grandparents told them the stories. Others replied, "we didn't think that stuff was so important to remember" or "that was too long ago to remember." Finally, two of the Elders, on separate occasions reprimanded me: "Well, that's your job now isn't it? Go on out there and find out!"

None of this discussion is intended in any way to provide fodder for those historians who forcibly, or secretly harp, that oral history is unreliable. Numerous studies demonstrate that where indigenous oral histories exist, they are strong, and that in their own right they can stand on their own as legitimate methods, sources, and forms.[9] Here I am describing a different kind of situation – gaps in the collective memory. So how does a community lose pieces of its collective memory? How do the details of significant historical events, events that shaped the current realities and dynamics of a community, disappear from the collection of past stories held by our Elders? Bernard Lewis tells us that the history of events, movements, persons, or ideas that were forgotten at a certain stage may in fact have been rejected by the communal memory for some reason.[10] A closer look at the historical experiences of the Home Guard Cree of Norway House helps shed some light.

By the late 1840s the Home Guard Cree of Norway House had endured and adapted to a century of colonial intrusion and cultural adaptation. The shift from a single-sector to a dual-sector economy found them entrenched in a global market system that little appreciated or respected their unique ways of life. The arrival of Methodist missionaries in 1840 attracted further settlement, placing even greater stress on available resources, and soon thereafter, the fur trade began its decline. These series of events eventually left the Home Guard Cree vulnerable with few options. By 1875 starvation reduced many of these once self-sufficient people to dependence on welfare from the HBC and the Methodist mission.[11]

The missionaries' arrival was timely. While they offered a new way to make a living, it came at a costly and distressing price. The history of Indian missions is well known. Christian missionaries were (and still are) colonial agents *par excellence*, demanding nothing less than total cultural transformation and forcefully condemning Aboriginal customs and religions as heathen and sub-human. Albert Memmi explains that colonizers are preoccupied with imposing urgent change and drive it home with a vengeance: "The mechanism of this remolding of the colonized is revealing in itself. It consists, in the first place, of a series of negotiations. The colonized is not this, is not that. He is never considered in a positive light; or if he is, the quality which is conceded is the result of psychological or ethical failing."[12]

Many of those who convert eventually internalize this indictment – they come to view their own culture and history as strange and become receptive to even more colonial pressure. Peter Nabokov and others tell us that for memory "to endure, someone somewhere must continue to bear witness, must intuitively resist the demands of archive and media in favour of the interactive, oral narrative." Oral history is called into being during and for interpersonal situations.[13] Add enforced residential school internment to their colonized past, and alienation from community, family, the past, and self pervades.[14] Writing about alienation, Frantz Fanon explains: "Historical conditions which confront men always structure their actions: 'Men make their own history, but they do not make it as they please; they do not make it under circumstances chosen by themselves, but under circumstances directly encountered, given and transmitted from the past.'"[15]

Over time the "oppressed learn to perceive the cause of their oppression in their own inferiority, their power of resistance weakens."[16] Then, as Albert Memmi explains: "As soon as the colonized adopts [the values of the colonizer], he similarly adopts his own condemnation. In order to free himself, at least so he believes, he agrees to destroy himself."[17] As his own institutions die he scarcely believes anymore in the remnants that do remain because he is faced with "daily confirmation of their ineffectiveness."[18] In time he "draws less and less from his past" and eventually forgets his own folk heroes, leaders, and sages: "At most, he may be able to give us a few names, in complete disorder, and fewer and fewer as one goes down the generations. The colonized seems condemned to lose his memory."[19]

Fanon summarizes the experience of alienation in colonial contexts in his well-known dictum: "Colonialism is not satisfied merely with holding a people in its grip and emptying the native's brain of all form and content. By a kind of perverted logic, it turns to the past of the oppressed people, and distorts, disfigures, and destroys it."[20] The situations presented by Fanon and Memmi represent extreme colonial experiences. No one can deny that the experience of colonization is traumatic – displacements, depopulation, alienation, powerlessness, demoralization, internalized hatred – the forces of colonialism not only rape the land; they violently assault the body, spirit, and mind of the colonized.

While the degrees and impacts of colonial encounters vary across time and space, there is no denying that the overall effects are long-lasting. Studies by Bonnie Duran, Eduardo Duran, and Maria Yellow Horse Brave Heart, describe the impact of colonialism on indigenous peoples as "historical trauma or intergenerational trauma," the contemporary symptoms of which include disproportionately high rates of "alcoholism, poverty, learned helplessness and dependence, violence, and the breakdown of values that correlate with healthy living."[21]

A handful of studies have been done on the impact of historical trauma on the collective memory of a people. Raymond Fogelson's study of Cherokee memories of the 1830 "Trail of Tears" demonstrates in this instance that the Removal event was so traumatic that it was denied: "the Removal experience was so degrading, so incredible, so brutally real that it became unreal to the Cherokee mind."[22] Thus, despite the abundance of written documentation left by non-Cherokee eyewitnesses, there were practically no Cherokee oral accounts of the event itself. In a study of Holocaust survivor testimonies, Naomi Rosh White explains that Holocaust survivors often slip into silence. "For some," she claims, "silence has its source in the pain from which the survivor seeks protection."[23] "Silence can be a sanctuary which protects speakers from themselves and from their listeners. It encloses feelings and experiences that may attract censure because they are unfamiliar, alien or threatening to the listener. The sense of impotence and powerlessness ... feelings of having been defiled, diminished and humiliated may remain unspoken because the listener's response may be disbelief, contempt, abandonment, misunderstanding or pity."[24]

Rosh White speaks of "anguished memory," which recovers the sense of being divided, of living in more than one world at a time. She speaks of "humiliated memory," which reveals a "besieged self" who, as in the past, is unable to act in the present because memory and the process of narrating offer no rescue from uncompensated and uncompensatable loss. "'Unheroic memory' reveals the 'diminished self' with its deprivation of moral agency and its partially traumatized or maimed self-esteem, the long-term impact of which is a fractured, fragmented self."[25] Within the historical context of colonialism, it is a testament to people's spiritual strength and tenacity that so much oral history still exists in our communities.

Ethnohistorians are in the business of historical reconstruction – they seek to recover the history of events, movements, persons, and ideas that have been largely neglected by conventional scholarship. They also strive to correct errors and reach deeper understandings. But theirs is an objective and generally distanced pursuit of knowledge. Their initial questions are seldom informed by experience, generational or direct. Most ethnohistorians begin their research in the archives and later end up in community, if at all. On the other hand, many Indigenous historians begin at community and end up at archives. The distinctions and implications of these two methodological approaches have not been seriously considered, but they should be. We all recognize that the kinds of questions we ask inform our methodologies, which in turn inform, impact, or dictate the outcome. For scholars doing Indigenous historical research, a significant question to ask at the outset is, how the forms and content of their work compare or contrast when the questions are framed in an archive and when questions are framed by the community oral history.

Students of Indigenous oral histories are well aware that each community has its own ways – its own forms and methods – of keeping and transmitting knowledge about the past through the generations. Some oral historical accounts are rigidly formulaic; others less so. And, while the forms of transmission have received considerable scholarly interest from folklorists, linguists, and students of literature, for example, they are studied as objects rather than as teachings to be applied or adhered to. What very few recognize is that oral traditions are unique among peoples and can be used as templates for the textual representations of oral historical accounts. In communities where we have templates for form, we also have direction on content. We have the community's point of view or determination of what constitutes a significant historical event or person, which in many cases differs from an outside perspective.

In the case of the Fisher River, however, the priorities of the research team were determined by what we did not know or what was missing in our collective memories. Another paradox is that while many of the details we sought had been lost, the traditional storytelling form is alive and well. In fact it was the pervasiveness of the oral tradition form in the community, the storytelling tradition and the great storytellers, that initially led us to believe that there must be lots of oral history – that the Old People would have lots of stories about the treaty and the migration from Norway House.

So, our Old People are great storytellers, and they want their book to be filled with great stories, and my questions become more pointed – the Indian and the academic in me engage: "Would not using our oral tradition storytelling forms to textually represent non-traditional (non-Indian) sources undermine or bastardize traditional and scholarly integrity? Would this not be an exercise in inventing tradition?"

Bernard Lewis, Eric Hobsbawm, and Terrence Ranger provided some help here.[26] Hobsbawm explains that the "strength and adaptability of genuine tradition is not to be confused with the 'invention of tradition.' When the old ways are alive, traditions need be neither revived nor invented."[27] If history has demonstrated little else, it has shown that we are a strong and adaptable People. Thus, the tasks of tribal historians are to recover the past and to present it to the public in a form that meets the approval of the people whose histories and lives it represents. Recovered history is a process of reconstructing the forgotten past, which Bernard Lewis explains, is a "modern and European task."[28] Tribal historians, like ethnohistorians, glean our data from all possible locations, but unlike most ethnohistory, our questions and ideally our textual products, are directed by community. In the end, the problem is not whether or not to write narrative history, but rather what kind of narrative history would be most appropriate – what forms and literary strategies could be borrowed to write our recovered histories in a way that respects the integrity of tribal oral traditions and the academy?

Thirty years ago this would have been a lonely venture, but the challenges and inroads made by Hayden White and other critical theorists, by literary critics and New Historicism, are pushing historians to think more critically about what we do, how we do it, and the limits of our potential.[29] Way out in the front are our own people, our literary and intellectual greats like Gerald Vizenor, N. Scott Momaday, and Maria Campbell, who have been writing in the oral tradition for a very long time. They teach by doing, which has helped pave the way for my generation to return home and learn to write from our own places.

So there I was, at once filling in the gaps in our oral history with Eurocentric documentary records and listening to the taped interviews of the Old People over and over again to feel the rhythm of their voices, to discern the local nomenclature and their unique Cree-English syntax. Trying to disassociate from my modernist social science training, I strove to adopt a creative literary approach, so I could write our histories the way the Elders told me to. As always, I found temporary respite in a conventional historical method – I kept doing research. One afternoon while learning about whitefish pemmican, I presented one of our Elders with my dilemma – "Lena, how can I write our histories in our own words when most of the information we have about our past comes from journal books written by fur traders and missionaries?" The immediate look on her face struck me – it was one of those "what a dumb question" kind of looks. Then, staring me straight in the eyes, she said, "Just take it!" "Just take it?" I replied, a little dumbfounded. "Yes, just take it!" "Listen girl," she said, "they took our memories from us, now you go on and take those memories back, and make them ours again."

Sifting through the thin stained pages of missionary journals, I searched for the ancestors of the Fisher River Muskego-wininiwak – the People I knew. Historical imagination, some call it – reading through the lines, between the words, across the cultures, into the minds, and searching through their eyes for narrative wisps of the Ochēkiwi Sīpi past.

Sitting on his worn-out couch, Old Alec raised his eyes and slapped his hands together … "Ahow!" he started, "We come from up north, us. Where the muskeg and rock, and the caribou and the moose, they meet. That's what old Jim he told me when I was a kid working the boats with him. Back then some of us were known as asiniwininiwak, Rock Cree Peoples. Now we are all known as muskego-wininiwak, Swampy Cree Peoples. How we came to be, one from the other, now that's a long story ..."

Ekosi.

NOTES

1 My thanks to Chief David Crate, former chief Lorne Cochrane, and the Fisher River Councils and Education Authorities for their constant support and encouragement for the oral history project. Most of the interviews with Elders were conducted by Fisher River university students over the course of five summers from 1990 to 1995. The author acknowledges the tremendous efforts they made toward the project and extends a special thanks to Tanya Cochrane, who stuck with it from the very beginning and is now the Fisher River Heritage Centre coordinator. Without the enthusiastic support and efforts of the Elders living at Fisher River this project could never have happened. Another special thanks to Verna J. Kirkness, Jennifer S.H. Brown, and Michael Cottrell for providing invaluable comments and advice on the earlier draft of this chapter. I thank you all, kinanaskomatinawaw.

2 The Reverend John H. Ruttan, *Report on Norway House Mission: 54th Annual Report of Missionary Society of the Methodist Church of Canada, June 1877–June 1978* (Toronto, 1878), xvii–xviii.

3 Provincial Archives of Manitoba (PAM), MG12, B1, Alexander Morris Papers, no. 783: Indians of Rossville to Alexander Morris, 25 June 1874.

4 The earliest baptism, marriage, and death records for the Methodist mission at Rossville and later missions are housed in the Provincial Archives of Manitoba.

5 Personal reminiscences differ from oral histories because they are specific to life experiences of the teller – they include direct observation and to a large degree are autobiographical in nature. Oral histories, on the other hand, while they may contain autobiographical details, are stories about significant events and persons from the more distant past.

6 Interviews conducted with Elders from the previous generation have proved invaluable especially the stories on family migrations to Fisher River. A special thanks to Verna Kirkness for providing a copy of an interview she did in 1967 with her late grandfather James Kirkness (1871–1975).

7 Alexander Morris, "Lake Winnipeg Treaty No. Five," in *The Treaties of Canada with the Indians of Manitoba and the North-West Territories including The Negotiations on which they were based* (1880 reprint. Saskatoon: Fifth House Publishers, 1991), 343.

8   United Church Archives, Personal Papers (UCA PP) John Semmens, fonds
    3204, box 1, file 1, "Under the Northern Lights: Notes on Personal History,
    1850–1921," 30, 31; Ruttan, "Report on Norway House Mission," xvii–xviii.
    The Hudson's Bay Company reported that the government hired two good
    boats (York) and one condemned boat, to take forty families to Fisher River.
    Provincial Archives of Manitoba, Hudson's Bay Archives (PAM HBCA)
    B.154/a/71, Norway House Post Journal, 5 September 1877, fo. 62.

9   The scholarly literature on the tenacity of Indigenous oral histories of events
    and peoples of the distant past is vast and has a long history in and of itself.
    See for example, Gordon Day, "Roger's Raid in Indian Tradition," *Historical
    New Hampshire* 17 (June 1962): 3–17; and "Oral Tradition as Complement,"
    Ethnohistory 19, no. 2 (1972): 99–108; Bernard L. Fontana, "American Indian
    Oral History: An Anthropologist's Note," *History and Theory* 8, no. 3 (1969):
    366–70; Angela Cavender Wilson, "Grandmother to Granddaughter: Gen-
    erations of Oral History in a Dakota Family," *American Indian Quarterly* 20,
    no. 1 (1996): 7–13.

10 Bernard Lewis, *History: Remembered, Recovered, Invented* (New York: Simon
    & Schuster, 1987), 12.

11 See, for example, PAM, HBCA B.154/a/71 Norway House Post Journal, 27
    March 1875, fo. 10; ibid., 27 July 1977, fo. 59.

12 Albert Memmi, *The Colonizer and the Colonized* (Boston: Beacon Press,
    1967), 84–5.

13 Peter Nabokov, "Present Memories, Past History," in *The American Indian
    and the Problem of History*, edited by Calvin Martin (New York: Oxford Uni-
    versity Press, 1987), 145.

14 Numerous studies of the residential school experience and the impact of that
    experience on contemporary First Nations communities have been done,
    many of which incorporated the personal reminiscences of the inmates. For
    example, see Jean Barman, Yvonne Hebert, and Don McCaskill, eds., *Indian
    Education in Canada, Volume 1: The Legacy* (Vancouver: UBC Press, 1986);
    Linda Jaine, ed., *Residential Schools: The Stolen Years* (Saskatoon: University
    of Saskatchewan Extension Press, 1993); Celia Haig-Brown, *Resistance and
    Renewal: Surviving the Indian Residential School* (Vancouver: Tillacum Li-
    brary, 1988); J.R. Miller, *Shingwauk's Vision: A History of Native Residential
    Schools* (Toronto: University of Toronto Press, 1996).

15 Renate Zahar, *Frantz Fanon: Colonialism and Alienation* (New York: Monthly
    Press, 1974), 5.

16 Ibid., 19.

17 Memmi, *The Colonized*, 121–2.

18 Zahar, *Frantz Fanon*, 37.

19 Memmi, *The Colonized*, 102–3.

20 Frantz Fanon, *The Wretched of the Earth* (1961. New York: Grove Weidenfeld,
    1991 reprint).

21 Bonnie Duran, Eduardo Duran, and Maria Yellow Horse Brave Heart, "Native Americans and the Trauma of History," in *Studying Native America: Problems and Prospects*, edited by Russell Thorton (Madison: University of Wisconsin Press, 1998), 61.

22 Raymond D. Fogelson, "The Ethnohistory of Events and Nonevents," *Ethnohistory* 36, no. 2 (1989): 143.

23 Naomi Rosh White, "Marking Absences: Holocaust Testimony and History," in *The Oral History Reader*, 1st edition, edited by Robert Perks and Alistair Thomson (New York: Routledge, 1998), 176.

24 Ibid., 176.

25 Ibid., 180.

26 Lewis, *History: Remembered*; Eric Hobsbawm and Terence Ranger, eds., *The Invention of Tradition* (New York: Cambridge University Press, 1983).

27 Hobsbawm and Ranger, *Invention of Tradition*, 8.

28 Lewis, *History: Remembered*, 13.

29 See, for example, Robert Berkhoffer, Jr, *Beyond the Great Story: History as Text and Discourse* (Cambridge: The Belknap Press of Harvard University, 1995).

14

I Can Hear Lois Now: Corrections to My Story of the Internment of Japanese Canadians

Pamela Sugiman

Until recently, the internment of Japanese Canadians in the Second World War was one of many stories hidden from public history. Scarcely heard were the voices of the twenty-two thousand women, men, and children who were removed from their homes, labelled enemy aliens, dispossessed of property and personal belongings, and relocated by the Canadian government.[1] Of the interned, 75 percent were naturalized or Canadian-born citizens. "Framed by race," Canadians of Japanese descent were "produced as outsiders" in their own country.[2]

Over the past two decades, however, this collective amnesia has been partially remedied. In 1988 the National Association of Japanese Canadians (NAJC) reached a redress agreement with the government of Canada. The details of the agreement included: an official acknowledgment of the wartime injustices, compensation payments to eligible surviving persons of Japanese ancestry, payment to the Japanese Canadian community to support the community's well-being or to promote human rights, and funding for the establishment of a Canadian Race Relations Foundation. In so far as redress lent legitimacy to people's wartime memories, the years following the settlement witnessed an outpouring of films, memoirs, and scholarly studies, all of which document the racial politics and personal impact of the internment on the *Issei* (first-generation pioneers), *Nisei* (second-generation, Canadian-born), *Sansei* (third-generation), and *Yonsei* (fourth-generation).

My own research of well over a decade has been a part of this liberation of memories and reconstruction of history. Though I was not an eyewitness to the war, as a child I gathered fragmented memories of the internment vicariously through my family.[3] My father was in his early twenties when Japan bombed Pearl Harbor in 1941. A rebellious young man who was born and raised in Vancouver, he resisted the orders of the RCMP to leave his hometown. For this, he was picked up, detained in the city's Immigration Building, and subsequently incarcerated in a prisoner of war camp in Petawawa, Ontario. My mother was a young woman when the government confiscated and soon afterward sold her family's ten-acre berry farm in Haney, British Columbia. After being held for several months in Hastings Park in the former livestock building in the Pacific National Exhibition fair grounds, the Matsuoka family were sent to live for four years in Rosebery, one of the smallest and most northerly sites of internment. As an adult, educated and politicized by the literature that grew out of the redress struggle, I attempted to situate my family's memories in a wider social and political framework. With my daughter in tow, I embarked on a pilgrimage to the sites of internment. In addition, I pored over thousands of old letters and government reports housed in government archives and I conducted oral history interviews with seventy-five *Nisei* women and men.

Needless to say, this project is close to my heart. My efforts to "give voice to the voiceless" were motivated in part by an affinity toward, and feelings of empathy for the *subjects* of my study.[4] My research has, without question, also been guided by a desire for social justice. Fortuitously, while in the final stages of my fieldwork, I was approached by the NAJC. When asked to join its National Executive Board, I eagerly accepted the appointment, feeling that it was time to give back to a community that had so generously opened up to me. The role of advocate, I believed, would complement that of scholar.

Over time, one of the harsh lessons that I have learned, however, is that when we combine personal and academic motives in research on living communities we sometimes run into complications.[5] In the process of collaboration and in trying to fairly represent a community of people, we must also be prepared to listen to voices that are dissenting, words that are cutting, and the expression of ideas that we may view as damaging to our own political projects. As discussed by many oral historians,[6] we need to consider how ideological clashes may affect the relationship between interviewer and narrator, the conversational narrative, and our vision of history.[7]

In her study of women of the Ku Klux Klan, Kathleen Blee specifically raises questions about how we can establish rapport with "politically abhorrent informants," interpret accounts that are "distorted," and present benign memories that mute "past atrocities."[8] Such dilemmas, as Antoin-

ette Errante states, may also have implications for our selection of informants and our use of their memories.⁹ These challenges have also led me
to reflect on the emotional impact that the interview and respondents
may have on the researcher herself. As noted by Ruth Behar, when a researcher writes about an emotional connection to our academic research,
this emotional investment becomes part of the public domain, leaving the
researcher vulnerable to charges and attacks from unsympathetic subjects
and bystanders.¹⁰

A MESSAGE FROM LOIS

These are issues that I was forced to confront several years ago when I
received an angry email message from a stranger, a *Nisei* woman named
Lois Hashimoto, who had read one of my articles on the internment. At
the time, Lois lived with her husband in Laval, Quebec. Like many other
Nisei, when Japan attacked Pearl Harbor, Lois (then a teen) and her family
were forced by the government, under the War Measures Act, to leave
their home in British Columbia. She was then housed temporarily in
Hastings Park in Vancouver before being transported to an internment
site in the Slocan Valley. After spending four years in Slocan, she headed
east of the Rockies to build a new home in the province of Quebec. The
only alternative to resettlement outside British Columbia was deportation
to Japan. Her letter to me began:

> I am a 77-year old who spent four years in Slocan. There is a serious
> flaw in your study in that you based your study on false premises.
> What, exactly, do you mean when you say, "[though] many decades
> have since gone by, Japanese Canadians continue to live with the
> injustices of the past?" What examples do you have to justify such
> a sweeping statement about thousands of us whom you have never
> met, let alone known.

Lois directly laid her charge. Much of my writing about the internment
has highlighted the emptiness of life, confiscation of property, denial of
opportunity, violation of rights, and enduring losses. Lois remembered
these times differently. About her years in Slocan, she wrote: "It was truly
an exciting time, even if you think you know better than someone who actually lived it." She further accused me of constructing a one-dimensional,
oppressed "internee" and referred to my statement about the silences
of the past as "utter nonsense." Lois ended her letter on a sarcastic note,

writing, "[Thought] you might be interested in the thoughts of one not so silent 'victim' of the 'most devastating event' in JC lives." [11]

My initial reaction to this message was one of hurt and dismay. I felt crushed. After all, I had a strong investment in my project, as a scholar, an advocate, and most important, as a bearer of memories of the wartime injustices. Furthermore, since my days as a young academic, I have been steeped in the literature on feminist process and have long believed in the democratizing potential of the oral history interview. [12] In my internment study, I thereby sought to establish a unity with my interviewees. At the outset, all of them were women of my mother's generation, then in their eighties and nineties, and so I felt a sense of kinship. In some, I even observed gestures, expressions, and cultural idiosyncrasies that were reminiscent of my mother, grandmother, and the many female relatives and family friends that I encountered as a child. With both *Nisei* women and men, I also assumed bonds based on a shared racial identity and community history. As a *Sansei*, I lacked experiential authority but I was not simply a bystander either.

My childhood memories had informed these interviews, and they became even more potent as I framed them in a political critique of racism in Canadian history and the internment in particular. I thus broke down in tears as I read Lois's harsh assessment of me and her invalidation of my work. Lois's message threw me off balance. Her accusations made me question my skills as an oral historian, my ethical obligations as a researcher, and the value of my research to a community about which I cared deeply. Her indictment placed me in a category that I had emphatically sought to avoid: that of a detached academic who, in the interests of furthering my own political or professional objectives, not only spoke for, but also misrepresented the subjects of my study. Early in this project, I foresaw a need to address an asymmetry of power between academic interviewer and working-class narrator. I was prepared for criticism or disinterest on the part of *Hakujin* (non-Japanese) audiences, but I did not anticipate receiving such disparaging words from someone within my own cultural community. I was caught off guard by such an unequivocal assertion of authorial control from an elderly woman whom I had never met. [13]

At first, I was tempted to fire off a defensive reply, informing this stranger that my analysis was an academically rigorous one based on in-depth interviews with dozens of *Nisei* with whom she had never spoken, and that although she herself had been interned, she did not have the perspective that I had developed as a scholar. It would have been easy to pathologize Mrs Hashimoto, dismiss her as a cranky, ignorant old woman, or demonize her as a right-wing fanatic. But on rereading her message, the ethical and professional dilemmas it raised made me pause. Lois's letter spoke to questions about sharing authority,[14] highlighted the importance of self-reflexivity on the part of the researcher, and it prompted me to contemplate the analytical value of personal memory.[15] Rather than simply defend my work, I tried to better understand her perspective. I invited Lois to say more.

She quickly responded to my invitation and her second message was written in a different tone than the first: "Thank you for replying so courteously and thoughtfully to my ill-tempered email. I confess that I was happily surprised to hear from you – I am more accustomed to being ignored, or being written off by earnest *sansei* Redress activists as someone in denial of my internment pain:-)!!" Lois's reply made me realize that she passionately wanted to comment on the public representation of her generation. How could I write about giving voice and sharing authority but proceed to marginalize, censor, or dismiss a woman who wanted to engage with me, even if I regarded her views as misguided, heretical, and dangerous to my larger political objectives? If I viewed her interpretation of the past with such skepticism, how could I highlight the concept of personal memory as fluid, subjective, interpretive – as being at the heart of oral history? In writing a comprehensive analysis of *Nisei* memories, did I not have a responsibility to listen to Lois? And if so, in what ways would her story shape my interpretation of the memories of others whom I had interviewed? What is the relationship between one woman's memories and a community's collective memory?

Lois and I corresponded for the next three and a half years. In the first two years, she sporadically sent email messages, mailed me a couple of books, and copied me on various items of correspondence. She voiced her political opinions and promoted her causes, but we also complained about the weather, shared health concerns, and spoke of family vacations and celebrations. Several winters ago, I visited Lois at her home in Quebec. There, I gathered six hours of oral testimony, and conversed with her (and her husband) for many more hours, over lunch and dinner.[16]

VOICE AND TRUTH

Lois was a working-class woman. She described herself as an "underachiever" partly because she was forced to leave school suddenly with the outbreak of war, when her formal education was limited. Her first job was as a seamstress in Morgan's department store. Before retiring, she worked in customer service at the Hudson's Bay Company. In the course of more than a decade, Lois gained some visibility, if not notoriety, within the Japanese Canadian community and in the wider Montreal area because she expressed her views publicly, often in the form of letters to the editors of newspapers and to local and national-level politicians. Lois was especially critical of some prominent community members who played leading roles in the struggle for Redress, notably the nationally acclaimed novelist Joy Kogawa, author of the classic work *Obasan*, Audrey Kobayashi, a highly regarded and outspoken anti-racist academic, and the Miki brothers, Art (former NAJC president) and Roy (professor emeritus of literary studies).

As Karen Olsen and Linda Shopes note, in our sensitivities to inequalities, academics may "overestimate our own privilege, even our own importance, in the eyes of the people we interview." But in fact, they observe, most interviewees "seem not especially overwhelmed, intimidated, or impressed with us at all."[17] Although she was a working-class woman with limited formal schooling, Lois was by no means intimidated by me. She contested my authority from the outset. While she frequently mentioned her failing memory, and expressed frustration at being unable to find the right words to articulate her views, she never questioned the veracity of her memories. Likewise, her sense of efficacy did not wane. Lois's authority was rooted in her direct experience of the war. She was an eyewitness and I was not. Likewise, I deferred to her age (she was my elder) and generational status (she was a *Nisei* and I a *Sansei*). Given that she had shared her thoughts with me (via the Internet) for years, by the time we sat down for a face-to-face interview, I was prepared for her rehearsed narrative.[18] Indeed, at times, I wondered if she approached the life story interview as simply another opportunity to step onto her political platform.[19]

In both her spoken narrative and written correspondence, Lois drew on the concepts of voice and representation. She claimed that the hegemonic voices of the Redress activists, human rights advocates in the NAJC, and *Sansei* academics (such as myself) now dominate public discourse. In her view, the Redress activists, in particular, were responsible for authoring and promoting our history as one of suffering, hardship, and injustice. Indeed, critical remarks about the activists are woven throughout her narrative. While Lois admitted that the government's decision to intern Japanese Canadians was unfair, she believed that the costs of our wartime treatment have been greatly exaggerated by a generation that was born after the war. Lois reiterated these views in many email messages: "A phenomenon that intrigues me is the tendency of *Sansei* activists ... to assume they know more about the nature of racism than we who experienced, and overcame the most overt case of racism in Canadian history. I mean, that's pretty funny, don't you think?"[20]

EPITOMIZING PERSONAL MEMORIES[21]

Lois was a bright and knowledgeable woman. She had done some reading on Japanese Canadian history, perhaps more than most, and was therefore aware of the range of internment experiences. One's placement during the war depended largely on age, sex, socio-economic position, religion, and family status. Lois was among the majority of Japanese Canadians who were interned in a ghost town in the BC interior. A smaller number of families that had sufficient economic resources relocated to the so-called self-supporting camps and, in effect, assumed the costs of their own internment. As compared to the ghost town internees, the "self-supporting" groups had fewer government-imposed restrictions. However, they were more isolated, without a community of Japanese Canadians, and lacked even a rudimentary infrastructure. Those who spent the war years on sugar beet farms in Manitoba and Alberta likewise faced physical and social isolation and harsh living conditions. In addition, they had to perform back-breaking labour in exchange for keeping their families intact. Reinforcing existing sex- and age-based divisions, the British Columbia Security Commission (BCSC) separated many young and middle-aged men from their families and exploited their labour in road or lumber camps. Men who displayed even mild resistance were incarcerated as prisoners of war (POWs). POWs spoke of poor nutrition, hard labour, harsh weather, loneliness, and occasional acts of rebellion. Some *Nisei* men, in an attempt to assert their national loyalty, also had unique and complex memories of war as soldiers in the Canadian Army.

Lois recognized that these varied experiences of internment produced a multiplicity of memories and it was important to her that these voices be evenly represented in public history. Yet, at the same time, she confessed: "I'm not a historian ... I could just write about *my* personal experience of internment." Throughout her interview and in all of her writings, she prioritized her personal memories, highlighting fun, carefree days, friendship, and opportunity.

Indeed, Lois's memories of fun and frivolity took on a symbolic meaning in her life story narrative. They epitomized her experiences during the war and resettlement years and were so powerful in personal memory that they shaped her interpretation of history.[22] The hardship stories that were voiced during and after the Redress campaign, she believed, were therefore a gross distortion of historical truth. She commented: "Slocan was fun. Right from the get go, it was fun! We got there and there were people meeting us." Lois attributed these happy times in part to youth. As a girl during the war, she did not shoulder the worries and responsibilities of her elders. Lois readily admitted that the experiences of her mother and father must have been different than hers, but added that, as a fourteen-year-old, she was pretty "self-centred" and unaware of what her parents (and other *Issei*) were going through. For instance, she explained: "My husband's father lost his logging camp ... But people like me, I didn't lose anything. I mean I was fourteen years old. What did I lose that's of monetary value?" She articulated these same sentiments more fully in her written essay "Go East, Young Ladies!" In this composition, she responded to ideas that had been expressed by a *Sansei* human rights activist: "I DID experience the forced assimilation of Japanese Canadians into mainstream Canada and can assure her [a *Sansei* activist] that far from being the humiliating and traumatizing event that she imagines, it was for me and I'm sure for many other Nisei, an exhilarating and liberating experience." She continued: "I knew that not being allowed to finish my school year in 1942, and being forced out of our home in Queensborough, and having to live for two months in a converted horse stall in the Hastings Park livestock exhibition hall was not exactly experiencing Democracy's finest hour. But after our arrival in the internment camp of Slocan, it was impossible to maintain any sense of outrage, because quite simply, I was enjoying myself too much." This was Lois's defining statement about the internment. As her narrative unfolded, I could see that this epitomizing memory of enjoying herself was the foundation for her vision of the history of her generation.[23]

VISIONS OF HISTORY

In my second meeting with Lois I detected that she was trying to move me from the position of passive listener to that of active participant. As a result, in spite of my efforts to minimize my role in shaping the conversational narrative, our format shifted at points from monologue to dialogue. Posing direct questions, Lois left me little choice but to share my opinions, if only coyly. Yet the more Lois proclaimed her conservative anti-NAJC views, the more difficult it became for me to fully express my own; and my level of discomfort became heightened, as did my feelings of ambivalence about my growing involvement with this woman. I dreaded to imagine what my fellow NAJC board members would think about our relationship and wondered if our association would throw into question my credibility with the critical factions of our small ethnic community.

As our conversational narrative progressed, Lois persisted in her efforts to minimize internees' "suffering" and downplay the long-term damages of the government's wartime policy. She did this in part by prioritizing historical acts of injustice and experiences of suffering. For example, she sought my reaction after comparing the millions of fatalities during the war to the property losses and uprooting of Japanese Canadians:

> LOIS: They [Redress activists] just talk about the internment. The injustice that was done to our, you know, they just talk as though it was separate from the war. I mean, over fifty million people were killed and died in horrible ways. What was our suffering compared to that? *I mean, don't you see that, Pam?*
> PAM: Do you think that the internment was necessary, a necessary part of the war?
> LOIS: Well, of course not! But it was still part of the war. It would not have happened if Japan hadn't bombed Pearl Harbor. How many innocent people died in Pearl Harbor? Where's the anguish over that? You know, why don't these people ever feel bad about that?

Lois further argued that the Redress campaign was redundant because Japanese Canadians had already won back their citizenship rights by 1949, when they secured the federal franchise and were permitted to return to the west coast. Again, weighing the suffering of internees and struggles of the Redress activists against the military casualties of the Second World War, and in defence of "democracy," she argued:

> [It's] not because of the Redress that you and I have done all the right things, freedom of Canadian citizenship. It's the fact that, I mean, what if Japan and Germany had won the war? What more racist countries were there than Japan and Germany? And how many, forty thousand Canadians died to grant us, to make sure we had our rights and freedoms. And we got all the rights and freedoms. By 1949 ... we had a right to move back to the Coast. It wasn't the Redress that got us that ... It's not the Redress that brought us the democratic rights.

Echoing one of the myths that had been promoted by BC politicians in their attempts to justify the uprooting, Lois maintained that Japanese

Canadians were interned for their own protection – protection against racism in the wider society: "Well, with Slocan there was no hardship ... It was like a, never-never ... because we were taken out of the real world. The rest of Canada was fighting a war. We were kind of secluded. We were separated from the racism that was ... outside the camps."

Another theme that emerged in Lois's life story was that of redemption. Echoing the long-standing "blessing-in-disguise" aphorism, Lois presented evidence not only of the survival of Japanese Canadians, but also of their educational and material successes in the postwar years, outcomes that she attributed to the wartime uprooting and dispersal. The view that past adversities (such as the internment) are ultimately for the good of a community serves different functions. It may help people define themselves in the present period, with dignity, as individuals who have triumphed in the face of adversity.[24] It is also a way of bringing "coherence" to a life story.[25] Lois admitted that, for some, there had been injustice and hardship but with more conviction, she spoke of the triumph of the *Nisei* and their *Sansei* offspring. In doing so, she also vehemently rejected the label of victim, declaring: "[The] internment, it didn't crush me. It didn't make me feel ashamed ... It was just part of my life experience and I know it was wrong and I know it hurt a lot of people. But this was a fact." About the community as a whole, she similarly stated: "[We] were treated so unjustly but we didn't let it crush us. We persevered and we didn't just survive, you know, we flourished." And in one of only a few references that she made to the *Nisei* who were interned as agricultural labourers, Lois commented: "[People] that went through, sugar beet farms, well, they did back-breaking work ... They went all through that and they weren't crushed by it. They won't become alcoholics and they persevered and they survived. I mean, I'm awfully proud of that ... The fact that they went on to be doctors and sociology professors." The reference to sociology professors was, of course, aimed specifically at me.

In extending the blessing-in-disguise argument, Lois also spoke of the assimilation of Japanese Canadians. Proudly, she observed that we are now among the most assimilated groups in this country. In her view, this is precisely because of the government's wartime policy. In 1944, after declaring the innocence of Japanese Canadians, Prime Minister Mackenzie King announced the government's decision to disperse them throughout the country. According to King, dispersal was in the community's best interest: "The sound policy and the best policy for the Japanese Canadians themselves is to distribute their numbers as widely as possible throughout the country where they will not create feelings of hostility."[26]

This policy of dispersal was effective. Prior to the war, 95 percent of Japanese Canadians (22,096) resided in the province of British Columbia. By 1947 this figure had dropped to 6,776. Not long after the war's end, the community was scattered throughout Canada.[27] Lois's views of these demographic shifts were far more sanguine: the assimilation of Japanese Canadians was another positive outcome of the internment. She stated: "Most of my friends, the friends that I've talked with, they say, looking back they say, 'It was the best thing that happened to us, that we were assimilated into the nation.' Without exception, my friends say that." While she recognized that their assimilation was "forced," Lois also saw it as a unique opportunity for Japanese Canadians to become rapidly integrated into the dominant society. Restating her argument, she remarked: "[In] the final analysis, [internment] was the best thing that could have happened to us. I mean would you really like to live the way we did in, all those completely Japanese communities? *Is that what you would like for yourself?*"

Lois's reasoning was tautological, though. Her analysis of the internment was based on her retrospective knowledge of the postwar educational and material gains of many members of the community. In her view, because the *Nisei* not only "survived," but "flourished" in the face of unjust treatment, the latter had facilitated their present-day success. In telling her life story, she repeatedly zigzagged between past and present, and she was most loquacious when she situated herself in contemporary political debates.

Not surprisingly, Lois was unmoved by my suggestion that subsequent generations have felt the injustices of the past and they have since left psychic scars on some *Nisei*. She rejected this interpretation for it was inconsistent with her blessing-in-disguise conclusion. When I introduced the idea, she retorted: "I don't buy that!" Shifting the focus from subjective experience to socio-economic outcomes, she reminded me: "Japanese Canadians of all the ethnic groups have the highest average income ... They've done well! I mean, no, I don't buy that. I don't. No. That's not true ... I just don't buy that. To me, it doesn't make sense. I mean we left the camps and we didn't dwell on that. Internment, you know? We just got on with life. And we overcame. Japanese Canadians are the most successful visible minority group. I mean, I think everyone has accepted us. I think Statistics Canada has proved that, you know. So, so, no." Lois was speaking to an audience of more than one. Her views were not just intended for me. Rather, she was making a case for the respectability and redemption of Japanese Canadians to the public, at large.

FRAMING PERSONAL MEMORIES IN CONTEMPORARY
POLITICAL DISCOURSE

Lois was not the first, nor was she the only *Nisei* to talk about having fun at an internment site or to speak of the uprooting as a blessing in disguise. Before meeting her, I interviewed several other women who had also spent their teen years in Slocan. Some of these women offered similarly nostalgic memories of friends, flirtations, and dancing to the music of the Big Bands. The difference between their narratives and the one articulated by Lois, however, was in the way they framed and interpreted their personal memories. While Polly Shimizu, for instance, remembered good times, she balanced these memories with richly detailed descriptions of terrible living conditions, cruel acts of racism, and the violation of her citizenship rights. Kay Honda likewise contextualized her fond memories in a poignant discussion of the suffering that she felt all around her.[28] While Lois recognized the suffering of others, she did not express it as part of her personal memory; nor did this knowledge inform her sense of a collective memory, her interpretation of the internment, or her vision of history.

What is also unique about Lois's life story is that it is densely woven into a contemporary public debate about racism and racialization. As she related her wartime experiences, she presented a counternarrative to that which has been popularized by the Redress activists. Lois drew on her personal memories to legitimate two related beliefs. One: she believed that although some groups have experienced racism, many others have exaggerated its effects. Two: racism, in Lois's view, is something that we as individuals can overcome. The conclusion she drew is that collective efforts to fight against racism are thereby unwarranted. Many of Lois's personal memories served to legitimate these beliefs. For example, she asserted: "I never had problems with race, I don't know. Oh, when my kids were little ... in grade one, and on the way to school, some little French boy would say, '*Chin, chin, macarine*,' but her reaction was to just whirl around and yell at him, yell right back at him. And they stopped [*laughing*]." Again distancing herself from the subjects of racism, she stated: "I didn't have the experience of being called 'Jap'; I was sure others did but I didn't. I mean, we'd go shopping. We went to a movie several times. But it was just kind of normal. That was *my* experience."

Consistent with these views, Lois proceeded to express her opposition to various struggles to challenge racial discrimination in Canada, past and present. She was critical, for example, of employment equity measures, the contemporary redress campaigns of Aboriginal groups (around residential schools), and the Chinese Canadian campaign to seek reparations for the Head Tax. About the latter, she stated:

> I don't think they [Chinese Canadians] should have got redress because at that time ... we were still evolving ... At that time, when the Chinese were coming [into Canada] ... we didn't have this ... anti-racism. But the important thing is that these Chinese people came anyways, and they paid the exorbitant head tax. And despite that racism, they still came. Why? Why did they do that? ... They felt that despite all that hardship and the racism [they had] hopes for a happier future for their kids here in Canada. And so you've got to admire their tenacity, you know, the fact they took it and they worked hard ... and managed to survive and just persevere. But look where they are now. I mean, their hopes were realized.

The more Lois moved from personal memory to direct assertions of her political position on current issues, the more I squirmed.[29]

There is a striking consistency in Lois's narrative from beginning to end. Her memories of life as a fourteen-year-old during the war, as a young woman in the postwar period, and later as a mother and grandmother all supported her ideological position. While she did not deny the existence of racism in Canada generally, she claimed that personally, she never experienced it. Furthermore, Lois maintained that like Japanese Canadians, other racialized or colonized groups, whether Chinese Canadians or Aboriginal, had to find ways of stoically coping on an individual basis. Her life story from childhood to old age was a coherent one. There were no victims in her narrative, and everyone was or could be an agent of their own fate. These arguments are consistent with a wider, neoliberal politics, in which meritocracy and the myth of individualism explain away racism as a purely personal outcome, the result of individual failure or inadequacy.[30]

CONCLUSION: ONE VOICE AMONG MANY

Why did I want to hear Lois's life story? Was I attempting to assert my authorial control in response to her attacks on my published work? Did I set her up, in an attempt to use her memories as an example of a counter-narrative to the view made public by the Redress Committee? Was I prepared to listen to her with a smile and seeming neutrality, only to critically dissect her life story later, in the privacy and safety of my own study? Was

I simply assuaging my feminist conscience and proving my commitment to democratic process by *giving* her voice?

In part, I wished to hear and understand Lois precisely because we were in such fundamental disagreement. Years ago, E.P. Thompson wrote: "It is only by facing into opposition that I am able to define my thought at all."[31] Like Thompson, I believed that Lois's contrary views would help me to sharpen my own. More important, I felt an ethical and professional responsibility to listen to this voice. Lois took the initiative not only in composing that first email message to me, but also in maintaining communication over the years. And, for well over a decade, she generated binders and file folders of written memoirs, letters, and statements of opinion. These efforts demonstrated a deep-felt concern about the representation of her community.

What did I learn from Lois? My exchanges with her taught me lessons about the relationship between researcher and narrator, as well as the interview frame itself. As Blee found, it can be fairly easy to establish rapport, even with a narrator whose views are "politically abhorrent."[32] I would not describe Lois's views as "abhorrent." However, I did find her opinions highly objectionable. Not only had I devoted most of my academic career to the kind of anti-racist work of which she spoke so disparagingly, but many of the targets of her criticism were people whom I have long regarded as icons in the community.

Yet, as Olsen and Shopes note, oral history interviews are "highly framed encounters" that are "not governed by the rules of ordinary interaction."[33] The interview presents us with a "social space where normal power relationships get blunted."[34] In such a context, the "power of the personal interaction" can override the "critical judgment" of the oral historian. Beyond our political differences, my relationship with Lois was shaped by my concerns about the practice of oral history (letting the narrator construct her or his own narrative), her status as an eyewitness and my senior, as well as the generosity and openness that she displayed in our interpersonal exchanges. After all, she not only gave me access to all of her private papers, but also welcomed me into her home, fed me, baked me cookies, and treated me to dinner at a local restaurant.

In turn, I remained empathetic throughout our interviews. Never did I suggest that she was wrong; though in the hope of avoiding misrepresentation or deception, I did mention at the outset that I disagreed with her interpretation. But in fact, so subtle was I in expressing my dissenting views that after many exchanges, Lois asked me what exactly we disagreed about? After visiting her in Laval, I was convinced more than ever of the value of the face-to-face interview. Hearing Lois's voice, observing her mannerisms and facial expressions, and noting when she would get up to eagerly retrieve her scrapbook of photos gave me a fuller sense of who she was as a human being. Meeting her in person enabled me to detect her ardency, frustrations, limitations, and vulnerabilities, and this understanding has helped me become a more empathetic researcher.[35]

Should Lois's story remain off the record? Clearly, her narrative raises tensions that many of us do not wish to air in public. She exposed political differences within our community: the conservative voices in conflict with progressive ones, those who wish to narrow the NAJC's mandate to community development (sushi-making, *taiko* drumming, and flower arranging) as opposed to advocates of a human rights agenda. Her narrative further reveals the unsavoury reality that even people who have been racially oppressed may be critical of anti-racist activism, and may themselves promote or perpetuate racist thinking.[36] Lois chose to highlight her positive, uncomplicated memories of internment and resettlement in postwar Canada. These memories give credence to a neoliberal agenda that highlights an ethic of individualism and downplays the role of systemic discrimination and structural inequalities in shaping people's life choices. In doing so, she minimized the negative and enduring impact of the wartime events and trivialized the efforts of some *Nisei* and many *Sansei* to challenge the government's actions.

Lois passed away unexpectedly in January 2010. I learned about her death weeks later. I could have dropped this project with Lois, kept her interviews locked away, or simply treated her as an informant, thereby selectively drawing on her memories. But rather than dismiss or diminish her voice, I wish to put her memories on record. Lois's story has enhanced my analytical understanding of Japanese Canadian history and deepened my reflections on the practice of oral history. Lois forced me to listen deeply, and to consider an interpretation of history that was inconsistent with my own. And these practices – deep listening and inclusiveness – are at the heart of oral history.[37] Granted, all research, oral history included, is built on bias and selectivity. But when we select or omit participants and stories for purely ideological reasons, then our practices become dubious and our analyses ultimately limited.

If we wish to uphold the value of personal memory, we cannot exclude memories from our accounts because they are inconsistent with public memory or diverge from what we view as historical truth. If a stranger presents us with her personal truths, with memories that are sincere, we cannot look away. Rather, we must take up the challenge and consider how they bear on our interpretation of history and how they stand up to the memories of others. My writing is inspired by my advocacy but, as an oral historian, I must allow the personal narrative to unfold under the direction of the narrator. If I view memory as being at the heart of oral history, then I must be prepared to learn from an interviewee's memories, even if they do not cohere with my own.

This is not to say, however, that researcher/advocates never make strategic choices. Twenty-odd years ago, in the heat of the campaign for Redress, I may have decided to keep Lois's memories off the record. Back then her words could have been more damaging to the political cause; more persuasive in the absence of a strong critical discourse. However, it now seems time to air the divisions within our community, to offer accounts that reveal the nuances of the war and resettlement years, and the complex ways in which racism has affected the second generation. It is time to enrich the story of internment. Lois agreed, pleading with me to write a complex history. Paradoxically, *she* urged *me* to be more than a conduit for a political cause: "You have a wealth of real memories narrated to you by people who generously shared their experiences with you – and they are far more valuable and real than the vicariously felt emotions of sansei Redress activists. You have the ingredients for an interesting and enlightening book."[38]

After listening to Lois, in seriously considering this woman's perspective on her own life, I listened somewhat differently to the narratives of the seventy-four other *Nisei* women and men I interviewed. And when I now read overly theorized, polemical writings authored by those whom Lois would call "earnest Sansei," I say to myself, "I can hear Lois now!" In a way, Lois acts as my conscience in the practice of oral history. She reminds me to consider all voices of the past. She taps me on the shoulder when I am swayed by deterministic accounts that lack empirical grounding, and when I romantically envision historical victims without a human dimension. Lois has given me a heightened sense of nuance in oral history practice. And her death does not exempt me, because her voice is not an isolated one. While the details of her life story, the idiosyncratic nature of its telling, and the form and development of her narrative are particular, Lois's repertoire of memories and interpretation of history may be understood as part of a larger political analysis.

Over time, I grew to like and respect this somewhat irascible woman. But do I agree with her description of the past? As noted earlier, my objective is not to establish the veracity of any individual's memories of her or his own life. I do, however, believe that if we wish to escape the post-modernist trap of positing ever-shifting realities, we need to make some claims about history.[39] As Iwona Irwin-Zarecka writes, there is a "baseline historical reality."[40] Lois's memories are meaningful, without doubt. But when she extrapolated from her personal memories to make statements about the community as a whole, I believe she was on shakier ground. The memories of my many *Nisei* interviewees, in addition to my reading of thousands of censored letters that were written by Japanese Canadians in the 1940s, have led me to a starkly different understanding of the war years – it was a time that was marked sometimes by fun and frivolity but also by deep suffering, loss, pain, anger, and wounds that have never fully healed.

I am not arguing that Lois's memories are inaccurate or that she is a *Nisei* "in denial." I am saying that memory is selective, partial, and shifting. Oral history can be both unreliable and revelatory. According to Blee, it is unreliable because of the subjectivity of personal memory, because of its gaps, its faultiness, its lapses.[41] But at the same time, as Alessandro Portelli notes, it is revelatory because "[what] informants believe is indeed a historical *fact* (that is, the fact that they believe it), as much as what really happened."[42] What does Lois's narrative reveal? I cannot nor do I wish to psychologize Lois. As a sociologist, however, I can attempt to situate her memories. Lois's narrative tells us about the relationship between personal memory and a wider public discourse. As Ronald Grele states, personal memories are neither static nor spontaneous. Memories of the past are situated in contemporary ideological beliefs and cultures, and they are crafted over time.[43] I can only speculate on the extent to which Lois's present-day political agenda shaped her personal wartime memories, and on the ways in which her position on current political debates, in turn, was a product of her early experiences as a Japanese Canadian internee. However, unlike most narrators, Lois demanded interpretive authority of her life story, and with authorial voice, she framed her personal memories in contemporary ideological debates around racism, human rights, and political redress. In the words of Gary Y. Okihiro, oral history offers ordinary individuals a way of evaluating their lives in relation to the historical meta-narrative.[44] Lois's narrative, then, is as much a comment on the social conflicts that have marked Canadian history as it is a definition of her individual self. It is not only a description of the past but also an ideological statement on the contemporary world in which she lived. Lois attempted to immortalize her personal memories, carve out her identity,

and define a new social identity for the women and men of her generation[45] and, in her narrative, this is a world in which structure does not set
limits, "race" no longer matters, and the individual is triumphant.

NOTES

1 At the beginning of the war, the government passed Order in Council PC
365, which designated an area one hundred miles inland from the west coast
a "protected area." On 4 March 1942, the government formed the British
Columbia Security Commission (BCSC), a civilian body that was given the
power to execute a "systematic expulsion" of all persons of Japanese origin
from the area that lay within this zone. See Roy Miki and Cassandra Kobayashi, *Justice in Our Time: The Canadian Redress Settlement* (Vancouver/
Winnipeg: Talonbooks/National Association of Japanese Canadians, 1991),
20–4.

2 Roy Miki coined the term "framed by race" in *Redress: Inside the Japanese
Canadian Call for Justice* (Vancouver: Raincoast Books, 2005), 13–37.

3 See Antoinette Errante, "But Sometimes You're Not Part of the Story: Oral
Histories and Ways of Remembering and Telling," in *Feminist Perspectives on
Social Research*, edited by Sharlene Nagy Hesse-Biber and Michelle L. Yaiser
(Oxford University Press, 2003), 411–37.

4 Daniel James, *Doña María's Story: Life, History, Memory, and Political Identity* (Durham: Duke University Press, 2000), 138.

5 Sherna Berger Gluck, "Advocacy Oral History: Palestinian Women in Resistance," in *Women's Words: The Feminist Practice of Oral History*, edited by
Sherna Berger Gluck and Daphne Patai (New York: Routledge, 1991), 214.

6 Kathleen Blee, "Evidence, Empathy, and Ethics: Lessons from Oral Histor-
ies of the Klan," in *The Oral History Reader*, 2nd edition, edited by Robert
Perks and Alistair Thomson (London: Routledge, 2006), 322–31; Katharine
Borland, "'That's Not What I Said': Interpretive Conflict in Oral Narrative
Research," in *The Oral History Reader*, 2nd edition, edited by Perks and
Thomson, 310–21; Gluck, "Advocacy Oral History," 205–19; Tracy E. K'Meyer
and A. Glenn Crothers, "'If I see some of this in writing, I'm going to shoot
you': Reluctant Narrators, Taboo Topics, and the Ethical Dilemmas of the
Oral Historian," *Oral History Review* 34, no. 1 (2007): 71–93; Valerie Yow, "Do
I Like Them Too Much? Effects of the Oral History Interview on the Inter-
viewer and Vice-Versa," *Oral History Review* 21, no. 1 (1997): 55–79.

7 On the conversational narrative, see Ronald Grele, "History and the Languages of History in the Oral History Interview: Who Answers Whose Questions and Why," in *Interactive Oral History Interviewing*, edited by Eva M.
McMahan and Kim Lacy Rogers (New York: Routledge, 1994), 2.

8 Blee, "Evidence, Empathy and Ethics," 324, 328.

9 Errante, "But Sometimes You're Not Part of the Story."

10 Ruth Behar, *The Vulnerable Observer: Anthropology That Breaks Your Heart* (Boston: Beacon Press, 1996). Also see chapter 4 in this *Reader*.

11 Personal correspondence between Lois Hashimoto and the author, 3 May 2006.

12 See Susan Geiger, "What's So Feminist About Women's Oral History?" *Journal of Women's History* 21, 1 (1990): 169–82; Judith Stacey, "Can There Be a Feminist Ethnography?" in *Women's Words*, edited by Gluck and Patai, 111–19; Joan Sangster, "Telling Our Stories: Feminist Debates and the Use of Oral History," in *The Oral History Reader*, 1st edition, edited by Robert Perks and Alistair Thomson (London: Routledge, 1998), 87–100.

13 For a related discussion, see Kathryn Anderson and Dana C. Jack, "Learning to Listen: Interview Techniques and Analyses," in *Women's Words*, edited by Gluck and Patai, 19.

14 See Michael Frisch, *A Shared Authority. Essays on the Craft and Meaning of Oral History* (Albany: SUNY Press, 1990); Kathleen M. Ryan, "'I Didn't Do Anything Important': A Pragmatist Analysis of the Oral History Interview," *Oral History Review* 36, no. 1 (2009): 25–44; Lorraine Sitzia, "A Shared Authority: An Impossible Goal?" *Oral History Review* 30, no. 1 (2003): 87–101; Special Issue of the *Journal of Canadian Studies* 43, no. 1 (spring 2009).

15 See Andrea Doucet, "'From Her Side of the Gossamer Wall(s)': Reflexivity and Relational Knowing," *Qualitative Sociology* 31, no. 1 (2008): 73–87.

16 Lois Hashimoto, interview by author, Laval, QC, 16–17 December 2008.

17 Karen Olsen and Linda Shopes, "Crossing Boundaries, Building Bridges: Doing Oral History among Working-Class Women and Men," in *Women's Words*, edited by Gluck and Patai, 196–7.

18 See James's discussion of the "performative" aspects of a narrative in *Doña María's Story*, 183–5.

19 Gluck notes that individual consciousness is rarely revealed through the recitation of a political platform. Gluck, "Advocacy Oral History," 209.

20 Personal correspondence between Lois Hashimoto and the author, 6 May 2006.

21 E. Culpepper Clark, "Reconstructing History: The Epitomizing Image," in *Interactive Oral History Interviewing*, edited by Eva M. McMahan and Kim Lacy Rogers (New York: Routledge, 1994), 20, 26. Writing in 1969, K. Burke (cited in Clark) introduced the concept of an "epitomizing image" to describe an episode that symbolically represents the "course of the plot." Certain anecdotes, says Clark, are so "salient" that the researcher cannot dismiss them. To this end, Linda Shopes states that "iconic stories" are "concrete, specific accounts that 'stand for' or sum up something the narrator reckons of particular importance." See Shopes, "Making Sense of Oral History," http://historymatters.gmu.edu (accessed 23 June 2014).

22 See Marigold Linton, "Phoenix and Chimera: The Changing Faces of Memory," in *Memory and History: Essays on Recalling and Interpreting Experience*, edited by Jaclyn Jeffrey and Glenace Edwall (Lanham: University Press of America, 1994), 81.

23 In turn, her personal narrative is governed by a particular vision of history. See Marie-Francoise Chanfrault-Duchet, "Narrative Structures, Social Models, and Symbolic Representation in the Life Story," in *Women's Words*, edited by Gluck and Patai, 77–92.

24 See Kim Lacy Rogers, *Life and Death in the Delta: African-American Narratives of Violence, Resilience, and Social Change* (New York: Palgrave, 2006).

25 Charlotte Linde, *Life Stories: The Creation of Coherence* (New York: Oxford University Press, 1993).

26 *Debates*, House of Commons, 4 August 1944, as cited in Miki and Kobayashi, *Justice in Our Time*, 50.

27 Audrey Kobayashi, *A Demographic Profile of Japanese Canadians and Social Implications for the Future* (Ottawa: Department of the Secretary of State, 1989), 6; Miki and Kobayashi, *Justice in Our Time*, 105.

28 Both Polly Shimizu and Kay Honda were outspoken advocates of Redress. See Pamela Sugiman, "Memories of Internment: Narrating Japanese Canadian Women's Life Stories," *Canadian Journal of Sociology* 29, no. 3 (2004): 359–88.

29 In their study of second-generation, grown children of Korean and Vietnamese immigrants in the United States, Karen Pyke and Tran Dang argue that "by accepting and internalizing mainstream racist values and rationales," the second-generation often ends up justifying the oppression of their own ethnic group, albeit often unintentionally. Pyke and Dang, "'FOB' and 'Whitewashed': Identity and Internalized Racism Among Second Generation Asian Americans," *Qualitative Sociology* 26, no. 2 (summer 2003): 151.

30 See Christopher Robbins, "Racism and the Authority of Neoliberalism: A Review of Three Books on the Persistence of Racial Equality in a Color-blind Era," *Journal for Critical Education Policy Studies* 2, no. 2 (2004), available at: http://www.jceps.com (accesed 23 June 2014).

31 E.P. Thompson, "An Open Letter to Leszek Kolakowski," in E.P. Thompson, *The Poverty of Theory* (New York: Monthly Review Press, 1978), 186.

32 Blee, "Evidence, Empathy, and Ethics," 328.

33 Olsen and Shopes, "Crossing Boundaries," 195–6.

34 Ibid., 196.

35 Lois was deeply embarrassed when she read the transcripts of our interviews. She felt that she had been incoherent, never finishing a sentence or thought, and failing to find the correct words to express her ideas. Despite my insistence that she had been lucid, Lois spent days writing out fuller explanations of her spoken words.

36 See Gluck, "Advocacy Oral History," 205–19; Claudia Koonz, *Mothers in the Fatherland: Women, the Family, and Nazi Politics* (New York: St Martin's Griffin, 1988); Anna Sheftel and Stacey Zembrzycki, "Only Human: A Reflection on the Ethical and Methodological Challenges of Working with 'Difficult' Stories," *Oral History Review* 37, no. 2 (2010): 191–241.

37 For more on oral history and the art of listening, see Bronwen Low and Emmanuelle Sonntag, chapter 12 in this *Reader*.

38 Personal correspondence between Lois Hashimoto and the author, 6 May 2006.

39 For a persuasive discussion of oral history, feminism, and material analysis, see chapters by Joan Sangster (chapter 5) and Kristina R. Llewellyn (chapter 6) in this *Reader*.

40 Iwona Irwin-Zarecka, *Frames of Remembrance: The Dynamics of Collective Memory* (New Brunswick, NJ: Transaction Publishers, 1994), 102.

41 Blee, "Evidence, Empathy, and Ethics," 324.

42 Alessandro Portelli, "What Makes Oral History Different," in *The Oral History Reader*, 2nd edition, edited by Perks and Thomson, 36.

43 Ronald Grele, "Movement Without Aim: Methodological and Theoretical Problems in Oral History," in *The Oral History Reader*, 1st edition, edited by Robert Perks and Alistair Thomson (London: Routledge, 1998), 38–52.

44 See Gary Okihiro, *Whispered Silences: Japanese Americans and World War II* (Seattle: University of Washington Press, 1996).

45 Claudia Salazar, "A Third World Women's Text: Between the Politics of Criticism and Cultural Politics" in *Women's Words*, edited by Gluck and Patai, 93–106.

Contested Memories: Efforts of the Powerful to Silence Former Inmates' Histories of Life in an Institution for "Mental Defectives"

Claudia Malacrida

In 2005, when Alberta celebrated its provincial centennial, official commemorations deployed images of wholesome families, wide open spaces, explorers, homesteaders, ranchers, and oilmen. This was history in revision and re-membrance; depictions of humble, hard-working, and decent White folks facing the challenges of a wild country, civilizing the unruly land, and building communities were used to represent the true history of the province. However, silence has prevailed concerning other memories that could have been invoked as part of the history of "taming the west," including the history of eugenics and institutionalization in Alberta. Michener Centre, which opened its doors in 1923 as the Provincial Training School, was a total institution for the incarceration of developmentally disabled children and adults in Alberta that sat at the very centre of Alberta's eugenic past. Despite this, Michener's official history describes the Centre's function as a "training school for the academic, vocational, and personal development of retarded children and young adults" and argues that the institution was a benevolent improvement for services to children and their families.[1]

Legal petitions brought against the government of Alberta in regard to eugenic sterilizations that occurred in the Michener Centre under the direction of the Alberta Eugenics Board,[2] and oral histories collected from individuals who were interned at Michener Centre,[3] contest these sanitized, official memories of institutionalization. Although these contested memories are specific to one institution, the practices of institutionalization and segregation they describe reflect broader discourses and practices that circulated in Europe and North America during much of the twentieth century, relating to science, eugenics, and fitness. As such, these memories tie into and support other marginalized recollections. They are important memories to access, not only for those who survive these experiences, but also for those who, because of innocence or ignorance, may repeat the mistakes already made.

At a recent conference on "The Role of Memories in Social Change," several presenters discussed the importance of collective memories in providing groups of people with a sense of identity and belonging, and the role of telling these memories in changing the broader history of a society. Examples such as the way that Jewish survivors' memories of the Holocaust gave birth to a new nation-state and strengthened and altered Jewish identity,[4] and the role of memory work in forging a collective sense of both pride and bereavement among Australian Aboriginal people[5] were offered as evidence of the power of memories from the margins to shift the broader social history. The oral history project with Michener Centre survivors discussed in this chapter was motivated by such beliefs about the power of memories from the margins to contribute to identity formation and to change collective, dominant memories. This chapter offers an examination of the efforts of the powerful to obstruct this particular rewriting of history from the margins. These obstructionist efforts by those in power pose challenges to a naïve belief that simply "wishing to tell the truth" about these hidden memories is sufficient grounds for motivating authorities to permit such memories to be told. Instead, changing collective memories through the telling of marginal history is something that the powerful are actively and effectively able to resist.

HISTORICAL CONTEXT

Prior to engaging in a discussion of the barriers encountered in this historical research project, it will be helpful to provide some background concerning Michener Centre and its establishment and continuance. In 1923, a former private girls' school (subsequently used as a recovery institute for "shell-shocked" First World War veterans) was purchased by the Alberta government and was refurbished and reopened as Provincial Training School (PTS), an institution for the residential care and training of "mentally defective" Albertans.[6] Upon opening, PTS housed 108 residents under the age of eighteen years, and comprised a single building on the outskirts of the small town of Red Deer, Alberta. By the early 1970s, the complex had taken on the name of Michener Centre, and comprised some sixty-six buildings on over three hundred acres of land, with a resident population – not only of children under eighteen, but also of adults of all ages – that exceeded 2,300 individuals.[7] The phenomenal growth of the institution does not necessarily reflect general population growth in Alberta, but is tied rather to the increasing normalization of segregating individuals with developmental disabilities[8] in the West during the early twentieth century.[9] It should also be noted that, although the institution's initial designation as a Training School might indicate that education, training, and preparation for community living were central institutional goals, the centre operated less as a school than as a prison. Indeed, even in the "official" history of the institution, the government itself acknowledged that fewer than 20 percent of all children admitted to Michener were *ever* provided any formal education.[10] Further, individuals who were generally admitted to the institution in early to middle childhood were not released at the age of adulthood. Instead, residents were transferred at eighteen years of age from the "school" side of the Michener campus to Deer Home, a long-term "care" facility for adults. In practice, then, many individuals lived at Michener Centre virtually their entire lives, from childhood through adolescence and adulthood to death.

Training and education were the given reasons for Michener's existence but eugenics played a central role in establishing and sustaining the institution. During the first half of the twentieth century, a belief that "feeble-mindedness" could be attributed to poor genetic material prevailed in the minds of social reformers, government officials, and medical and scientific practitioners throughout the Western world.[11] At Michener Centre, institutionalization, segregation, and eugenics were intimately linked. The lifelong internment of "mental defectives" in a virtual fortress set at distance from a small rural town, and the reportedly almost obsessive arrangements for sexual segregation within the Michener Centre functioned as a covert, passive form of eugenics; "defective" individuals segregated in these ways posed little risk of "polluting" the social body with their offspring.

More overt eugenics programs also operated within the Michener Centre. In 1928, just five years after the opening of the Provincial Training School, the Province of Alberta implemented the Sexual Sterilization Act and established the Alberta Eugenics Board. The Board held regular quarterly meetings to hear "sterilization order cases" inside the Michener compound, and although things started slowly with "only" sixteen sterilizations performed in 1930, by the time of the Board's closing, it was approving between thirty and forty involuntary sterilizations per year, most of them on Michener residents.[12] The Michener population was particularly vulnerable following a 1937 amendment to the Act that made obtaining consent from individuals identified as "mental defectives" redundant, since such individuals were considered *de facto* incapable of granting consent.[13] Further, while the eugenics doctrine swept the Western world during the first half of the twentieth century, Alberta's (and Michener's) eugenics program operated longer than most others, only ceasing with the repeal of the Act in 1972.[14]

In the 1960s, a series of philosophical and structural changes in the Alberta Child Welfare system, stemming in part from negative media exposure, led the Alberta Government to commission an inquiry into system reform.[15] The resulting Blair Report made 189 recommendations for service improvement, including reducing the numbers of inmates[16] in mental facilities and finding places for these people in the community.[17] The response of the Michener Centre was less assiduous than might have been hoped: while on the one hand programs and strategies were put in place for the eventual "normalization" (the term used in official documents relating to communitization) of former inmates, many of these individuals found their new "community" homes in a number of purpose-built group homes that were installed directly on the Michener campus.[18] The institution's ambivalence over communitization is also evidenced in institutional records relating to injuries and deaths during attempted runaways[19] that occurred during the communitization transition. In one such record, for example, the Institution's Charge Nurse states clearly that the best way to avoid harm to residents is not to provide them with more freedom and support for the transition from institutional life, but instead to "return to previous lock-down practices" on the wards.[20] Thus, at both the institutional level and at the level of individual administrators and staff, the closure of the institution was a goal only reticently embraced.

The life histories, interviews of ex-workers, and archival records that comprise the data for this project cover the period between 1965 and 1985, and therefore include these years of ostensible transition towards communitization and a "kinder, gentler" set of institutional practices. However, as I have written elsewhere, the daily routines of the Michener Centre remained for the most part dehumanizing and oppressive for those who lived inside the institution's walls, regardless of the institutional rhetoric.[21] Thus, the memories of those who lived in and worked at the institution, and the hidden official records contained in the institutional archives offer a stark counter-narrative to the official institutional memory.

THE POLITICS OF ORAL HISTORY

In social research, telling life stories and reconstructing memories has relatively recently become a legitimate research strategy. Arthur Frank, for example, argues for the strength of narrative in health research in claiming one's personal memories and telling one's own experiences as a counter-narrative to the dominant medical model. In that dominant model, patients are conceived as little more than their diseases or conditions, and patients' subjective knowledge is regarded as irrelevant to the understanding or treatment of illness and disability.[22] The power of narrative to reclaim and refashion knowledge by making one's memories public thus offers individuals an opportunity to bear witness to their experience, to affirm personal perspectives on illness and disability as real and legitimate, and to challenge dominant health care ideologies.[23] In addition, these narratives provide a politicized reading of relations of power, offering the patient an opportunity to bear witness to harms suffered, and drawing on the perspectives of subordinated individuals to expose the workings of power and domination within the medical encounter.[24] Mike Bury notes that narrative and memory work is not limited only to those who are ill or operating against the medical model, but rather that a politics of narrative can be used by a broad range of people who have been harmed or marginalized by powerful institutions,[25] including such places as the Michener Centre.

The individuals who initiated this oral history project, many of them Michener survivors, understood the importance of telling marginalized memories. Roy Skoreyko,[26] who survived over twenty years of institutional life, was a central motivator in getting this project started. During his interview, he noted: "I feel that it's time the people listen to our stories and I think that eventually if you can get this [project] going ... hopefully this will help, this tape will help to educate people, so something like this will never happen again, so people with disabilities will never be abused again."

Roy adds another element to the theoretician's arguments for the power of narrative and memory reclamation. In Roy's analysis, not only does retelling and remembering have the power to legitimate the individual's memories and perspectives, but reclaiming these memories by telling them from the perspective of the survivor has two other strengths. First, this memory work has the power of conveying a cautionary tale against institutionalization both past and future; and second, it produces an emancipatory message of empowerment for individuals with disabilities by evidencing that history from survivors' perspectives matters. In short, telling memories from the margins is a political act.

Disability scholar Susan Wendell has argued that memory work from the perspectives of individuals with disabilities is crucial to the construction of an emancipatory disability history.[27] By this, Wendell means that distanced and purportedly objective knowledge constructed by historians, sociologists, and disability scholars falls short. Indeed, although researchers have begun to expose the systematic institutionalization, degradation, and eugenicization of disabled individuals that occurred in the West during much of the twentieth century,[28] most of these histories exclude accounts from those who, having survived these practices, can tell us about the intimate mechanisms of disability oppression at its most profound level. Emancipatory history that comes from the positions or standpoints of survivors draws on the assertion that telling one's memories serves the purpose of naming hurts, describing exploitation, acknowledging power relations, and remembering history as it actually occurred for those most oppressed by it, rather than reproducing memories that may serve dominant interests.

This chapter speaks to the challenges and barriers encountered in research that has the capacity to produce memories of the institution that are potentially damaging to those in authority. The memories I have sought to access come from institutional survivors, and they also include purportedly publicly-accessible materials relating to the institution, including archival records and the grounds of the institution itself.

ACCESS ISSUES AND ORAL HISTORIES

While the value of reclaiming memories from the perspectives of those who have suffered most is clear, it has not been easy to gain access to such memories. This was abundantly clear at several junctures in conducting this research. Many of the individuals who were released from Michener Centre in the community-living movement of the 1970s and 1980s had been legally wards of the institution while living at the institution. Some were individuals whose parents or other family members had died, leaving the institution with sovereign authority over the inmate. Others were individuals whose families had abandoned them to the institution from the very beginning, handing legal authority over to Michener administration upon institutionalizing the child. Clearly, the Institution could no longer morally, legally, or ethically sustain its authority over these individuals once they were deinstitutionalized and living in the community. On the other hand, decades of institutional abuse, isolation, and confinement left many of the survivors without the skills or resources necessary for negotiating survival outside. A solution was created for this dilemma through the formation of regional Offices of the Public Guardian, which were established by the Government of Alberta to provide "appropriate decision-making mechanisms for individuals who are unable to make personal non-financial decisions for themselves ... to ensure the rights of these individuals are protected."[29]

In the early stages of the project, when I approached several Offices of the Public Guardian to seek permission to recruit research participants, this role of protection seemed instead to operate as obstruction; my offers to provide information sessions, and my requests to send former inmates Calls for Participation were consistently refused. Inevitably, such refusals were justified by claims that the Public Guardian Office was protecting Michener survivors from having to relive their experiences. However, one can also imagine reasons other than paternalism for keeping these individuals from telling their stories; in "protecting" individuals from telling painful memories, one government office effectively refused my access to individuals who might have negative things to say about another government office, in effect protecting the dominant, sanitized official history of Michener Centre. They also effectively denied these individuals their rights to refuse or agree to tell their own marginalized memories of life in the institution.

Finally, the protectionism of the Public Guardian offices also potentially meant that the most marginalized survivors have been barred from participating in this research project. Because Public Guardianship orders affected individuals who were deemed to be less independent and less intellectually capable, only survivors who were able to act as their own legal guardians have been able to tell their memories in this project. In turn, this may also mean that the survivor memories that are being told in this research reflect experiences in wards that were less oppressive than average. In Michener Centre, residents were segregated in wards according to hierarchies of disability from "High Grades" to "Low Grades," and it is likely that the participants in this project enjoyed better living conditions within the institution than others who, both during their time in the institution and once they were released back into the community, were perceived as less intellectually competent.

PROTECTIONISM IN THE INSTITUTION ITSELF

The ability of privileged and powerful social actors to obstruct an emancipatory history of Michener Centre has been evidenced in numerous
ways throughout this project. In 1999, early in the research, I spoke with
the then-current manager of Planning and Communications at Michener
Centre, asking about the status of the institution and whether Michener
Centre would be willing to provide access to their on-site archives. I will
return to the question of the archives later. As to the current institutional
status, the manager informed me that, although officially the Michener
Centre "discouraged" admission and supports communitization, there
were still at that time a few admissions every year, and a total population
of almost 550 residents, all adults committed for long-term residency. The
manager also expressed that, tying in with Michener Centre's role as one
of the largest employers in the area, the Board at that time would actually
have liked to increase admissions. In other words, although there was a
large grassroots movement during the 1970s and 1980s seeking to close
such institutions, the Michener Centre continues to exist, has until recently expressed an interest in strengthening its role on the one hand as
an institution for the internment of disabled people and, on the other,
as a major employer of non-disabled people.[30] Finally, this Michener
representative noted that Michener itself had been wanting to write another history of the centre (an official government history of the Michener Centre was produced in 1985), this time with a focus on how the
centre has acted as a career stepping stone for many Albertans schooled
at Michener Center as MDNs, or "Mental Deficiency Nurses," in a two-
year training program that ended in 1973, just as Michener was winding
down its eugenics program. In other words, at the time of our discussion,
it was clear that there persisted a desire on the part of the institution to
continue to produce its own, sanitized memories of institutional life and
institutional purpose.

When asked about the eugenics program at Michener, the manager's
response was not to deny that such things had ever happened: it would be
impossible to do so in light of several high-profile court cases successfully
launched against the Alberta government for unlawful and involuntary
sterilization.[31] Rather, the communications manager stated, "That wasn't
Michener Centre. That was the provincial government. We just went
along with it because we had to. In fact, we'd be happy to have the *truth*
told."[32]

In light of Michener's stated ambitions to expand its operations, and its desire to produce its own sanitized memories, it is not surprising that the institution failed to cooperate with the survivors' oral history project. In the spring of 2001, I and two research collaborators appealed to the current Michener Centre Board of Governors, asking for a tour of the grounds. I had never seen the facilities where the survivors' experiences took place, and I thought it would be important to see the hallways, dormitories, solitary confinement cells, medical examining rooms, and other spaces that figured so poignantly in the survivors' stories. We were asked to attend a Board meeting held on the Michener Campus. There are two points worth noting concerning this request: first, the Michener Centre is a public institution, funded by public dollars, and it is in theory neither an asylum nor a prison. It is a "care facility," and as such, members of the public are not typically barred from being on the campus. In fact, in the past two decades, a number of recreational facilities, including a theatre, a swimming pool, and a gymnasium, have been built on the Michener campus, and these are open to the general public on a daily basis. Thus, our request was as much a courtesy as a requirement. A second point concerns the makeup of the Michener Board at the time. The Board was composed of nine members, all of them acting as volunteers. These individuals, from various districts across Alberta, included small business owners, management consultants, members of philanthropic societies, and, in some cases, sitting members of other disability advisory committees reporting to government. Thus, these Board members represented not only qualities of ideal citizenship, but they were individuals who had been selected by government for service on the Board because of their high moral and social standing. One might thus reasonably expect such a civic-minded group to support the idea of seeing historical justice done.

Nonetheless, our request to the Board was not well received. After what seemed like an interminable wait in a cool, dark, echoing hallway, we were invited in to present our request to a stone-faced group seated around a long, polished table. When we finished, one Board member noted that he "had some concerns about the project particularly in relation to its potential to continue to create an inaccurate impression about the current nature of … Michener," while another indicated "history is important but … how [would] the project be placed in the context of the society at the time?"[33] Each of these responses implied that, while history might be good to know, *this* history would not: *this* history would instead pose a threat to the desired, official memory, and to the legitimacy of the institution in the present moment. In other words, echoing Roy's earlier insights, these men also understood the political potential of memories from the margins. Predictably, some weeks later we received a polite letter barring our access to the Michener campus.

ARCHIVAL RESEARCH AND ACCESS ISSUES

The research project discussed here stems from an earlier project initiated by members of Alberta Association for Community Living, which sought to collect life histories of survivors as a means of expressing and honouring the experiences of those individuals institutionalized and often involuntarily sterilized at Michener Centre. As the project has developed, my own research has taken on a broader historical treatment, and has expanded to interviews with former employees, and includes archival research on institutional records. These institutional records include daily record logs, proceedings of sterilization hearings, minutes of disciplinary committees for staff members, budgets, lists of escape attempts and resulting actions, admission notes, and experimental treatment records, all of which pertained to the survivor narratives.

My experience in obtaining access to these archival materials provides another example of how the powerful are able to constrain or erase undesirable memories. In 1999, when I first spoke with the communications manager at Michener, these records were housed primarily at the institution itself. It is not surprising in light of the institutional response to the research that I was not provided access to the privately held records held on the Michener campus. Since then, virtually all remaining records[34] relating to the institution have been transferred into the public archives of the Province of Alberta. Although one might hope that transfer would result in easier access to Michener's historical records by researchers and claimants against the institution, this has not been the case.

In 1996 the provincial government implemented the Freedom of Information and Protection of Privacy Act (FOIP), designed "to allow any person a right of access to the records in the custody or under the control of a public body subject to limited and specific exceptions."[35] Thus, any records that were archived after 1996 are subject to the Act, while materials archived before the law came into effect are not "protected" by the Act. In practice this means that the few files from Michener Centre that were placed into the "public" archive prior to 1996 are completely open to citizens and researchers. However, the vast majority of the institutions' records were archived once the protectionist law was enacted. As with the question of whose memories were being protected when we sought access to the grounds of Michener Centre or to recruit volunteers among survivors living under guardianship orders, the question of whose privacy is being protected with the FOIP law bears some scrutiny. In effect, when an individual seeks information that is FOIP-protected, that person must make application to the government for clearance, after which the archivist then painstakingly goes through each record that is requested, erasing any names that are in the record, and writing in the phrase "Section 17(1)" where each name would have appeared. Obviously, this is a very time-consuming process. It is also a very expensive one. My first request to the FOIP officer was for one daily record book taken from each ward within the Michener Centre, the proceedings of staff meetings taken during two sample years, some records of medical experiments conducted on-site over the period of one year, and some assorted correspondence. It should also be noted that, because applicants are not actually able to view the contents of the files and boxes before making requests, my selections were quite arbitrary, and quite "thin"; I fully expected to return for additional materials on the basis of the results of this first *Request for Access*. Mercifully, the archivist did not immediately fill my request, but instead sent a fee estimate for this first round of archival materials. That initial estimate totalled over thirteen thousand dollars, a sum that would be prohibitive to most researchers and certainly to most institutional survivors who might want to learn about the attitudes, practices, and systems that operated to oppress them during their years in the institution. It is not unreasonable to speculate that, in this case at the very least, Alberta's FOIP Act is operating not to provide citizens with access to hidden and marginal memories, but instead to protect public bodies from citizens' (and particularly marginalized citizens') access to these institutional records.

LEGITIMATION AND MARGINAL VOICES

As noted earlier, the Michener history project was initially designed to draw on oral histories provided by institutional survivors, stemming from a consideration that oral histories permit "insider perspectives" that are best positioned to provide a counter-narrative to dominant historical accounts.[36] Centring the study on personal histories was also seen as critical because, as Elizabeth Bredberg has argued, much of disability history has been taken from the perspective of the institutions that were most oppressive to persons with disabilities, and even when disability histories have been constructed from an explicitly emancipatory perspective, they have continued to focus on institutional practice without including the voices of the individuals most affected by those practices.[37] Therefore, expanding the data sources for this project from oral histories to archival materials represents something of a compromise to me, both methodologically and ethically. It is thus important to offer a rationale for this decision, and to provide an accounting of the potential advantages to the project of including additional sources.

While the decision to expand data sources was not made because of any inconsistencies in or doubts about the survivor narratives – I have never doubted that their stories are honest, accurate reflections of shared experiences – it is also true that triangulating data sources has been something of a concession to the imagined skepticism that such histories will engender among others. The Michener survivors' narratives, like many other survivor narratives, expose previously hidden stories of physical, sexual, economic, psychological, medical, and legal abuse, and like other survivor stories about these kinds of abuse, the potential for discrediting such memories is high. From Sigmund Freud, whose patients' reports of sexual abuse from male relatives were so discounted as to form the basis of his theory of oedipal desire and penis envy, to current debates over "false memory syndrome" that continue to keep vulnerable individuals from disclosing the harms done to them, relatively powerful social actors have consistently had the capacity to discredit and silence the memories of those in the margins. Individuals with intellectual disabilities may be especially vulnerable to such discrediting strategies precisely because they are so devalued and stigmatized. For example, researchers have argued that individuals with intellectual disabilities are especially prone to persuasion by researchers and therapists, particularly when claims of abuse have been involved.[38] Finally, some have argued that this susceptibility to influence has led to false accusations simply to please interviewers and investigative workers.[39] In many ways, these "discrediting" claims are as dangerous to the construction of an emancipatory disability history as are the obstructionist actions encountered in the Michener history project. Thus, despite possible methodological and ethical disadvantages, I have opted to include multiple, triangulated data sources as a pre-emptive strategy; these methods will hopefully preclude any possibility of powerful and interested parties discrediting the Michener survivors' oral histories. Nonetheless, on a personal level, I remain ambivalent about this choice; while the inclusion of alternate sources will hopefully pre-empt delegitimation by those who might be interested enough to discredit the survivors' stories, the politics of this inclusion stand in contradiction to the emancipatory goals of the original project.

DISCUSSION

In the end, the memories accessed in this oral history project have been highly constrained: I have only been able to reach people who are articulate enough, and free enough, that they can engage in the research process without the barriers of "protection" by their legal guardians. I have only been able to see the hallways and exteriors of the buildings where the survivors lived. I have only been able to view a fraction of the archival materials, and this is because a sympathetic woman in the provincial archives saw the importance of accessing the institution's hidden memories, and began working with me in creative and accommodating ways.

Nonetheless, despite all these barriers, it is undeniable that twenty-one interviews with institutional survivors, several hundred pages of archival material, and several interviews with ex-workers from Michener Centre have tapped into a rich vein of silenced and delegitimated memories. These materials contain the promise of constructing a new, emancipatory set of memories relating to institutionalization, allowing us to understand that the official memory of the Michener Centre is not the only version available. By way of example, Michener survivors' stories have provided us with rich materials with which to understand how social control operated within the institution, with particular reference to disciplinary practices in time-out or "quiet" rooms.[40] In the survivors' accounts, a picture emerges of brutality and humiliation, rather than the accounts of controlled behavioural management protocols that might be offered in traditional clinical and institutional accounts. Instead, survivors' stories allow us to see that a central purpose of the time-out rooms at Michener Centre was the intimidation of all inmates and the construction of divisions between inmates who avoided punishment and those who were "foolish" enough to "invite" it. In the data provided by survivors, then, we can see multiple and nuanced ways of exercising power and control, in ways that dominant historical accounts would never permit.

Thus, survivor narratives allow us to understand that although the institutionalization of people with disabilities may have seemed like benign paternalism and well-intentioned, if faulty, social engineering from the outside, the practices of the Centre instead led to systematic deprivation, isolation, violent and dehumanizing treatment, and willful exploitation for those who were unfortunate enough to find themselves on the inside. Further, it seems almost certain that making these survivor narratives public holds the potential to not only rewrite the history of the institution, but also to change the ways that people think and act concerning institutionalization. We can make these speculations in part because of the tenacity with which the powers that be have struggled to "protect" their own versions of the past; if survivors' memories had no such potential, then those in authority would not be working so hard to silence them.

Finally, in light of the research and discourse on acquiescence and the skepticism that has been levelled against the claims of individuals with intellectual disabilities, it is important to consider the relative social value of these two groups. Individuals with intellectual disabilities, because of their social positions and their economic, cultural, and social capital, are vulnerable to discrediting. Conversely, those who enjoy economic, social, cultural, and intellectual dominance have been able to tell their own histories, to obstruct the telling of marginal memories, and to be relatively immune to both scrutiny and discrediting. While there has been considerable speculation on the motives of vulnerable individuals and on the veracity of their narratives, there has been virtually no discussion of the "false memory syndromes" of the powerful institutions and social actors who seek to prevent marginalized histories from becoming known. Most certainly, it is time for such a discussion to begin.

NOTES

1 Public Affairs Officer, Roland Michener Recreation Centre. "Michener Centre: A History, 1923–1983" (Edmonton: Government Publications, 1985), 31. (In the following cited as "Michener Centre.")

2 Jana Grekul, Harvey Krahn, and Dave Odynak, "Sterilizing the 'Feeble-minded': Eugenics in Alberta, Canada, 1929–1972," *Journal of Historical Sociology* 17, no. 4 (2004): 359.

3 Claudia Malacrida, *A Special Hell: Institutional Life in Alberta's Eugenic Years* (Toronto: University of Toronto Press, 2015).

4 Edward Tiriyakian, "Reflections on the Dialectic of Memory and History" (paper presented at "Memories in Action: The Role of Memories in Social Change," the International Sociological Association Interim Conference. WG 03: *The Body in the Social Sciences*, Rome, Italy, 2005).

5 Diane Hafner, "The Past in the Present: Lamalama Relationship to Memory and the Old People" (paper presented at the International Sociological Association Interim Conference. WG 03: *The Body in the Social Sciences*, Rome, Italy, 2005).

6 Although the general descriptor for inmates was "mental deficiency," in fact there were six possible classifications for admission to the institute at this

time: a child could be admitted on the grounds of being an idiot, an imbecile, a moron, constitutionally inferior, psychopathic, or "mentally deficient and psychopathic" ("Michener Centre," 1985).

7 "Michener Centre," 1.

8 In Canada, the term "developmentally disabled" is used to describe individuals with intellectual challenges, while in the United Kingdom, "learning disabled" is more typically used.

9 See, for example: Nicole Rafter, *Creating Born Criminals* (Urbana: University of Illinois Press, 1997); Angus McLaren, "The Creation of a Haven for 'Human Thoroughbreds': The Sterilization of the Feeble-Minded and the Mentally Ill in British Columbia," *Canadian Historical Review* 67, no. 2 (1986): 127–50; and Daniel J. Kevles, *In the Name of Eugenics: Genetics and the Uses of Human Heredity*, 3rd edition (Cambridge: Harvard University Press, 1995).

10 "Michener Centre," 10.

11 Angus McLaren, *Our Own Master Race: Eugenics in Canada, 1885–1945* (Toronto: McLelland & Stewart, 1990).

12 Deborah C. Park and John P. Radford, "From the Case Files: Reconstructing a History of Involuntary Sterilisation," *Disability & Society* 13, no. 3 (1998): 317–42.

13 Bill No. 45 of 1937 *An Act to Amend the Sexual Sterilization Act*, 3rd sess., 8th Alberta Legislature, 1937. Retrieved from "Our Future, Our Past: The Alberta Heritage Digitization Project," http://www.ourfutureourpast.ca/law/page.aspx?id=29806387 (accessed 24 June 2014).

14 McLaren, *Our Own Master Race*.

15 "Michener Centre," 19.

16 The official history of the Michener Centre refers to individuals who live or have lived in the Institution as "residents" or as "trainees"; however, given the carceral qualities of the institution and its relative dearth of educational focus, "inmate" more accurately describes the status of these people within the institution.

17 Alberta Alliance on Mental Illness and Mental Health, "Good People ... Good Practices ... No System: A Discussion Paper," (Edmonton: AAMIMH, February 2000) http://aamimh.ca/Portals/aamimh/Public/goodpeople.pdf (accessed June 23, 2014).

18 "Michener Centre," 21.

19 From the available archival records, it appears that, during 1973 alone, two individuals drowned, and one person died of hypothermia while attempting to escape.

20 Anonymous, *Letter Re: Elopement of x.* (2 June 1973). Government of Alberta Public Archives, Accession GR1990.0212, Box 4a. Red Deer.

21 Claudia Malacrida, "Bodily Practices as Vehicles for Dehumanization in an Institution for 'Mental Defectives,'" in "Embodied Action, Embodied

Theory: Understanding the Body in Society," edited by Claudia Malacrida, special issue, *Societies* 2, no. 4 (2012): 286–301.

22 Jurate A. Sakalys, "The Political Role of Illness Narratives," *Journal of Advanced Nursing*, 31, no. 6 (2000): 1469–75. Also, Arthur W. Frank, "Why Study Peoples' Stories? The Dialogical Ethics of Narrative Analysis," *International Journal of Qualitative Methods* 1, no. 1 (2002): 1–9.

23 See, for example, Arthur Kleinman, *The Illness Narratives: Suffering, Healing and the Human Condition* (New York: Basic Books, 1988); Kathy Charmaz, "'Discovering' Chronic Illness: Using Grounded Theory," *Social Science & Medicine* 30, no. 11 (1990): 1161–72; and Martha Balshem, *Cancer in the Community: Class and Medical Authority* (Washington and London: The Smithsonian Institution Press, 1993).

24 Sakalys, "The Political Role of Illness Narratives," 1474.

25 Balshem, *Cancer in the Community*, 142.

26 Mr Skoreyko is one of the initiators of the project. He has been the vice-president of the Alberta Leadership Today Society and a prominent member of the Alberta chapter of People First. He asked that his real name be used.

27 Susan Wendell, *The Rejected Body: Feminist Philosophical Reflections on Disability* (New York and London: Routledge, 1996), 31.

28 See, for example: Ian Dowbiggin, "Keeping This Young Country Sane: C.K. Clarke, Immigration Restriction, and Canadian Psychiatry, 1890–1925," *The Canadian Historical Review* 76, no. 4 (1995): 598–627; Stefan Kuhl, *The Nazi Connection: Eugenics, American Racism, and German National Socialism* (New York: Oxford University Press, 1994); Park and Radford, "From the Case Files"; John P. Radford "Eugenics and the Asylum," *Journal of Historical Sociology* 7, no. 4 (1994): 462–73; and McLaren, "The Creation of a Haven for 'Human Thoroughbreds.'"

29 Government of Alberta, "Alberta Human Services," Office of the Public Guardian: Information, http://www.seniors.gov.ab.ca/services_resources/opg/index.asp (accessed 23 June 2014).

30 In 2013 the Alberta government announced its intention to remove 125 residents from Michener, with the goal of closing the institution. In early 2015, protests by unionized workers and community members led Jim Prentice, the provincial premier, to announce his government's decision to keep Michener open.

31 Grekul, Krahn, and Odynak, "Sterilizing the 'Feeble-minded,'" 380.

32 Judy Mason, Manager, Planning and Communication, Michener Centre, 30 August 1999.

33 Michener Board, "Michener Board Minutes," 2001.

34 In 2003 a fire in the main building of Michener Centre caused enormous destruction of these historical materials. From a more recent discussion with the new executive director of Michener Centre, I understand that these

water-soaked materials have been saved, in freezers, in hopes that someday they can be retrieved for historical use.

35 Province of Alberta, *Freedom of Information and Protection of Privacy Act, Revised Statues of Alberta 2000* (Edmonton: Alberta Queen's Printer, 2013), Section 2a, p. 11.

36 Dan Goodley, "Tales of Hidden Lives: A Critical Examination of Life History Research with People who have Learning Difficulties," *Disability & Society* 11, no. 3 (1996): 333–48.

37 Elizabeth Bredberg, "Writing Disability History: Problems, Perspectives and Sources," *Disability & Society* 14, no. 2 (1999): 189–201.

38 Lynn Ahlgrim-Delzell and James R. Dudley, "Confirmed, Unconfirmed, and False Allegations of Abuse made by Adults with Mental Retardation who are Members of a Class Action Lawsuit," *Child Abuse & Neglect* 25 (2001): 1121–32. Finlay and Lyons also acknowledge that the open-ended methods of oral histories are likely less prone to "acquiescence" than positivist, fixed-response interviews. W.M.L. Finlay and E. Lyons, "Acquiescence in Interviews with People Who Have Mental Retardation," *Mental Retardation* 1 (2002): 25.

39 Ahlgrim-Delzell and Dudley, "Confirmed, Unconfirmed, and False Allegations," 1127; Max Scharnberg, "Frailty, Thy Name Is Memory: An Inverse Witch Trial in Denmark," *IPT Journal* 8 (1996): 10.

40 Claudia Malacrida, "Discipline and Dehumanization in a Total Institution: Institutional Survivors' Descriptions of Time-out Rooms," *Disability & Society* 20, no. 5 (2005): 523–37, 525.

16

"Don't Speak for Me": Practising Oral History amid the Legacies of Conflict[1]

Joy Parr

How should oral historians retune our practice when we are conducting research amid the legacies of conflict? Guided by what anthropologists and oral history practitioners have written about their fieldwork, I have been reflecting on the issues involved in collecting and presenting the testimonies of participants and witnesses whose lives were shaped by such legacies. My own historical research engaged these questions, sometimes in unexpected ways. I work now as a health geographer among residents unsettled by environmental change and the uncertain aftermath of industrial activity. I began as a historical researcher learning of and from the child immigrants who came to Canada between 1868 and 1924 to work as agricultural labourers and domestic servants.[2] I listened to them and followed the rich and rare paper trail of letters and case records left in the files of the state and philanthropic institutions that had sponsored their migration. I knew elders who had come to Canada as Home Children when they were my neighbours in rural Ontario. However I only established relationships with them as human subjects after we met in Britain, when they were visiting the British orphanages in search of home and I was reading the case records documenting their displacement. From the start of my work as an oral historian, I was interviewing people carrying a considerable legacy of pain, labouring under burdens of barely suppressed and thoroughly repressed memories. This point of departure gave a distinctive turn to how I weighed my responsibilities to the profession and to those who helped me, as well as to how I framed my pedagogy as a graduate teacher.[3]

Lately, I have published *Sensing Changes: Technologies, Environments, and the Everyday, 1953–2003*, a book founded in six case studies; five rely upon oral histories, my own and from public repositories.[4] Our colleague, John Milloy, a Trent University historian of Canada's aboriginal peoples, writes that on ethical grounds he did not seek out oral histories for his research on Indian residential schools.[5] Ten years ago, amid the water contamination in Walkerton, Ontario, I too chose, on ethical grounds, to work from the documentary detritus alone, a decision I still do not regret.

Donna Haraway, in her "scholarly comedy,"[6] invokes the modest witness, a creature whose genesis dates from the Scientific Revolution, as testifier "to matters of fact."[7] "S/he is about telling the truth, giving reliable testimony, guaranteeing important things – while eschewing the addictive narcotic of transcendental foundations." To render accounts that mirror reality, this kind of witness must be invisible, the modern, "legitimate and authorised ventriloquist ... adding nothing from his mere opinions, from his biasing embodiment ... inhabiting the culture of no culture." Haraway criticizes the use of this pretense of modesty as a trick to distinguish the modest witness from the curious gawker, whose authority is authenticated by the naked, "unadorned [and] factual" qualities of her or his rhetoric. The account that results from this kind of unengaged witnessing "ceases magically to have the status of representation and emerges simply as the fact of the matter."[8]

At once tacit and beyond reproach, the modest witness guides the research practice of the scientists and medical professionals with whom we work, and through the Tri-Council Policy Statement inflects our own practice by informing our relationships with the Research Ethics Board in some of our universities. Traces of deference to the proper comportment of the modest witness are abundant in the methodological literature of oral history as we seek to be known as delivering "the fact of the matter." Edward Said, channelling Vico, notes how this "rhetoric of intellectual disinterestedness" serves political ends and demeans the people we study.[9] We live in times when our practice is suspect. For example, a review recently characterized an eminent biographer as "far more sympathiser and intellectual co-dependent than an even mildly neutral oral historian."[10] We have taken refuge in methodology, hoping that a thick barrier of safeguards will protect us from what Johannes Fabian identifies as charges of "intellectual distortion, historical contingency and the lure of special interests."[11] Such preoccupations with the techniques of knowledge procurement, arising from our need to defend our practices, will not treat the epistemological challenges inherent in communication between those who know and we who wish to know, upon which our work depends. They but re-represent as objective the very inter-subjectivities that we should be pursuing as analytical challenges.

Paula Hamilton and Linda Shopes, among our leading theorists and practitioners, worry that oral historians have adopted an approach that "too often fetishizes the interview process," a practice that can occlude "the social and cultural processes that have shaped subjectivity." They argue that oral history must be more than "an archival activity," that it is necessarily "a deeply social practice connecting past and present."[12] Valerie Yow parsed the way through "Ethics and Interpersonal Relationships in Oral History Research" by acknowledging that we as oral historians enter domestic spaces and workplaces "as collectors and preservers of accounts of human experience for generations to come" and recognizing that narrators' "evasiveness and omissions" can "destroy the credibility of the history we write, rendering it useless as a contribution to understanding the historical phenomenon under scrutiny." Yow concedes that "in an ongoing project the researcher wants to get something from the narrator to further a purpose outside the relationship" and serves as "a facilitator for the revelation of information of historical significance," while simultaneously in a relationship of trust with the individual narrator. She finds her resolution in the fiduciary relationship that binds narrator and historian in trust "for a full, honest testimony."[13]

Shopes observes: "collaboration is a responsible, challenging and deeply humane ideal for some oral history work, but in certain kinds of projects, beyond a basic respect for the dignity of all persons, it seems not an appropriate goal."[14] She shares the concerns of a colleague, reflecting upon her work with women of the Ku Klux Klan. Kathleen Blee suggests that such an invocation of trust "reflects implicit romantic assumptions about the subjects of history from the bottom up that are difficult to defend when studying ordinary people who are active in the politics of intolerance, bigotry or hatred."[15]

One resolution Shopes offers is to narrow the frame of the research designs for oral history projects, to organize the task around a historical problem rather than a series of life-history interviews, and to define the universe of narrators broadly, persistently asking ourselves, "whom am I missing?" Her interviews thus reflect and reveal more broadly and deeply "both the internal complexity of the community under study and its relationship to a broader historical process." Within this more closely specified compass, she counsels courage: "approach interviews in a spirit of critical inquiry ... asking the hard questions that may cause discomfort, that address difficult or controversial topics, that may reveal ruptures in the community." "Oral history," she insists, "is long haul work ... It requires a commitment of years" to weather "complicated and at times contentious ... negotiation, give-and-take."[16]

Conducted from this stance, oral history is like ethnography. We cannot appease the modest witness. We are seeking not objectivity but a highly disciplined subjectivity. As Nancy Scheper-Hughes concludes, reflecting upon a long, controversial and distinguished career in ethnography, the question of "losing one's objectivity in the field is really quite beside the point. Our project is centrally about translation and, like any form of translation, has both a predatory and a writerly motive." As a student of Ireland, she turns for guidance to the insights of the Nobel Laureate poet Seamus Heaney. Translation, Heaney asserts, harkening to analogies from Irish history, can be like a Viking raid yielding imitations as a form of booty; or it can be a process of settlement. "In settling in with the work," Heaney advises, "you stay with it a long time, identify with it in an imaginative way: you change it and it changes you."[17]

For oral historians, this advice speaks to Shopes's judgment, which in our current conjuncture is of considerable moment: "It is a mistake to rely solely on visually skimming or electronically searching transcripts for a sense of what interviews contain or for specific information and useful quotes."[18] The use of digital indexing packages to facilitate such skimming may be a cutting-edge technical version of what in the past could have merited condemnation as source mining.

Some anthropologists have gone down a similar path. For them this practice has meant "working as overseers of large teams of assistants on big research projects." This practice, as Ruth Behar, a Jewish, Cuban, and American ethnographer, and other naysayers among the ethnographers contend, tends "to depersonalise one's connection to the field, to treat ethnographic work (only a small part of which is done personally by the principal investigator) as that which is 'other' to the 'self' and to accumulate masses of data that can be compared, contrasted, charted, and serve as a basis for policy recommendations, or at least as a critique of existing practices." Working with large digitized databases can be a refuge from charges of immodesty, a convincing attempt to defend against accusations of engagement unseemly for scholars. Some anthropologists have, instead, found safe havens from these threats in the "starkly unpeopled" terrain of high theory. Others "have retreated to history, to the quiet of the archives and the study of the past, where presumably an observer can do less damage, not have to be quite so disturbingly present."[19] This resort will not work for us as oral historians; we have already been there, done that. Anthropologists may respond that my argument merely has brought us back to where they were when James Clifford published his classic essay "On Ethnographic Authority," twenty-seven years ago.[20] I can only respond that this is where we oral historians find ourselves, and our question must be: what should we do now? What can we learn from ethnographers' struggles with engagement? How are we appropriately to be present in that portion of our practice among participants and witnesses who come forward and engage us, for these may be people who both know what they would tell and know what they would have us tell.

Clifford's question was: "How, precisely, is a garrulous, over-determined cross-cultural encounter shot through with power relations and personal cross purposes circumscribed as an adequate version of a more-or-less discrete 'other world,' composed by an individual author?"[21] Shopes's advice to us about specifying more closely our research questions while broadening our universe of narrators can make this challenge less daunting. Yet the issues that Ivan Karp and Martha Kendall highlight in their classic essay "Reflexivity in Field Work" remain. Field workers must be fair to the society they study and conform to the standards of their academic colleagues. This is a "profoundly alienated" mode of existence, which some anthropologists judge makes the greatest of their tribe both the "freest" and "the most troubled of the social scientists."[22] In *The Vulnerable Observer*, Ruth Behar, who amid these conflicting obligations distrusted her own authority, found the stance "constantly in question, constantly on the point of breaking down."[23] Many ethnographers of the next generation follow the counsel of Philippe Bourgois "to venture into the 'real world' not just to 'interview' people but to actually participate in their daily life and to partake of their social and cultural reality."[24] For them listening entails a "compassionate pact," a "contract of testimony." Anthropologists who follow this practice now tend to refer to themselves as "engaged observers," bound by a joint responsibility to both voice and listen civilly but critically while not eschewing the hard questions.[25] Such a concern with "retooling the interpersonal politics of research," Kay Warren affirms, involves "an engagement with local agendas" and the "more interactive process subject to long-term negotiation, reciprocities and collaboration," which Shopes has advocated.[26] Engagement twinned with confrontation and hard questioning – this is surely a lonely and alienating route to commit to in fieldwork.

Ronald Grele and Alessandro Portelli offered us guidance along this path early on. By 1975, Grele had grown troubled by the irenic, unquestioning stance that oral historians had adopted as collectors from the community chroniclers who preceded them. He declared forthrightly that this sad condition had "resulted in a situation of endless activity without goal or meaning," in "movement without aim ... [and that] oral history interviews are constructed, for better or for worse, by the active intervention of the historian." We initiate the conversation and we can understand the narratives that emerge by attending to (in the senses both of "tending to" and "paying attention to") the relationships embedded there. Grele notes three kinds of relationships: (1) in the narratives' "linguistic, grammatical and literary structure"; (2) in the interaction of the interviewer and the interviewee, a process more akin to a performance than "a literary product created alone and as a result of reflective action," and which "cannot be divorced from the circumstances of its creation, which is one of audience participation and face to face confrontation"; and (3) the relationships among the speaker, her own historical consciousness, and the interviewer, whose "cultural vision and cognitive structure" is the gateway through which readers and listeners have access to the narrator's world.[27] These relationships bind the historian in both the creation and the analysis of the narratives.

If we are privy only to the digitized transcripts produced from interviews, not the processes and context that informed their making, how will we make good use of the information accumulating in digital archives? When any witness is interviewed, we have an obligation to those to whom we listen to proceed deliberately, prudently, and with all due care not to leave the memoryscape littered carelessly. How will these relationships with participants, which must crucially inform our analytical work, weather the profound transition to a different information technology, an excising transition which in the knowledge culture of our time is "both tacit and beyond reproach"?

Portelli candidly acknowledges that his fieldwork is "a form of political intervention, because it encourages an effort at self-awareness, growth, and change for all those involved ... unlike hard data or archives."[28] As political work, he contends, "the interview implicitly enhances the authority and self-awareness of the narrator, and may raise questions about aspects of experience that the speaker has never spoken or even seriously thought about."[29] "Because people will not talk to you unless you talk to them, will not reveal themselves unless you reveal yourself," the oral historian must be an engaged interlocutor.[30] Portelli rejects the "view of political militancy as the annihilation of all subjective roles" for its ironic similarity to traditional historians' non-involved posture, the view from the Archimedes point, and Haraway's modest witness. He calls the ethnologists' "compassionate pact," the "contract of testimony" entailed by listening, an "assumption of responsibility" such that, as the work proceeds, "the historian becomes less and less a 'go-between' from the working-class to the reader, and more and more a protagonist."[31] In Portelli's protean and powerful "There's Gonna Always Be a Line," his informant, Mrs Cowens, the great-granddaughter of slaves, carried across the generations a burden of history which marked them both: "I don't trust you, you know ... So I was raised; my grandmother always told us I don't care what nobody say, I don't care how good they look, how good they talk, you gonna always be black. There's gonna always be a line." That line marked him, a European intellectual, and it registered the distance and difference between him and his African American interlocutor. I first heard this assertion, in a recruiting meeting for the Canadian Institute for Academic Research, from a First Nations physician raised in Toronto's Regent Park who had referenced his father's influence on his own life choices. Addressing me directly across the table, he said, "Don't speak for me." I did not doubt him, but I did not know I had. I have since learned that this sort of intervention is a common way in which settler Canadians learn of the line from First Nations colleagues and narrators. As Portelli notes, such civil and generous gestures at once affirm the line and speak across it.[32]

Let us define vulnerable narrators as those who agree to speak with us not knowing what they will tell. Dori Laub, a Holocaust survivor and psychiatrist, writes of these narrators as initially "testifying to an absence," "a known event" that the narrator experienced but had not fully integrated into his or her consciousness, so that the listener is "the blank screen on which the event comes to be inscribed for the first time." The listener does not become the witness but, as witness to the witness, is the enabler of the testimony. Witnesses, like good campers, must avoid leaving litter behind, be both "unobtrusive, non-directive, and yet ... present, active, in the lead." What does speaking across the line do to them or for them? What does it do to us and for us? How is this listening, and its compact of testimony, different?

Laub spelled out these "Hazards of Listening" in his advice to interviewers for the Yale Holocaust Archive.[33] These risks have troubled me, as they have other oral historians. Minimally, this process creates a "juxtaposition of stories" that is "not a historical narrative, and that, in some sense ... annuls historical narrative."[34] In Europe, Central America, and Latin America "producing testimony has become a crucial therapeutic tool"; but Behar describes the undercurrent of this predation, this participant-observation, as oxymoronic: "when the grant money runs out ... go back to your desk, write down what you saw and heard. Relate it to something you've read by Marx, Weber, Gramsci, or Geertz and you're on your way to doing anthropology" and oral history.[35] Or not.

Victoria Sanford, who works in sites of violence in Central America, notes that "survivors come forward to give testimonies not only to denounce a violent past but also to claim a future of peace."[36] Is our compact to cross the line to be "a passage through difference, or the Broken Promise"?[37] When "something powerful is at stake," are there reasons and ways to practise amid "actually existing social suffering," to respond to narrators' needs?[38] Liisa Malkki, who works in Rwanda and Burundi, counsels us to adopt "a caring form of vigilance,"[39] to simply listen without pretensions to being authenticating experts, investigators, or inquisitors who ask hard questions.[40] Is it possible through "a practical politics of solidarity" to be present merely, simply, circumspectly as an enabler of the testimony, in times and places where the "everyday is a state of emergency"?[41]

In "On Suffering and Structural Violence," Paul Farmer, a physician and theologian whose practice has been divided between the Harvard Medical School and the highlands of Haiti, draws a distinction between "explaining" and "making sense of suffering": "Certain kinds of suffering are readily observable ... the suffering of individuals whose lives and struggles recall our own tends to move us; the suffering of those who are distanced, whether by geography, gender, 'race' or culture, is sometimes less affecting." And further: "Structural violence all too often defeats those who would describe it" because it is "'exoticised' as 'lurid'"; because its sheer weight makes it "more difficult to render." Facts and figures objectify the sufferers, render them anonymous, without "voice, let alone rights, in history." Case studies "reveal suffering ... but to explain suffering one must embed individual biography in the larger matrix of culture, history and political economy." Farmer contends that we must create "more fine-grained and systematic analyses of power and privilege in discussions of who is likely to suffer and in what ways."[42] Here I borrow and recast Behar's self-depiction in *The Vulnerable Observer*.[43] Oral history, like ethnography, is a: "voyage through a long tunnel ... troubled by the insight that is always arriving late, as defiant hindsight, a sense of the utter uselessness of writing anything and yet the burning desire to write something ... At the end of the voyage, if you are lucky, you catch a glimpse of a lighthouse, and you are grateful.[44] Emerging from such a long tunnel, can a historian "act morally as a memory critic," asking the hard questions? In such a conjuncture, is the modest witness due deference? Or, alternatively, should we listen "without looking for what [we] know is not to be found?"[45]

In "Poetics and the Politics of Witnessing," Jacques Derrida insists on this "fact of the matter": that those who are in the presence of witnesses, which is the most we can claim as oral historians, are but "third persons," the "addressees of the testimony." The witness affirms:

> rightly or wrongly ... that was or is present to me, in space and time (thus sense-perceptible), and though you do not have access to it, you, my addressees, *you have to believe me* ... [A] historian does not seriously, as a scholar, ask me to *believe* him or her. Bearing witness is not through and through and necessarily discursive. It is sometimes silent. It has to engage something of the body, which has no right to speak. With this attestation, there is no other choice but to *believe* it or *not believe* it. Verification or transformation into proof, contestation in the name of "knowledge," belong to a foreign space ... no one *can*, which is to say, no one *must*, no one *ought* bear witness for the witness, replace the witness, defend the witness ... one *must* not bear witness *for* the witness. The judge, the arbiter, the historian also remains a witness of a witness.[46]

"Don't speak for me." Like Seamus Heaney, "you stay with it a long time, identify with it in an imaginative way: you change it and it changes you." Still, that which is "sense perceptible" to the witness alone eludes us. As fieldworkers, we may be lonely, alienated, and alone, but among those who come to us from vulnerable populations we are but witnesses to the "essential solitude of the witness." In this authority, we cannot and must not claim to share.

NOTES

1 This chapter initially was presented as a Keynote Address to the 89th Annual General Meeting of the Canadian Historical Association/La Société historique du Canada, Concordia University, Montreal, 31 May 2010. My heartfelt thanks to Grey Osterud, a former American editor of *Gender and History* and a resilient and reflective fieldworker in oral history. Her freelance editorial work transformed this writing from plenary entertainment to scholarly chapter when the task confounded me. I recommend her scholarly writing on the rural women of nineteenth- and more recently twentieth-century New York.

2 Joy Parr, *Labouring Children: British Immigrant Apprentices to Canada* (Montreal and Kingston: McGill-Queen's University Press, 1980); revised edition (Toronto: University of Toronto Press, 1994).

3 I infer, from their early theoretical and methodological writing on oral history, that at least two of my former students (who may reject the inference) subsequently had to bridge the distance bequeathed by this unconventional formation. See chapter 3 by Nancy Janovicek and chapter 10 by Alexander Freund in this *Reader*.

4 Joy Parr, *Sensing Changes: Technologies, Environments, and the Everyday, 1953–2003* (Vancouver and Toronto: UBC Press, 2010).

5 John Milloy, *A National Crime: The Canadian Government and the Residential School System, 1879–1986* (Winnipeg: University of Manitoba Press, 1999). Milloy is professor of history at Trent University. His speciality is the study of aboriginal Canadian history. In January 2010, he was appointed Director of Research, Historical Records and Report Preparation, for the Truth and Reconciliation Commission of Canada and since July 2010 has continued as Special Advisor on Research to Justice Murray Sinclair, chair of the Commission.

6 Donna Haraway, *Modest_Witness@Second_Millennium.FemaleMan©_ Meets_OncoMouse™: Feminism and Technoscience* (New York: Routledge, 1997).

7 Ibid., 15.

8 Ibid., 22–6, 33.

9 Michael Herzfeld, *Anthropology Through the Looking Glass: Critical Ethnography in the Margins of Europe* (Cambridge and New York: Cambridge University Press, 1987), 189; Giambattista Vico, *New Science of Giambattista Vico*, translated by Thomas Goddard Bergin and Max Harold Fisch (Ithaca: Cornell University Press, 1968); and Edward W. Said, *Covering Islam: How the Media and the Experts Determine How We See the Rest of the World* (New York: Vintage, 1987), 127–31.

10 Roger Morris, "Clinton: The paths not taken: Taylor Branch is far more sympathiser and intellectual co-dependent than an even mildly neutral oral historian," *Globe and Mail*, 21 November 2009, F11.

11 Johannes Fabian, *Anthropology with an Attitude: Critical Essays* (Stanford, CA: Stanford University Press, 2001), 13, 18, 19.

12 Paula Hamilton and Linda Shopes, *Oral History and Public Memories* (Philadelphia: Temple University Press, 2008), ix, viii.

13 Valerie Yow, "Ethics and Interpersonal Relationships in Oral History Research," *Oral History Review* 22, no. 1 (summer 1995): 51–2, 57–8, 65.

14 Linda Shopes, "Sharing Authority," *Oral History Review* 30, no. 1 (2003): 109.

15 Kathleen M. Blee, "Evidence, Empathy, and Ethics: Lessons from Oral Histories of the Klan," *Journal of American History* 80, no. 2 (September 1993): 597.

16 Linda Shopes, "Oral History and the Study of Communities: Problems, Paradoxes, and Possibilities," *Journal of American History* 89, no. 2 (September 2002): 596, 597.

17 Nancy Scheper-Hughes, *Saints, Scholars, and Schizophrenics: Mental Illness in Rural Ireland* (Berkeley: University of California Press, 1991), 318–19.

18 Shopes, "Oral History and the Study of Communities," 592.

19 Ruth Behar, *The Vulnerable Observer: Anthropology that Breaks Your Heart* (Boston: Beacon Press, 1996), 25.

20 James Clifford, "On Ethnographic Authority," *Representations* 2 (spring 1983): 118–46.

21 Ibid., 120.

22 Ivan Karp and Martha B Kendall, "Reflexivity in Field Work," in *Explaining Human Behaviour: Consciousness, Human Action, and Social Structure*, edited by Paul F. Secord (Beverly Hills: Sage Publications, 1982), 269, 270.

23 Behar, *Vulnerable Observer*, 21.

24 Philippe Bourgois, "Confronting Anthropological Ethics: Ethnographic Lessons from Central America," *Journal of Peace Research* 27, no. 1 (1990): 45; and Philippe Bourgois, "Ethnography's Troubles and the Reproduction of Academic Habitus," *Qualitative Studies in Education* 15, no. 4 (2002): 417–20.

25 Asale Angel-Ajani, "Expert Witness: Notes toward Revisiting the Politics of Listening," in *Engaged Observer: Anthropology, Advocacy and Activism*, edited by Victoria Sanford and Asale Angel-Ajani (New Brunswick, NJ: Rutgers University Press, 2006), 87.

26 Kay Warren, "Perils and Promises of Engaged Anthropology: Historical Transitions and Ethnographic Dilemmas," in *Engaged Observer*, edited by Sanford and Angel-Ajani, 220.

27 Ronald J. Grele, "Movement without Aim: Methodological and Theoretical Problems in Oral History," in Ronald J. Grele, *Envelopes of Sound* (Westport, CT: Greenwood Press, 1975), 127–54. Judith Butler, *Gender Trouble: Feminism and the Subversion of Identity* (London: Routledge, 1990), *Bodies that Matter: On the Discursive Limits of "Sex"* (London: Routledge, 1993), and *Excitable Speech: Politics of Performance* (London: Routledge, 1997); Elizabeth Clark, *History, Theory, Text: Historians and the Linguistic Turn* (Cambridge, MA: Harvard University Press, 2004); and Renate Holub, *Antonio Gramsci: Beyond Marxism and Postmodernism* (London: Routledge, 1992).

28 Alessandro Portelli, "Memory and Resistance," in Alessandro Portelli, *The Battle of Valle Giulia: Oral History and the Art of Dialogue* (Madison: University of Wisconsin Press, 1997), 52.

29 Ibid., "Oral History as Genre," in *Battle of Valle Giulia*, 4.

30 Ibid., "Memory and Resistance," 52.

31 Ibid., "What Makes Oral History Different," in *Battle of Valle Giulia*, 57, 72–3.

32 Ibid., "There's Gonna Always Be a Line: History-Telling as Multivocal Art," in *Battle of Valle Giulia*, 37, 39.

33 Dori Laub, "Bearing Witness or the Vicissitudes of Listening," in *Testimony: Crises of Witnessing in Literature, Psychoanalysis, and History*, edited by Shoshana Felman and Dori Laub (New York: Routledge, 1992), 57–8, 80, 71–3.

34 Annette Wieviorka, *The Era of the Witness* (Ithaca: Cornell University Press, 2006), 144, 110.

35 Behar, *Vulnerable Observer*, 27, 5.

36 Victoria Sanford, "Excavations of the Heart: Reflections on Truth, Memory, and Structures of Understanding," in *Engaged Observer*, edited by Sanford and Angel-Ajani, 37.

37 Dori Laub, "An Event Without a Witness: Truth, Testimony and Survival," in *Testimony*, edited by Felman and Laub, 88.

38 Bourgois, "Ethnography's Troubles," 419.

39 Liisa H. Malkki, "News and Culture: Transitory Phenomena and the Fieldwork Tradition," in *Anthropological Locations: Boundaries and Grounds of a Field Science*, edited by Akhil Gupta and James Ferguson (Berkeley: University of California Press, 1997), 94–9.

40 Angel-Ajani, "Expert Witness," 82, 87.

41 Philippe Bourgois, "Foreword," in *Engaged Observer*, edited by Sanford and Angel-Ajani, xii, citing Walter Benjamin, "Critique of Violence," in *Walter Benjamin: Reflections*, edited by Peter Demetz (New York: Schocken, 1978), xi.

42 Paul Farmer, "On Suffering and Structural Violence," *Daedalus* 125 (1996): 272, 279, reprinted in Paul Farmer, *Pathologies of Power: Health, Human Rights, and the New War on the Poor* (Berkeley: University of California Press, 2003). He cites Rebecca S. Chopp, *The Praxis of Suffering: An Interpretation of Liberation and Political Theologies* (Maryknoll, NY: Orbis Books, 1986), 2.

43 Behar, *Vulnerable Observer*, 3.

44 Wieviorka, *Era of the Witness*, 131–3.

45 Ibid.

46 Jacques Derrida, "Poetics and the Politics of Witnessing" in Jacques Derrida, *Sovereignties in Question* (New York: Fordham University Press, 2005), 76–9, 82, 90–1.

Postscript

Ronald J. Grele

There was a time – I remember it well – when one could talk about national differences in the practice of oral history: the influence of archival traditions in the United States, the new social history in Great Britain, the role of ethnography in Scandinavia and folklore in Finland, the historical role of the thought and politics of Antonio Gramsci in Italy, the concern with the Nazi era in Germany, the collection of life histories in Poland and Cuba. That day has passed. As the popularity of historical interviewing and the internationalization of the practice have exploded, the world of oral history has become far more varied in terms of fieldwork, theory, and presentation, but less varied regionally. Of course what was actually going on then was much more complicated but it did seem as if these larger trends explained the world of oral history. In my memory, oral history in Canada was defined by diversity. Perhaps in no area of the world was there so much fieldwork in such a wide variety of practices. As in the United States, many projects were mounted by various governmental and private archives. There were also projects in ethnic history, social history, and what was then termed Native American studies, a field where the boundaries between oral history and oral tradition, history and anthropology, seemed to meet. As elsewhere, there were individual scholars who conducted interviews as part of the research leading to the publication of their various studies. Unique to Canada was a fruitful concern with sound and a group of fieldworkers who self-consciously described themselves as aural historians. Located for the most part in British Columbia, the home of the World Soundscape Project at Simon Fraser University established by R. Murray Schafer, aural history was a strong enough component of oral history work in Canada to induce the leaders of the national association to call it the Oral/Aural History Association. Any survey of the

348 · Ronald J. Grele

then Canadian scene would have to include the broad and long-lasting influence of the programming of the Canadian Broadcasting Corporation, which for many years broadcast personal memoirs, as well as the unique sound trilogy of Glenn Gould. In maritime Canada those who called themselves oral historians were also folklorists or very close to folklorists. And in francophone Canada, at Laval and Montreal universities, life-history sociologists were part of the broad international movement of oral historians.

The essays in this *Reader* reflect that continuing diversity. Given the rich traditions of oral history in Canada, the editors were wise to try to maintain that diversity. But it does make any judgment on the volume of essays, as a volume, difficult if not impossible. Some of our authors are concerned with fieldwork practices varying from instructions on interviewing to copyright or the more complicated issue of ethical guidelines. Many have chosen to report upon their own fieldwork and the complications engendered in the conduct of either their research or their interviews, particularly the complex relationships involved. Quite naturally several articles report on work in indigenous communities, or ethnic communities, or with Holocaust survivors or victims of genocide, while still others touch on new fields of historical inquiry and the special role that oral history plays in the development of those fields. Some essays are very local in focus, others raise universals. It is, in the words of Gerard Manley Hopkins, a "pied beauty." What, then, can we say about oral history in Canada? Even more problematic, what can an outsider say?

This variety comes to us at a time and in a form that make it possible for us to see common concerns. What is the form of our time? There is no space here to trace the complex and convoluted history behind the nature of the cultural determinants of a change that elsewhere I have described as a move from data to text. A minor key in the human sciences in the post–Second World War era of the seeming triumph of a certain view of the world, that transformation is now the unstated assumption of a concern with subjectivity, narrative, self, relational responsibility, and the relations of power inherent in the minutia of daily life. For the oral historian, much of this was recently summed up by Lynn Abrams in *Oral History Theory*. Essentially the argument is that in order to understand the particular ways in which evidence of the past is constituted and framed within the oral history interview, we must look to the construction of narrative, memory, ideas of the self, performance, and issues of empowerment as they are expressed in the dialectical relationship of interviewer and interviewee. This way of looking at evidence is the tide that explains the currents that move these essays and measures their ebb and flow. Rather than pointing to individual essays to make this point I draw your attention to the citations and footnotes mobilized by the authors. It is remarkable that so little of an earlier social science literature on interviewing and interviewing methodology shows up, while so many familiar names such as Bakhtin, Derrida, Foucault, Haraway, Butler, Behar, James, and, of course, Passerini and Portelli, as well as other old friends are scattered throughout. In some of these essays the authors do refer to work in social science disciplines but usually to work that is qualitative or textual.

Canadian oral historians are, of course, not alone. This way of referencing our work is not unique to these essays. It is clearly seen in any review of the citations in many of the articles in our leading journals. A look at the contents of the various handbooks of interviewing now on the market shows quite clearly that more traditional ways of judging interviewing in terms of representation, validity, and a more distanced and contemplative research method has been replaced in journals devoted to oral history by a much more subjectivist approach. Again, all of this is simply a small and local example of a much larger alteration in how we think about our work specifically, and history more generally. In 1985, when Arthur Danto compared his thoughts on the relationship of history and science in the introduction to *Narration and Knowledge* to his thoughts in his earlier *Analytic Philosophy of History*, he noted that whereas in his first volume his concern was the ways in which history could be thought of as a science, his second, published after Thomas Kuhn, was concerned with science as history. "There now really was a unity of science, in the sense that all science was brought under history rather than, as before, history having been brought under science." While it might be too grandiose to claim that humanists, including oral historians, are constructing a Bowditch to steer us toward a science of the subjective, it does seem that we have embarked on a journey to those shores, and a few points are raised here that might help us to refine our understanding of intersubjectivity, the deep current of most of these essays, three of which explore in some detail important aspects of the historiographical issues that emerge in oral history in light of this transformation.

This theoretical paradigm shift was accompanied in historical study, and especially oral history, by a decided alteration of focus in the wake of what came to be called "the new social history." It was only logical, given the potential of the tape recorder and the political urge for a history from below, that oral history would play a key role in this change. It is not surprising, then, that the literature on oral history as it emerged in the 1960s and 1970s was intensely concerned with the role of those whose histories, and their importance, had been ignored by professional historians: members of the working class, racial and ethnic minorities, women, and gays. In this sense oral history was to play a key role in the intellectual reorientation of the profession itself – that it was, in the words of Paul Thompson, a movement. Not only was there a transformation in the way one thought about history; there was a transformation of the object and purpose of study.

Joan Sangster encourages us to situate our "oral history praxis" in this changed context – "academic, political, and social" – which now shapes our research. The use of the term "praxis" is crucial because it directs our attention to the politics of the practice and the way those politics relate to the theoretical concerns noted above, and the intersection of that theory with the movement orientation of early oral history. With an intimate knowledge of the development of the "new" social history in Canada, she shows us complex and shifting relationships of our understandings of a more subjectivist theory, the urge to recuperate the social and cultural histories of heretofore ignored populations, and the ways in which together they served to decentre power in the historical profession. It has been clear to many of us that the move to subjectivity in oral history was very much a project of the New Left. Sangster's essay, while intensely focused on issues in Canadian history, is a wonderful example of an exploration of this connection. It has the added joy of her insights into the convoluted manner in which social history and cultural history were interwoven, the obvious example set by the work of E.P. Thompson, and into the way the patterns of that warp and weft illuminate the development of feminist historiography. In a deep structural sense we can see how we have moved, in Carol Feldman's words, from an epistemological stance (how to expand our knowledge of what happened) to a more ontological understanding (how does an understanding of who I am and how I came to be who I am find expression in the events occurring at a certain time in a certain place). In her reflections on her own work through these years Sangster sets a template for many of the essays that follow.

In a different venue Sangster, as quoted here by Kristina R. Llewellyn, warned against the "post-structuralist" tendency to accent form over context in theories of narrative that diminish the attempt to understand social (and cultural) patterns in the analysis of texts. In focusing attention on her own work reading the oral history narratives of women teachers she collected, as well as those of other feminist scholars, Llewellyn highlights issues of the definition of self, power inequities in the interview process, the problem of intersubjectivity, historical construction, and metaphor to move us beyond language to the study of "life." She reminds us once again that our mission is to see the emergence of self within a set of historically contingent vectors. For oral historians, the linguistic turn is always a matter of telling stories about event and place, since event is the metric of time while place is the metric of space. In this manner we re-contextualize the text. One might argue that this imperative in oral history is what prevents the hegemony of a postmodernist discourse to adequately describe what it is that we do.

Alexander Freund sets for himself a different problem. If indeed, our thinking about the oral history interview moves toward more collaborative understandings, then the knowledge produced derives from the meeting of the parties to the interview – from the process of that interview – a process of struggle over interpretation that begins with the initiation of the project design and continues through to the end product. He outlines for us current best practices and then notes some of the special features of the oral history: its production through recorded sound, its orality, the particularities of memory, the discussion in the here and now about the then and there, and the negotiations involved in every stage of the process. Of special interest is his discussion of his own attempts to use archived interviews produced at a time when text and its creation were not widely considered questions. How can we tease evidence of this creation from the limited record of the genesis of the archive, and from the texts in that archive? What must we know about the oral history process of that time in order to maximize our use of the archive?

Among of the most significant issues raised by many of these essays are the current complexities of the long debate, brilliantly explored by Jan Vansina, over what oral traditions can tell us about the history of a people. Three of these essays, in one way or another, continue that exploration, and the subtle problems inherent in the complex and seeming contrary literature constructed for the most part by anthropologists and historians. Brian Calliou, working the oral-history side of the street, explores in some detail the methodology of oral history interviewing in aboriginal communities, paying particular attention to the role of folk history and ethnohistory in the reconstruction of the past when the written record is sparse, and the legal and political imperatives give weight to oral histories as evidence buttressing land claims in Canadian courts.

Winona Wheeler, conscious of her situation as an academic, as a land claims researcher, and as a member of the community in which she is working, faced the challenge of "how to write the story in the voices of the Elders ... when the oral history has so many gaps." What happens when, given a history of "colonialism," of relocation and dislocation, "a community loses pieces of its collective memory"? It is in such cases that storytelling and oral traditions take on heightened importance. But, she asks, "Would not using our oral tradition storytelling forms to textually represent non-traditional (non-Indian) sources undermine or bastard-ize traditional and scholarly integrity? Would this not be an exercise in inventing tradition?" How does history become tradition and tradition become history?

There has always been a very thin line between oral tradition and oral history. That line has been made even more tenuous, and increasingly important, in Canada, in light of various court decisions, particularly *Delgamuukw* v. *British Columbia*, which have made it necessary for "the Canadian legal system to 'adapt the laws of evidence so that the Aborig-inal perspective on their practices, customs and traditions and on their relationship with the land, are given due weight by the courts'" (Calliou). These decisions have brought to the public arena questions of the rela-tions between tradition and history. The question is, how does metaphor become evidence? It is not a new question. It has been inherent in a broad range of the discussion of history and narrative over many years.

It is the question behind the elegant article by Julie Cruikshank. Openly disputing the notion that stories can be mined for the "facts," using the questions about narrative raised by Bakhtin, Walter Benjamin, and Harold Innis, a Canadian economic historian whose work is new to me, she sets a task of the examination of local metaphor and local narrative conventions to move beyond time-worn arguments about the reliability of oral history. These she identifies as: the argument that oral traditions speak to local rather than global distinctions, the positioning of oral nar-rative on the "mentalist" divide of an idealism, materialism dichotomy, and postmodern relativism.

Through a close and detailed symptomatic reading of two examples of stories told to her, whose hidden meanings were not the responses she had hoped to get from those telling the stories, she explores in, to my mind, an astonishingly careful and complex manner the not-so-hidden but often ignored deeper structure of those tales. Listening carefully to those stories and, in one case, a story about a story, Cruikshank reveals to us that the stories "aren't simply elaborate mental constructions. They are as grounded in everyday, material conditions as they are in local ideas and practices. Nor are oral traditions in any way natural products. They have social histories and they acquire meanings in the situations in which they emerge, in situations where they are used, and in interactions between narrators and listeners. They have their roots in ancient narratives but contemporary tellings emerge in settings where powerful forces impinge directly on local experience." In this way, as Jacques Atali would say, metaphor is not just a rhetorical figure but a vicarious image that we actually behold in place of a concept. Narrative structures penetrate the consciousness surrounding events much as theories penetrate observations in science. This is the way metaphor becomes evidence to the historian.

One of the most fascinating aspects of the argument is that it rests on an examination of the basic structure of a very special kind of conversation that is an oral history. Many of our authors focus their attention on the incredibly complicated and tender negotiation of the mediations involved in the relationships that emerge in the interview (conversation) between the interviewer and the interviewee, between the subject and the public, and especially between the parties to the interview and their individual and collective pasts. In some sense every interview is unique and the forms can vary enormously. Here some studies report on a one-to-one relationship, while others report on situations where third and maybe fourth parties were added to the mix on either side of the mike, bringing alternative subjectivities to the interview, sometimes moulded by generational experiences (Freund, Zembrzycki), sometimes by alternate visions of what happened in the past (Sugiman), sometimes mediated by the end product of the interview: an archive, a book, a classroom presentation, a museum exhibit (Low and Sonntag, Zembrzycki and High). In some cases the interviewers were close members of a community or shared the same experiences as those they interviewed, in some cases strangers. In all cases, however, the relationship between the differing notions of the past on the part of the interviewer/historian and the interviewee/narrator was in question. We understand the past through our study, our reading, our examination of documents; the people we talk with understand the past through experience, and while they may be able to understand the past as we do (if they do the reading), we will never understand the past as they do.

Let us look at two of the fieldwork reports. Alexander Freund set out to talk with three generations of a German-Canadian family about the Nazi past and their way of understanding and giving meaning to that history. Let us begin with the recognition, common to all oral history, and, perhaps, to all communication, that each of the participants brings his or her history to the conversation. It's like playing the old childhood game of how many people are involved in this conversation. Each person has had a conversation over the years with themselves about who they are both individually and collectively. They have had lifelong conversations with family and friends in which a social self was defined and redefined. They have had conversations with others about themselves as members of a collective, as Germans, as Canadians, as German Canadians, as women, and as members of a generation, a family, and other collective identities based upon a lifetime of social interaction. Lastly, they have had a series of conversations about how they have been placed in history and have defined themselves within the larger forces shaping their histories such as, in this case, Nazism, but also class, race, gender, etc. Each has constructed a history that is always a smorgasbord of all of those conversations, overlapping, held in tension, and contradicting one another. These conversations are an amalgam of lived lives. Within the space and time of the interview these relations of one to the other are revealed and explored, as well as their individual and collective relations with Freund, both as an individual and as a representative of another world for which their thoughts will become public knowledge. Each of our four personalities has a personality of his or her own, and it should not surprise us that each has such a different story to tell.

An essay describing a different but equally complex set of relationships in the interviewing process is Stacey Zembrzycki's report on her fieldwork as her Baba (grandmother), who was quite important in gaining her admission to members of the Ukrainian community, joined her in the actual process of interviewing. Here, our first comment must rest upon the relationship between Zembrzycki and her "Baba," then the relationships of both to the various members of the community with whom they talked – some friends of Baba, some strangers, some members of the community who shared memories and politics with Baba, some who did not. What struck my eye in this complexity is the description of how the relationship of researcher to grandmother changed in the process of the project to such an extent that Zembrycki had to limit her Baba's participation in it. I am sure that throughout the life of the project the relationships between interviewers and informants also changed in subtle and not so subtle ways, as it does in most of the long-term projects we embark upon; it reminds us once more how important the sociocultural practices behind our fieldwork are. That point is brought home by Sugiman, who discovers rather late in her project that what seemed to be a community story with a Talmudic seal was indeed a story open to disagreement and reinterpretation. In all cases the end result is a need for reconsideration of our fieldwork practice.

A number of our authors categorize these problems as questions of "shared authority." The term comes, of course, from the work of Michael Frisch and has, as Linda Shopes argues, become a mantra for discussions of fieldwork in oral history. Frisch's use of the term was, and is, a wonderful way to help us understand an important aspect of the collaboration and the "complex sources of historical interpretation" in the oral history process. As a rubric covering all of the process, however, it has its limits. Building upon methodological reservations of Shopes and Paula Hamilton, and attuned to the political point of Alessandro Portelli's marvellous essay "There's Always Gonna Be a Line," Joy Parr puts before us major reservations, especially when working with vulnerable populations. Her essay is replete with wise insights drawn from a wide range of readings in fieldwork methodology and textual analysis, and deserves to be read again and again for its richness. Our particular concern here is, in the words of Shopes, quoted by Parr, that the concern with shared authority fetishizes the interview process and draws our attention away from the ways in which people are related to their history and cultures.

My own concerns are somewhat different but I feel that they do resonate with Shopes's critique and Parr's strong reservations. I don't think that any of us would deny the affective aspect of interviewing. In some cases it is the major part of our work and its joy. It really is a lot of fun having an excuse to talk with people, and an exciting intellectual experience to speak with them about their pasts. But likewise, we can never deny that the conversation takes place because we are interested in complicating our view of that past – our special role. Before we can begin to understand the complex set of relations emerging from this project, it is necessary that we be clear in placing them within that task. My own view is that we must first begin with the product not the experience. Our task must begin with the text. How has that text been created and how do the social relations, only one set of relations involved, help us understand that text. Why do three generations of women in the same family have such widely divergent interpretations of the historical experience? Not only is this an interesting question about the cultural transmission of memory, history, and myth, but it is a clue to our next question as well. Interpretation is never-ending, but interpretation is always our starting point. One sets out to do fieldwork with a question. That question arises from an interpretation.

There is another, more practical reason to start one's analysis of the relations in the interview with the text rather than the experience; in almost all reports on the experience, we have only the testimony of the fieldworker and rarely of the storyteller. Within the text we find the partner. That is the object of our symptomatic reading, or listening. And as I have explained elsewhere (*Envelopes of Sound*) we are also interested in questions of language and ideology. We must always recognize the nature of the power relations involved in such discussions and the forms in which they are constructed with the special cultural tools available, beyond issues of rapport, to both parties to the discussion of the construction of a usable past. In that light, in order to analyze the personal relations of the interview I think we can also rely upon an already existing literature, whether it be in ethnomethodology, conversational analysis, speech communication, information theory, or some other branch of the social sciences.

What, then, can we make of shared authority? Certainly it has in many, many cases been a wonderful and insightful concept to guide us in our practice. I think we have to go back to the brilliance of Frisch's work. To begin a reread, we have to note Frisch's own understanding of what he was doing, uncovering who was the author in an oral history and asking "what does that mean for understanding how interviews can actually be a source for history as distinct from historical data?" His interest was in interpretative authority, its generation, and the method of uncovering the shared interpretation within the cultural and political dimensions of a struggle for a more democratic historical consciousness. Frisch was particularly concerned with the public dimension of oral history, perhaps its intrinsic teleology. It is noteworthy that most of the essays that follow his introduction, in which he sets out the idea of shared authority, concern public presentation and a working imaginatively back from that public presentation to uncover the struggle over interpretation and the way that struggle informs our pasts and our present. That public dimension should never be forgotten; the subtitle of the work is, after all, *Essays on The Craft and Meaning of Oral and Public History*. Parr is surely correct that shared authority is problematic as a means of understanding representation for witnessing, and for understanding the limits of language and knowledge in the effort to explain experiences such as the holocaust. As a guide for our understanding of the public exhibition of the end product of the process, however, it is a valuable tool and a constant reminder of a commitment to a more democratic practice.

This is the third dimension of this volume that I want to consider here – the public dimension. In one sense public uses of oral testimony are regulated by the legal and somewhat more contentious ethical boundaries that have been set by various regulators: copyright, here discussed by Jill Jarvis-Tonus, and the Tri-Council Policy Statement, Ethical Research

Involving Humans, the implications of which are carefully and critically discussed by Nancy Janovicek. In the first, Jarvis-Tonus quite usefully, I think, briefly compares Canadian, US, and UK law. Here I think it is also wise for us to refer again to the admission of oral histories as evidence in cases of land claims. This, I think, is a unique aspect of Canadian law. It may be that the relative newness of the Canadian Charter of Rights and Freedoms (1982) allows a flexibility to the highest court of the land to re-imagine the nature of evidence, a flexibility that would be almost impossible in other nations such as the United States, with hundreds of years of case law, but the rulings do give an added public dimension to the role of oral history in the culture. In addition, despite the reservations of many scholars about the guidelines set by the Tri-Council Policy Statement, it should be noted that the drafters avoided the distinction about the nature of scientific research contained in the guidelines for institutional review boards in the United States.

Archival practice, always predicated upon a public forum, was at one time a major impetus in oral history, especially in the interviewing of political and cultural elites. It is still a major impetus but now is increasingly endowed with a differing sense of responsibility and mission. Two essays in the *Reader* draw our attention to this process. In the mission outlined by Elise Chenier to preserve lesbian history we can clearly see the importance of the building of an archive where, for many reasons, the historical record is almost non-existent, and where members of the community set out purposely to hide their history and whatever material does survive is of an ephemeral nature. This archive is, in the words of Ann Cvetkovich, an archive of feeling. In building that archive Chenier argues that the involvement of the community is crucial. Not only will the end result of the archive be the creation of a public record but the process itself will serve to create a community.

Claudia Malacrida extends that drive for a public record to the documentation of the inner world of a public carceral agency. In this context the oral history archive being built is an act of contestation of the power to conceal and the pervasiveness of suppression inherent in such agencies, in this case the Provincial Training School (Michener Centre) in Alberta. Established to provide residential care and training of those defined as mentally defectives at a time when such a definition was infused with the ideology of eugenics, the centre was, in effect, a prison. Most of us can easily recognize the place. We all have memories of just such an institution within our own neighbourhoods. We would like to believe that they no longer exist, that the dehumanizing and oppressive daily routines that once defined such "care" are artifacts of the past. But we simply have to look closely at our modern prisons to see how that past lingers.

Oral history interviews with staff, administrators, social scientists who applied their theories to the treatments under study, and especially with people who lived through the horrors of such institutions can serve to bring into the public consciousness a powerful counter-narrative to the discourse on disability and legitimate marginal voices. Malacrida catalogues the barriers to the mounting of such projects in the face of determined efforts of powerful actors to thwart the attempt: from legal and bureaucratic hurdles, to denigration of the abilities of former inmates to speak for themselves or to interpret their experiences, to outrageous fees for permission to consult records. Given the hurdles she faced, her concluding message that it is time for a discussion to begin on the ways in which powerful institutions and social actors have prevented "marginalized histories from becoming known," brings us face to face with some of the political and social limits to the attempt to build a public archive of oral histories.

Building a public archive of oral histories can be a passive activity. While available to researchers and community, the public activities of the collection staff are frequently limited in many ways: budget, imagination, lack of staff, and institutional restrictions, among others. Issues raised by ambitious audience development are usually not as complex or as contentious as projects that have emerged in public history. In this *Reader* the most interesting and in many ways fruitful considerations arise from the remarkable work of the Centre for Oral History and Digital Storytelling at Concordia University. The Centre, in its various projects, is, to my mind without doubt, one of the most sophisticated and active public history programs in the world. The historians on the staff (both professional and community) have mobilized an ongoing program to present the results of its interviewing to a wide variety of audiences in a wide range of forms: films, art and museum exhibits, radio programming, community education projects, walks, and other venues for public testimony. The articles describing these public performances, especially the article by Stacey Zembrzycki and Steven High describing their work on the Montreal Life Stories project interviews with Holocaust survivors, allow us to make a few generalizations about what this all means.

Firstly it is clear that historical interpretation is open-ended. There is no seal on historical discourse. Public history is collaborative and involving. There is the freedom to agree to share or demur. There is an acknowledgement of difference. It is, in the words of Portelli, "an experiment in democracy." While "When I Was Your Age," is focused on survivor testimony, its collection, interpretation, and presentation, and the involvement of members of the community in almost every stage of the process calls our attention to many of the questions at the heart of oral history practice. A close reading of the essay and its particularities is, of course, its own reward but I want to take this opportunity to speculate a bit on some of the points made by the authors.

The authors ask the question, why have the people they have recorded agreed to be interviewed? The answer here is, of course, local to the project but we might all ask, why do people agree to be interviewed? Why is it, generally, so easy to secure their agreement? To be sure we have all had invitations refused, and we have all had, even worse, an agreement to be interviewed and a refusal to respond in any meaningful manner to our questions, but, for the most part responses are positive. Now, sometimes it might be to be kind to a grandchild, or to help the kids, or to right what has been a slight, to give in to pressures from companions, but there is something deeper. I really believe that people agree to be interviewed because they think history is important. While they might be speaking to us, they are involved in a larger conversation with their pasts. In culture, history seems to be a way of organizing a life, and plotting a future. Jerome Bruner has argued that "we have no other way of describing 'lived time' save in the form of a narrative." The oral history interview is a chance to tell the world our story. It is a rare opportunity.

Zembrzycki and High talk about storytelling spaces but, of course, each space has an audience, and their essay is as much about audience (telling stories) as it is about collecting stories. In some very profound manner oral history is teleological. There is always an end product in the genre, as Portelli argues. This means that there is always an audience; and more, the mode of sharing varies with audience, the setting, and the medium of the telling. In this manner the text is recontextualized. As Bronwen Low and Emmanuelle Sonntag show us in their remarkable essay, sharing has its own meaning in the world of sound – listening. Considering Jean-Luc Nancy's concept of listening, they call upon us to consider a much more active and engaged mediation between presenter and audience. We have any number of studies on the orality of oral history but usually from the speaker's position (the difference between speaking and reading, between voice and writing). What is of interest here is the view from both positions in the mutuality of listening. We are back to first principles, the converse generated by conversation.

Zembrzycki and High are at pains to tell us that they are as interested in what happened before and what happened after the violence of the Holocaust experience. The focus, they tell us, is on the life remembered, not the event as such. Linda Shopes, concerned, as is Parr, about what she calls the fetishism of the interview moment, has suggested that stressing a life history has diverted attention from the historical problem. While this is perhaps an understandable reaction, the work at Montreal shows us what we would lose. Surely there must be a limit to context, but also surely that limit need not be so narrow. If one had the time and space, other questions could be explored: private versus public memories, the new meanings that such a range of public activities and role reversals gives to questions of outsider/insider, the use of the Greenspan interview template as the first mediation in the interview process, and a range of questions for those of us dealing with vulnerable populations.

As should be evident, I am an outside commentator. The task I set for myself when I began this essay was to place this *Reader* within the context of my memories of the oral history movement in Canada, and try to give the articles a symptomatic reading in order to uncover how they represent the state of oral history at this moment. If I have succeeded it is only because the work of our authors has allowed such a reading. While I am pretty sure of most of my judgments about where these essays stand in the field, I am less sure of where they stand in Canadian historiography. But this I know: they do speak to the vibrancy of the movement.

Additional Readings in Canadian Oral History: 1980–2012

Kristina R. Llewellyn and Dana Nowak

This readings list was compiled in the fall of 2012 through the authors' extensive searches in social sciences and humanities library databases for published works in the field of oral history starting from 1980 (when the area of study experienced resurgence) and with a Canadian subject focus. Keyword searches associated with oral history were inclusive of, but not exclusive to, oral tradition, narrative, storytelling, and folklore. Some additions were made to the bibliography on the basis of the authors' knowledge of other published works. This is a partial list of Canadian oral history publications. The search methods limited the findings for chapters in edited collections and articles published in journals outside of the social sciences and humanities. An annotated version of these readings is available in Vol. 33 of *Oral History Forum d'histoire orale* at www.oralhistoryforum.ca. References for oral histories in Canada pre-1980 and for international oral history publications are available at the Canadian Oral History Association webpage www.canoha.ca. Articles published in *Oral History Forum d'histoire orale* since 1974 are accessible online at www.oralhistoryforum.ca and not listed here.

Anderson, Kim. *Life Stages and Native Women: Memory, Teachings, and Story Medicine.* Winnipeg: University of Manitoba Press, 2011.

Ashley, Susan L.T. "Negotiating Narratives of Canada: Circuit of Communication Analysis of the Next Stop Freedom Exhibition." *Journal of Canadian Studies* 45, no. 2 (2011): 182–204.

Aubé, Mary Elizabeth. "Oral History and the Remembered World: Cultural Determinants from French Canada." *International Journal of Oral History* 10, no. 1 (1989): 31–49.

Beardy, Flora. *Voices from Hudson Bay: Cree Stories from York Factory*. Montreal: McGill-Queen's University Press, 1996.

Benkoff, Ahna. "Inside Memory: A Story of Living in the Past and Present of a Social and Cultural Movement." *Qualitative Inquiry* 12, no. 5 (2006): 886–907.

Bennett, John, and Susan Rowley, eds. *Uqalurait: An Oral History of Nunavut*. Montreal: McGill-Queen's University Press, 2004.

Biggs, C. Lesley, and Stella Stephanson. "In Search of Gudrun Goodman: Reflections on Gender, 'Doing History' and Memory." *Canadian Historical Review* 87, no. 2 (2006): 293–316.

Bird, Patricia. "Hamilton Working Women in the Period of the Great Depression." *Atlantis* 8, no. 2 (1982): 125–36.

Boschma, Geertje, Olive Yonge, and Lorraine Mychajlunow. "Gender and Professional Identity in Psychiatric Nursing Practice in Alberta, Canada, 1930–75." *Nursing Inquiry* 12, no. 4 (2005): 243–55.

Botros, Ghada. "Religious Identity as an Historical Narrative: Coptic Orthodox Immigrant Churches and the Representation of History." *Journal of Historical Sociology* 19, no. 2 (2006): 174–201.

Botting, Ingrid. "Understanding Domestic Service Through Oral History and the Census: The Case of Grand Falls, Newfoundland." *Resources for Feminist Research* 28, no. 1 (2000): 99–119.

Bowerbank, Sylvia, and Dolores Nawages Wawia. "Literature and Criticism by Native and Metis Women in Canada." *Feminist Studies* 20, no. 3 (1994): 565–81.

Brink, Jack W. "The Lessons of Buffalo Bird Woman: Faunal Abundance and Representation from Plains Oral History." In *Archaeology on the Edge: New Perspectives from the Northern Plains*, edited by Brian Kooyman and Jane H. Kelley, 157–86. Calgary: University of Calgary Press, 2004.

Brown, Michael P. "The Work of City Politics: Citizenship through Employment in the Local Response to AIDS." *Environment & Planning A* 26, no. 6 (1994): 873–94.

Brydon, Anne. "Dreams and Claims: Icelandic-Aboriginal Interactions in the Manitoba Interlake." *Journal of Canadian Studies* 36, no. 2 (2001): 164–90.

Buhler, Sarah. "'I Chose Some Cups and Saucers': Gender, Tradition, and Subversive Elements in My Grandmother's Life Stories." *Ethnologies* 21, no. 1 (1999): 47–63.

Burrill, Gary. *Away: Maritimers in Massachusetts, Ontario, and Alberta: An Oral History of Leaving Home*. Montreal: McGill-Queen's University Press, 1992.

Cavanagh, Sheila L. "Female-Teacher Gender and Sexuality in Twentieth-Century Ontario, Canada." *History of Education Quarterly* 45, no. 2 (2005): 247–73.

Chenier, Elise. "Hidden from Historians: Preserving Lesbian Oral History in Canada."*Archivaria* 68 (fall 2009): 247–69.

Churchill, David S. "Mother Goose's Map." *Journal of Urban History* 30, no. 6 (2004): 826–52.

Clark, Jessica, and Thomas D. Isern. "Germans from Russia in Saskatchewan: An Oral History." *American Review of Canadian Studies* 40, no. 1 (2010): 71–85.

Clow, Michael, and Peter MacDonald. "The Rise and Decline of Trailcutting on the Miramichi, 1960–1990: A Perspective Based on Oral History." *Acadiensis* 26, no. 1 (1996): 76–91.

Corman, June. "Gendered Career Paths for Saskatchewan Educators: A Century of Change." *Atlantis* 35, no. 1 (2010): 92–107.

Cruikshank, Julie. *Do Glaciers Listen? Local Knowledge, Colonial Encounters and Social Imagination.* Vancouver: UBC Press, 2005.

– *The Social Life of Stories: Narrative and Knowledge in the Yukon Territory.* Vancouver: UBC Press, 1998.

– "Claiming Legitimacy: Prophecy Narratives from Northern Aboriginal Women." *American Indian Quarterly* 18, no. 2 (1994): 147–67.

– "Oral Tradition and Oral History." *Canadian Historical Review* 75, no. 3 (1994): 403–18.

– "Oral Tradition and Material Culture: Multiplying Meanings of Words and Things." *Anthropology Today* 8, no. 3 (1992): 5–9.

– *Life Lived Like a Story: Life Stories of Three Yukon Native Elders.* Lincoln: University of Nebraska Press, 1990.

Csonka, Yvon. "Changing Inuit Historicities in West Greenland and Nunavut." *History & Anthropology* 16, no. 3 (2005): 321–34.

Davey, William, and Richard MacKinnon. "Nicknaming Patterns and Traditions among Cape Breton Coal Miners." *Acadiensis* 30, no. 2 (2001): 71–83.

Davis, Rocío G. "Locating Family: Asian Canadian Historical Revisioning in Linda Ohama's *Obaachan's Garden* and Ann Marie Fleming's *The Magical Life of Long Tack Sam.*" *Journal of Canadian Studies* 42, no. 1 (2008): 1–22.

Dean, Jonathan. "'These Rascally Spackaloids': The Rise of Gispaxlots Hegemony at Fort Simpson, 1832–40." *BC Studies* 101 (1994): 41–78.

– "The 1811 Nass River Incident: Images of First Conflict on the Intercultural Frontier." *Canadian Journal of Native Studies* 13, no. 1 (1993): 83–103.

Desdouits, Anne-Marie. "Quand de 'maudit' le carillonneur devient 'benit': La réécriture du populaire par le savant." *Ethnologies* 21, no. 1 (1999): 193–207.

Devlin, Sheila. "Working with Water: Goulais Mission Memories." *Canadian Journal of Native Studies* 22, no. 2 (2002): 269–326.

Dick, Ernest. "'The Valour and the Horror' Continued: Do We Still Want Our History on Television?" *Archivaria* 35 (1993): 253–69.

Duffin, Jacalyn. "The Quota: 'An Equally Serious Problem' For Us All." *Canadian Bulletin of Medical History* 19, no. 2 (2002): 327–49.

Edmondson, John, and R. Douglas Edmondson. "Memories and Reflections on the Dieppe Raid of 19 August 1942." *Canadian Military History* 13, no. 4 (2004): 47–61.

Epp, Marlene. *Mennonite Women in Canada: A History.* Winnipeg: University of Manitoba Press, 2008.

Evans, Simon M. *The Bar U and Canadian Ranching History*. Calgary: University of Calgary Press, 2004.

Fay, Terence, Nichole Vonk, and Gwyn Griffith. "Oral Sources for Religious History." *Historical Studies* 77 (2011): 71–84.

Fiske, Jo-Anne. "From Customary Law to Oral Traditions: Discursive Formation of Plural Legalisms in Northern British Columbia, 1857–1993." *BC Studies* 115 (1997): 267–88.

Flynn, Karen. "'I'm Glad That Someone Is Telling the Nursing Story': Writing Black Canadian Women's History." *Journal of Black Studies* 38, no. 3 (January 2008): 443–60.

Fogerty, James E. "Filling the Gap: Oral History in the Archives." *The American Archivist* 46, no. 2 (1983): 148–57.

Freund, Alexander. "Troubling Memories in Nation-Building: World War II Memories and Germans' Inter-Ethnic Encounters in Canada after 1945." *Histoire Sociale/Social History* 39, no. 77 (2006): 129–55.

– and Laura Quilici. "Using Oral History to Explore Subjectivity in the Narratives of German and Italian Women in Vancouver, 1947–1961." *Canadian Issues/Thèmes Canadiens* 18 (1996): 49–59.

– and Alistair Thomson, eds. *Oral History and Photography*. New York: Palgrave Macmillan, 2012.

Friesen, T. Max. "Analogues at Iqaluktuuq: The Social Context of Archaeological Inference in Nunavut, Arctic Canada." *World Archaeology* 34, no. 2 (2002): 330–45.

Ghent, Jocelyn. "Canada, the United States, and the Cuban Missile Crisis." *Pacific Historical Review* 48, no. 2 (1979): 159–84.

Gleason, Mona. "Between Education and Memory: Health and Childhood in English Canada, 1900–1950." *Scientia Canadensis* 29, no. 1 (2006): 49–72.

Greenhill, Pauline. "English Immigrants' Narratives of Linguistic and Cultural Confusion: Examples of Ethnic Expression from Ontario." *Ethnic & Racial Studies* 15, no. 2 (1992): 236–65.

– and Peter Narvaez. "Afterword: The Journal of American Folklore and Americanist versus Canadianist Traditions." *Journal of American Folklore* 115, no. 456 (2002): 283–92.

Guard, Julie. "Authenticity on the Line." *Journal of Women's History* 15, no. 4 (2004): 117–40.

Guimond, Eric, Gail Guthrie Valaskakis, Madeleine Dion Stout, eds. *Restoring the Balance: First Nations Women, Community, and Culture*. Winnipeg: University of Manitoba Press, 2009.

Haefeli, Evan, and Kevin Sweeney, eds. *Captive Histories: English, French, and Native Narratives of the 1704 Deerfield Raid*. Amherst: University of Massachusetts Press, 2006.

Hak, Gordon. "The Harvest Excursion Adventure: Excursionists from Rural North Huron–South Bruce, 1919–28." *Ontario History* 77, no. 4 (1985): 247–65.

Hallman, Dianne. "Telling Tales In and Out of School: Twentieth-Century Women Teachers in Saskatchewan." *Saskatchewan History* 49, no. 2 (1997): 3–17.

Hammerton, James. "The Quest for Family and the Mobility of Modernity in Narratives of British Migration to Australia and Canada since 1945." *Global Networks* 4, no. 3 (2004): 271–84.

– "Migrants, Mobility and Modernity: Understanding the Life Stories of Post War English Canadian Immigrants, 1945–1971." *British Journal of Canadian Studies* 16, no. 1 (2003): 160–9.

Hardill, Kathy. "From the Grey Nuns to the Streets: A Critical History of Outreach Nursing in Canada." *Public Health Nursing* 24, no. 1 (2007): 91–7.

Hesse, Jürgen, ed. *Voices in Exile: Refugees Speak Out: An Oral History*. White Rock, BC: Thinkware Publishers, 1994.

High, Steven. "Sharing Authority: An Introduction." *Journal of Canadian Studies* 43, no. 1 (2009): 12–34.

– *Industrial Sunset: The Making of North America's Rust Belt*. Toronto: University of Toronto Press, 2003.

– and David Lewis. *Corporate Wasteland: The Landscape and Memory of Deindustrialization*. Ithaca: Cornell University Press, 2007.

–, Jessica Mill, and Stacey Zembrzycki. "Telling Our Stories/Animating Our Past: A Status Report on Oral History and Digital Media." *Canadian Journal of Communication* 37, no. 3 (2012): 1–22.

Hollenberg, Donna Krolik. "At the Western Development Museum: Ethnic Identity and the Memory of the Holocaust in the Jewish Community of Saskatoon, Saskatchewan." *Oral History Review* 27, no. 2 (2000): 85–127.

Hornborg, Anne-Christine. "Visiting the Six Worlds: Shamanistic Journeys in Canadian Mi'kmaq Cosmology." *Journal of American Folklore* 119, no. 473 (2006): 312–36.

Hulan, Renée, ed. *Native North America: Critical and Cultural Perspectives*. Toronto: ECW Press, 1999.

Iacobelli, Teresa. "'A Participant's History?': The Canadian Broadcasting Corporation and the Manipulation of Oral History." *Oral History Review* 38, no. 2. (2011): 331–48.

Iacovetta, Franca. "From Contadina to Worker: Southern Italian Immigrant Working Women in Toronto, 1947–62." In *Looking into My Sister's Eyes: An Exploration in Women's History*, edited by Jean Burnet, 195–222. Toronto: Multicultural History Society of Ontario, 1986.

– *Such Hardworking People: Italian Immigrants in Postwar Toronto*. Montreal: McGill-Queen's University Press, 1992.

Iseke-Barnes, Judy. "Grandmothers of the Métis Nation: A Living History with Dorothy Chartrand." *Native Studies Review* 18, no. 2 (2009): 69–104.

– "Living and Writing Indigenous Spiritual Resistance." *Journal of Intercultural Studies* 24, no. 3 (2003): 211–38.

Jackson, Paul. *One of the Boys: Homosexuality in the Military during World War II*. Montreal: McGill-Queen's University Press, 2004.

Juchnowicz, Katarzyna. "Reflections of Oral Traditions in Contemporary Native Writing: Ruby Slipperjack's *Honour the Sun*." In *Aboriginal Canada Revisited*, edited by Kerstin Knopf, 270–89. Ottawa: University of Ottawa Press, 2008.

Kennedy, John. "At the Crossroads: Newfoundland and Labrador Communities in a Changing International Context." *Canadian Review of Sociology & Anthropology* 34, no. 3 (1997): 297–317.

Kenny, Michael. "A Place for Memory: The Interface between Individual and Collective History." *Comparative Studies in Society & History* 41, no. 3 (1999): 420–37.

Kirshenblatt, Mayer, and Barbara Kirshenblatt-Gimblett. *They Called Me Mayer July: Painted Memories of a Jewish Childhood in Poland before the Holocaust*. Berkeley: University of California Press, 2007.

Kukharenko, Svitlana. "Negotiating Magic: Ukrainian Wedding Traditions and Their Persistence in Canada." *Canadian Slavonic Papers* 50, nos. 1–2 (2008): 55–74.

Kulchyski, Peter, and Frank James Tester. *Kiumajut (Talking Back): Game Management and Inuit Rights, 1900–70*. Vancouver: UBC Press, 2007.

Labrie, Vivian. "Quand Ti-Jean rencontre Dieu: les sept étapes de la vérité." *Journal of Canadian Studies* 27, no. 3 (1992): 75–99.

Laugrand, Frédéric, Jarich Oosten, and François Trudel, eds. *Apostle to the Inuit: The Journals and Ethnographic Notes of Edmund James Peck, the Baffin Years, 1894–1905*. Toronto: University of Toronto Press, 2006.

Li, Peter. "The Use of Oral History in Studying Elderly Chinese-Canadians." *Canadian Ethnic Studies* 17, no. 1 (1985): 67–77.

Lischke, Ute, and David T. McNab, eds. *Walking a Tightrope: Aboriginal People and Their Representations*. Waterloo: Wilfrid Laurier University Press, 2005.

Llewellyn, Kristina R. *Democracy's Angels: The Work of Women Teachers*. Montreal and Kingston: McGill-Queen's University Press, 2012.

– "Gendered Democracy: Women Teachers in Post-War Toronto." *Historical Studies in Education* 18, no. 1 (2006): 1–25.

– "Performing Post-War Citizenship: Women Teachers in Toronto Secondary Schools." *Review of Education, Pedagogy, and Cultural Studies* 28, no. 3 (2006): 309–24.

Lockerby, Earle. "Ancient Mi'kmaq Customs: A Shaman's Revelations." *Canadian Journal of Native Studies* 24, no. 2 (2004): 403–23.

Long, John. "Narratives of Early Encounters between Europeans and the Cree of Western James Bay." *Ontario History* 80, no. 3 (1988): 227–45.

Lotbinière, Pauline. "Des wampums et des 'petits humains': récits historiques sur les wampums Algonquins." *Recherches Amérindiennes au Québec* 23, no. 2 (1993): 53–68.

Lovisek, Joan. "Transmission Difficulties: The Use and Abuse of Oral History in Aboriginal Claims." In *Papers of the Algonquian Conference* 33, edited by H.C. Wofart, 251–70. Winnipeg: University of Manitoba Papers of the Algonquian Conference, 2002.

Lutz, John Sutton. *Makúk: A New History of Aboriginal-White Relations.* Vancouver: UBC Press, 2008.

Lyle, Dick. "The Contributions of Margaret Conrad to Public History in Canada." *Atlantis* 34, no. 2 (2010): 34–42.

Lyons, Natasha, Peter Dawson, et al. "Person, Place, Memory, Thing: How Inuit Elders Are Informing Archaeological Practice in the Canadian North." *Canadian Journal of Archaeology* 34, no. 1 (2010): 1–31.

Macfie, John. *Tales from Another Time: Oral History of Early Times in Parry Sound District.* Parry Sound: Hay Press, 2000.

MacLaren, Ian. "'Caledonian Suttee'? An Anatomy of Carrier Cremation Cruelty in the Historical Record." *BC Studies* 149, no. 3 (2006): 3–37.

MacLennan, Anne F. "Women, Radio Broadcasting and the Depression: A 'Captive' Audience from Household Hints to Story Time and Serials." *Women's Studies* 37, no. 6 (2008): 616–33.

MacLeod, Peter. "The Anishinabeg Point of View: The History of the Great Lakes Region to 1800 in Nineteenth-Century Mississauga, Odawa, and Ojibwa Historiography." *Canadian Historical Review* 73, no. 2 (1992): 194–210.

Majhanovich, Suzanne, and Goli Rezai-Rashti. "Marginalized Women: Minority Women Teachers in Twentieth-Century Ontario." *Education & Society* 20, nos. 2–3 (2002): 61–72.

Maloney, Sean M., and John Llambias. *Chances for Peace: Canadian Soldiers in the Balkans, 1992–1995: An Oral History.* St Catharines: Vanwell, 2002.

Marsden, Susan. "Adawx, Spanaxnox, and the Geopolitics of the Tsimshian." *BC Studies* 135 (2002): 101–35.

McCarthy, Martha. *From the Great River to the Ends of the Earth: Oblate Missions to the Dene, 1847–1921.* Edmonton: University of Alberta Press, 1995.

McCrady, David G. *Living with Strangers: The Nineteenth-Century Sioux and the Canadian-American Borderlands.* Lincoln: University of Nebraska Press, 2006.

McKeen, Carol, and Alan Richardson. "Education, Employment, and Certification: An Oral History of the Entry of Women into the Canadian Accounting Profession." *Business & Economic History* 27, no. 2 (1998): 500–21.

McLeod, Neal. *Cree Narrative Memory: From Treaties to Contemporary Times.* Saskatoon: Purich Publishing, 2007.

McNab, David. "Who Is on Trial? Teme-Augama Anishnabai Land Rights and George Ironside, Junior: Re-Considering Oral Tradition." *Canadian Journal of Native Studies* 18, no. 1 (1998): 117–33.

– "'The Promise That He Gave to My Grand Father was Very Sweet': The Gun Shot Treaty of 1792 at the Bay of Quinte." *Canadian Journal of Native Studies* 16, no. 2 (1996): 293–314.

McNeil, Bill. *Voices of a War Remembered: An Oral History of Canadians in World War Two*. Toronto: Doubleday Canada: 1991.

McNeil, Daniel. "Finding a Home While Crossing Boundaries: Black Identities in Halifax and Liverpool." *International Journal of Canadian Studies* 31 (2005): 197–235.

McPherson, Kathryn. *Bedside Matters: The Transformation of Canadian Nursing, 1900–1990*. Toronto: Oxford University Press, 1996.

Milewski, Patrice. "Perilous Times: An Oral History of Teachers' Experience with School Inspection in the 1930s." *History of Education* 41, no. 5 (2012): 637–56.

– "'I Paid No Attention to It': An Oral History of Curricular Change in the 1930s." *Historical Studies in Education/Revue d'histoire de l'éducation* 24, no. 1 (2012): 112–29.

Militz, Helga. "Mündliche Erzähltradition und Prosaliteratur im Französisch-sprachigen Kanada." *Zeitschrift für Kanada-Studien* 12, no. 1 (1992): 153–70.

Miller, Jim. "Owen Glendower, Hotspur, and Canadian Indian Policy." *Ethnohistory* 37, no. 4 (1990): 386–415.

Mogadime, Dolana. "Racial Differential Experiences of Employment Equity for Women Teachers: One Teacher's Narrative of Resistance and Struggle." *Journal of Black Studies* 39, no. 1 (2008): 85–108.

Namaste, Viviane. "Beyond Leisure Studies: A Labour History of Male to Female Transsexual and Transvestite Artists in Montreal, 1955–1985." *Atlantis* 29, no. 1 (2004): 4–11.

Ndejuru, Lisa. "Sharing Authority as Deep Listening and Sharing the Load." *Journal of Canadian Studies* 43, no. 1 (2009): 5–11.

Neufeld, David. "Parks Canada, the Commemoration of Canada, and Northern Aboriginal Oral History." In *Oral History and Public Memories*, edited by Paula Hamilton and Linda Shopes, 7–30. Philadelphia: Temple University Press, 2008.

Oetelaar, Gerald A., and David Meyer. "Movement and Native American Landscapes: A Comparative Approach." *Plains Anthropologist* 51, no. 199 (2006): 355–74.

Parker, Mike. *Running the Gauntlet: An Oral History of Canadian Merchant Seamen in World War II*. Halifax: Nimbus, 2003.

Parr, Joy. *The Gender of Breadwinners: Women, Men and Change in Two Industrial Towns*. Toronto: University of Toronto Press, 1990.

– "The Skilled Emigrant and Her Kin: Gender, Culture, and Labour Recruitment." *Canadian Historical Review* 68, no. 4 (1987): 529–51.

Pickles, Katie. "Exhibiting Canada: Empire, Migration and the 1928 English Schoolgirl Tour." *Gender, Place & Culture: A Journal of Feminist Geography* 7, no. 1 (2000): 81–96.

Piper, Liza. "Subterranean Bodies: Mining the Large Lakes of North-West Canada, 1921–1960." *Environment & History* 13, no. 2 (2007): 155–86.

Podruchny, Carolyn. "Werewolves and Windigos: Narratives of Cannibal Monsters in French-Canadian Voyageur Oral Tradition." *Ethnohistory* 51, no. 4 (2004): 677–700.

Potvin, Maryse. "Second-Generation Haitian Youth in Quebec. Between the 'Real' Community and the 'Represented.'" *Canadian Ethnic Studies* 31, no. 1 (1999): 43–72.

Preston, Chris. "A Past of Tragic Stories: The (Non-)Treatment of Native Peoples' Oral Histories in Canada." *Undercurrent* 2, no. 1 (2005): 54–64.

Preston, Susan. "Exploring the Eastern Cree Landscape: Oral Tradition as Cognitive Map." In *Papers of the Algonquian Conference* 31, edited by John D. Nichols, 310–32. Winnipeg: University of Manitoba Papers of the Algonquian Conference, 2000.

Purdy, Sean. "Bertold Brecht, Public Housing, and Oral History." *Oral History Review* 29, no. 2 (2002): 83–6.

Pylypchuk, Mary Ann. "The Value of Aboriginal Records as Legal Evidence in Canada: An Examination of the Sources." *Archivaria* 32 (1991): 51–77.

Repo, Satu. "Rosvall and Voutilainen: Two Union Men Who Never Died." *Labour/ Le Travail* 8 (1981): 79–102.

Rimstead, Roxanne. *Remnants of Nation: On Poverty Narratives by Women.* Toronto: University of Toronto Press, 2001.

Roy, Patricia. "'Active Voices': A Third Generation of Studies of the Chinese and Japanese in British Columbia." *BC Studies* 117 (1998): 51–61.

Runte, Hans R. *Writing Acadia: The Emergence of Acadian Literature 1970–1990.* Atlanta: Rodopi, 1997.

Rutherdale, Robert. "Fatherhood, Masculinity, and the Good Life during Canada's Baby Boom, 1945–1965." *Journal of Family History* 24, no. 3 (1999): 351–73.

Sangster, Joan. *Through Feminist Eyes: Essays on Canadian Women's History.* Edmonton: Athabasca University Press, 2011.

– *Earning Respect: The Lives of Working Women in Small-Town Ontario, 1920– 1960.* Toronto: University of Toronto Press, 1995.

– "Telling Our Stories: Feminist Debates and the Use of Oral History." *Women's History Review* 1, no. 5 (1994): 5–28.

Scott, Colin. "Encountering the Whiteman in James Bay Cree Narrative History and Mythology." *Aboriginal History* 19, no. 1 (1995): 21–40.

Seixas, Peter. "Visual History Reviews." *Canadian Historical Review* 80, no. 4 (December 1999): 687–706.

Sigurdsson, Gisli. "What Does a Story Tell? Eddi Gíslason's (1901–1986) Personal Use of Traditional Material." *Canadian Ethnic Studies* 34, no. 2 (2002): 79–89.

Silverstein, Cory, and Zeek Cywink. "From Fireside to TV Screen: Self-Determination and Anishnaabe Storytelling Traditions." *Canadian Journal of Native Studies* 20, no. 1 (2000): 35–66.

Sing, Pamela V. "'J'vous djis enne cho', là: Translating Oral Michif French into Written English." *Quebec Studies* 50 (2010): 57–80.

Smith, Helen, and Pamela Wakewich. "Regulating Body Boundaries and Health During the Second World War: Nationalist Discourse, Media Representations and the Experiences of Canadian Women War Workers." *Gender & History* 24, no. 1 (2012): 56–73.

– "'I Was Not Afraid of Work': Female War Plant Employees and Their Work Environment." In *Canadian Environments: Essays in Culture, Politics and History*, edited by Robert C. Thomsen and Nanette L. Hale, 229–47. New York: Peter Lang, 2005.

Smyth, Elizabeth M., and Linda F. Wicks. *Wisdom Raises Her Voice: The Sisters of St. Joseph of Toronto Celebrate 150 Years: An Oral History*. Toronto: Sisters of St Joseph of Toronto, 2001.

Srigley, Katrina. *Breadwinning Daughters: Young Working Women in a Depression-Era City, 1929–1939*. Toronto: University of Toronto Press, 2010.

– "Clothing Stories: Consumption, Identity, and Desire in Depression-Era Toronto." *Journal of Women's History* 19, no. 1 (2007): 82–104.

– "'In Case You Hadn't Noticed!' Race, Ethnicity, and Women's Wage-Earning in a Depression-Era City." *Labour/Le Travail* 55 (2005): 69–105.

Stanley, Anna. "Citizenship and the Production of Landscape and Knowledge in Contemporary Canadian Nuclear Fuel Waste Management." *Canadian Geographer* 52, no. 1 (2008): 64–82.

St-Onge, Nicole. "Memories of Metis Women of Saint-Eustache, Manitoba, 1910–1980." *Native Studies Review* 17, no. 2 (2008): 45–68.

– "Variations in Red River: The Traders and Freemen Metis of Saint-Laurent, Manitoba." *Canadian Ethnic Studies* 24, no. 2 (1992): 1–21.

Storey, Robert. "'They Have All Been Faithful Workers': Injured Workers, Truth, and Workers' Compensation in Ontario, 1970–2008." *Journal of Canadian Studies* 43, no. 1 (2009): 154–85.

Struthers, Roxanne, and Cynthia Peden-McAlpine. "Phenomenological Research Among Canadian and United States Indigenous Populations: Oral Tradition and Quintessence of Time." *Qualitative Health Research* 15, no. 9 (2005): 1264–76.

Sugiman, Pamela. "'Life is Sweet': Vulnerability and Composure in the Wartime Narratives of Japanese Canadians." *Journal of Canadian Studies* 43, no. 1 (2009): 186–218.

– "'A Million Hearts from Here': Japanese Canadian Mothers and Daughters and the Lessons of War." *Journal of American Ethnic History* 26, no. 4 (2007): 50–68.

– "Memories of Internment: Narrating Japanese Canadian Women's Life Stories." *Canadian Journal of Sociology* 29, no. 3 (2004): 359–88.

– "Passing Time, Moving Memories: Interpreting Wartime Narratives of Japanese Canadian Women." *Histoire Sociale/Social History* 37, no. 73 (2004): 51–79.

Sutherland, Neil. *Growing Up: Childhood in English Canada from the Great War to the Age of Television*. Toronto: University of Toronto Press, 1997.

- "The Triumph of 'Formalism': Elementary Schooling in Vancouver from the 1920s to the 1960s." *BC Studies* 69 (1986): 175–210.
Thom, Brian. "The Anthropology of Northwest Coast Oral Traditions." *Arctic Anthropology* 40, no. 1 (2003): 1–28.
Treat, James. *Around the Sacred Fire: A Native Religious Activism in the Red Power Era: A Narrative Map of the Indian Ecumenical Conference.* New York: Palgrave Macmillan, 2003.
Tremblay, Mary. "Going Back to Civvy Street: A Historical Account of the Impact of the Everest and Jennings Wheelchair for Canadian World War II Veterans with Spinal Cord Injury." *Disability & Society* 11, no. 2 (1996): 149–69.
–, Audrey Campbell, and Geoffrey Hudson. "When Elevators Were for Pianos: An Oral History Account of the Civilian Experience of Using Wheelchairs in Canadian Society. The First Twenty-Five Years: 1945–1970." *Disability & Society* 20, no. 2 (2005): 103–16.
Verma, Archana B. *The Making of Little Punjab in Canada: Patterns of Immigration.* Thousand Oaks, CA: Sage Publications, 2002.
Vest, Jay. "The Oldman River and the Sacred: A Meditation Upon Aputosi Pii'kani Tradition and Environmental Ethics." *Canadian Journal of Native Studies* 25, no. 2 (2005): 571–607.
Wakewich, Pamela, and Helen Smith. "The Politics of 'Selective' Memory: Re-Visioning Canadian Women's Wartime Work in the Public Record." *Oral History* (autumn 2006): 56–68.
Wall, Sharon. *The Nurture of Nature: Childhood, Antimodernism, and Ontario Summer Camps, 1920–55.* Vancouver: UBC Press, 2009.
Wallace, Birgitta. "The Norse in Newfoundland: L'Anse Aux Meadows and Vinland." *Newfoundland Studies* 19, no. 1 (2003): 5–43.
Westman, Clinton. "Homesteading in Northern Alberta During the Great Depression: A Life History Approach." *Prairie Forum* 32, no. 1 (2007): 167–89.
Wheeler, Winona. "Reflections on the Social Relations of Indigenous Oral Histories." In *Walking a Tightrope: Aboriginal People and Their Representations,* edited by Ute Lischke and David T. McNab, 189–214. Waterloo: Wilfrid Laurier University Press, 2005.
- "Indigenous Voices, Indigenous Histories – Part 1: The Othering of Indigenous History." *Saskatchewan History* 50, no. 2 (1999): 24–7.
- "Indigenous Voices, Indigenous Histories – Part 3: The Social Relations of Oral History." *Saskatchewan History* 51, no. 1 (1999): 29–35.
Wickwire, Wendy. "To See Ourselves as the Other's Other: Nlaka'pamux Contact Narratives." *Canadian Historical Review* 75, no. 1 (1994): 1–20.
Widdis, Randy William. *Voices from Next Year Country: An Oral History of Rural Saskatchewan.* Regina: Canadian Plains Research Center/University of Regina, 2006.

Wong, Alan. "Conversations for the Real World: Shared Authority, Self-Reflexivity, and Process in the Oral History Interview." *Journal of Canadian Studies* 43, no. 1 (2009): 239–58.

Zembrzycki, Stacey. "There Were Always Men in Our House: Gender and the Childhood Memories of Working-Class Ukrainians in Depression-Era Canada." *Labour/Le Travail* 60 (2007): 77–105.

– et al. "Oral History and Adult Community Education: Notes from the Field." *Oral History Review* 38, no. 1 (2011): 120–35.

Contributors

BRIAN CALLIOU is the director of the Banff Centre's Indigenous Leadership and Management program area, which designs and delivers leadership and organizational development programs for Indigenous leaders. Brian is Cree and a member of the Sucker Creek First Nation in the Treaty 8 area of northern Alberta. He completed a BA, LLB, and LLM at the University of Alberta.

ELISE CHENIER is an associate professor in the Department of History at Simon Fraser University, where she specializes in the history of sexuality, oral history, and Canadian history. She is the founder of two digital archives, and teaching and learning tools that feature oral history: Interracial Intimacies: Sex and Race in Toronto, 1910–1950, www.interracialintimacies.org, and Archives of Lesbian Oral Testimony, www.alotarchives.org.

JULIE CRUIKSHANK, professor emerita at the University of British Columbia, lived in the Yukon Territory for more than a decade, working with indigenous women who were eager to record their life stories. Her books include: *Life Lived Like a Story* (in collaboration with Angela Sidney, Annie Ned, and Kitty Smith, 1990), *Reading Voices* (Douglas & McIntyre, 1991), *The Social Life of Stories* (UBC Press, 1998), and *Do Glaciers Listen?* (UBC Press, 2005). She was elected to the Royal Society of Canada in 2010 and appointed as an Officer of the Royal Society of Canada in 2012.

ALEXANDER FREUND is a professor of history and holds the chair in German-Canadian studies at the University of Winnipeg, where he is also co-director of the Oral History Centre. He is co-president of the Canadian

Oral History Association and former co-editor of *Oral History Forum d'histoire orale*. Recent publications include *Oral History and Ethnic History* (Canadian Historical Association, 2014); *Beyond the Nation? Immigrants' Local Lives in Transnational Cultures* (edited; University of Toronto Press, 2012); and, co-edited with Alistair Thomson, *Oral History and Photography* (Palgrave, 2011).

RONALD J. GRELE is the former director of the Columbia University Oral History Research Office. He is the author of *Envelopes of Sound: The Art of Oral History*, and a former president of the (US) Oral History Association.

STEVEN HIGH is Canada Research Chair in Oral History and co-director of Concordia University's Centre for Oral History and Digital Storytelling. He is author or lead editor of seven books, including *Beyond Testimony and Trauma* (UBC Press, 2015), *Oral History at the Crossroads* (UBC Press, 2014), *Remembering Mass Violence* (University of Toronto Press, 2013), and *Occupied St John's* (McGill-Queen's University Press, 2010). He was also lead researcher on the Montreal Life Stories Community-University Research Alliance.

NANCY JANOVICEK is associate professor of history at the University of Calgary. She is the author of *No Place to Go: Local Histories of the Battered Women's Shelter Movement* (UBC Press, 2007) and co-editor of *Feminist History in Canada: New Essays on Women, Gender, Work and Nation* (UBC Press, 2013).

JILL JARVIS-TONUS is counsel with Bereskin & Parr and head of the firm's New Media/Copyright practice group. Her practice focuses on all areas of copyright and trademark law, particularly as they relate to new media and digital products and services. She has a particular interest in the entertainment industry and educational fields.

KRISTINA R. LLEWELLYN is associate professor in the Department of Social Development Studies at Renison University College, University of Waterloo, and associate member of the Department of Sociology and Legal Studies, as well as the Women's Studies Program at the University of Waterloo. She is a former co-editor of *Oral History Forum d'histoire orale*. Her areas of research include history, education, gender, and citizenship. She is the author of *Democracy's Angels: The Work of Women Teachers* (McGill-Queen's University Press, 2012).

BRONWEN LOW is an associate professor and graduate program director in the Department of Integrated Studies in Education in McGill University's Faculty of Education. Her research interests include the implications and challenges of popular youth culture for curriculum theory, literacy studies, and pedagogy; community-media projects and pedagogies; translanguaging and the multilingual Montreal hip-hop scene; and the pedagogical implications of the life stories of Montrealers who have survived genocide and other human rights violations. Her books include *Slam School: Learning through Conflict in the Hip-hop and Spoken Word Classroom* (Stanford University Press, 2011) and, with Chloe Brushwood Rose and Paula Salvio, *Community Media Pedagogies: Listening in the Commons* (forthcoming, Routledge).

CLAUDIA MALACRIDA researches on the body, sexuality, disability, motherhood, and social control at the Department of Sociology, University of Lethbridge. She is the author of several books, including *A Special Hell: Institutional Life in Alberta's Eugenic Years* (University of Toronto Press, 2015), which draws on oral histories of Michener Centre survivors. A website on the project can be found at www.eugenicsnewgenics.com.

JOY PARR is professor emerita of geography at Western University. She is a Canadian historian of work, gender, and technology. She is author of *The Gender of Breadwinners* (University of Toronto Press, 1990), *Domestic Goods* (University of Toronto Press, 1999), and *Sensing Changes* (UBC Press, 2010; winner of the Canada Prize, 2011). More information on this latter work can be found at www.megaproject.uwo.ca.

NOLAN REILLY is a professor of history and co-director of the Oral History Centre at the University of Winnipeg. He is co-president of the Canadian Oral History Association and former co-editor of *Oral History Forum d'histoire orale*. He conducted his first oral history interviews in 1976 in Amherst, Nova Scotia. His engagement with community public history and oral history research has continued unabated since his first experience many years ago with the citizens of Amherst.

JOAN SANGSTER teaches in gender and women's studies at the Frost Centre for Canadian Studies and Indigenous Studies at Trent University. She has published monographs on women and the Canadian Left; law and criminalization; and women, work, and the labour movement. Her most recent books are *Transforming Labour: Women and Work in Postwar*

Canada (University of Toronto Press, 2010) and *Through Feminist Eyes: Essays on Canadian Women's History* (AU Press, 2011).

EMMANUELLE SONNTAG is an information scientist and sociologist. She is pursuing her PhD in sociology on the topic of Listening at Université du Québec à Montréal (UQAM). She tweets @lvrdg on listening, information literacy, information technologies, education, life stories, and radio.

PAMELA SUGIMAN is professor and chair of the Department of Sociology at Ryerson University. She is currently doing comparative research on the memories of working-class women and their livelihoods from girlhood to old age, in different regions of Canada. Sugiman is also leading the oral history research cluster of the research project, "Landscapes of Injustice," a large multi-disciplinary initiative that seeks to deepen our understanding of the dispossession of Japanese Canadians.

WINONA WHEELER is a member of the Fisher River Cree Nation in Treaty No. 5 territory, though her family hails from George Gordon's First Nation in Treaty No. 4 territory. She has been a professional historian and a professor of Indigenous studies for over twenty-five years, with research interests in the history of Indigenous-Newcomer relations, Indigenous oral histories, colonialism and anti-colonial studies, land claims, and Treaty Rights. She is currently an associate professor and the department head of Native studies at the University of Saskatchewan. She is a mother and a grandmother, and lives near Duck Lake, Saskatchewan, with her husband Tyrone Tootoosis, fourteen horses, four dogs, eight chickens, and two cats.

STACEY ZEMBRZYCKI is an affiliate assistant professor in the Department of History at Concordia University. A modern Canadian oral and public historian of ethnic, immigrant, and refugee experience, she is the author of *According to Baba: A Collaborative Oral History of Sudbury's Ukrainian Community* (UBC Press, 2014) and its accompanying website: www.sudburyukrainians.ca; and is co-editor of *Oral History Off the Record: Toward an Ethnography of Practice* (Palgrave Macmillan, 2013), winner of the 2014 Oral History Association Book Award.

Index

Aboriginal languages, in interviews, 37–8
Aboriginal peoples and culture. *See* indigenous cultures and peoples
abuse and violence, ethics, 85
academic debate, in oral history, 4, 14, 28–30
academic research, methodology, 31
accuracy, 10, 193
activism, 14–15, 241–2
agreements, in copyright, 111–12
Akan, Linda, 38–9
Alaska Highway, 185–6, 193–4
Alberta, 318–19, 320–1, 324–5, 327–8. *See also* Michener Centre
Alberta Association for Community Living, 327
Alberta Eugenics Board, 318, 320
Allison, Fred H., 234
American Oral History Association, 221, 227
analog audio recordings: digitization, 214, 220, 223; loss and archiving, 201–2, 207–8, 214, 222; use and reuse, 222–4, 351
analytical methods, 41–2
Anderson, Kathryn, 146
Andrews, Margaret, 13
anonymity, 79–82, 226–7. *See also* privacy
anthropologists, 12, 29, 338–9
appearance, women teachers, 151–3
Archive of Lesbian Oral Testimonies (ALOT), 202, 211–13

archives and archiving: access to oral history projects, 218; analog recordings, 223–4, 351; and consent, 82; copyright, 113–14; of data, materials, final reports, 44; in indigenous communities, 44; of interviews, 81–2; lesbian oral history, 202, 203, 206–8, 212, 357; Michener Centre issues, 325, 327–9, 357; role in oral history, 13, 218, 291–2, 337, 357–8
Archives lesbiennes de Montréal–Traces, 206–7
archivists, role, 6, 13
Assmann, Jan, 161–2
"aural" history, 7, 347–8
authors and authorship, copyright, 99–100

Baba (Olga Zembrzycki): biography, 55–6, 63–4; dominating interviews, 59–60; as intermediary, 58–9, 60–3, 64–5, 66–7, 68, 354; as interviewee, 54; as interviewer, 59–60; not at interviews, 63; relationship with interviewee, 53–4, 55–7, 60–1, 67, 354; stories from, 53, 56–7, 59, 62; subjectivity, 65
"bad fits," 152
Bakhtin, Mikhail, 147, 152, 181–2, 183–4
Band Councils, for consent, 33, 74, 87
Barrett, Michèle, 147
bearing witness, in classroom, 248–52
Behar, Ruth, 299, 338, 339, 340–1, 342–3
Benjamin, Walter, 182, 184, 194

Bettman, Batia, 249, 260
bias. *See* subjectivity
Blee, Kathleen, 298, 313, 337
Bloom, Leslie, 145
body language, women teachers', 149–50
Bolgar, Ted, 249, 252
Boston College subpoena, 90
Bourdieu, Pierre, 187
Bourgois, Philippe, 339
breach of confidence, 109–10
British Columbia, 28, 347–8
Bruckert, Chris, 90–1
Buffalo Women's Oral History Project, 205
Bultz, Paula, 240, 246, 252, 254–6
Bury, Mike, 322

Canadian Copyright Act, 98–9, 100–1, 103, 112–14
Canadian Gay Archives, 206
Canadian Lesbian and Gay Archives (CLGA), 206–7, 214
Canadian Oral History Association (COHA), 6–7, 213, 214
Canadian Oral History Association (COHA) Journal, 6, 120
Canning, Sophie (pseudonym), 149, 153
Carroll, Jock, 101–2
case law, copyright, 101–3, 105–7
Casey, Kathleen, 147
cataloguing information, 40
CBC and Canadian Radio Broadcasting Commission (CRBC), 6
Centre for Oral History and Digital Storytelling, 358
child survivor activism, rise, 242–4
Chinese Canadians, redress, 309
Chong, Hazel, 146, 151–2
classroom. *See* education field and classroom
Clifford, James, 339
collaboration, 55, 58–61, 67, 337–8. *See also* shared authority
collective interview, 37, 290–1
collective memory: description, 162; gaps, 288–9, 351–2; loss through colonialism and trauma, 289–91; Ochékiwi Sīpi Cree, 287–9, 292, 293–4; and social change, 319
colonialism, 183, 289–90

communication, interactive nature, 132
communicative memory, 160–2, 165, 175–6, 353–4
Communist Party of Canada (CPC), 123
community, 68n2, 241
community history, lesbians and gays, 203, 204, 213
conceptualization of project, in PGOH, 221–2
confidentiality: and copyright, 109–10, 112; and regulations, 89–91; TCPS, 73, 79, 81–2; TCPS2, 80–4
conflict legacies, 335
consent: and archiving of data, 82; from Band Councils, 33, 74, 87; free and informed, 84–6; identity of participants, 80–1, 83; lesbian oral history materials, 208–10, 213; negative aspects, 84–5; recommendation for TCPS2, 83–4
contested memories, 318–19
contradictory information, 36–7, 65, 78–9, 125
conversations, copyright, 105–7
Co-operative Commonwealth Federation (CCF), 123
copies, copyright, 113–14
Copinger and Skone James on Copyright, 105
copyright: Canadian Copyright Act, 98–9, 100–1, 103, 112–14; case law, 101–3, 105–7; and content, 101–3; and copies, 113–14; Copyright Modernization Act, 112–14; fair dealing, 112–13, 115; general principles, 98–9; and oral history, 99–101; for orators (*see* orators); and ownership, 101–7; performers, 114; in PGOH, 227; protection terms, 103; recent changes, 112–14; summary of law, 104–8; written agreements terms, 111–12
Copyright Modernization Act, 112–14
courts: closed and open-ended questions, 31–2; copyright, 100, 101–2, 113; indigenous oral history, 11–12, 25, 27–8; methodology for evidence, 31. *See also* law and legal aspects
credibility of oral history: concerns, 231–4; indigenous peoples, 25, 27–8, 29–30, 351–2, 357

Cree. *See* Home Guard Cree; Ochēkiwi Sīpi (Fisher River) Cree
critical theories, 10
Cruikshank, Julie, 29, 39, 86–7
cultural memory, definition, 162
culture, in colonialism and trauma, 289–90

Danto, Arthur, 349
data: analysis, 41–2; orality in PGOH, 230–1; secondary uses and consent, 81–2, 83–4
Davis, Madeleine, 205, 206
defamation, 108–9
Delgamuukw case, 25, 27
denial, and trauma, 290–1
Derrida, Jacques, 143, 343
Dick case, 28
difficult knowledge, teaching and learning, 267
digital technologies: access to interviews, 13, 220; and copies, 113; copyright, 101, 113; and interest in oral history, 17; and research relationships, 340
digitization: of analog audio recordings, 214, 220, 223; lesbian oral history, 202, 214; quality issues, 224; use and reuse, 220–1, 351
dignity, 76, 77, 91–2
disabilities, people with, 322–3, 328–9, 331
discourse, women teachers' oral histories, 142, 147–50
discrepancies and contradictions, 36–7, 65, 78–9, 125
the Donovan, Sudbury (ON), 56–7
Dorris, Michael, 181
Dutton, Ron, 206

education field and classroom: of difficult knowledge, 267; Holocaust (*see* Holocaust education); human rights violations, 267–8, 270–1, 272, 273–9; life story interviews, 267, 272; listening practice and theory, 269–70, 272–3; and oral history, 13–14, 267. *See also* pedagogy; women teachers oral histories
Elders and their knowledge: access to, 44; conversation pattern, 38–9; cooperation with researchers, 33–4; copies of record-

ings and transcripts, 40, 43; discrepancies in, 36–7; dissemination and future use, 43–4; importance and credibility, 25, 26, 27, 28; interview process and methodology, 31–2, 35–9; protocols and cultural factors, 32, 34–5; questions for, 31–2, 33, 36–7, 39; repetition in topic, 38–9; simultaneous interviewees, 37
emotion and emotional impact, 133, 298–9
empty speaking, 172, 173
English language, in interviews, 37–8
epitomizing, 193
Eppert, Claudia, 270–1
equipment for recording, preparation, 35
Errante, Antoinette, 299
ethics: anonymity and use of names, 226–7; bureaucratic issues, 75, 85, 88–9, 92–3; in development of oral history, 8–9, 76–9, 91–2; evolution of, 93; free and informed consent, 84–6; indigenous peoples, 8, 84, 86–8; and interpretation, 78, 89–90; interviewee-researcher relationship, 77, 336; lesbian oral history, 209; of listening, 275–6; in medical model, 75; PGOH, 226–7; privacy and confidentiality, 79–84; in publications, 86; regulatory and legal power, 89–91; secondary uses of data, 81–2, 83–4; and silences, 78–9; subpoenas, 90; in testimony, 270–1. *See also* research ethics boards (REBs); *TCPS* (first edition); *TCPS2*
ethnographers, 12, 338
ethnohistorians, 291, 292
eugenics, 318–19, 320–1, 323, 325. *See also* Michener Centre
Euro-Canadians, views of indigenous peoples, 26
the everyday, in oral story/narrative, 181, 182, 188, 195
evidence. *See* truth
explicit memory, 172

"fair comment," 109, 111

gender, 122–4, 141, 143–4, 147
generations, communicative memory, 162, 353–4. *See also* three-generational interviews

German Canadians: identity, 159–60; reuse of 1970s interviews, 219–20, 222, 226, 228–30. *See also* Hiebert family

"giving voice," 14

Gould Estate v. *Stoddart Publishing Co.*, 101–2

Greenspan, Henry, 60, 241, 272

Grele, Ronald J.: conversational narratives, 10; on engagement and relationships, 339–40; on interpretation, 232–3; on the interview, 224–5; on memory, 125, 313

Grenke, Arthur: indexes of interviews, 229–30; method, 228–9; relationship with interviewees, 226; reuse of research and interviews, 219–20, 222, 223–4, 235

Haché, Alfred, and Jessie, 13

Hager v. *ECW Press Ltd. et al.*, 102–3

Halbwachs, Maurice, 162

Hamilton, Paula, 337

hand gestures, 36

Haraway, Donna, 145, 336

harm to participants, and ethics, 85–6

Harstock, Nancy, 151

Hartmann, Heidi, 144

Hashimoto, Lois: as help to research, 310–13; invalidation of researcher, 299–301; justification for internment, 305–6; personal memories, 299, 303–4, 305, 308, 311–13; positive outcomes of internment, 303–4, 306–7, 311; and racism, 308–9; on redress activism, 302–3, 305–6, 308–9. *See also* internment of Japanese Canadians

health research, 322

Heaney, Seamus, 338, 343

Hemingway case, 105–7

Hiebert, Irma: biography, 159, 162–4; family and Nazi Germany stories, 159–60, 165–72; narrative structures, 172–3

Hiebert family: description, 159, 162–4; foundational stories, 164–72, 175; harmonization and conflict, 175–6; narrative structures, 172–5

High, Steven, 120, 213

historians: copyright ownership, 101–2; criticism of and opposing views to, 299–301, 309–12; engagement with research, 339–41; interpretation of oral history, 77–8; line between participants, 341–2; as listener, 342–3; and oral history relationships, 145–7, 340; personal motives, 298–9; practice of oral history, 310–12; responsibility to participants, 335–7; role in oral history, 145–7, 336–8; subjectivity, 336–9

historical research, and *TCPS2*, 88–91

historical truth, 66–7, 142, 143–7

Hobsbawm, Eric, 292

Holmes, Michael, 102–3

Holocaust education: bearing witness, 248–52; child survivor activism, 242–4; educational activism and practices, 241–2; eyewitness accounts, 239; in the family, 251–2; interviews and process, 241–3, 244–7, 359–60; March of the Living program, 257–60; Montreal Life Stories project, 240–2; museum interpretation, 252–6; origins of, 243; silence of survivors, 243–4, 290–1; survivors as educators, 240, 241–2, 243, 244, 248–56, 257–8, 260; survivors interviewing survivors, 244–7

Home Children project, 335

Home Guard Cree, 289

Hotchner, A.E., 105–6

Hudson's Bay Company (HBC), 286

human rights violations: teaching and learning, 267–8, 270–1, 272, 273–9; testimony and chain of testimony, 270–2, 277

Iacovetta, Franca, 80

identity, construction in women, 142, 150–3

identity of participants, 73, 75, 80–1, 83, 89–90. *See also* anonymity; privacy

immigration, 11, 335

implicit memory, 172

inconsistencies and contradictions, 36–7, 65, 78–9, 125

indexes, 40, 229–30, 338

Indian Residential Schools, 12, 85

indigenous cultures and peoples: colonialism and missionaries, 289–90; credibility and acceptance of oral history, 25,

27–8, 29–30, 351–2, 357; and development of oral history, 11–12; and ethics,
8, 84, 86–8; historical reconstruction,
285, 291–3; homogenization and variety
of stories, 181; law and legal aspects,
11–12, 25, 27–8, 352, 357; methodology
of oral history, 25–6, 31–44; need for
oral history, 26–8; oral history research,
11–12; oral story/narrative (see oral
story/narrative); oral tradition (see oral
tradition); and other evidence, 30–1;
traditional history, 28–9; transmission
of oral history, 181–2, 291–2; views
in history-writing, 26–7, 28–30. See
also Elders and their knowledge; First
Nations, Inuit, Métis; Native North
America; Ochēkiwi Sīpi (Fisher River)
Cree; Yukon Territory
individual memories: importance, 30; in
internment of Japanese Canadians, 299,
303–4, 305, 308, 311–13; vs. multiplicity
of, 303–4, 312–13; as problem, 233–4
information sources, 33
informed consent, and ethics, 84–6
ininiwag dibaajimowag: First Nations
Men's Digital Stories on the Intergenerational Experiences of Residential
Schools, 12
Innis, Harold, 181–2, 183, 184–5
Institutional Review Boards (IRBs), 92
intellectual disabilities. See disabilities,
people with
Interagency Panel on Research and Ethics,
73, 83–4, 92
intermediary in interview, 34; Baba as,
58–9, 60–3, 64–5, 66–7, 68, 354
internment of Japanese Canadians: assimilation and dispersal policy, 306–7;
contradiction of researcher, 299–301;
ghost towns and supporting camps, 303;
hiding and redress of, 297; justification
for, 305–6; oral history interviews, 298;
personal memories in, 299, 303–4, 305,
308, 311–13; positive outcomes, 303–4,
306–8, 311; and racial discrimination,
308–9; reconstruction, 297–8; redress
activism, 302–3, 304–6, 308–9. See also
Hashimoto, Lois

interpretation: background and development, 5, 9–10; concepts, 142; and
emotion, 133, 298–9; ethics policies, 78,
89–90; in Holocaust museum, 252–6; by
interviewer, 77–8; intuitive, 42; value,
232–3, 359; variety of, 355
interpreters, in interviews, 38
interpretive patterns, in Hiebert family,
172–3
interview: collaboration in, 55, 58–61, 67,
337–8; copyright ownership and terms,
101–2, 103–4; development of practices,
6–8; and difficult experiences, 66–7,
125; influences in, 225–6; listening
when reusing, 229–31; location and
atmosphere, 35–6; oral character, 230–1;
as PGOH, 218; post-interview, 39–44;
post-structuralist view, 127, 128; power
relationship (see power relationship);
pre-interview, 32; preparation, 31–3;
process and methodology, 35–9, 54;
and purpose in oral history, 9, 218, 337,
351; reliability and acceptance of, 130;
reuse, 218–20; setting of, 225–6; silences
in, 65–6, 78–9, 149–50; simultaneous
interviewees, 37; social context, 129,
132; social history, 9–10, 79; steps in, 7;
strategies, 227–9
interviewee: agreeing to interview, 359;
collective method, 37; helping with
interviews, 58–9; and intermediary, 59;
in knowledge creation, 146–7; orators
and legal aspects (see orators); prompting questions, 36; relationship with
inverviewer (see interviewer-interviewee
relationship); shared authority, 8, 146;
silences and omissions, 65–6; speaking
for and listening to, 341–3; as starting
point of inquiry, 131–3; subjectivity, 77;
unity of findings, 150–1
interviewer: attitude and behaviour,
36, 54; awareness of in PGOH, 226;
benefits from interviews, 77; control
by intermediary, 59–60; insider status,
53, 55, 57–8, 65, 354; interpretation
of oral history, 77–8; in knowledge
creation, 146–7; life story of and oral
history, 55–8; protocol with Elders,

34–5; relationship with inverviewee (*see* interviewer-interviewee relationship); role, 7, 8; subjectivity, 54, 65, 67, 77; training, 227–9. *See also* historians

interviewer-interviewee relationship: engagement of historian, 340; ethics, 77, 336; in Holocaust project, 245–7; importance in oral history, 10, 348–9, 353; influences in interview, 225–6, 304–5, 337–8, 355–6; and listening, 272; and opposite views, 302, 310–12; in orality of interview, 231; in PGOH, 224–6; shared authority and kinship in, 53–4, 55–7, 58–61, 67, 354; women teachers oral histories, 145–7; working-class oral histories, 124

intuitive interpretation, as data analysis, 42

Inuit. *See* First Nations, Inuit, Métis

invasion of privacy, 110–11, 112

Ivry, Liselotte, 248–9, 258–9

Jack, Dana, 146

Japanese Canadians. *See* internment of Japanese Canadians

Jerry Falwell v. *Penthouse International Limited*, 107

Jewett, Pauline, 8

Ḵaax̱'achgóok story and song, 189–91

Kendal, Fred, 30

Kennedy, Elizabeth, 205, 206

kinship: in interviewer-interviewee relationship, 53–4, 55–7, 60–1, 67, 354; in Yukon Territory, 186–7

Klondike gold rush, 185, 186, 193

knowledge, in women teachers' oral histories, 142, 143–7

Krysia (Holocaust educator), 245–6

labelling, of interview data, 40

labour: in postwar schools, 143–4; working-class historians, 10–11, 121–4, 126–7, 130–1. *See also* working-class oral histories

LaClare, Leo, 6

Lamer, Chief Justice, 27–8

language: and gender, 141, 147; interactive nature, 132–3; in interviews, 37–8; in

post-structuralism and materialism, 142, 147–50, 350. *See also* discourse

Laub, Dori, 341

law and legal aspects: ethics and confidentiality, 89–91, 93; indigenous claims and oral history, 11–12, 25, 27–8, 352, 357; oral history in Canada, 9; in PGOH, 227; of privacy, 82–3. *See also* copyright; courts

Learning and Evaluation Situations (LES), 268, 274–9

Left (political), in early oral history, 122–3, 350

Lenihan, Patrick, 10

"lesbian," meaning, 212

Lesbian Herstory Archives (LHA), 204–5

lesbian oral history: analog recordings, 201–2, 207–8, 214; Archive of Lesbian Oral Testimonies (ALOT), 202, 211–13; archives and archiving, 202, 203, 206–8, 212, 357; collection and preservation, 202, 203, 208, 210; consent for use and legal constraints, 208–10, 213; digitization, 202, 214; and ethics, 209; funding and grants, 208, 214; interviews from later twentieth century, 201–2; Lesbian Herstory Archives (LHA), 204–5; Lesbians Making History (LMH), 206, 208, 209; male volunteers domination, 204–5, 206–7; projects in Canada, 201–3, 206–8, 210–13, 214–15; Queer History Project (QHP), 210–11; questionnaire and responses, 202–3, 207; recommendations, 213–15; US projects, 204–5

lesbians and gays, 149, 202–6

Lesbians Making History (LMH), 206, 212

Levine, Gil, 10

liability, *TCPS* and *TCPS2*, 73, 74, 75, 91

libel, 108–9

libraries, as sources, 33

Life Stories of Montrealers Displaced by War, Genocide, and other Human Rights Violations project, 266, 267–8. *See also* Montreal Life Stories project

life story interviews: in education, 267, 272; Fortunoff Video Archive formula, 245; of human rights violations, 267–8; and interviewer, 55–8; Montreal Life Stories project, 240, 242, 272; testimony and chain of testimony, 270–1, 272; and three-generational interviews, 161; use of, 228

Lightning, Richard, 38

Lightning, Walter, 38

Likert scale, 41

Lindeman, Yehudi, 244, 245, 246–7

"linguistic turn," 141, 351

listener, 231, 341–3

listening: definition and theories of, 266–7, 269–70, 272–3, 278; ethics, 275–6; by historians, 342–3; as interaction, 272–3, 359; loss of, 266; in oral history, 272–3; pedagogy of, 266–7, 269–70, 272–8; as relation to self and other, 278–9; in reuse of interviews, 229–31; by students in schools, 269; in testimony, 270–2, 277, 341–3

Little, Margaret, 130

Living Testimonies project, 244–5, 247

local authority, in methodology, 33–4

local history, 65

long-form census, 83

long-term memory, 233, 234

loss of detail, 172, 173

McCardle, Bennett Ellen, 30

MacDonald, Maria, 207

McMahan, Eva M., 225

Magnotta, Luka, 90

Malkki, Liisa, 342

March of the Living program, 257–60

marginalized groups and views: discrediting of, 329, 331; in indigenous cultures, 87–8; memories of, 322–3, 328–9; in oral history, 9, 77; participation, 324, 326–7, 328–9

materialist approach: and feminism, 141–2, 153; and identity, 142, 150–3; and language, 142, 147–50; and truth, 142, 143–7; women teachers oral histories, 142–53; working-class oral histories, 127, 131

Matschke, Anne, 61, 62–3

medical sector, 322

Memmi, Albert, 289, 290

memory: change in, 234; collective (see collective memory); communicative, 160–2, 165, 175–6, 353–4; construction and

reconstruction, 128–9, 322; in family, 159–60; functioning of, 161–2; implicit and explicit, 172; inclusion of all views, 311–12; individual (see individual memories); loss in the colonized, 289–91; for marginalized, 322–3, 328–9; multiplicity of vs. individual, 303–4, 312–13; and narrative, 193–5; and official ideologies, 322; in oral history, 126, 128; reclaiming, 322–3; reliability, 233–4; subjectivity, 313; understanding of, 78; and women's experiences, 78, 124–6, 128–9

Methodists at Norway House (MB), 286, 287, 289

methodology: background research, 32–3; cooperation with community, 33–4; description and steps, 5, 25–6, 31–44; development, 7; for dignity and protection, 91–2; goals and objectives of project, 31–2, 34; interview process, 35–9, 54; in PGOH, 221–9; post-interview process, 39–44; preparation and planning, 31–3; procedures and standards, 221; production stages, 221–2; recordings, 36; in shared authority, 60–1, 65–6; and subjectivity in interview, 54

Métis. See First Nations, Inuit, Métis

Michener Centre: access to memories and buildings, 323–8, 330–1, 357; archives, 325, 327–9, 357; Board of Governors, 326–7; communitization transition, 321; contested memories, 318–19; current policy, 325–7; data sources expansion, 329; education and segregation, 320; eugenics programs, 320–1, 325; history and description, 318, 319–21, 324; internment policy, 320, 323, 330; official memories, 318, 319, 321, 325, 326–7, 330–1; project details, 319, 327, 329, 330; protectionism over survivors, 324–7; sterilizations, 318–19, 320–1; survivors memories, 321, 322, 324

migrants and ethnicity, 11, 335

Millroy, John, 336

missionaries, impact, 289–90

Mitchinson, Wendy, 80

modest witness, 336, 338

Moharty, Chandra, 151

moiety, in Yukon Territory, 186–7
Montreal Holocaust Memorial Centre
(MHMC), 241, 242–3, 244; survivors as
interpreters, 252–6
Montreal Life Stories project, 240–2, 267–8,
272, 273–4
moral bond, in interviews, 8
moral rights, 111–12
Morrow, Justice, 28
Morton, Arthur S., 5–6
movement history, 121
museum interpretation, by survivors,
252–6
myths, in family, 175

Nabokov, Peter, 289
names, discrepancies in, 37
Nancy, Jean-Luc, 269–70, 359
narrative: and data analysis, 41–2; homogenization and variety, 180–1; and
memory, 193–5; power and official
ideologies, 322–3; role, 180, 182. See also
oral story/narrative
narrative structures, of family stories,
172–6
narrativity, 132
National Association of Japanese Canadians (NAJC), 297, 298
Native North America, 184–6, 187, 193–4.
See also Yukon Territory
Nazi Germany: explicit and implicit
memories, 172; family memories,
159–60, 161; Hiebert family foundational
stories, 165–72; in narrative structures
of families, 172–5; three-generational
interviews, 161–2
Nestle, Joan, 204–5, 206
non-Aboriginals, views of indigenous
peoples, 26
No Place to Go, 80–1
Norkunas, Martha, 272–3
Norway House (MB), 286, 289

objectivity, 7–8, 145
Ochēkiwi Sīpi (Fisher River) Cree:
collective memory, 287–9, 292, 293–4;
description and history, 285–6, 287–8;
interviews and gaps in events, 287–9,

351–2; oral history and history projects,
287; textual and documentary records,
287, 293; writing of history, 287, 292, 293
Okihiro, Gary Y., 313
Olsen, Karen, 146, 302, 310
"On Suffering and Structural Violence"
(Farmer), 342
open-ended questions, 31–2, 41
oral history: academic debate, 4, 14, 28–30;
changes in, 348–50; criticisms, 29;
definition, 3, 4–5, 30–1, 294n5; development in Canada and global context, 5–8,
10, 11–13, 15–17, 119–24; as dialogue, 10;
diversity in Canada, 347–8; interpretive
concepts, 142; methods, 5; opposing
views and approaches, 131–2, 310–12; vs.
oral tradition, 86–7, 352; periodization
and shifts, 119–20, 125–6; purposes, 9,
26–7, 31–2, 79, 91, 221; quality of projects,
221–2; relationships in, 340; reuse of
collections, 218–20; types, 30
Oral History Committee of the Canadian
Historical Association, 6
Oral History Forum d'histoire orale, 120
orality of data, 230–1
oral story/narrative: analysis, 182; documentation, 181, 187–8; and the everyday,
181, 182, 188, 195; homogenization and
variety, 180–1; and the local, 181, 182, 186,
352; northwestern Canada, 181–2; place
and meaning, 184, 193–4; as reference
points for other events, 186, 188, 189–91,
192–4; role and purposes, 180, 188, 191,
194–5, 352–3; theoretical attention and
debate, 180–1, 182, 188; transmission,
180, 181–2, 183–4; women in Yukon,
186–8, 189–93, 194–5
oral tradition: and colonialism, 183–4; convergence in analysis, 181; evaluation and
historical value, 180–1; and historical
reconstruction, 292–3; vs. oral history,
86–7, 352; role, 183–4, 351; writing of, 12,
287, 292, 352
orators: authorship and copyright, 99–100,
101, 104, 105–8; breach of confidence,
109–10; invasion of privacy, 110–11;
slander and libel, 108–9
outline, of report, 42

ownership, and copyright, 101–7

Palys, Ted, 91
Parent, Collette, 90–1
partiality. *See* subjectivity
participant: anonymity and confidentiality, 80–1; harm to and ethics, 85–6; identity, 73, 75, 80–1, 83, 89–90; modest witness, 336, 338; responsibility towards, 335–7; speaking for and listening to, 341–3; *vs.* subject, 76; use of names, 226–7
Passerini, Luisa, 10, 143, 232
Paulette case, 28
Pauls, Nancy: biography, 159, 162–4; family stories, 165, 167–72; German-Canadian identity, 159–60; narrative structures, 172–3, 174, 175. *See also* Hiebert family
pedagogy: of human rights violations, 274–9; learning tools, 268; of listening, 266–7, 269–70, 272–8; testimony and chain of testimony, 270–2, 277. *See also* education field and classroom
performers, copyright, 114
permission, for interview, 33, 35
personal memories. *See* individual memories
PHOH. *See* process-generated oral history (PHOH)
political history, and origins of oral history, 120
politics, 119, 121–4
Portelli, Alessandro: description of oral history, 79; on engagement of researcher, 340–1; ethics, 88; and misremembering, 10; oral quality of interviews, 231; role of oral history, 218–19, 359; on subjectivity, 126, 232, 313; on truth, 66–7
post-interview methodology, 39–44
post-structuralist theory: and feminism, 141–2, 153; and identity, 142, 150–3; and language, 142, 147–50, 350; and truth, 142, 143–7; women teachers oral histories, 142–53, 350–1; working-class oral histories, 127–8, 131
power relationship: and dominant ideologies, 322–3; feminist historians, 145–6; in oral history and interview, 14, 55, 77, 91, 225, 272, 356; and shared authority,

145–6, 272, 356; teachers in postwar schools, 144; working-class women, 128
pre-interview preparation, 32
preliminary meeting, with Elders, 34–5
preservation and presentation, as part of oral history, 5
primary sources, 26, 30, 39–40, 234–5
privacy: importance and issues, 80, 81; invasion, 110–11, 112; legislation, 82–3; recommendation to Panel, 83–4; *TCPS*, 73, 79, 81–2; *TCPS2*, 79–84
private records, consent, 84–5
process-generated oral history (PGOH): description, 218; ethical and legal aspects, 226–7; example, 219–20; interviewer-interviewee relationship, 224–6; interview strategies and interviewer training, 227–9; missing data, 223–4; orality of data, 230–1; project conceptualization, 221–2; technology and recording media, 222–4; transcriptions and summaries, 229–30; use and reuse of collections, 218–20
production stages of oral history, 221–2
professionalism, in women teachers, 148–9
Provincial Training School (PTS), Alberta, 319–20. *See also* Michener Centre
Public Guardian offices, Alberta, 324

qualitative research, ethics, 75
Quantz, Richard, 148
Quebec, human rights violations education program, 268, 274–9
Queer History Project (QHP), 210–11
queers. *See* lesbians and gays
questions: closed and open-ended, 31–2, 41; copyright, 100, 101, 103–4; development for interview, 33; prompting of interviewee, 36; and social context, 129; and transcripts, 40

race, women teachers, 146, 151–2
recordings: availability in future, 43–4; copies and original, 40; copyright, 100, 104; development, 5–6; methodology, 36; preparation, 35; sound recordings, 98–9, 100, 103–4; transcription, 39; video, 35, 222–3. *See also* analog audio recordings

recovery, 9, 121, 122, 131, 134

recuperation, 121, 125, 129–30, 134

redress activism and Redress campaign, 302–3, 304–6, 308–9

reel-to-reel tapes, 222–3

relativism, 145

release form, 35, 50n60, 227

remembering. *See* memory

repetition in topic, 38–9

report writing, 41, 42–3

research: definition in *TCPS* and *TCPS2*, 75–6; as methodology of project, 32–3

researchers. *See* historians

research ethics boards (REBs): and anonymity and consent, 79, 80–2, 227; privacy legislation, 82–3; procedural issues, 89; risks and harm, 85–6; schedule for interview, 85; *TCPS* and *TCPS2*, 73, 75–6, 79, 92

research participant. *See* participant

residential schools, 12, 85

respect and trust, 84

retrospectivity, 234–5

Riordan, Michael, 4, 209

risks, and consent, 84–5

Ritchie, Donald, 225, 234

The Role of Memories in Social Change conference, 319

Rosenberg, Gabriele, 176

Rosh White, Naomi, 290–1

Ross, Becki, 208

Rousmaniere, Kate, 144

St Mary's Ukrainian Catholic Church (Sudbury, ON), 55, 57, 61–3

Sandford, Victoria, 342

Sangster, Joan, 77, 141

Saskatchewan Indians and the Resistance of 1885: Two Case Studies (Stonechild), 26–7

schedule for interview, 85

Scheper-Hughes, Nancy, 338

Schondorf, Rena, and Mayer, 249, 251

schools. *See* women teachers' oral histories

Schrag, Zachary, 92

Schulz, Karla: biography, 159, 162–4; family stories, 165, 167–72, 176; German-Canadian identity, 160; narrative structures, 173–4. *See also* Hiebert family

Schwartz, Musia, 250, 251

secondary sources, definition, 234

secondary uses of data, 81–2, 83–4, 231

Secretariat on Responsible Conduct for Research (SRCR), 91

self-identity, 152–3

Sensing Changes: Technologies, Environments, and the Everyday, 1953–2003 (Parr), 335–6

sexuality, history, 201

Sexual Sterilization Act (Alberta, 1928), 320–1

Shafer, Robert, 27

shared authority: in activism, 14–15; challenges and limitations, 8, 65–6, 355–7; concept, 54–5; control of interview, 59–60; development with intermediary, 60–1; and education, 272; in interviewer-interviewee relationship, 53–4, 58–61, 67, 354; with lesbian and gay community, 204; methodology, 60–1, 65–6; need for, 55; positive aspects, 61, 62–3, 65, 66, 67; possibilities of, 358–60; power relationships, 145–6, 272, 356

Sher, Olga, 251, 252, 253–4

Shopes, Linda: interviewer-interviewee relationship, 146, 302, 310; shared authority and collaboration, 54, 67, 337, 355; subjectivity and oral history process, 337–8, 339, 360

short-term memory, 233, 234

Sidney, Angela: biography, 188–9; life stories in Yukon, 186–8, 189–91, 194; local and global events, 186–7, 188

silence (of survivors/victims), 243–4, 290–1

silence (as act), while learning, 269–70

silences (in interviews), 65–6, 78–9, 149–50. *See also* unspoken

Simon, Roger, 270–1

Simon Fraser University, lesbian archives, 211–12

Skoreyko, Roy, 322–3

slander, 108–9

Smith, Dorothy, 131–2, 151

Smith, Kitty: biography, 191–2; carvings, 192–3, 195; life stories in Yukon, 186–8, 191–3, 194–5; local and global events, 186–7, 188

Smith, May Hume, 192–3
social capital, 187, 189
social change, 319
social context, influence, 128–9, 132
social history: anonymity in, 79–80; in development of oral history, 9–11, 14, 120, 122–4, 350; and interviews, 9–10, 79
socialism, 123
solidarity, women teachers, 151
Sound Heritage program (Provincial Archives of BC), 13
sound recordings, copyright, 98–9, 100, 103–4
Spalter-Roth, Roberta, 144
standpoint theory, in feminism, 151
Statistics Act, 83
Stonechild, Blair, 26–7
story and stories. See narrative; oral story/narrative
storytelling, 38–9, 161, 184
subject, vs. participant, 76
subjectivity: definition, 232; of historian, 336–9; and interpretation, 232–3; in interview, 67; interviewee, 77, 313; interviewer, 54, 65, 67, 77; of memory, 313; as oral history element, 119, 125–6, 127, 129, 132, 134, 349–51; as problem, 231–3; usefulness, 232–3
subpoenas, ethics cases, 90
Sudbury (ON), Ukrainians in, 53, 55–7, 58, 59, 60, 61–4, 65–6
suffering, listening to, 341–2
Sugiman family, internment, 297–8
summaries, in PGOH, 229–30
Supreme Court of Canada, 11–12, 25, 27–8, 100, 113
survivors: power of memory and story, 322–3, 330–1. See also Holocaust education; human rights violations; Michener Centre

tapes/cassettes. See analog audio recordings
TCPS (first edition): confidentiality, 73, 79, 81–2; core values, 75–6; criticisms, 73, 75, 92; definition of research, 75; First Nations, Inuit, and Métis, 73, 87–8; and liability, 75

TCPS2 (second edition of Tri-Council Policy Statement: Ethical Research Involving Humans): bureaucratic issues, 85, 89, 92–3; confidentiality and privacy, 79–84; and consent, 85; core values, 75–6; definition of research, 75–6; description, 73; evolution of, 93; First Nations, Inuit, Métis, 74, 88; historical research, 88–91; improvements, 73–4, 75–6, 92–3; at institutional level, 89; and liability, 73, 74, 91; regulatory and legal power, 82–3, 89–91, 93; secondary uses of data, 82
teachers, postwar schools, 143–4. See also women teachers' oral histories
testimony and chain of testimony, 270–2, 277, 341–3
Theobald, Marjorie, 142
"There's Gonna Always Be a Line" (Portelli), 341
Thiessen, Angela, 164
Thiessen, Janis, 81
Thompson, Paul, 77, 145, 230, 233, 350
three-generational interviews: and communicative memory, 161–2, 353–4; Hiebert family's stories, 165–72; narrative structures, 172–5; as tool, 176
time periods, and retrospectivity, 234–5
topic question, 32–3
totalization, 145
tradition, invention of, 292–3
traditional gifts, for interviewees, 34
transcriptions: additional commentary, 40; archiving and cost, 13; availability in future, 43–4; copyright, 103–4; in digital format, 340; editing, 39, 227; in PGOH, 229–30; in post-interview, 39–40; silences and the unspoken, 149–50; sole reliance on, 338
translation, and transcription, 39
transpeople. See lesbians and gays
trauma, and denial, 290–1
Treasure, Julian, 266, 278
treaties, 26
Treaty and Aboriginal Rights Research library, 44
tri-council policy, development, 8–9

Tri-Council Policy Statement: Ethical Research Involving Humans (TCPS). *See* TCPS (first edition); TCPS2
trust and respect, 84
truth, 66–7, 142, 143–7
Twohig, Peter, 83–4

Ukrainian Labour Farmer Temple Association (ULFTA), 63
Ukrainians: communities within, 53, 57, 63–4, 70n21; interviews in project, 55, 70n21; project planning and priorities, 55; public archive, 53, 64; in Sudbury (ON), 53, 55–7, 58, 59, 60, 61–4, 65–6. *See also* Baba (Olga Zembrzycki)
United Kingdom Copyright Act and law, 101, 104–5, 108
United States: case law, 357; copyright law, 105–7, 108; ethics, 75, 90, 92; legal questions in oral history, 9, 357
universities, liability and institutional support, 90–1
University of Ottawa, confidential records case, 90–1
the unspoken, 149–50, 230–1. *See also* silences (in interviews)

Vancouver (BC), queer history project, 210–11
Vansina, Jan, 351
video recordings, 35, 222–3
violence and abuse, ethics, 85
Volosinov, V.N., 132
von Plato, Alexander, 174

Warren, Kay, 339
We Are Here package, 268
Weiler, Kathleen, 152
Weissman, Aerlyn, 211
Welzer, Harald, 161–2, 172, 174, 175–6
Wendell, Susan, 323
Wheeler (Stevenson), Winona, 28, 29
Whig narrative, 120, 128
Williams, Raymond, 122, 130–1
Wilson, Angela Cavender, 29
Wolf, Eric, 180
women: anonymity and consent, 80–1; commitment to interviews and oral

history, 129–30; and human agency, 133; identity construction, 142, 150–3; life stories in Yukon, 186–8, 189–93, 194–5; and power relations, 128; silences, 78–9, 125; TCPS approval, 87–8; understanding of past events, 78, 124–6, 128–9; vision of society, 151
women's historians, 11, 121, 122–4, 129–30
women teachers' oral histories: appearance of women, 151–3; and authority, 144; and discourse, 142, 147–50; and identity, 142, 150–3; post-structuralism and materialism, 141–53, 350–1; and professionalism, 148–9; and truth, 142, 143–7; unity of findings, 150–2
Worden, Doreen, 81
working-class historians, 10–11, 121–4, 126–7, 130–1
working-class oral histories: change in oral history writing, 119; early projects and grass-root endeavours, 122, 123–5; interviewees as starting point of inquiry, 132–3; in 1970s, 122–5, 134; in 1990s and beyond, 125–7; politics in, 119; post-structuralism and materialism, 127–8, 131; and power relations, 128; and recovery, 9, 121, 122, 131, 134; recuperation, 125, 129–30, 134; shifts in, 131, 133–4; understanding of, 128–9
written word: for cross-referencing, 42; indigenous oral history, 28, 287, 292, 351–2; and oral history, 12, 28, 133, 187

Yow, Valerie, 337
Yukon College, opening, 191
Yukon Territory: documentation of stories, 181, 187–8; impact of Euro-Americans, 185–6; key events of nineteenth and twentieth centuries, 185–6, 187, 193–4; kinship and matrilineal lines, 186–7; oral tradition, 184–5; songs of Tlingit, 190–1; transmission of stories, 181–2; women's life stories, 186–8, 189–93, 194–5

Zeitlin, S.J., 164
Zembrzycki, Olga. *See* Baba (Olga Zembrzycki)
Zoltak, Sidney, 243–4, 250, 251–2, 260